Lenin
The Heritage We (Don't) Renounce

Edited by
Hjalmar Jorge Joffre-Eichhorn
and Patrick Anderson

Published by
Daraja Press
https://darajapress.com/
Wakefield, Quebec, Canada
In association with
KickAss Books

Lenin: The Heritage We (Don't) Renounce

© 2024 Hjalmar Jorge Joffre-Eichhorn & Patrick Anderson
All rights reserved
Copyright of all texts, translations and images
are retained by the respective authors

ISBN: 9781998309047

Editors: Hjalmar Jorge Joffre-Eichhorn & Patrick Anderson
Cover Design: Johann Salazar

Library and Archives Canada Cataloguing in Publication
Title: Lenin : the heritage we (don't) renounce / edited by Hjalmar Jorge
 Joffre-Eichhorn, Patrick Anderson.
Other titles: Lenin (Wakefield, Québec)
Names: Joffre-Eichhorn, Hjalmar Jorge, 1977- editor. | Anderson,
 Patrick, 1970- editor.
Description: Includes bibliographical references.
Identifiers: Canadiana 20240288041 | ISBN 9781998309047 (softcover)
Subjects: LCSH: Lenin, Vladimir Il'ich, 1870-1924—Anniversaries, etc.
Classification: LCC DK254.L447 L475 2024 | DDC 947.084/1092—
 dc23

Macht kaputt, was euch kaputt macht.
(Ton, Steine, Scherben)

We call communism the real movement,
which abolishes the state of things.
(Marx & Engels)

Many fall along the way, which only makes the wishes
of those who remain even more urgent.
(Antonio Gramsci)

To work, everybody to work,
the cause of the world socialist revolution
must and will triumph.
(Lenin)

Contents

Preface: The Cult is Dead, Long Live the Cult!   xi

1. Obituary for Lenin   1
   KYRGSOC

2. Cabral and Lenin: An Ideological Conversation   4
   Abel Djassi Amado

3. This too is Leninism: Military Marxisms in Africa   8
   Adam Mayer

4. The Wreaths of Lenin   13
   Adrien Minard

5. Me and the Lenin Museum   16
   Aimo Minkkinen

6. Lenin and Mao   19
   Alain Badiou

7. Invocation of Lenin   23
   alejandra ciriza

8. Lenin, Dialectics, and Trans Liberation   26
   Alex Adamson

9. Lenin and Artificial Intelligence   29
   Alex Taek-Gwang Lee

10. My Lenin   32
    Alexander Vatlin

11. Lenin, Liberated Woman of the East   34
    Anara Moldosheva

12. To Blow (Up) The Mausoleum   37
    Anatoli Ulyanov

13. Lenin, Labriola and the Historical Nodes of International Communism   40
    Andrea Bonfanti

14. Moscow is Just Two Steps Away   43
    Andrés Carminati Ciriza

15. Encountering Lenin in Iceland (and Once in Denmark)   45
    Árni Daníel Júlíusson

16. A Letter to Lenin in Lagos   48
    Baba Aye

17	'Baking Books' – Practising Revolutionary Theory Through Bread *Baran Caginli*	53
18	On the Day in Skopje When Anarchists for Lenin Became a Possibility ... *Ben Watson*	55
19	Pupils at the Same School, Enemies in 1917: Lenin and Kerensky *Bill Bowring*	58
20	Lenin, the (un)making of a critical legal theorist *Camila Vergara*	61
21	A Feminist-Socialist View of Lenin and the Soviet Revolution from the Río de la Plata *María Cecilia Espasandín Cárdenas*	65
22	Holiday Haunts for Progressive Travellers. Lenin's Guide to Europe *Chris Read*	68
23	Lenin and Black Power *Christian Høgsbjerg*	73
24	Lenin met Makhno (Or Did He?) *Colin Darch*	76
25	Lenin: Building Hope *Constantino Bértolo*	79
26	Lenin on Women's Emancipation and Sexuality *Daria Dyakonova*	82
27	Richter and Gus *David McIlwraith*	85
28	Lenin, Psychoanalysis and Free Love *David Pavón-Cuéllar*	88
29	Lenin's Enduring Influence on the Struggle against Imperialism in Africa *Demba Moussa Dembélé*	93
30	How the Soviet Union Saved the Caribbean without Colonisation *Earl Bousquet*	96
31	Reclaiming Lenin in Iran: Challenging Male Dominance in the Revolutionary Movement *Elsaa and La'al*	99
32	Snapshot of the Statues *Esther Leslie*	101

33	"Vilici": The Theoretician of Hegemony in Antonio Gramsci's Prison Notebooks *Fabio Frosini*	104
34	Lenin's Vanguardist Party: Reflections on the Nigerian Revolution *Femi Aborisade*	107
35	Back to Zimmerwald *Franco 'Bifo' Berardi*	110
36	How I cooked soup with Lenin *Frigga Haug*	113
37	Lenin's Vision: Awakening of the Masses to Socialist Future *Gal Kirn*	117
38	Lenin, Partisan of the Conjuncture *Gavin Walker*	120
39	Lenin and the Weltgeist: A Philosophical Reflection *George Sotiropoulos*	123
40	Consciously Revolutionary Workers Do Not Fall From Heaven *Gianni Del Panta*	126
41	One of the Creators of the 20th Century *Göran Therborn*	129
42	The Mass Psychology of the Renunciation of Lenin *Gordana Jovanović*	131
43	A Century of Lenin in Tunisia (1924-2024) *Habib Kazdaghli*	134
44	Lenin's Battles *Helena Sheehan*	139
45	Between the Poetry of Revolution and the Prose of State Formation: Lenin in Memoriam *Himani Bannerji*	142
46	I Do Not Know *Ian H. Birchall*	145
47	Lenin's Dream *Ian Parker*	148
48	Lenin and Nyerere – A Conversation in the Heavens *Issa Shivji*	151
49	Dictator Lenin vs. Democrat Churchill? *Jacques Pauwels*	156

50	V.I. Lenin and Black Liberation *Joe Pateman*	159
51	Leninists *John Holloway*	163
52	Dear Lenin *J. Moufawad-Paul*	165
53	José Carlos Mariátegui and Lenin *Juan E. De Castro*	168
54	Lenin Never Quoted Lenin *Juan Dal Maso*	171
55	Sasha and Volodya in Sri Lanka *Kanishka Goonewardena*	174
56	With friends like these... *Kaveh Boveiri*	177
57	Lenin and the Living Dialectic *Kevin B. Anderson*	180
58	Too soon! Too late? It's Time! *Lars T. Lih*	183
59	"All and Sundry" *Leo Zeilig*	186
60	Lenin and the Long Journey to the East: The Case of Qu Qiubai *Luka Golež*	190
61	Lenin's Way Out *Mahir Ali*	193
62	Lenin in Bakhmut *Marc James Léger*	196
63	The Need to Dream and the Importance of (Re)Believing in Lenin *Marcela Magalhães*	199
64	Lenin and the deep history of Inner Eurasia *Marcus Bajema*	202
65	Ecological Leninism and Proletarian Agency *Matt Huber*	206
66	Lenin Against Stalin: The National Question *Michael Löwy*	209
67	Lenin and the Invention of Politics *Michael Neocosmos*	212

68	President Putin is somewhat right *Michał Kozłowski*	215
69	Hiding *Minna Henriksson*	218
70	Thinking (in) the conjuncture *Natalia Romé*	222
71	Eulogy of Lenine by a Cuban Marxist *Natasha Gómez Velázquez*	225
72	Lenin Will Rise Again Like a Phoenix *Naweed*	228
73	Lenin on the Moon *Nicholas Bujalski*	231
74	Lenin and Great Russian Chauvinism *Nigel C. Gibson*	235
75	The Star of Lenin Still Shines *Olya Murphy*	239
76	Lenin on the Buses *Owen Hatherley*	242
77	Lenin: Responding to Catastrophe, Forging Revolution *Paul Le Blanc*	247
78	The Three Tragedies of Vladimir Ilyich Lenin *Peter Hudis*	250
79	Lenin in Thailand *Puangchon Unchanam*	253
80	Six Links of Leninism *Redrock*	256
81	Building Strength in the Weakest Link: Lenin and the Philippines' Internationalist Solidarity *Regletto Aldrich Imbong*	259
82	Against the Capitalist Scaremongers from 1917 to 2024, 2025, etc. *Richard Gilman-Opalsky*	262
83	Lenin and Me *Ronald Grigor Suny*	265
84	Whatever Would Lenin Have Said? – We Owe Him an Answer! *Ronald Matthijssen*	268

85	Lenin on Women and Social Reproduction ... in Vietnam *Ly Hoang Minh Uyen (Sally Mju)*	273
86	Lenin on Imperialism: Wrong But Also Right *Sam Gindin*	276
87	Lenin as Method *Sandro Mezzadra*	280
88	'Lenin' is the Name of a Man *Sara Katona*	283
89	On the Eve of Revolution, When Ilyich Visits Rosa... *Sevgi Doğan*	287
90	Publishing as Scaffolding *Sezgin Boynik*	291
91	Words: 26 October 1917 *Sheila Delany*	294
92	Lenin at His Worst... Or at His Best? *Slavoj Žižek*	295
93	What to Do with *Chto Delat?* *Soma Marik*	297
94	The Finest Statue of Lenin Ever Made *Stefan Gužvica*	303
95	Lenin's *"Left-Wing" Communism* and ISO-Zimbabwe in the Late 1990s Working-Class Struggles *Antonater Tafadzwa Choto*	306
96	Lenin's Legacy – An Alternative to Capitalism *Tamás Krausz*	309
97	Lenin, Theorist of the Integration of the National, Colonial and Social Questions *Thierno Diop*	312
98	The Vanguard Question *Will Cameron*	315
99	What Lenin Did Not Say *Wladislaw Hedeler*	318
100	Lenin's Death in China *Xianxin Yuan*	320
101	Eleven Theses on the Contemporaneity of Tovarish Lenin *Yağmur Ali Coşkun*	323

102	Lenin of February 24th *Yevgeniy Fiks*	327
103	"Truth [is] Not in 'Systems'": *Our* Politics of the Event *Yutaka Nagahara*	328
104	Lenin's Time *Jodi Dean*	333
	About KickAss Books	336
	About Daraja Press	337
	Bibliography	338

List of Images

Postcard: "Building the Mausoleum"   x
(Artist: Olga Della-Vos-Kardovskaya)

Collage: Wreaths of Lenin   12
(Source: *Leninu. 21 ianvaria 1924*)

Drawing: "En octubre tu fuiste mía ... y ahora todo es melancolía"   22
(Artist: Valentín Carmín)

Photo: "Baking Lenin"   52
(Artist: Baran Caginli)

Image: "Lenin of February 24th"   72
(Artist: Yevgeniy Fiks)

Envelope "Republique du Niger, 1974"   92
(Artist: Unknown)

Drawing: "Todo es ilusión, menos, el poder"   116
(Artist: Valentín Carmín)

Painting: Lenin   138
(Artist: Laya Hooshyari)

Postcard: "Funeral of V.I. Lenin Red Square"   162
(Artist: A.I. Kravchenko)

Postcard: "The Appassionata"   182
(Artist: V.I. Masik)

Lino prints: "Hiding"   218
(Artist: Minna Henriksson)

Image: "Lenin on the Moon"   231
(Artist: V.A. Khovaev)

Postcard: "Gorki 23 January 1924"   246
(Artist: V.A. Serov)

Postcard: "Sad News. 21 January 1924"   272
(Artist: Y.N. Tulin)

Drawing: Rosa Luxemburg   286
(Artist: Ernst Jazdzweski)

Photo: Lenin Monument in Mohács   302
(Source: Ády)

Image: "Lenin of February 24th"   326
(Artist: Yevgeniy Fiks)

Postcard: "Death of the Leader" (Artist: S.D. Merkurov)   335

Artist: Olga Della-Vos-Kardovskaya

Preface: The Cult is Dead, Love Live the Cult!

One had to study very hard during those years, to reread Lenin sedulously, to learn to link up the past with the present, to learn how to live with Ilyich without Ilyich.
(Nadezhda Krupskaya)

Comrade workers and peasants! I have an important appeal to make: do not turn your sadness regarding Lenin's death into an external veneration of him. Do not build monuments and palaces in his name, do not carry out splendid ceremonies in his memory, etc. – he gave little significance to these things when he was alive [...]. Remember how much poverty there still is [...] in our country. If you want to perpetuate the name of Vladimir Ilyich Lenin – build nursery schools, shelters, houses, schools, libraries, clinics, hospitals, homes for the disabled, etc...., and, most importantly: do all you can to put his teachings into practice.
(Nadezhda Krupskaya)

Amen, Nadezhda Konstantinovna, Amen. Let's face it, comrade-readers: The man Lenin is dead, has been for a long time, will be forever. "Old truths that are ever new." "Our immediate task"? Accept it and radicalise our orphanhood. Mayakovsky said it best:

Yes!
Yes!
Ye-s-s!
We can,
        will believe it ----
                      that bulletin does not lie!

Ok, he did not say this. He said the opposite, but then he was dead wrong.[1] Lenin died, Lenin is dead, Lenin will be dead. "A valuable admission." The soon-to-be ex-Tovarish Trotsky was arguably the most clairvoyant of all Leninist moirologists: "Lenin is no more. We have lost Lenin. The dark laws that govern the work of the arteries have destroyed his life. [...] no miracle occurred where science was powerless." And so he died. Back on January 21, 1924, at exactly 6:50pm. A long, short, and in recent decades – many would say since late 1991 – increasingly disgusting and unbearable century ago. Hasn't been seen since (his buddy Zinoviev was right: "[Lenin] understands also how to rest") except in the Stalinist "special mould" of (nowadays fast falling) "monuments and palaces in his name," and of course zombified and brain dead in that highest stage of scientific powerlessness-cum-"left-wing childishness," the venerable and miraculous mausoleum. "The world is one big boil. And the worst thing is that even those who want to change it are starting to stink" (Ferdinand Lassalle aka Stefan Heym). Pablo Neruda begs to differ: "Thank you, Lenin, for the energy and the teachings, thank you for the firmness, [...] thank you for the air, the bread and the hope." Thank you

---

[1] See V. Mayakovsky's "We don't believe": "No! No! No-o-o! We can't, won't believe it ---- that bulletin lies!"

for the air? WTF? Now that is cultish. Should have followed your own advice, compañero Pablo:

> Lenin, to sing to you
> I must say farewell to words:
> I must write with trees, with wheels,
> with plows, with cereals.

Speaking of trees, *der Genosse* B. Brecht once wrote:

> As Lenin went, it was
> As if the tree said to its leaves
> I am off.

A bit schmaltzy, but cool, right? Lenin, the Tree – Bonsai? Hyperion? – cannot be grasped, however, without first accepting what may just be the founding statement of early pantheistic Ecological Leninism, "remarked somewhere" by Comrade Karl Radek, one of the most prolific Bolshevik eulogists (e.g. of Liebknecht, Reissner, Dzerzhinsky): "Like everything else in nature, Lenin was born, has developed, has grown." He "forgot to add": ... and was posthumously futurised into a ... "slap in the face of public taste,"[2] i.e. an emasculated Communist cucumber. That same Brecht, ever the virile *Besserwisser* (know-it-all), was not amused:

> The mistakes and errors of some Futurists are obvious. They placed a giant cucumber on a giant cube, painted the whole thing red and called it: Lenin's portrait. [...] The picture was not supposed to remind us of anything from the old, cursed times. Unfortunately, it didn't remind us of Lenin either. These are terrible events. But that doesn't make those artists right whose pictures now remind us of Lenin, but whose style of painting in no way recalls Lenin's manner of struggle.[3]

Can't win for losing, comrades. And wo/man, have we reds been at the receiving end of bitter defeats in recent decades. "Truly, [we] live in dark times!" "And still [we] eat, [we] drink" and we struggle-worship.

Coming back to Bertolt B's lament, we would like to believe that the quote above is not yet another episode of the Left's supremely honed, ever tedious, but at times necessary capacity for movement-destroying infighting, but rather a Brechtian appeal to de-phallicise and thus de-alienate Herr Ulyanov – ain't no phallic road to Communism[4] – akin to the categorical imperative our sister-amauta Nadezhda Krupskaya decreed: that is, "to learn

---

[2] See Burliuk, David; Kruchenykh, Alexander; Mayakovsky, Vladimir and Victor Khlebnikov (1917), "A slap in the face of public taste," *Marxists Internet Archive*. Available online.
[3] Brecht, Bertolt (1967), *Gesammelte Werke 19*. Frankfurt: Suhrkamp: 291-292. (Translation: the editors.)
[4] Inspired by Budgen, Sebastian (2020), "The Phallic Road to Socialism," *Salvage*. Available online.

to live with Ilyich without Ilyich,"⁵ "to learn to link up the past with the present" and in the process to engage in a bit of perpetuating of Lenin's name by doing "all [one] can to put his teachings into practice," by "recall[ing] Lenin's manner of struggle."

"Where to begin?" Great question, Ili. Building (public) schools, shelters, libraries and hospitals everywhere is definitely a great beginning, middle and end. "Peace, Bread, Land" still sounds pretty basic – and radical again – as well (ask the Palestinians). "Expropriate the expropriators"? Absolutely. "From each according to their ability, to each according to their needs"? Да, Да, Да. For all of this to be remotely possible, however, "what is to be done" is communisting, i.e. organising comradeship in order to hang out with each other, chug down a few vodkas, dance the Appassionata and (grave)dig our way towards the bright and shiny Communist future. Or something like that. If "the point is [still] to change [the world]," the truth is that we need each other. Being together precedes struggling together.⁶

The shamelessly immodest purpose of this book is to be an active part of this process of communisting; in our case, an unapologetically Leninist one. "To stand on the rock of the word 'we' amidst the sea of boos and outrage."⁷ 100 years since VIL died, we had to do something, together with others: more than 100 comrade-others, as it turned out, hailing from 50+ countries and all continents, from Afghanistan to Zimbabwe. Not all of them die-hard disciples, but each and every one of them responding to Krupskaya's request to "reread Lenin sedulously" in order to help liberate the old Ilyich from the musty, petrifying solitude of his mausoleum and to invite him back into the "real movement, which abolishes the state of things" in the here and now, i.e. our multiple, intersecting struggles against all types of capitalist-colonial-heteropatriarchal-ableist oppression and for the rekindling and strengthening of the new Communist horizon.

While many on the contemporary Left continue to disavow any association with Tovarish Lenin, *Lenin: The Heritage We (Don't) Renounce* – inspired by Lenin's 1897 article (without the bracket) – affirms the opposite: that there will be no revolution without Vladimir Ilyich among our rank-and-file comrade-ancestors. Or, in the words of Himani Bannerji, one of the book's authors, "We neglect Lenin's voice at our own peril."

Enjoy the read and (re-)take action.

Hjalmar & Patrick

---

5 *Spasibo bolshoi* to *Tovarish* Nicholas Bujalski – see also his cosmic contribution in chapter 73 of this volume – who drew our attention to Krupskaya's request, which can be found in her *Reminiscences of Lenin*.
6 Inspired by Simon, Joshua (ed.) (2019), *Being Together Precedes Being. A Textbook for The Kids Want Communism*. Berlin: Archive Books.
7 See "A slap in the face of public taste."

1. Obituary for Lenin

KYRGSOC

Generally, an obituary intends to reconcile the reader with the idea that the deceased is gone forever, concluding this person's life path. However, Lenin would not be Lenin if he gave us the peace of mind to do so, even 100 years later. He stubbornly refuses to be buried, in every sense, blistering our eyes with what is left of him.

As such, a posthumous evaluation of Lenin is difficult to accomplish in a few words. Lenin was the leader of the world's first successful socialist revolution, one that fundamentally altered the course of the 20th century. Yet, clearly, there were revolutionaries before and after Lenin – many of whom achieved their goals. It is hence strange to suggest that we leftists should value him just because he was the first.

In more general terms, Lenin's personality attracts us with its contradictory nature and the impossibility of fitting it into any predetermined framework. Whenever someone tries to bring together the numerous biographical facts of his life (Lenin is arguably the most studied person in history), they can thus never add up to any type of whole picture.

Let us try, then, to briefly highlight what we consider the most essential elements of Lenin's legacy. Lenin fought for socialism and democracy, never once in his life retreating from his political ideals. At the same time, he built a vanguard party – a political sect, really – whose reins he never relinquished, not even for a second. Lenin's administrative abilities and Bolshevik discipline underpinned the decisive success of the October Revolution. This was a period when all other political groups – chained to ideological dogma – were terrified of taking power, afraid of historical responsibility. Although the Paris communards had also seized power years before, their example showed that gaining power is not enough, but holding and unleashing it is crucial. This is where the Bolsheviks were truly able to walk across thin ice, managing not only to emerge from both the Civil and World Wars victorious but (and this is another paradox) preserving the former Russian Empire in its initial borders with only a few exceptions. The ongoing war in Ukraine and the recent exodus of refugees from Artsakh must hence seem to the liberal philistine the result of a terrible historical mistake, almost as if the notion of the 'Empire' had not been definitively dismantled but rather undergone a profound transformation.

This gift for 'revolutionary management' is entirely tied to both Lenin's personality – which we want to admire – and to his astonishing methods, which we are scarcely prepared to put into practice in the modern world: initiating splits, weaving intrigues (to the detriment of the sense of solidarity so beloved by today's Left), and even applying simple common sense. Lenin was always a true Machiavellian in his party struggle, a political animal ruthless to his comrades.

In his 1902 *What is to be done?*, Lenin defended the position that the attempt to create a revolution based on grassroots democratic principles was fruitless. He thus declared the necessity of the existence of a professional revolutionary layer. A little later he criticised Gorky and Bogdanov for establishing what for him was nothing but a factional "workers' school" in Capri. That is, the aspiration to build a universally equal society was paradoxically combined in Lenin with what can be interpreted, at best, as negative democratism, designed to keep the group of chosen from making mistakes and binding them instead through mutual accountability and responsibility to a common decision. Ultimately, the entire Soviet state began to work according to this logic — forcibly or naturally.

At the same time, Lenin's principles, rooted in Marxist theory and shaped by his distinctive utilitarian approach to politics, never became a dogma for Lenin himself. In fact, it would be challenging to find a greater opportunist in politics who did not hesitate to change his positions when it was most necessary. Yesterday's worst enemies could well become the close allies of tomorrow, as happened in the case of Trotsky in 1917. Hopes of building a socialist economy, dashed by the War Communism disaster, were easily replaced by a New Economic Policy, essentially restoring capitalism, which even after his death bore fruit by keeping the workers' state afloat. In other words, Lenin easily discarded the erroneous and unnecessary, but never lost sight of the main goal of the entire labour movement – the destruction of class society – without fear of being labelled inconsistent or insufficiently radical.

It is noteworthy that this political instinct, though bearing the mark of truly "diabolical insight," is the product of rational analysis, which is reflected in Lenin's numerous texts. Lenin is the direct heir of Marx in this regard, the bearer of the Hegelian claim to a complete understanding of the world and the confirmation of this claim in practice. Even Lenin's polemical texts stubbornly refer us to Marxist philosophical and political economy categories, making this kind of political discussion the norm in the Bolshevik milieu.

Moreover, whenever there were any gaps in theory, Lenin rolled up his sleeves and rushed to fill them, spending months in libraries, sometimes to the detriment of direct political work. The childishly amusing phrase, "the Marxist doctrine is omnipotent because it is true" could not have been espoused by a man who even for a second doubted what he was doing.

This all-conquering confidence in the power of theory – the power of human reason – defines the path that Lenin and the Bolsheviks travelled, from small circles and newspapers to overthrowing the entire existing world order, questioning the centuries-old foundations of mutual exploitation and oppression for the first time. The appealing glow of all that Lenin achieved is the lustre of victory over circumstances at any cost, even when the odds are infinitesimally small.

Such confidence, 100 years later, is utterly devoid in today's Left. Over time, leftism has increasingly become a way of life, rather than a way of thought. Lenin, conservative in his personal life but boundlessly radical in his political life, is the mirror opposite of the modern left. We, sensing the problem, hating capitalism, try magically, like wizards, to draw attention to its problematic nature and just as magically to overcome it, marginalising both ourselves and our ideas. Lenin, on the other hand, did what had to be done to win without being able to look back. That is why we cannot bury Lenin yet – he will be a living reproach to all of us for a long time to come.

KYRGSOC is an organisation of leftists united by fanning the flames of Marxism in Kyrgyzstan.

Translated from the Russian by many, with support from modern technology.

2. Cabral and Lenin: An Ideological Conversation

Abel Djassi Amado

Amílcar Cabral (1924-1973) was born in Guinea-Bissau and lived most of his childhood and adolescence in Cabo Verde. In 1945, he departed to Portugal to study agronomy. Despite the right-wing dictatorship in Portugal, Cabral was highly involved in the political underground in Lisbon, where anti-fascist and anticolonial materials widely circulated. Cabral became acquainted with Marxism-Leninism, mostly through colleagues and friends affiliated with the illegal Portuguese Communist Party. In the late 1950s, in Bissau, then 'Portuguese' Guinea, Cabral founded the African Party of the Independence of Guinea (-Bissau) and Cabo Verde (PAIGC); in 1963, the PAIGC launched the national liberation armed struggle. This war would last ten years, resulting in the independence of Guinea-Bissau in 1973, the collapse of the dictatorship in Portugal, and the decay of her colonial empire, with Cabo Verde gaining independence in 1975. Cabral proved to be the main political leader, military commander, chief diplomat, and ideologue-in-chief of the liberation movement.[1]

If Lisbon was where Cabral met Lenin, Guinea-Bissau became the main theatre for creatively applying many lessons from Lenin's political thought and life. Cabral's own work stood on two basic principles: theory and practice are intimately intertwined; and while lessons can be drawn from other political experiences, blind importation of politico-ideological models is to be categorically rejected.

In this sense, Cabral was never an orthodox Marxist-Leninist, though he frequently used that theoretical framework and terminology to grasp the sociopolitical environment, organise the liberation struggle, and propose a blueprint for its aftermath. That is to say, the development of Cabral's political thought surely passed through the avenue of Marxism-Leninism. Yet, to reduce Cabral to Marxism-Leninism is to underestimate its theoretical uniqueness and originality.

In general terms, many scholars have noted the influences of Lenin on Cabral's political life.[2] Cabral himself acknowledged this importance, calling Lenin the "living example of a combatant for the cause of Humanity, for the economic and therefore national, social and cultural liberation of mankind."[3]

---

[1] See, e.g., Chabal, Patrick (2003), *Amílcar Cabral: Revolutionary Leadership and People's War*. Trenton: Africa World Press & Amado, Abel Djassi (2021), "The União Nacional in Cabo Verde, 1937-1945: Local Politics in an Imperial Political Party," *Portuguese Literary & Cultural Studies*, 36/37, 129-155.

[2] See, e.g., Nzongola-Ntalaja, George (1984), "Amílcar Cabral and the Theory of the National Liberation Struggle," *Latin American Perspectives*, 11(2), 43-54 & McCulloch, Jock (2020), *In the Twilight of Revolution: The Political Theory of Amílcar Cabral*. London: Routledge.

[3] Cabral, Amílcar (1970), "Une Lumière Féconde Éclaire Le Chemin de La Lutte," *Arquivo Amílcar Cabral*.

Moreover, Cabral noted that Lenin's works were of such significance that even those who opposed his politics read him: "Now it is not uncommon to hear politicians – even the most anti-socialist – quote Lenin or boast of having read his works."4 For Cabral, Lenin's "life and behaviour as a <u>humane personality</u> (*"personalité humaine"*) contains lessons and examples useful to all national liberation fighters."5 It follows that Lenin served as a model for revolutionary ethics. As a man of uncompromising and unconditional devotion to the political cause of liberating oppressed groups, his behaviours were to be emulated lest the liberation struggle fail.

On the other hand, as mentioned above, instead of a mechanical importation of Marxism-Leninism, Cabral maintained a critical conversation with its core ideas and principles, judiciously cherry-picking precepts depending on their theoretical usefulness to explain and understand the specific conditions of the colonial situation and the subsequent anticolonial struggle in Guinea-Bissau and Cabo Verde. Cabral's dialogue with Lenin was deeper and far more engaging, however, in two main subjects: imperialism and vanguardism.

Regarding the former, in his 1917 *Imperialism, the Highest Stage of Capitalism,* Lenin sought to unpack the development of financial capital and the competition for territories and resources around the globe by major European powers, including on the African continent. While Lenin's theory had a major impact on Cabral's political thought, the latter sought to expand and adapt it to the situation he was experiencing. In his text, Lenin observed that Portugal, though Europe's sick man, maintained her colonies only because it served the interests of the United Kingdom: "Great Britain has protected Portugal and her colonies in order to fortify her own positions in the fight against her rivals, Spain and France." Cabral, on the other hand, focused on contemporary Portugal to understand "piracy reorganised," i.e. modern imperialism.

He distinguished two main forms of imperialist domination: direct domination or political control through colonialism, and indirect domination through neocolonialism or economic control.6 While Lenin might have spent considerable ink discussing the former, he did not live to experience the latter. Like Frantz Fanon and Kwame Nkrumah, Cabral understood that so-called political independence was a sham, a plot devised by erstwhile colonial powers to maintain control over African territories and resources. Therefore, like Nkrumah, Cabral realised that crude imperialism was not the final stage of capitalism; rather, political independence in the former colonies translated into a new stage of domination, neocolonialism, or "rationalised imperialism."7

The question that puzzled Cabral was why Portugal was stubbornly keeping her colonies and not granting them political independence. He

---
4 Ibid.
5 Ibid (underlined in the original).
6 Cabral, Amílcar (2008), *Unity & Struggle: Selected Speeches and Writings.* Pretoria: Unisa Press, 159.
7 Cabral, Amílcar (1969), *Revolution in Guinea: Selected Texts.* New York: Monthly Review Press, 60.

concluded that it was because Portugal lacked "*neocolonising power.*" As put bluntly by Cabral, "[i]n analysing the problems of African independence we can say that independence was given to colonised countries by the colonial powers as a means of securing the indirect domination of colonised peoples. But Portugal does not possess the necessary economic infrastructure that will allow her to try decolonisation in this manner. She cannot decolonise because she cannot neocolonise."[8] Essentially, for Cabral, neocolonialism, as an innovative system of domination, can be only imposed by those who can. Weak powers, as was the case of Portugal, clung to bygone practices of direct political control. In this regard, Cabral added a novel dimension to the understanding of imperialism.

Another important contribution was its dismantling. Like Lenin, Cabral likely asked, "What is to be Done?" His response, given at the First Solidarity Conference of the Peoples of Africa, Asia and Latin America in Cuba, was emphatic: "There is an African proverb very common in our country [...]: 'When your hut is burning, it is no use beating the tom-tom'. [...] this means that we are not going to succeed in eliminating imperialism by shouting or by slinging insults, spoken or written, at it. For us, the worst or best we can say about imperialism, whatever its form, is to take up arms and struggle."[9] However, he also noted that the barrel of the gun must be accompanied by the barrel of the pen, "the weapon of theory," i.e. political action and ideological development are two sides of the same coin.

It is in this context that a second Leninist political principle had a major impact on Cabral's political work: the notion of vanguardism. Vanguardism was not simply a theoretical framework of the struggle but a practice of organisation. More than a collection of ideas of how to procede politically, it entails the application of these ideas as part of the modus operandi of the revolutionary organisation. The struggle for national liberation was not easy and demanded uncompromising commitment – particularly to those in leadership positions. Thus, Cabral developed the notion of the "*os melhores filhos da nossa terra*" (best sons and daughters of our land), according to which the political leadership of the liberation movement, notwithstanding the fact that "everyone must struggle," should be in the hands of the committed few, "whatever their origin, and wherever they come from."[10]

However, where Cabralian vanguardism arguably goes beyond the Leninist is that in the latter vanguardism essentially *preceded* revolution. In other words, the vanguard constituted the committed few who could accelerate the revolutionary process. In Cabral's understanding, vanguardism did not only precede the start of the liberation struggle. Rather, it was an organisational principle developed to *maintain* the revolutionary fire. As such, the principle of "best sons and daughters of our people" is consciously formulated against the backdrop that the liberation struggle constituted a

---

8 Cabral, Amílcar (1973), *Our People Are Our Mountains: Amílcar Cabral on the Guinean Revolution*. London: Committee for Freedom in Mozambique, Angola and Guinea, 14.
9 Cabral 2008: 153.
10 Ibid: 105.

protracted war that would likely take years until the final victory. Hence, the vanguard of this political process – "constantly embellished by [the] people" – must be capable of bearing any political, material and moral costs that derive from it and, perhaps more importantly, "prepar[e] new militants to carry [the struggle] on, if need be": "The strength of our party is only effective if we, the leaders, are able to open the way for the youth to progress, [...] other youth who are still behind, in their hundreds, in their thousands, to take over and to bring the best forward to lead." Cabral's vanguardism thus stands on the principle that political leadership must entail sacrifices. To such desideratum, vanguardism coincides with a revolutionary ethics grounded on the notion of "class suicide," insofar as the leading class must be willing to go as far as eliminating itself as a class in order to best advance the interests of the people.[11]

By way of conclusion, the lessons developed by Lenin and Cabral in their own times are very much current. Their uncompromising and absolute devotion to a revolutionary cause is a trait that must be highlighted in today's world, characterised by neoliberal totalitarianism disguised as democracy. The struggle for a radically better, just and fair world demands a small group of best sons and daughters, placing collective well-being and interests well above their own. While the struggle is in essence a collective endeavour, and the role of the masses is undoubtedly important, committed leadership is the sine qua non for its success.

Abel Djassi Amado is an associate professor of political science and international relations at Simmons University. He researches on the politics of language in West Africa/Cabo Verde, Amílcar Cabral, and the political history of national liberation in Cabo Verde and Guinea-Bissau.

---

11 Ibid: 105.

3. This Too is Leninism: Military Marxisms in Africa

Adam Mayer

The Left in general, and the Western socialist Left in particular, is accustomed to view the police and the military as the enemy. Allende's broken glasses, and literally millions of our martyrs from Germany to Indonesia, remind us how imperialist violence has used armed platoons against us again and again. Junta is an especially terrible word for us, for we are reminded of Franco, South American right-wing dictators, and by extension Mussolini, the Nazis, the Black Hundreds of Tsarist Russia, Chiang Kai-shek, the apartheid South African army, Mobutu, Sani Abacha, Bokassa, Eyadéma, and all their ilk in Africa.

But Lenin taught us that monopoly capital rules through imperialism, which in the neocolonial context means domination also through war or the threat of war. Therefore, if we stick to our Western notions of 'cops and punks,' comrades against the police, comrades against the army dichotomy, we miss crucial aspects of working-class emancipation historically. We may also fail to grasp what is currently going on, especially in West Africa in the context of the fight against imperialism. If we as Marxists look beyond the classical industrial working class as the sole revolutionary force and consider also the peasantry and informal sector workers as potential revolutionaries, as many of us do, we should equally accept the necessity of armed platoons that belong to the working class on the African continent. Not enough unionised comrades in industry? Class conscious peasants, informal workers, market women have attacked colonialist occupiers on African soil, and radical states built radical armies on the continent.

The Western Left has debated, and will probably debate forever, whether the Soviet experiment, the Chinese People's Republic, the Vietnamese experience, the Lao People's Democratic Republic or the Romanian socialist state had enough socialist content in them to qualify for 'our' sympathy. This in itself is sad, of course, but perhaps inevitable. But it is completely absurd to think that the Red Army or the People's Liberation Army were, in their essence, the same as the whites and imperialist armies that they were fighting, that they fought for 'bureaucratic rule' or 'Stalinism' or social fascism, that there have not been armies in history that belonged to the working class. As a matter of fact, none other than Trotsky built the Red Army, and fought tooth and nail against comrades who wanted to rid it of the 'professional elements,' the old Tsarist officers who ensured its capacity as a fighting force. Importantly, the Red Army thus built fought off French, American and British mercenary armies on Soviet soil, as well as the Russian proto-fascists. Without the People's Liberation Army and its fight against the Japanese imperialists and the Chinese warlords, the PRC would not have come about. China might well have been balkanised and a neocolonialist puppet until this day.

In South America and in Africa, Marxist guerrillas fought (and often won) many wars from the Congo through Angola to Mozambique, Cape Verde, 'Portuguese' Guinea, and other places. But before the 1990s, let us not forget that Africa also had Marxist-Leninist, or African Marxist states from Ethiopia to Benin, Burkina Faso, and states which built very close ties to the PRC (from Mauritania to Uganda, Zambia and Tanzania). These states built real armies when political power already belonged to the victorious socialists or the new radical class constellations. Some of them subsequently fought wars of consequence, as when Tanzania chased away Idi Amin's mad rightist terror, or when Angola fought off Jonas Savimbi's secessionist cause.

One of these states has been ridiculed as 'champagne Marxists' (Congo Brazzaville) because its leaders did not sever economic ties with imperialism, another has been derided as mere voluntarists because they did exactly that (Burkina Faso), as mad Stalinists (Ethiopia), as Islamists (Sudan) or, in the case of Benin, as faux Marxists due to the bronze statues and military help that North Korea provided.

Today, a number of African states – Mali, Guinée, Burkina Faso, Niger – aim to eliminate imperialist rule and exploitation via popular military governments. At the same time, popular movements in democratic socialist fashion from Kenya to Nigeria, from Sudan to Namibia thrive and oppose sub-imperialism. We Leftists and especially Leninists cannot, and should not, simply eliminate the West Africans from our horizon, and even sympathy, as they are fighting the Leninist fight of national liberation against what Kwame Nkrumah called multilateral imperialism, and more specifically against *Francafrique*, an exploitative system that Toyin Falola has recently named "permanent colonialism." Falola is no Communist; let us not be more mainstream than liberals.

Trade unions, student movements, pro-democracy movements under sub-imperialist African 'liberal democracies' such as Senegal, Nigeria, or Kenya, definitely draw on Lenin as an inspiration, as Maina wa Kinyati, Issa Shivji, Leo Zeilig, Baba Aye, or Pascal Bianchini have shown so convincingly. It would thus be a mistake to follow the hegemonic mainstream of academia in labelling military Marxisms as a contradiction in terms, even if the Marxist theory of military Marxisms seems to be less explicit than in more uncontested areas. Resisting neoliberalism, NGO rule and elite brutality in multiparty or one-party systems by strikes and protests, comes to us naturally. Rallying behind soldiers does not, but I would argue that this is our dialectical responsibility, our responsibility as Marxists.

Contrary to what is usually alleged in the literature there even exists Marxist theory on military coups, and partially, on military Marxism of the African variety. None other than Ruth First, the South African Marxist feminist anti-apartheid fighter and martyr, had written early on a 700-page volume on African military governments (*The Barrel of a Gun*), with an eye for detail and a meticulous avoidance of distant, Western attitudes and lack of sympathy for the emancipatory efforts contained within some of those military interventions.

In other words, Lenin's understanding of imperialism and colonialism, Cabral's notion of class suicide (of the petty bourgeoisie), Sankara's focus on the peasantry (we must remember that the peasantry is by far the single most important class component in Africa's armies), Nkrumah's concept of neocolonialism and Ruth First's marked lack of disdain for soldiers (especially the ones who fight against imperialism) should weigh on our own appreciation of the phenomenon of military Marxism too.

Some African Marxist countries, such as the Ethiopian People's Republic, built vanguard parties in the Leninist fashion (prematurely and at the behest of the USSR, mistakenly as it turned out). Others relied on the army itself for the mechanics of government, or on village committees, guerrilla organisations, urban organisations, or an alliance of different parties (such as in state-socialist Madagascar under Ratsiraka, where the multiparty system was kept but each had to subscribe to socialist ideals). All that seemed to melt away after 1989 amid structural adjustment programs in Africa. Recently, however, these ideas have been reappearing in countries across Africa, and we must not be neutral when ECOWAS or France want to attack them militarily. Their fight is Lenin's fight.

Finally, a recurrent 'concern' of Western observers and even Leftists is whether today's capitalist Russia or state socialist China, instrumentalises African radical sentiment to gain ground against the West in Africa. Do they fuel the resurgence of African radicalism? Do they want West Africa to go to Wagner instead of the French legions? Of course, they do all that. But as with social movements in general, great power backing does not constitute the reason behind the phenomenon. Coal miners in England did not strike because Gorbachev secretly sent them funds in his first years in power, they went on strike because of what Thatcher was doing to them. In the same vein, West Africa's officers are no Russian or Chinese stooges. They are fighters for national liberation because of what France does to them, namely the most naked and overtly 19th-century-style imperialism that exists today on the face of the planet.

At the time of writing this short essay, with France reportedly planning an invasion of Niger, the only way West Africa's much abused 'former' French colonies may stand up to a vivacious imperialism, is by playing great powers against each other, and by finally severing their abusive, exploitative Western ties, so as to gain agency, dignity, and the right to be masters of their own fate.

"My generation does not understand this: How can Africa, which has so much wealth, become the poorest continent in the world today? And why do African leaders travel the world to beg?" asked Ibrahim Traoré, the young Burkinabe military head of state, before he pledged armed support for neighbouring Niger in the face of the impending ECOWAS invasion. His anti-imperialist deliberations struck at the heart of the neocolonialist mechanisms which are underdeveloping Africa. Niger then raised uranium prices by

300%: just the kind of step that Kwame Nkrumah, or indeed Lenin, would have recommended.

Adam Mayer is Assistant Professor at Széchenyi István University Hungary and the American University of Iraq Baghdad. He is the author of Naija Marxisms: Revolutionary Thought in Nigeria *(Pluto Press, 2016), and is currently working on a book under the title of* Marxist Africa: Militant and Military Marxist Theory, 1957-2020.

Source: *Leninu. 21 ianvaria 1924*

4. The Wreaths of Lenin

Adrien Minard

I had been looking for this weird volume for a long time. It was finally a local bookseller and bagpipe player whom I met in a Georgian restaurant in Paris who told me the good news. Yes, he had the book and was ready to sell it for a good price. Soberly titled *Lenin, January 21, 1924*, it is a systematic collection of all the offerings placed by his coffin during his burial[1] – around 900 works listed and photographed, a large majority of them funeral wreaths, but also textile compositions, embroideries, portraits, banners, flags, posters and carpets. So many artefacts which show the intensity of emotion aroused by Lenin's death. According to Nina Tumarkin, more than half a million people from all over the country passed by the bier between January 23 and 26 in the Hall of Columns of the House of the Unions where the lying-in-state took place in Moscow.[2] As Zinoviev put it in his funeral speech: "Have you ever before seen such a beautiful, united mass of people, a living giant wave of hundreds of thousands of proletarians who organise themselves on the streets, who day and night stand and wait in this winter storm for their turn to pay their respects to the remains of the leader?"[3]

After years of war, epidemics and famine, this collective mourning ceremony served as a type of catharsis for a population hard hit by a decade of suffering. Certainly, Lenin's funeral was carefully organised by a special commission headed by Dzerzhinsky, chairman of the OGPU, to mobilise Soviet citizens and avoid a political crisis. However, we would be wrong to see it retrospectively as nothing more than an indoctrination enterprise. The size of these crowds and especially their sense of creativity reveal a true spirit of spontaneous communion and a deep popular attachment to Lenin.

Each delegation of mourners came with a piece of art, whether naive or sophisticated, but always modelled according to a particular know-how and inspired by a specific sensibility, highlighting their professional status.[4] Miners from Donbass sculpted a bust of Ilyich from a big piece of coal. The workers of the Profintern Factory in Bryansk arranged around an icon of him all the metal products of their plant such as chains, compasses, drills and taps. Those from Saransk made a wreath with the farming implements they usually forged for their "peasant brothers." The employees of the Tula munitions factory combined an oak branch, with cartridges instead of acorns, and laurel leaves with bullets. Despite the atmosphere of grief, such creative effervescence recalls the early days of the revolution, when avant-garde

---

1 Commission of the Central Executive Committee of the USSR for the Perpetuation of the Memory of V.I. Ulyanov (1924), *Leninu. 21 ianvaria 1924*. Moscow: Goznak.
2 Tumarkin, Nina (1997), *Lenin Lives! The Lenin Cult in Soviet Russia*. Cambridge: Harvard University Press, 140.
3 Ibid: 154.
4 Malysheva, Svetlana (2020), "Funeral Wreath to the Leader: Grief for Lenin and the Practices of Soviet Self-Representation," *Bulletin of Perm University*, n°4 (51), 87-94, in Russian.

artists embarked on all kinds of agitprop experiments. This time, it was ordinary people who customised their offerings, with inscriptions, various winter plants, work tools, little hammers and sickles from odds and ends.

Even before the funeral, the authorities were overwhelmed by the tremendous accumulation of all these works and decided to store most of them in a hall in the Kremlin. But in the days that followed, a question arose: what to do with all these relics? The most fragile ones were starting to deteriorate. In response, the special commission, soon renamed the Commission for the Immortalisation of Lenin's Memory, decided to restore them and to make a complete inventory which would be published in 13,000 copies. All wreaths were photographed, described as precisely as possible and divided into different groups according to the social status or institutional affiliation of the depositaries. In the end, they were listed in a meaningful top-down order: first government agencies, then Party organisations, trade unions, workers' and peasants' collectives, Red Army regiments, cooperative societies and finally children – who were also active participants in the ceremony, rather than poor little victims of official propaganda.[5]

Nonetheless, it was not just about celebrating the memory of a great man, but above all a question of power. This somewhat morbid catalogue, absolutely unique in its kind, was supposed to stop time and freeze for eternity this moment of popular mobilisation, the most important since 1917. Hence, the new Bolshevik government sought to perpetuate this fervour by making the cult of Lenin the basis of its legitimacy. This project probably took shape on the very day of Lenin's death, when the sculptor Sergei Merkurov went to the late leader's bedside and created a death mask, plaster copies of which would soon be venerated in Lenin museums across the country.[6]

Such practices were reminiscent of funerary rituals intended to honour monarchs and nobles during the despised old regime, but Soviet authorities did not hesitate to divert imperial traditions to achieve their own goals. By way of example, shortly after the funeral, in February 1924, the Commission received an anonymous letter of complaint sent from a state farm located in the Mozhaysk district. Their authors, almost illiterate but very angry, denounced a blasphemous act: the large wreath of porcelain flowers placed next to Lenin's coffin in the name of the Moscow Regional Land Department was a second-hand wreath which had already been used during the burial of Prince A. G. Shcherbatov in 1915. An official had just removed the ribbons and added the inscription "To the leader of the working people, the implacable enemy of the oppressors."[7]

But, as is well known, they went even further. Instead of being buried, Lenin's body was then displayed inside a glass sarcophagus placed in a temporary wooden mausoleum built on Red Square, so that more people

---

[5] Leiderman, Daniil and Sokolovskaia, Marina (2021), "'Poor, Poor Il'ich': Visualizing Lenin's Death for Children," in Marina Balina and Serguei Alex. Oushakine (eds.), *The Pedagogy of Images. Depicting Communism for Children*. Toronto, University of Toronto Press, 420-421.
[6] Neumeyer, Joy (2015), '*The Final Struggle*': *The Art of the Soviet Death Mask*. Berkeley: University of California.
[7] Malysheva 2020: 89.

could see it. In late March 1924, after endless debates, and despite opposition from Krupskaya, Trotsky and Bukharin, it was decided to launch an experimental procedure – still ongoing – aimed at lastingly preserving its physical appearance with frequent injections of chemical substances.[8]

The book that emerged from this stunning mix of faith and science resembles a macabre entomology treatise. At a time when 'Leninism' was beginning to be crudely fossilised as an official doctrine for the purposes of political combat, each testimony of devotion to Lenin was scrupulously classified, as if it were necessary to bring order and discipline to the turmoil caused by his death. During his lifetime, a sort of cult had developed, largely from below, in the form of popular art which led to a proliferation of his representations. But as Stalin and his supporters expanded their control over the Party, the production of propaganda artifacts bearing the image of Lenin became more and more standardised. Statues and portraits had to be created by academic artists and approved in high places.[9]

Fast forward to the 21st century, after the killing of 130 people in Paris by three ISIS commandos in November 2015, it was decided to archive thousands of messages, drawings and various objects found among flowers and candles in the spontaneous memorials that appeared in public spaces.[10] For several years now, researchers have looked into this type of collection, which apparently dates back to the 2004 Madrid attacks.[11] Yet, even though circumstances and motivations are extremely different, the precedent of Lenin's funeral remained unnoticed. The Soviet authorities did not keep all the offerings left by mourners, but by making their detailed catalogue they attempted for the first time to account for the massive scale of a collective grief. However, this sort of paper mausoleum, made within the framework of a strictly codified cult, could also appear as a tomb of the revolution.

Adrien Minard (Paris), independent researcher and collector of Soviet artifacts, is the author of Bouzloudja. Crépuscule d'une utopie *(B2, 2018).*

---

[8] Yurchak, Alexei (2015), "Bodies of Lenin: The Hidden Science of Communist Sovereignty," *Representations*, 129(1), 116-157.
[9] Silina, Maria (2015), "Memorial Industry: V. I. Lenin Commemoration in Soviet Russia from 1924 until today," International Conference *"Sites of Memory of Socialism and Communism in Europe*, Bern. Available online.
[10] Gensburger, Sarah & Truc, Gérôme (2020), *Les mémoriaux du 13 novembre*. Paris: Éditions de l'EHESS.
[11] Santino, Jack (ed.) (2006), *Spontaneous Shrines and the Public Memorialization of Death*. New York: Palgrave Macmillan.

5. Me and the Lenin Museum

Aimo Minkkinen

I stumbled upon Lenin while studying at Tampere University at the end of the sixties. Someone had thrown a pile of Lenin's *The State and Revolution* into the student dormitory bin. I picked them up and read one. It really made an impression on me. Lenin wrote: "states, which possess a military apparatus expanded as a consequence of imperialist rivalry, have become military monsters that are exterminating millions of people." And Lenin has never let go of me since.

Lenin never finished the book, but he wrote that it was far more "pleasant and useful to go through the 'experience of revolution' than to write about it." After reading this, I decided to go into the Soviet Union to learn how Lenin's revolutionary thoughts about a democracy that comes from the bottom, from the people, were applied in practice.

I took along my girlfriend Lea on the trip that became a nine-year honeymoon in Moscow. Before departure, I learned the basics of the Cyrillic alphabet and three words of Russian: *terpenije, terpenije, terpenije* (patience, patience, patience). This turned out to be an appropriate attitude. It was very hard to live in the new Soviet conditions. We also brought with us a good deal of socialistic enthusiasm.

In Soviet Russia, I ran into Lenin on every corner. He had become some kind of harmless idol. It was as if he had replaced Santa Claus as a storybook figure. Lenin himself once said that history had shown several times that after a revolutionary dies, there is an attempt to turn them into "harmless icons, to canonise them, so to say, and to hallow their names to a certain extent for the 'consolation' of the oppressed classes and with the object of duping the latter, while at the same time robbing the revolutionary theory of its substance, blunting its revolutionary edge and vulgarising it." The Soviet reality showed that Lenin was right.

I therefore decided to study the real Lenin and his thinking. After preparatory studies, I studied historical materialism for five years at Moscow University's Faculty of Philosophy and then proceeded with a doctorate at the Academy of Social Sciences on Lenin's concept of peaceful coexistence between states with different societal systems. The teachers were very good.

After what I'd read and experienced, it was painfully obvious that Lenin had been turned upside down in the USSR. He was made into the complete opposite of what he had actually been about. Instead of developing civil society, Soviet Russia had grown the bureaucratic state machinery into a gargantuan monster, and in the process Stalin had locked up Lenin under house arrest in the village of Gorki and Lenin's thoughts under the umbrella of official Marxism-Leninism.

But there was one place where Lenin's real thoughts and intentions were taken seriously: the Lenin Museum in Tampere, Finland. I thus decided to return and work there. I thought that it was important to tell the truth about

Lenin: his national policy, the right to self-determination of nations, international solidarity, the fight for peace, against imperialism and great Russian chauvinism.

The Tampere Lenin Museum was opened on January 20, 1946, the day before the anniversary of Lenin's death. Unlike Soviet museums and Lenin museums elsewhere, the Tampere Museum was never an institution of the Communist Party; instead, it was maintained by the Finnish-Soviet Friendship Society and the original initiative to found it came from the Society's Tampere branch.

The Museum is located in the Tampere Workers' Hall, the building where Lenin had promised in 1905 and 1906 that he would work to promote Finland's freedom. Finland was then an autonomous part of the Russian empire. Here Lenin met Stalin for the first time.

As we know, after the revolution Lenin made good on his word. The agreement that acknowledged Finland's independence was the first international agreement signed by the newly formed Bolshevik government, led by Lenin himself. After that, other countries also acknowledged Finland's independence.

In his 1919 "Draft Programme of the R.C.P. (B)" Lenin said: "Look at Finland; she is a democratic country, more developed, more cultured than we are." Finland had to be granted independence because, according to Lenin, the Finnish people thought that "the Muscovites, the chauvinists, the Great Russians, wanted to crush the Finns." Hence, Lenin proclaimed, "it had to be done." In other words, the Finnish people and Lenin had a common enemy, the Russian czarist regime. This united us.

Nonetheless, many of Lenin's own comrades in the party criticised his principled stance on nationality politics, particularly when he authorised certain territorial concessions for Finland. Lenin had to listen to some plainly chauvinistic counterarguments because of his stance: "There are excellent fisheries there, and you have surrendered them." In response, Lenin said: "Scratch some Communists and you will find Great Russian chauvinists." It is these events that are remembered, displayed, and studied at the Tampere Lenin Museum, showing the historical developments and struggles leading up to Finland's independence.

In later years, Mikhail Gorbachev's perestroika had a liberating effect on the museum's activities and programme. It was no longer necessary to have Lenin on a pedestal, and the Soviet Union did not need to be looked at through rose-tinted spectacles. Therefore, from the 1980s onwards there were several special, temporary exhibitions dedicated to themes including the cult of Lenin and the history of faked photographs during the Stalin time (when Trotsky, Bukharin and others suddenly vanished from Soviet photos).

After the fall of the Berlin Wall, discussions on closing down the Tampere Lenin Museum began in 1990 in several Letters to the Editor columns of newspapers, at the city council and the national parliament. Consequently, the museum's allowance was cut and its existence hung in the balance. Fortunately, the museum received support from those who appreciated its historical significance.

Today the Lenin Museum in Tampere is still going strong, attracting countless visitors from around the world. The museum became my fate, my life's work. And for that, the formal and informal education I received in Moscow laid an excellent foundation.

Lenin never dies.

Aimo Minkkinen Ph.D. was the director of the Tampere Lenin Museum between 1989 and 2013.

6. Lenin and Mao

Alain Badiou

I would like to describe here the striking continuity between how Lenin, shortly after the insurrectional victory of 1917, viewed the very young communist revolution in Russia, and how Mao Tse-tung, in the 1960s and 1970s, after twenty years of practice of power by the Chinese Communist Party, reflected on the political results of this power.

As our starting point, let us begin with Lenin's view of the transition from the still bourgeois revolution of February 1917 to the complete takeover of power by the Communist Party, completed in effect at the beginning of the 1920s.

For Lenin, a bourgeois revolution in Russia in 1917 was only a belated catching up to what had already taken place in France, England and Germany. A victory, within the rigorous framework of Marxism, cannot be the simple alignment of the laggards with the already dominant state of things. This is why the main measures he proposes, in theses 6 to 8 of the famous text known today as the "April Theses," relate to the property system. First, one must attack what remains of the feudal order, namely large land ownership, I quote: "Nationalisation of all lands in the country, the land to be disposed of by the local Soviets of Agricultural Labourers' and Peasants' Deputies." Then, the financial power of Capital is broken: "The immediate union of all banks in the country into a single national bank, and the institution of control over it by the Soviet of Workers' Deputies." More generally: "[O]ur immediate task [is] to ... bring social production and the distribution of products at once under the control of the Soviets of Workers' Deputies." It is indeed a question of giving definitive meaning to Marx's formula in the Manifesto: "The theory of the Communists may be summed up in the single sentence: Abolition of private property." And this, which is a long-term historical program for Marx, becomes, in the movement of the Russian revolution, for Lenin, "our immediate task," that which, for there to be the beginning of a victory, must occur "at once."

What should be noted, however, is that, in this text, Lenin in no way proposes the general "nationalisation" of the means of production. He uses the term in relation to land ownership, but this is because this property remains, in Russia, of a feudal type. For the rest, obviously, there must be a single national bank. But it must be under the control of the Soviets of Workers' Deputies. And in general, whether it concerns land ownership, industrial production or the distribution of products, everything must be handed over immediately, not by "nationalisation" to the state power of the Communist Party, but to the assemblies that the revolution created, namely the peasant and worker soviets.

As such, victory does not ultimately reside in the disappearance of private ownership of the means of production and exchange, which is the negative or destructive phase of victory, but rather in a collective appropriation of these means by popular assemblies, and not by a central state.

In other words: for Marxism, as Lenin sees it, the decisive criterion of victory cannot be primarily, and even less solely, negative. Rather, it depends decisively on the new order of things, in this case on the affirmative and irreversible creation of an effectively collective form of appropriation.

In his final texts before his death at the beginning of 1924, Lenin doubts whether the Russian Revolution was really a victory, given the restoration, not of real popular power over the management of things, but of a bureaucracy that copied the traditional forms of the State. He intensifies polemical interventions, far removed from a sense of historic victory. He declares, on the contrary, that "the tasks constituting the core of the socialist revolution have been relegated to the background." He ends up taking a stand against the power to whose apparent victory he contributed so greatly: "Our state apparatus is so deplorable, not to say wretched, that we must first think very carefully how to combat its defects." He goes as far as to question the importance of the Party, of his party. What he says on this subject is truly prophetic, given that we know what, gradually, from the 1930s onwards, this party, under the leadership of Stalin, will become: "Our party is perhaps at risk at this moment of falling into an extremely dangerous situation, that of the man who exaggerates his importance."

As is evident, Lenin in no way speaks of having achieved victory, even though the communists have wrested state power, and won the terrible civil war, which lasted more than three years, led by the counter-revolutionary bands, the Whites, armed and supported by Western powers, including the United States. In fact, for Lenin, the process of the victory of socialism has not, in practice, really begun. What is striking in this vision is that, for Lenin, neither the destruction of an adverse power nor the existence of a communist party at the head of the State, constitute in themselves a guarantee of victory.

We find this vision fifty years later, as one of the problems to be addressed by the Cultural Revolution in China. In this country, in 1966, almost twenty years after the overthrow of the military government of Chang Kai-Chek by the communist Red Army, the major means of production are removed from private property. And yet, Mao Tse Tung doubts that the country is really committed to a true communist perspective. He does not believe that the socialist State alone is capable of achieving the victory of communism. In other words, the political leadership of the country, through a merger between the State and the Communist Party, in no way constitutes a real victory. Mao said this: "without a communist movement, no communism." This means that victory presupposes a mass subjective and combative commitment in the direction of communism.

Here again, the overthrow of the old political and social order, the negative side of the revolutionary process, cannot be enough to speak of victory. The constant reality, outside the Party, if necessary, of vast popular movements, is necessary. Mao goes so far as to say that a new bourgeoisie is present in the State and Party apparatus. He notes that the salary hierarchy still has nine levels. He asks the fundamental question: the factories belong to the State, of course, but from the point of view of those who work there, are socialist factories really different from capitalist factories?

It is in this spirit that he will support, in opposition to the state bureaucracy and the conservative inertia of the Communist Party and the army, first a violent and anarchic movement of student youth, then the workers of the large factories, notably in Shanghai. The aim is to bring about, within mass movements themselves, a confrontation, albeit as peaceful as possible, between what will be called the "two paths," the communist path and the capitalist path. This struggle will reach all levels of society: universities, factories, businesses, administrations, and even certain sectors of the police and army.

Following almost ten years of unrest, movements and counter-movements, the capitalist path openly prevail after the death of Mao in 1976. Ultimately, if we can speak of victory, it can only be that of Deng Xiao Ping and his faction towards an explicit restoration of capitalism. Deng will indeed make two crucial pronouncements. The first is to fetishize "development" as the unique slogan of the times – meaning economic growth at any social cost, and in particular the creation of a gigantic reserve labour force that can be exploited at will. Deng's second principle, quite dialectical, is that the first stage of communism must be capitalism. In this regard, it ultimately amounts to a serious defeat of communism, which will be followed by its virtual historical disappearance.

From this point of view, we can understand that Mao, ageing and, like Lenin, finally defeated by the Party-State apparatus, ended up saying, "We haven't done much."

In other words: *If* we take the Marxist criterion of the two paths, the capitalist or the communist; private property and the concentration of Capital, *or* the collective appropriation of the entire production apparatus; the maintenance of national control of populations *or* the transnational future of politics; the acceptance of truly monstrous inequalities, *or* an effectively egalitarian vision; a strictly hierarchical organisation of work, *or* the participation of all in manual and intellectual tasks, in management tasks as well as in execution tasks. *If* these are the real orientations, and it is a question of ensuring that they prevail in public opinion as well as in political, economic and social reality, then a victory cannot be reduced either to the seizure of State power or to the nationalisation of the production apparatus. It is the masses themselves who, changing their position in the process, must be able to experience and define victory. Or again: there is a formalism of victory that must be distrusted. Its reality is much more difficult to construct and affirm because it is based on the effective transformation of the entire social system. A social system whose formal characteristics, defined by Marx as the historical existence of social classes with opposing interests, go back much further in history than capitalism, which has only existed for a few centuries – in other words, almost no time at all.

Alain Badiou is a French philosopher. Translation: Patrick Anderson.

Artist: Valentín Carmín

7. Invocation of Lenin

alejandra ciriza

> *On snow-covered lands*
> *and on stubbly fields,*
> *in smoky plants*
> *and on factory sites,*
> *with you in our hearts,*
> *Comrade Lenin,*
> *we build,*
> *we think,*
> *we breathe,*
> *we live,*
> *and we fight!*
> (Vladimir Mayakovsky)

En octubre tu fuiste mía ... y ahora todo es melancolía. In October you belonged to me ... now there is nothing but melancholy.

Impelled by the powerful image created by Valentín, we invoke Comrade Lenin.

Inspired by the indispensable words of Mayakovsky, we bring Lenin into this terrifying present that threatens to suffocate us in this small country of mine, located in the south of the South of our dark-skinned *Nuestramérica*, in Argentina, in the provincial city where I live in the mighty shadow of the Andes. Our present marked by the advance of the far-right leaves us without breath. And yet we breathe.

We want a conversation with Comrade Lenin. It is urgent, *camarada*... his *photograph on the whiteness of the wall* while fascism is once again raising its ugly head among the wretched of the earth, *lxs condenadxs de la tierra*, here in my Argentina, an empty little matchbox discarded on some forgotten footpath in the South of the world.

The images of Lenin: Multiple, recurring, potent, they summon our dreams, the dream that we hold on to with such determination – *la revolución*, the revolution, this eternal dream that illuminates our every step, even in ill-fated times like the one we currently inhabit. That is why the conversation is so urgent.

Lenin in the armoured train, *as his mouth jerks open in speech... the immense brow.*

Lenin face-to-face with the revolutions of 1917, and those that did not come after, and then those that did come ... much later from across the ocean, from this side of the world.

Lenin was besieged by the urgent need to think revolution and organise *las masas* in his country, the Russia of the brutal autocracy, of the repression unleashed against the starving people in 1905, of the sailors' mutiny on the Battleship Potemkin, of the hanging of generation after generation of fearless revolutionaries. Just like in this small country of mine, my country at the end of the world, ravaged by genocide, debt and famine, but illuminated by age-old, stubborn resistance. Perhaps this time too, hope may be lying in wait... somewhere.

Lenin confronts an all-devouring imperialism and the brutality of war, his lucidity refuting the idea of the possible compatibility between capitalism and workers' emancipation.

Lenin in his debates with the European Social Democrats during the Zimmerwald conference, his alliances with women like Clara, Inessa, Nadia, and Rosa.

But also the young Lenin, the third son of an enlightened, open and affectionate family, deeply attached to his *madre* and *padre*, to his *hermanas* Anna, Olga and Maria, and to his brothers, Dmitri the younger and Alexander the older.

Lenin a man deeply marked by his times and country of origin and at the same time a universal man, his revolutionary sensibility tied to the cataclysmic moment that was the hanging of his *hermano* Alexander at the hands of Tsarist barbarism, as well as the watershed of the singular and collective upheavals that propelled the proletarian revolutions, from that of 1905 to those of February and October 1917, under the dazzling light of the April Theses.

Lenin and the difficult construction of socialism after his return to Russia. The sleepless time, *awhirl with events*. The July days. All Power to the Soviets! The flight to Finland. *El Estado y la Revolución*.

Lenin writing, agitating, summoning. Peace, Bread, Land! Here and everywhere.

> *The tense*
> *creases of brow*
> *hold thought*
> *in their grip,*
> *immense brow*
> *matched by thought immense.*

Lenin encouraged the dream of revolution in times of looming defeat, carrying it out against all odds. Not because he did it alone...

> *A forest of flags,*
> *raised-up hands thick as grass...*
> *Thousands are marching*
> *with him...*

We want a conversation with Comrade Lenin, starting from here, from the South, from the affinity born of our readings of him, from the shared dreams of *revolución*, from the many defeats he experienced and overcame, and the ones we had to endure and overcome, we the wretched of the earth, *indixs, negrxs y mestizxs, amefricanxs,* children of Abya Yala, land of plenitude soaked in blood from the early 1920s *Patagonia Rebelde* of wool working peons and Tehuelches to the 1975 Red Snake of the Paraná Operation against disobedient industrial workers. We, who tried to storm the heavens and paid a heavy price. We, the inhabitants of the south of the South, want a conversation with Comrade Lenin, to *report to him* and share with him *this hellish work... as the day slowly sinks, as the night shadows fall.*

We want to bring him urgently into the present, sensitive as he was to women's rights and dissent in times of misogyny and regression.

Lenin and *las mujeres*, the women... first, those of his family, his mother and Anna, his older sister; the young Olga, who died of typhus in 1891; Maria, the youngest, all of them comrades in arms and emotional support throughout his life. Lenin, a brother of sisters considered as equals, born in a country where a woman could be sold in the same way as a horse.

Lenin and *las rojas*, those red, communist women who were his contemporaries and whose voices we have never stopped hearing: Nadezhda Krupskaya and Inessa Armand, close in love and ideas; Alexandra Kollontai, *compañera* and *interlocutora* in the construction of the Zhenotdel, so necessary to transform the daily lives of women workers and peasants; Rosa Luxemburg, in spite of everything, critical and supportive, the red eagle of the Revolution; Clara Zetkin, comrade of so many years...

Nosotras, beloved Lenin, we who ardently read your programme for the women of the Revolution, We who remember you today in our struggles for the right to abortion, We, *Nosotras*, invoke you, Vladimir Ulyanov, because your voice still resonates among us.

With you in our hearts,
Comrade Lenin,
we build,
we think,
we breathe,
we live,
and we fight!

alejandra ciriza *is a feminist activist and militant for memory, truth and justice, working as a philosophy teacher in Mendoza, Argentina.*

Translated from the Argentine Spanish by hjje.

8. Lenin, Dialectics, and Trans Liberation

Alex Adamson

Every birth and every death, far from being a protracted gradualness, is rather its breaking off and a leap from quantitative into qualitative alteration. Natura non facit saltum [nature does not make leaps], as the saying goes; and ordinary thinking, when confronted by a coming-to-be or a passing-away, believes that it has comprehended it conceptually by representing it, as we said, as a gradual emerging or vanishing... The belief that coming-to-be is gradual is based on imagining that what comes to be is already present to the senses or is in principle actual, only so small that it still escapes perception... Explaining coming-to-be and vanishing from the gradualness of alteration suffers from the tediousness typical of any tautology; the coming-to-be and the vanishing are presupposed as ready-made beforehand and the alteration is reduced to the mere mutation of an external difference, and in this way the change becomes in fact only a tautology. The difficulty confronting an intellect intent on this kind of explanation lies in the qualitative transition from a something into its other in general and into its opposite – a difficulty which the intellect meets by pretending that identity and alteration are the indifferent external identity and alteration of the quantitative sphere.
(Hegel, *Science of Logic*, 1812)

Leaps, Leaps, Leaps!

Man's consciousness not only reflects the objective world, but creates it.
(Lenin, "Conspectus on Hegel's *Science of Logic*," 1914-16)

Lenin's Bolshevik Party abolished the czarist anti-gay law and legalised abortion less than eight weeks after the October 1917 Revolution.
(Leslie Feinberg, 2004)

Lenin held that just when capitalism had reached this high stage of 'organisation,' monopoly (which extended itself into imperialism), was the time to see new, national revolutionary forces that would act as 'bacilli' for proletarian revolutions as well.
(Raya Dunayevskaya, *Philosophy and Revolution*, 1973)

Maybe a homosexual can be the most revolutionary.
(Huey P. Newton, 1970)

STAR is a very revolutionary group. We believe in picking up the gun, starting a revolution if necessary.
(Marsha P. Johnson, 1973)

Bringing together contemporary struggles for trans liberation and Lenin's legacy might seem surprising at first, but I argue along with trans communist Leslie Feinberg, that even if the explicit intentions of 1917 were not organised around gender self-determination, the underpinnings and aspirations of the Bolshevik revolution *are* compatible with trans liberation. Lenin's work should hence be re-evaluated in light of the burgeoning, though sometimes contradictory, movement for trans liberation. The quote "there are decades where nothing happens; and there are weeks where decades happen," is commonly attributed to Lenin to describe the experience of the Russian

Revolution, but it could equally apply to the experience of transitioning. The dialectics of transition follows the route that Hegel outlines in the *Science of Logic*. There comes a moment of qualitative *leap* on many levels at once – in one's consciousness, in the relationships one holds with others, and in one's experience of the world as one finally consciously takes part in one's own process of revolutionary becoming. The experience is not smooth, nor linear, but continues with fits, stops, starts, and leaps – such is the movement of the dialectic.

This account of dialectics, consistent with trans experience, gender self-determination, and the movement of revolution, is contrary to the mechanical account of dialectical materialism outlined in Lenin's *Materialism and Empirio-Criticism* (1909). Lenin would later distance himself from this account of dialectics – and its basis in Plekhanov rather than Marx – after he retreated to the Berne library in 1914 to study and reflect on the failures of the Second International to prevent WWI. In these years he carefully studied Hegel's *Science of Logic* and produced a significant body of notes and reflections on Hegelian dialectics that led him to infamously argue: "It is impossible completely to understand Marx's *Capital*, and especially its first chapter, without having thoroughly studied and understood the whole of Hegel's *Logic*. Consequently, half a century later none of the Marxists understood Marx!!" As Raya Dunayevskaya and Kevin Anderson have persuasively argued, Lenin's concepts of revolutionary defeatism and national liberation were heavily influenced by this study of Hegel. Breaking with the crude 'dialectical materialism' of Plekhanov is what enabled Lenin to write his most philosophically rich texts on the revolutionary nature of national liberation struggles, *State and Revolution*, and *Imperialism, the Highest Stage of Capitalism*. I argue similarly that a study of dialectics reveals the revolutionary basis of trans struggles, and the necessity of gender self-determination for the overcoming of *all* forms of alienation under capitalism.

The starting quote from Hegel on the truth of qualitative change as something fundamentally *not* gradual, but rather a radical coming-into-being of something new, is what inspired Lenin to write in his marginalia, "Leaps, Leaps, Leaps!" The mechanistic and positivistic thinking of the Second International is finally smashed for Lenin. This moment allows him to reorient his thinking on the nature of monopoly capitalism, revolutionary strategy, and the role of national liberation struggles as "'bacilli' for proletarian revolutions." He reverses his initial analysis of Hegel's dialectic as perniciously idealistic, instead arguing that Hegel's writings in the "Doctrine of the Concept" are actually some of the most useful for a materialist account of reality. The interplay of humanity and nature for Lenin finally comes together with Marx's notes on humanism and nature in the *1844 Economic and Philosophic Manuscripts*. Marx writes "*[The human being]* is directly a *natural being*. [...] But [the human being] is not merely a natural being; [they are] a *human* natural being. [They are] a being [for-itself], and therefore a *species-being*; and as such [they have] to express and authenticate [themselves] in being as well as in thought." Further, Lenin writes, "Man's consciousness not only reflects the objective world but creates it." Applying these insights to trans liberation, against various charges of 'unnatural-ness' – whether that be transgender existence *tout court* or gender-affirming medical interventions in particular – from a Marxist perspective, it should be clear that appropriating one's existence with what has been made possible by human labour is the most natural thing a human being can do.

Nevertheless, although trans liberation *should be* logically consistent with a Marxist-Leninist analysis, many who called themselves such in the 1970s and 1980s argued that LGBT people represented a counter-revolutionary manifestation of 'bourgeois decadence' – with some exceptions, like the Los Angeles Research Group's "Toward a Scientific Analysis of the Gay Question." Although Black Panther Party leader Huey Newton would come to the opposite conclusion – "maybe a homosexual can be the most revolutionary" – he only arrived at this position after meeting with Jean Genet and Sylvia Rivera. Rivera as a co-founder of STAR – the first trans sex-worker-led organisation offering shelter to queer and trans youth – attended the 1970 Revolutionary People's Constitutional Convention, organised by the Black Panther Party, and helped put gay power and trans liberation on the map of revolutionary politics in the United States. As another co-founder of STAR, Marsha P. Johnson put it, "STAR is a very revolutionary group. We believe in picking up the gun, starting a revolution if necessary." Dividing themselves against the assimilationist and upwardly mobile gay and lesbian organisations fighting merely for rights and inclusion into the imperialist capitalist state, STAR embodied a qualitative leap in both its analysis and strategy for revolution.

Current struggles for revolutionary trans liberation are similarly set against a politics of liberal inclusion viewing assimilation into an imperialist state as progress. That is to say, revolutionary trans liberation, just like the process of transition itself, requires the "withering away" of one's old self, one's old world, and a leap into something new. A world where colonial bourgeois gender norms are no longer enforced, and the material conditions requiring these rigid and so-called 'productive' forms of life and social relations are no longer in place. In the revolutionary spirit of Lenin, our continued fight to overthrow capitalist imperialism and its attendant forms of dehumanisation should be seen as one and the same as our fight for trans liberation.

Alex Adamson (he/they) is an assistant professor of philosophy at Babson College and a community organiser in the Greater Boston area.

9. Lenin and Artificial Intelligence

Alex Taek-Gwang Lee

In 2017, Russian President Vladimir Putin, addressing students at the commencement of the school year in Russia, underlined the significance of artificial intelligence (AI) by stating that it holds the key to the future, not only for Russia but for all of humanity.[1] He stressed the vast opportunities that AI presents, along with unpredictable threats, asserting that the individual or nation that excels in mastering AI will hold global dominance. Despite expressing the ambition to lead in this field, Putin accented the importance of avoiding monopolisation. He affirmed that if Russia were to achieve leadership in developing AI, it would willingly share its expertise with the entire world, drawing a parallel with its current approach to sharing nuclear technologies.

Here, Putin fell short in dispelling Lenin's legacy, even though he had previously criticised Lenin on numerous occasions. In this case, one of Lenin's renowned statements defined communism as "Soviet power plus the electrification of the whole country,"[2] a reference often linked to Lenin's emphasis on technology, including capitalist technology, as a vital element of communism. The contemporary resonance of Lenin's perspective on 'tech communism' is evident in Putin and figures like Peter Thiel, entrepreneur, and co-founder of PayPal and Palantir Technologies, who also financially contributed to the development of ChatGPT.

In the 2018 Cardinal Conversation with Reid Hoffman at Stanford University, the alt-right venture capitalist Thiel asserted that "AI is communist."[3] Specifically, Thiel accentuated the discernible dynamics of "centralisation" and "decentralisation" in both technology and politics. He characterised cryptocurrencies like bitcoin as embodying a libertarian ethos, while labelling AI, which plays a role in extensive data gathering across societies, as having "a communist nature." His point possibly alluded to Lenin's concept of "democratic centralism." What stands out in this characterisation of Bolshevik centralism is the intriguing notion that the connection between democracy and centralisation could be realised through what Lenin described as "professional revolutionaries." Who are these professional revolutionaries? According to Lichtheim, they are "a self-constituted elite."[4]

When Thiel labelled AI as communist, he might have envisioned an Orwellian dystopia governed by Leninist-like elites. Thiel's understanding of

---

1 See "'Whoever leads in AI will rule the world': Putin to Russian children on Knowledge Day." *RT*. Available online.
2 Lenin, V.I. (1974), "The Eighth All-Russia Congress of Soviets," in *Collected Works Vol. 31*, Moscow: Progress Publishers, 516.
3 Parker, Clifton B. (2018), "At Stanford, first Cardinal Conversation spotlights technology, politics," *Stanford News*.
4 Lichtheim, George (1970), *A Short History of Socialism*. New York: Praeger Publishers, 154.

communism is not new of course, and undeniably in line with Friedrich von Hayek's 1945 critique of central planning. Hayek pointed out that "the 'data' from which the economic calculus starts are never for the whole society 'given' to a single mind which could work out the implications, and can never be so given," and that consequently the vast and diverse knowledge that individuals hold, spread out across millions of minds, is impossible for any central authority to fully grasp.[5] Central planners, such as the bureaucrats in the USSR, are thus doomed to make unsuccessful decisions without understanding each person's preferences and unique potential. From this perspective, Hayek defined "competition" as "decentralised planning by many separate persons" and monopoly (or "organised industries") as "the halfway house" between centralisation and decentralisation. His solution to this is "the price system," in other words, market economies which showcase a remarkable capacity to process and consolidate dispersed information with (apparent) efficiency and effectiveness.

It is crucial to highlight in Hayek's argument that for him central planning is an attempt to square the circle, which is incompatible with "all truly social phenomena, language, and cultural inheritance." In short, his point is that central planners cannot understand the economic reality because they lack a method to accumulate the data of its actual mechanism. Hayek's solution to this failure is "the interactions of people each of whom possesses only partial knowledge."[6] Interestingly, his approach to economic reality seems to resonate with Lenin's own understanding of the relationship between economic theory and its actualisation in the context of "backward" Russia. In his 1918 "The Immediate Tasks of the Soviet Government," for example, Lenin described Taylorism (i.e. scientific management) as "a combination of the refined brutality of bourgeois exploitation and a number of the greatest scientific achievements in the field of analysing mechanical motions during work, the elimination of superfluous and awkward motions, the elaboration of correct methods of work, the introduction of the best system of accounting and control."[7]

However, he added to this argument that "the Russian is a bad worker compared with people in advanced countries. It could not be otherwise under the tsarist regime and in view of the persistence of the hangover from serfdom," and so "the task that the Soviet government must set the people in all its scope is – learn to work." Lenin proposed addressing the challenges in the Russian economy through the organisation of "self-constituted elites," empowering them to instil learning to work among the workers. Therefore, where Hayek emphasised the competition of "the price system" in the market, Lenin called attention to the socialist "organisation of competition"

---

5 Hayek, F.A. (1945), "The Use of Knowledge in Society," *The American Economic Review*, 35(4), 519.
6 Ibid: 530.
7 Lenin, V.I. (1974), "The Immediate Tasks of the Soviet Government," in *Collected Works Vol. 27*, Moscow: Progress Publishers, 259.

based on "all-out revolutionary enthusiasm" and coercion in form of "trial by court for those who violate labour discipline."

Importantly, Lenin viewed Taylorism as a provisional technology for the gradual building and consolidation of socialism through a strong workers' state. The paradox of Soviet Taylorism resided in its internal logic, wherein it required a robust state for its inherent negation – communism. At the same time, certain elements of Taylorism, including task decomposition, standardisation, and a focus on efficiency, laid the groundwork for the eventual incorporation of automation and the rise of AI. Lenin's perception of scientific management as a means to achieve socialist objectives led to a call for increased emphasis on learning. Over time, however, scientific management with the goal of automatising the state turned out to be not a matter of learning but of enhancing algorithmic affordances. The more data-driven scientific management logic is realised, the more workers adapt by accepting the machine's algorithms as normative. The result is a state of voluntary servitude where everything is judged according to computational data. In this sense, ironically, Lenin's idea of the proletarian state, seen as a transitional mechanism toward the ultimate elimination of the state through its own functions, has found greater application within neoliberalism than within historical socialism.

The state Lenin sought to dismantle has since undergone decentralisation through Hayek-inspired "competition," only to be supplanted by increasingly centralised big tech companies. As Yanis Varoufakis points out in *Technofeudalism: What Killed Capitalism*, the dominance of big tech monopolies appears to have replaced the fundamental tenets of capitalism with their platforms and rents – there are no more autonomous markets but only "techno-feudalism." With the growing prevalence of AI, we are fast entering an era where individuals can autonomously handle tasks that once required extensive collaboration. These self-managing, self-optimising individuals stand in stark contrast to Lenin's notion of self-appointed elites trying to organise the masses for the creation of a radically more just society. Instead, they willingly serve as enslaved labour to automated machines in order to enhance the profit of the 1%. In a scenario where capitalism increasingly operates without traditional workers, it would signify the termination of its prevailing mode of production.

In the contemporary landscape dominated by automation and computation, what is absent, in contrast to Lenin's era, is a socialist organisation. Considering the current wave of AI-driven automation as a contemporary iteration of the scientific management witnessed by Lenin, the imperative now is to re-think the lost cause of a socialist organisation with a clear political aim of communism. Lenin's task remains an unfinished project, and he continues to ask us what is to be done in the re(tro)volutionary era.

Alex Taek-Gwang Lee is a professor of cultural studies and a founding director of the Centre for Technology in Humanities at Kyung Hee University, Korea.

10. My Lenin

Alexander Vatlin

I do not count myself among Lenin's admirers, but rather the opposite. As an historian, I see how much Russia lost over the past century, as Lenin and his political heirs attempted to impose on the country a path to the future based not on that country's political experience but on their own interpretation of wise books, the classics of Marxism. The last of these heirs was Mikhail Gorbachev who declared that, under the conditions of perestroika, the Soviet Union would return to "Lenin's path to socialism." He thus remained true to the traditional algorithm, according to which this path should be sought not in real life, but in quotations from the *Complete Works* of the Bolshevik leader.

This time of invigorating hope ended quickly, but it left its mark on the life of every Soviet person of that era. I remember late autumn 1991, when the Communist Party was overthrown, and the USSR was in its last days. At that time, I was a research fellow at the Institute of Marxism-Leninism at the Central Committee of the CPSU (which, on the eve of the August putsch, had been renamed the Institute for the Theory and History of Socialism). My workplace was in a pompous building on the outskirts of Moscow, where another global project was once launched and eventually came to an end: the Communist International, which saw itself as the headquarters of the proletarian world revolution.

I came by car to take my books with me, an impressive library that I had amassed over the three years I had worked at the institute. Most of the books were gifts from foreign colleagues who brought or sent works that were banned in Russia before perestroika. Among these were books with Lenin's portrait emblazoned on the cover, often alongside Stalin or Trotsky, both of whom were unacceptable to the Soviet censors because they called into question the sacred truth of the 'uniqueness' of the origins and consequences of "Lenin's path."

But my story is not actually about these books, which seemed to me at the time to be an adequate rejection of a now obsolete Soviet dogma. As I walked through the floors of the deserted institute, not a single soul was to be seen, all the doors were wide open. Colleagues had long since taken with them everything they could use in their future lives; what they thought useless had been left in the hall. In this long passageway, reminiscent of a prison wing, lay blue and brown books in heaps, the volumes of the fourth and fifth editions of Lenin's *Works*. (As we soon learned, it was not, as the title suggested, the *Complete Works*, because many of Lenin's letters and writings, amounting on their own to several volumes, were still unpublished at the time.)

Hardly anything could surprise me anymore in those autumn days, but the scene before me was truly shocking. A more vivid symbol of the fall of a decaying system could scarcely be imagined. Until recently, a world power that considered itself the 'vanguard of advanced humanity' (a conceptual template that had been etched in our minds, and which we imagined we would carry with us until our dying day) had been firmly based on these volumes with Lenin's profile on the cover. Now, this 'ideological foundation' had collapsed and become nothing more than mounds of wastepaper.

More out of habit than by design, I searched through these heaps of books for what – may Marx forgive me! – seemed to me to be the "object of my labour" at the beginning of my scientific career. The history of the Comintern, the Russian view of the united workers' front, Lenin's testament – I remember these volumes as well today as I do the titles of the articles they contain. And now, right before my eyes, everything had become useless, consigned, to quote Trotsky, to "the dustbin of history."

As a staunch supporter of perestroika – and I am still convinced today of the positive character and inevitability of the reforms that were taking place at the time – I was shocked. For seven decades, had our grandparents and parents been "wanderers into the void" or worse, merely following the tune of the pied piper, who had become a catcher of souls? The life experience gained in subsequent years shows that we are still today looking for melodies that inspire us or put us to sleep. And those who enter the stage of history with us are hence not subject to the condemnation of their contemporaries, but only to the judgement of world history, as Nikolai Bukharin affirmed during his show trial.

To say that everyone living in Russia today possesses their own Lenin would not be true. For the vast majority, he simply does not exist: either he has been pushed out of historical memory by other issues, beliefs, or leaders; or the few pages devoted to him in school textbooks were inadequate to make him accessible at all. Lenin's name has not vanished from Russian cityscapes, streets and squares are named after him, his monuments still stand, but they no longer evoke those stormy emotions, neither hate nor reverence. And that is good. The 'leader of the world proletariat' has long since disappeared from the everyday political agenda (unlike Stalin, for example); he has ceased to be an instrument with which the still molten past can be reforged at will.

My Lenin, those ten or twelve volumes of the *Works* that I took with me that autumn from the temple of Marxism-Leninism, abandoned by its high priests, are still in my study today. When I open them to find a quote or to dive into the historical context of a century ago, I remember how they came into my possession. For me it is a reminder that the path *per aspera ad astra* also has an opposite vector. But anyone who has not walked this path to its end has no right to call themselves a historical figure. Lenin, on the other hand, undoubtedly numbers among those who, as Stefan Zweig aptly said, embody the "finest hour of humankind."

Alexander Vatlin is Professor of Modern History at Lomonosov Moscow State University.

11. Lenin, Liberated Woman of the East

Anara Moldosheva

*"Tell me,
Who is this Lenin?"
And I replied, quietly:
"Lenin is you."*
(Sergei Yesenin)

The obituary came into being as an elite form of remembrance, primarily to immortalise the 'services to society' of the rich and famous. Consequently, it isn't easy for me to write in this genre about Lenin in the type of revolutionary way he deserves. In any case, for the message to be revolutionary, according to Lenin, some type of organisation would be necessary. Instead, I am opting to share with the reader a 'sketch from life' informed by a personal (but inevitably political) perspective, with one important preliminary remark. Just as the conceptual space of Marxism possesses, as has often been pointed out, the great advantage that it can be interpreted in many different ways (as evidenced by Lenin's own work), so too its symbolic space should be open to unusual transformations in which much needed new ideas and images are stimulated.

My interactions with Lenin are quite regular and they are connected, strange as it may sound, with everyday housekeeping tasks, since these include washing the 'Lenin sitting in an armchair' statuette from our collection of Soviet-era porcelain. This almost ritualistic activity has its own name – 'bathing Lenin.' The other day, I was once again giving him a bath, thinking how I might write a Lenin obituary about the 'Asian question' in our assessment of Lenin's legacy, in light of recent debates about 'decolonisation' in our region, which in reality also means 'de-sovietisation.'

As is well known, anti-Leninist rhetoric has historically been based, among other things, on the idea that the 'dark side' of his political genius was an 'inborn' manifestation of his 'Asian' character, linked to 'oriental despotism' and so on. However, my aim here is not to expose this racist discourse, as important as this undoubtedly is in today's times. Rather, I want to appropriate the 'Asian Lenin' as a quintessential communist figure, always creatively responding to the current historical situation, in a state of constant praxis. In this sense, Lenin is 'undeniably Asian,' regardless of (or perhaps understanding dialectically) the many instances where he himself expressed prejudices against Asia.

This gesture of appropriation seems particularly symbolic in light of another important date. 1924 was not only the year of Lenin's death, it was also the year in which the Kyrgyz Autonomous Oblast came into being, as a direct result of Lenin's policy upholding the right of peoples to self-determination, including a secession from the federation and the formation of an independent state. It is from that moment that modern Kyrgyz statehood began, and simultaneously the grand project for the 'liberation of the women of the East,' represented as the most oppressed section of women in the Soviet Union. A project that, despite all its contradictions and complexities, achieved undeniable successes in the fields of labour, administration, education, health care, social protection and culture, and thanks to which my two grandmothers, my mother Clara (named after Clara Zetkin) and countless other women of their generations gained novel opportunities for an active and fulfilled life.

My own 'inherited' activities in the field of expanding women's personal and social possibilities occurred mostly in the period after the collapse of the Soviet Union, when a new politics entered the scene – the politics of 'gender' as promoted by international development agencies. It would be hard to call this politics 'women's liberation,' however, since the very notions of liberation and emancipation were hardly used any more. Not that we paid attention to this at the time – being super-confident in the new realities and the promises of 'gender equality' we thought we had been deprived of. How tragicomic we must have appeared to women activists from those parts of the world where the achievements of Soviet women we now ignored seemed like a distant dream. Today, having been actively engaged for many years with this 'gender politics,' it is difficult for me to disagree with the critique of so-called gender equality strategies, which, without a concrete political, social and economic programme, have turned out to be nothing more than "reformist bamboozling," that is, an empty ideological form with no relation to the "burning needs and shameful humiliation suffered by weak and powerless women under the bourgeois [capitalist] system," as denounced by Lenin in his conversations with Zetkin.

The paradox is that the facade of empty gender politics has often been inspired by originally left-wing, socialist ideas. A good example is the history of the annual march in Kyrgyzstan's capital Bishkek in honour of International Women's Day on March 8, around which a serious "discursive struggle" takes place year in, year out between conservatives and liberals, right-wing and left-wing groups, over slogans, symbols and women's history in our country. It is impossible to go into detail here, suffice it to say that as a result of this struggle, liberal feminists with their euphoric demands for 'rights,' 'democracy,' and nowadays 'decolonisation' have ended up colonising the agenda of the march, depoliticising the issue of women's rights, and leaving those of us who understand the "burning need" for more radical agendas with the task of rebuilding them on the base of the old Leninist programs, inspired by radically new ideas and visions.

Speaking of which, long ago F. Jameson observed that the main task of the Left (he was talking about the US-American left but that doesn't matter) seems to have become the invention of "new ideas to replenish the imagination and the political arsenal of an eclectic moderate political movement [...] whose bankruptcy follows swiftly on the disappearance of its secret source of inspiration."

This makes me think that perhaps we should ourselves "disappear" and then come back to life in a new capacity that stimulates the radical imagination and strengthens our collective ability to, in the words of Jameson, "name the alternative, name the solution, name the system." And why not attempt to do so through an operation as queer as bathing 'Lenin, the liberated woman of the East,' thereby potentially opening up new prospects of mutual penetration of various political traditions, along with new liberatory paths fraught with gaps, constraints and incommensurabilities? Of course, it is entirely possible that on this path neither side will end up recognising itself any longer, but isn't that precisely what radical imagination is about? After all, who on earth bathes Lenin...?

Anara Moldosheva is an independent bookstore worker and activist of the March 8 march, living in Bishkek, Kyrgyzstan.

Translated from the Russian by many.

12. To Blow (Up) the Mausoleum

Anatoli Ulyanov

It's a magnificent sunny day with a touch of snow.
(Lenin)

1

Anyone who writes about Lenin risks falling into the bowels of the Mausoleum. There, the lizards with sticky tongues crawl. Dripping and moaning, they lick Ilyich's remains until they shine like a ruddy banner. This oral admiration turns Lenin into an ontological corpse.

> Our beloved father! (...) We know that the hour will soon come when wreaths from all corners of the world will descend upon your heated grave. (...) It will forever flourish; it will never be barren. It won't be the morning summer dew that moistens it, but the tears of your children, who ardently loved you and will remain eternally loyal to you.
>
> *(from Grigory Zinoviev's memoirs)*

The icon of Lenin is the icon of death, which, much like an inverted crucifix, rejects the one it meant to venerate. I don't want to turn Lenin into a lollipop. I aim to expose the man of flesh behind the marbled mummy doll.

2

I was born far back enough to call the Soviet Union my birthplace, yet not as far as to experience the era of school dictations about Lenin.

Sliding from my mother's womb in the 1980s, I was entering the country that was exiting into a grave. This twilight state of the system shielded me from the cult of Lenin, whose portrait on my kindergarten wall was soon replaced by the Ukrainian poet Taras Shevchenko.

This is how I realised nothing is sacred; history moves forward, and the core of its movement is matter: the world of nature, humans, relations, practices, and things we produce with labour.

The Michael Jackson of global politics – neoliberalism – took Lenin's place in the post-Soviet child's bed. Triumphant, he waved his end of history in my face. His promise of pleasure drowned first the sickle, then the hammer in the limitless ocean of Pepsi.

It climaxed like capitalism always does – with a crisis and war. Russian tanks, adorned with Soviet symbols, invaded what Putin dubs "Vladimir Ilyich Lenin's Ukraine," my home, threatening to show Ukrainians "true decommunization."

3
"Lenin lived, Lenin lives, Lenin will live." (Vladimir Mayakovsky)

I never queued at the Mausoleum to gaze upon Lenin's corpse to realise that Communism was dead. But I felt the fisting performed with the free market's invisible hand.

Now, the entire post-Soviet space is a colossal Mausoleum, cradling the dismembered remains of the first workers' state. For over thirty years, the slurping sounds of the 'former republics' emanate from its depths. Their inhabitants, desperate to erase their past, are trapped in a ghostly loop, perpetually returning to what they desperately seek to flee.

I made it out into the 'free world' – the one Donald Duck promoted as an alternative to the "prison of nations." Here, I almost gave in to the urge to shrug it all off, like Atlas. But there is no getting away from the reality behind the glossy shopfronts.

I ran to a supposed paradise: a world where cops brutalise Black teens; veterans of endless wars rot under bridges; quality healthcare remains a mocking dream for the impoverished; inmates labour for pennies in prisons more crowded than the GULAG; students graduate indebted to bankers; and I, a colonial alien, find solace in being here, away from the trenches...

The facade shattered, and from the debris, Lenin winked. In his writings, I met not the towering idol but a mere comrade. An imperfect voice that ignites with a timeless message: another world is possible; the guiding stars are those who work.

4

Nothing indicates Lenin was a pleasant man. However, revolution doesn't call for pleasantries.

Diving into the sea of Lenin's ten million words, one biographer stumbled upon musings on the dialectical ideal of beauty and utility. Lenin finds it in the female breast. This observation is consistent with historical materialism but remains at odds with the Soviet narrative that depicts Lenin as an asexual hermaphrodite.

It delights me to picture Ilyich, hunched over his works, trying to reflect objective reality and suddenly grabbing a boob to make a point. His alleged 'asexuality' is a hypocrisy, a fabrication by prudes in their goody-goody icon-making. Their bronze Lenin is never horny. Nevertheless, according to Dmitry Manuilsky, the man had fifty shades of laughter – a clear indication of libido.

To break the myth of an unaroused Ilyich, consider reading his correspondence with his comrade and mistress, Inessa Armand. In December 1913, she wrote:

> We've parted, parted, my dear! And the pain is deep! (...) Nearly every endeavour here in Paris was entwined with thoughts of you. I wasn't in love with you back then, but I loved you so much. Even now, I would do without

kisses; just seeing you having a chat now and then would be a pleasure. It wouldn't hurt a soul. Why deprive me of this? (...) I adored hearing your words and watching you speak. Your face lit up, and it was easy to watch because you were blissfully unaware...

Now, let's hear the mating sounds of Lenin (1914):

Oh, how I long to kiss you a thousand times, greet you, and wish you well.

In a gesture of love, Lenin gifted Armand galoshes. After her death from cholera, he followed her coffin through Moscow, drowning in grief and tears, encircling his beloved with a wreath of white roses.

5

To understand Lenin's life, we must assess his death.

Neurophysiologist Valery Novoselov, who examined doctors' notes, medication lists, and autopsy records, argues that Ilyich died from syphilis – a condition far too scandalous for a 'moral icon.'

Back then, there was no penicillin. Syphilis was ravaging entire villages in Russia. The Simbirsk Province, where Lenin came from, was among the worst affected. The disease spread not just through sex but due to poor living conditions and even bites from street kids. Shockingly, 30% of syphilis cases in Russia were children. Orphaned and abused, they roamed the streets, confronting strangers: "Give me a coin, or I'll bite."

It doesn't matter if Lenin got it through such a bite, a dirty towel, or in bed. What matters is that syphilis is a disease that has a significant impact on one's mind. It affects memory and thinking, leading to paralysis, hallucinations, aggressive behaviour, and manic episodes.

These symptoms, present in Ilyich's medical records, were well exploited by his critics. Yet they highlight the human brain's resilience, given Lenin's productivity during his illness. Furthermore, this diagnosis clarifies Ilyich's edgy personality and, indeed, his mistakes, thereby liberating socialism from some ontological claims.

6

To be a Leninist is to peel Lenin from the sky, to strip him of his clouds, to shatter his icon.

The human Lenin leaves no room for retreat into his church, where we can wait for the Second Coming of a god that never existed.

Lenin's cause is a worker's cause. It is a daily commitment to engage in society, its transformation, and the liberation of workers.

To be a Leninist is to live, to act in the present, to make history.

A proper memorial to Lenin is not a monument but a practice.

Anatoli Ulyanov is a Soviet-born Ukrainian writer of Russian ethnicity, visual poet, and political refugee based in Los Angeles, California.

13. Lenin, Labriola and the Historical Nodes of International Communism[1]

Andrea Bonfanti

Why does an Italian student in Wuhan find a Chinese translation from Russian of Labriola? The short answer to this question is, of course: Lenin. The long answer, one that reveals a greater complexity, follows...

Sometime in 2018, I was in a tiny second-hand bookshop tucked away in an alley next to Wuhan University, where I was conducting my doctoral research. Weaving through the narrow spaces, I was surprised to discover a Chinese translation of a Russian work on the "first Italian Marxist," Antonio Labriola. *La-bu-li-ao-la-zhuan*: the biography of Labriola. As the note written on the flyleaf indicated, this book (which is simultaneously a fact and the expression of a relation in process) was gifted by Sun Kui, one of its editors, to comrade Xing Geng on 25 November 1987. Yet, the traces of this human interaction, however emotionally charged, could not satisfy my thirst to explain the historical connection between this volume and me, now.

After promptly purchasing the artefact, I started to realise the full scale of the puzzling issue and of the fascinating challenge ahead: the enigma required a deeper explanation than one based on the (nonetheless important) camaraderie between two Chinese communists. What was a booklet on Labriola, the first Italian Marxist, sure, but largely ignored outside of Italy, doing here? How did it end up on the dusty shelf of a tiny shop? What spatial and historical paths did it pass through, and what political significance do these continue to wield today?

My meeting with the book turned out to be an indicative node of a global network that in this case takes the form of the world history of the international communist movement in the 20th century (and more concretely or minutely the form of a paperback). This web finds in Lenin one of its great protagonists, and perhaps the first truly modern and global-globalising node. On the centenary of his death, to reflect synthetically and transversally, through this story, on these questions, without obviously arrogating the possibility of organically answering them here, is useful to mark the end of *one form* of communism and, perhaps, to rally comrades all over the world (and there are many of them) to the cause of a more equal and just society once again.

The first node in the network of the global history of 20th-century communism is in this case Labriola himself, evidently. Labriola (1843-1904) was an acute philosopher and minor politician during Umberto I's Italy who

---

[1] I have not included any bibliographical apparatus to avoid burdening a text which is very short in length and commemorative in form. I mention and thank those who have been formative, in excess or defect, but always constructive in dialectical confrontation, particularly for this piece: Luciano Canfora, Daniela Caterina, Umberto Cerroni, Cui Zhiyuan, Luka Golez, Antonio Labriola, Maksim Lavrik, Lenin, Lars T. Lih, Elliot O'Donnell, Silvio Pons, Sun Kui, Giuseppe Vacca, Wang Hui, Wang Zheng, Roman Zhalilov.

only encountered Marxism towards the end of his life. His morphological conception of the process of formation and transformation of society envisaged a very particular approach to the Marxist reading of the movement of history, placing human labour and its organisational form at the core of his visions, and thus eschewing certain deterministic catechisms within the Second International. Critical communism, as he understood it, stemmed from the conscious proletarian movement – mass and truly democratic – that was capable of burying the existing society, but from the cracks of which the genesis *in fieri* of a new society was already emanating.

The next node in this story is the 'encounter' between Labriola and Lenin, a crucial nexus of the interdependence of communists. It was a bookish and unilateral exchange: we find it in Lenin's personal correspondence. In a letter of 10 December 1897, now incorporated in volume 37 of the *Collected Works*, Lenin wrote to his sister Anyuta: "I am now reading the French translation of Labriola's *Essays on the Materialistic Conception of History*. It is a very sensible and interesting book. The idea came to me that you ought to translate it." In fact, in the article "Gems of Narodnik Project-Mongering," also dated 1897, the future Bolshevik had already expressed positive judgement towards a Labriola who mocked the utopians, against whom the "teachers" of historical materialism had always lashed out.

Under Lenin's impetus, the global network of communism continued to develop and intertwine the peoples of the world, internationally and intergenerationally. *Essays on the Materialistic Conception of History* was translated into Russian from French in 1898 and censored by the thugs of Nicholas II. Was Anyuta the translator? We don't know. But with the international communist movement, the net grew, and the nodes multiplied. Let us then move on to the next one, which brings us back, and closer, to where we are presently writing this piece (Beijing): the Chinese node.

In China, the first book on Labriola was published in 1984 by the People's Publishing House (PPH). It combines *In Memory of the Communist Manifesto* and the *Essays*. Neither is translated from Italian. The first text is a Chinese version of Franz Mehring's German translation; the second translates a Russian version from 1960. The imprint of the Dengist opening is evident, denoting the operation to introduce Italian Marxist to the Chinese reader. The preface is designed to place Labriola in the post-1978 framework that highlights the arrival of a new era, communism as the end of the class struggle, and respect for law and the State. On the same educational line, the second Chinese node (the one autographed by Sun Kui, which brought us here) was also a PPH publication, dated 1987. It is a translation from Russian of a short intellectual biography written by L. A. Nikitich and published for the Moscow Thought Press in 1980.

We have thus arrived, or returned, by progressive stratifications to the latest historical node of this story. That which, *by chance*, through the spatio-temporal vicissitudes of the 20th-century communist movement, has entangled our hands in its web in that second-hand bookshop in Wuhan.

So, what, if any, is the political meaning of all this? Any arguments must depart from the fact that *that* experience of a world communist movement is over: dead and now rightly the subject of more or less critical dissection. Without falling into a banal polemical discourse, the erstwhile horizon of the radiant future, which ultimately included suffocating workers and glorifying and rewarding leaders and parrots, must be adequately criticised and critically digested. Sacred Histories – even if supposedly communist – must be understood and overcome.

Despite this, or perhaps precisely in light of it, the traces of that history of global communism clearly indicate its progressive expansion, in time and space, and that today it reaches out to and touches all peoples of the world, as the stories and reflections contained in this collection prove. While the experience of communism in the 20th century is over and one cannot resurrect it, its many nodes nevertheless influence and unite us, as we continue to stumble in and be entangled by that dense network of interdependencies. A landscape is not made up solely of elements from the present but is also a stratification of works from the past. Recent sedimentations can 'only' (!) rest on it, changing its organic complexity.

After the Orwellian 1984 comes 1985. We, remembering Lenin, must strive for one which is neither a catastrophic continuation of neo-liberal capitalism nor an Oceania in a perpetual state of war. After a hundred years, Lenin lives on because he continues to be metabolised. The entanglements for the morphological movement and changes in society are ever more numerous. Our struggles grow thicker.

PS: The battle must continue, I repeat to myself, as I listen to the glorious workers of Picun (Beijing) reading poems and chanting songs. Comrades Sun and Xing are with us, I'm sure. And Lenin and Labriola too.

Andrea Bonfanti is a postdoctoral fellow at the Tsinghua Institute for Advanced Study in Humanities and Social Sciences, Tsinghua University (China).

14. Moscow is Just Two Steps Away

Andrés Carminati Ciriza

Sin embargo
queremos para nombrarlo palabras sólidas
que resistan en medio de la noche
los nuevos vientos del mundo
(Roque Dalton)

I was young in the 1990s. When my generation was coming into public life, the philosophy of capital was decreeing victoriously that the *"fin de la historia,"* the end of history, had arrived. The voracity of the market was gobbling up in record time the social wealth created by humanity's first workers' state. The echoes of the global counter-revolution and the symbolic and material power of the fall of the *muro de Berlin* shook the tectonic layers of all our rights and rebellions. It was then that it became clear to us that, despite the 13,467 km that separated Buenos Aires from Moscow, in reality, we were only two steps away from each other. Here too, in these lands where *Los Andes* and the Antarctic ice merge into one, the wealth created by the labour of generations was appropriated and plundered in the blink of an eye.

The verdict was carved in stone: socialism has failed, there is no alternative, Marx is dead and Lenin is the great culprit. The 'self-criticisms' followed soon after; the more lapidary, the more applauded. And if it was impossible to bury Marx entirely, he was now deemed permissible for innocuous, academicist intellectualism only. But there was nowhere to place *el rojo bolchevique*, the Red Bolshevik. There is no Lenin without his Revolutionary Party, now deemed obsolete, and neither is there a Lenin who does not intend to storm the Winter Palace – indeed the palaces of all four seasons, of the whole world.

And so, while imperialist capitalism – with its large monopolies, which Lenin described; its financial oligarchy, analysed by Lenin; its massive export of capital, studied by Lenin; and its division of the world, foreseen by Lenin – was expanding at unprecedented speed, the supposedly critical theories denigrated the now unmentionable Vladimir Ilyich Lenin. Thus began to flourish a multitude without a party in a polycentric, quasi-benign Empire and a world that could apparently be changed without taking power.

What was/is to be done?

When my generation took to the streets with so many questions on the 20th anniversary of the onset of the *dictadura genocida* in Argentina, it was among the demonised spectres of *nuestrxs desaparecidxs*, of our disappeared comrades and loved ones who had wanted to storm the heavens, that we were able to uncover a few traces. Every single one of their actions and writings was tinged with the signs of 'our Lenin.' On the back side of the commodified image of Che – which Capital, so full of itself as a result of its partial victory, now replicated en masse – we found the other end of the red thread informing our past-future. The rhythmic beats of the Cuban *son* and rumba held hidden keys: Fidel, Guevara and Celia Sánchez were our best interpreters of Russian.

La burguesía, like every ruling class, wants to dry up the subterranean rivers that link the Sierra Maestra with Tucumán, Túpac Amaru with Karl Marx, Spartacus, the Haitian Revolution, Vietnam and the emancipated future of all humanity. Yet the stubborn October breeze continues to whisper a message that we can hear if we pay attention: everything is illusion, except power; without the organisation of the subalterns, *lxs subalternxs*, the battle against the self-proclaimed masters of the world and their deadly über-commodifying voracity of everything alive cannot be won.

Oído, memoria, teoría, organización y acción. Hearing, memory, theory, organisation and action.

Andrés Carminati Ciriza is an historian and lecturer at a public university in Argentina, a Marxist from Nuestra América.

Translated from the Argentine Spanish by hjje.

15. Encountering Lenin in Iceland (and Once in Denmark)

Árni Daníel Júlíusson

The Vietnam War entered my consciousness with a copy of Newsweek in 1968. My father had been presented a subscription to the magazine, and through it, I saw the war. During that time there were also the May events in Paris in 1968 and the Warsaw Pact invasion of Czechoslovakia in August of the same year, all reported on TV, radio and of course in Newsweek. The Beatles, Bob Dylan and the Rolling Stones were the soundtrack, heard on the radio and played at friends' houses. At the age of nine, I felt that I must have started to breathe in the radical air (mostly because of the pictures and the music). We were living in the countryside in the north of Iceland, and my father was a teacher at the local school, just like my mother.

Some years later, when I was 16, I entered an organisation of communists in the northern town of Akureyri. I wanted to join a left-wing organisation, and the one I chose, because many people I knew were members, was called Einingarsamtök kommúnista (marx-lenínista), EIK (m-l) – The Union of Communists (Marx-Leninists). Although I had heard of Lenin before, I think it was only at that time I really became aware of him, in the aftermath of the great events in the period 1968-1973. The Vietnam War had been won by then. The Vietnamese people had beaten the US military, but it stayed on in Iceland and so many places elsewhere.[1]

I started to learn about the Russian Revolution and Marxism-Leninism in reading circles within the EIK (m-l). We had a strict revolutionary discipline, with weekly cell meetings and revolutionary secrecy, and were fully engaged in activism in the areas of labour rights, women's rights, anti-imperialism and student rights. We learned that Lenin was an enemy of all revisionists, especially Eduard Bernstein in Germany, who was his most hated enemy. We also learned that Lenin and the Bolshevik party were one of the few Social Democratic parties that had not betrayed the international working class by supporting their nation-state in 1914, as especially the German Social Democrats had done so fatefully – the same German Social Democrats that had been the teachers and hope of every party in Europe and elsewhere. We also learned that Stalin had been a faithful heir to Leninism, and Mao after that. Trotsky, on the other hand, was not viewed in a positive light.

The EIK (m-l) had close connections to the Norwegian party AKP (m-l), which still exists and is now called Rødt (Red); in many ways, Rødt continues the heritage of the 1968-1973 years, being the most left-wing party in Norway. EIK (m-l) in Iceland, on the other hand, was disbanded around

---

[1] The US military had come to Iceland in spring 1951. It stayed there at the Keflavik base until 2006.

1985, for a variety of reasons, including that many who were active in the organisation had become exhausted from years of intensive activism, and that one of the main drivers of that activism, the Vietnam War, was now over. A third reason was that many of the members of the organisation, often students who had now finished their studies, started to have families and careers and did not have as much time as before, which along with a change in political climate towards the right and neoliberalism, acted towards dissolution.

For a few years I wasn't political and studied history diligently at the University of Iceland, but when I got the chance, I started to look around at what was going on. I read a book by Alex Callinicos, the British Marxist, and started to think about Lenin and his heritage again. I did not agree with those who thought that his work had become undone when the Wall fell in 1989 and the Soviet Union was dissolved in 1991 – that everything that he had done had been for nothing. My very kind teacher in Copenhagen, the great historian Alex Wittendorff, made it one of his tasks when he started to lead my PhD work at the University of Copenhagen to show me through the Historical Institute library. As we walked past the collected works of Lenin, Wittendorff pointed at the books and said, "Now all this is useless. Those books are of no use anymore." Wittendorff had been one of the Danish class of '68, a very important and active radical social movement. Now he was disillusioned.

I came home to Iceland with a PhD (on Icelandic peasantry, 1300-1700) and started teaching at the University. Iceland was in the deep freeze of neoliberalism. Very little funding was forthcoming for the humanities and the social sciences. Instead, the neoliberal government started business universities with large endowments of state money, the people's money.

In 2003 the neoliberals succeeded in privatising all the banks. It took the new, private bankers only five years to sail all the banks to complete wreckage on the rocky beach of one of the greatest bankruptcies in history. Iceland was bankrupt; neoliberalism in Iceland was bankrupt with it. This happened in October 2008. Soon the people were on the streets. Every weekend they met at the city square, and their numbers grew and grew. In January 2009 the mass movement succeeded in ousting the neoliberal government and a new left-leaning government was elected in its place. It was the first of the great worldwide movements of the period 2008-2014 to become active, a beautifully successful urban siege of the modern kind, executed by a population that everyone thought had been lulled completely to sleep by the false promises of neoliberalism and the wonderful market. Then we had the Spanish movement, the Arab Spring, the Occupy Wall Street uprising, SYRIZA, Bernie Sanders, Podemos, Jeremy Corbyn. Some failed spectacularly, others not, and most have in some manner reawakened the spirit of radicalism, rebellion and revolution so dear to Lenin.

It was at this time that I encountered Lenin again. I was teaching a course with my colleague and friend Halldór Bjarnason, now sadly and far too early gone, on the history of imperialism 1500-1950 at the University of

Iceland in the spring semester of 2009. One of the books we decided to put on the reading schedule was Lenin's *Imperialism, the Highest Stage of Capitalism*, a text that was very pertinent to the subject matter of the course. Lenin was back! And what a comeback. Much of what he wrote seemed so right in the current circumstances – almost as if he had watched Icelandic neoliberal capitalism come to its sorry end in the financial crash and then decided to write about it. All the students agreed: it was like a very fresh and modern text, which reflected the recent history of Iceland to a surprising degree. But it was about capitalism at the beginning of the 20th century! Dear Wittendorff was wrong after all. Lenin had become a classic – at least in Iceland, with me and Halldór and our 40 students. The course was a one-off, but now a course I teach with others on the history of the Scandinavian countries serves as a lively venue for discussions of this sort.

In this way I came to know Lenin, beginning with an encounter that was to have a lasting impact, and then again and again in various circumstances. His constant legacy, which until recently had been sadly neglected by many in the revolutionary left, now seems to be experiencing a renaissance of sorts. In Iceland at least, following the events of 2008-2009, a new Socialist party has been organised, a radicalised wing of the labour movement has been active since 2018 and new radical media has grown up. Here the interest in the writings and legacy of Lenin (as well as Marx, Engels, Stalin and Mao) is growing fast. In this way, Lenin is being rediscovered as he truly was and is: a classic revolutionary.

Árni Daníel Júlíusson is a historian and musician affiliated to various academic institutions in Iceland, such as the University of Iceland and the Reykjavík Academy.

16. A Letter to Lenin in Lagos

Baba Aye

Dear Vladimir Ilyich,

Greetings comrade. I was thrilled to learn from your last letter that you are in Lagos. Even though you are there incognito, I am sure you would have had a taste of typical Nigerian hospitality from the warm-hearted working people in our pleasantly boisterous great city. Make sure you have some Nigerian jollof rice, if you have not been offered a plate of this delicious meal.

I couldn't but chuckle on reading that you will make a surprise appearance at the conference that Nigerian comrades intend to organise at Abuja in commemoration of the centenary of your death. I hope the conference goes ahead as scheduled; they postponed an earlier conference to commemorate the 200th anniversary of Karl Marx's birth several times. There will likely be many papers presented, eulogising how great you are, and even how we could learn from your politics, ideas and sense of organisation.

My fear though is that little will come out of the discussions. The 2018 Marx Conference seemed to hold much promise, but nothing serious emerged from it. To date, the organisers have not yet published the papers presented. A 'Conference on Marxism' WhatsApp group was its only 'concrete' outcome, and even that is now nothing more than any other WhatsApp group, neither enabling organisation nor promoting theoretical discussion.

Returning to your upcoming anniversary, a lot could undoubtedly be drawn from you and your legacy to better understand and deepen socialist theory and practice in Nigeria, a country which was formally a mere ten-year-old British colony when you died. So much water has passed under the bridge since then, but believe me when I say things have not been all that pretty, including as concerns the Nigerian left, which has been lagging behind the development of the working class for which it supposedly stands.

Nigeria in the 21st century is somewhat similar to the Tsarist Russia you knew and detested so much, in a few important respects. It is a regional power with a huge population, 70% of whom are under 30 years old. It is also a "prison of nations" with a statistically small but politically significant working class. And, while the country is formally a democracy, the powers of its president are almost as absolute as those of a Tsar. Besides, the country's thieving bourgeoisie, with its coterie of overfed parliamentarians and official advisors to the president nationally, and governors at the subnational level, are far more corrupt than Russian nobles were, before they were swept into the dustbin of history in 1917.

The similarities do not end on the side of the oppressor, however. The fighting spirit of the working class is remarkable. Workers have repeatedly shaken the country to its foundations with mass strikes, despite the trade union bureaucracy trying to hold them back, with a dozen nationwide general strikes this century alone! Young people have also repeatedly taken to the barricades, in revolt against anti-people policies in the past and against police dictatorship in recent times.

You might think that this is a ripe context for us to have a vibrant revolutionary movement of the left, like what you built with your fellow Bolsheviks. Alas! That is not the case. Many on the left today kid themselves with the illusion that they share some resemblance with the revolutionary party you built, even if just as caterpillars to the butterfly of tomorrow's Nigerian Bolsheviks. And of course, not a few of the leaders of these grouplets see themselves as some incarnation of you, only that the 'ignorant' working class are yet to appreciate that, despite the great battles this class has waged!

I would have found it funny, were it not so tragic, that none of the handful of revolutionary groups that still have any sense of life can boast of more than a few dozen members at best, in a country with over 200 million people. Yet, each sees itself as *the* vanguard that will lead a socialist revolution that is apparently just around the corner, in the minds of these so-called "friends of the people."

Truth be told, Vladimir Ilyich, things were not always as bad as this. We had parties like the Socialist Workers and Farmers Party (SWAFP) in the 1960s with up to five thousand members and the Imoudu Front of Nigeria (IFN) which operated underground with about two thousand members during the military dictatorships of the 1990s. But the movement suffered a terrible setback with the collapse of the Soviet Union. Several leading socialists abandoned revolutionary politics for human rights advocacy or even jumped ship to enter bourgeois parties and governments. Consequently, many left organisations and their circles just withered away.

The political decline and organisational collapse have also ruptured the fecund ties between theory and practice which you valued so much. We actually used to have a significant number of socialist activists who took their theory very seriously, such as Eskor Toyo, Ola Oni, Baba Omojola, Edwin Madunagu, Segun Osobo, Omafume Onoge, Ikenna Nzimiro, Mahmud Tukur, and Bade Onimode to mention a few. They thought and acted as members of collectives, which were in contention and collaboration at different times. Of those I just mentioned, only two are still alive. And while they remain true to their ideas, age appears to have robbed them of the virility of their theorisation.

Nowadays, theorisation is left to an ivory tower of thinkers with little if any ties to practical efforts, while clichés and slogans take the place of reflection for the praxis of our wannabe revolutionary groupuscules.

Having said that, I hope your visit will help rekindle the embers of our movement, though admittedly I am a bit sceptical. Most of the people you will meet at the conference in your honour are really no longer interested in changing the world. And just a few are still keen on even interpreting it in ways that could force them out of the comfort zone of the peace they have made with the system, whilst outwardly still condemning it.

Given that we all hold you in awe, you would be the one person who can convince those still bent on revolution on the need to set aside petty differences, unite around a shared revolutionary programme, and work with a singleness of purpose to provide political and ideological leadership for the working class. These are your defining qualities. Like Marx you were "before all else a revolutionist." These are the attributes I hope your visit will inspire once more in our movement.

Needless to say, I understand that you are not a magician. Despite the leap forward that your inspiring presence will hopefully provide, we have to seize the bull by the horns ourselves, to rebuild the movement. But it will be a spark which will set ablaze a fire in the Savana of working-class discontent and a beacon for millions of workers whose fighting spirit have been tested and can be trusted. I for one will be on top of the world, after a series of derailed attempts to forge a united fighting left since the Third All-Nigeria Socialist Conference was held twenty years ago.

So, Vladimir, you see why I am so overjoyed that you are in Lagos and needed to write to you before you head to Abuja (if the Conference is indeed confirmed). The organisers have no inkling of your being so nearby. My lips are sealed whilst I keep tabs on them to know if they are serious about going ahead. If they do, I will be waiting for you at the airport to take you incognito to the Conference venue. But if they postpone it, I'll be on the next flight to Lagos to see you. We have a lot to talk about on the current situation, whilst I treat you to the pleasures of Naija palm wine and fresh fish pepper soup.

Revolutionary regards,

Baba

Baba Aye is a member of the Socialist Workers League (SWL), Co-Convener of the Coalition for Revolution (CORE, Nigeria), contributing editor of the Review of African Political Economy (ROAPE), and Council member of the Progressive International (PI).

Artist: Baran Caginli

17. 'Baking Books' – Practising Revolutionary Theory Through Bread

Baran Caginli

> *She looked in, and there was Ilyich standing at a table eating a piece of black bread and herring to which he had helped himself. He was somewhat taken aback at the sight of the office cleaner, and said with a smile: "I felt very hungry, you know."*
> (Nadezhda Krupskaya)

In September 1980, the Turkish Armed Forces carried out the third successful military coup in the history of the Republic of Turkey. Consequently, the Parliament and the Government were dissolved, and all political parties were banned. They also raided homes, schools, and universities to eliminate any type of opposition.

As a high school student in Istanbul, my father was a member of a leftist youth organisation. The military police imprisoned and tortured him because of his involvement in political activities. When my grandfather heard about his son's incarceration, he travelled from Kars, a city in the Kurdish region of Turkey, to Istanbul to bring his son home. My father brought with him his library of forbidden Marxist-Leninist books. My grandfather, who was illiterate, did not recognise the books for what they were and saw no harm in taking them along. Upon their arrival, someone in the village warned my grandfather about the books: they were prohibited literature and, if found, they would all get arrested! To resolve the situation, my grandparents burned the books in their fireplace. But there were so many books that the constant fire made some people in the village suspect that something unusual was going on. To obscure their actions, my grandmother baked bread continuously for a week and gave it out to the whole village for free.

53 years later, I baked bread in the form of Lenin, Marx and Rosa Luxemburg in memory of my father's burned books. The bread was then shared among the visitors of the 'Kuvan Kevät' exhibition, which opened at the Helsinki Academy of Fine Arts in May 2023.

Ingredients for one Marx and either one Lenin or one Rosa Luxemburg loaf:

550g wheat flour
4.5 dl warm water
11g dry yeast
1 tablespoon of salt
Pinch of sugar

Directions:

    Mix the yeast with warm water, add a pinch of sugar, and mix well.
    Mix the flour and yeast-water mixture in a large bowl.
    Knead the dough slightly for 3-4 minutes.
    Cover the bowl with a lid or cling film and wait 45 minutes.
    Preheat the oven to 250 degrees Celsius with the ceramic moulds inside.
    After 45 minutes, mix the salt with 0.5 dl water and add to the dough.
    Knead the dough for 3-4 minutes.
    Cover the bowl with lid or cling film and wait 15 minutes more.

After 15 minutes, turn the dough out onto a surface that has been lightly sprinkled with flour and knead it gently.

Cut a piece from dough:

    - 550g dough for Marx mould.
    - 400g of dough for Lenin or Rosa Luxemburg.

Place the dough piece in the hot ceramic mould and bake in the oven for 20 minutes. Remove the semi-baked bread from the mould and keep the bread inside the oven for 10 minutes more without the mould.

And it is ready!

Baran Caginli (b. 1990, Istanbul) is a Helsinki-based visual artist.

18. On the Day in Skopje When Anarchists for Lenin Became a Possibility...

Ben Watson

Skopje – where giftshop trinkets have suffered gigantism, and loom over the people like acid-trip hallucinations. Skopje – where repro-hulks too huge to navigate the shallow mountain waters of the Vardar sit precarious and dry to provide drinking platforms for the wealthy. Skopje – where the young folk talk English to overcome the feud between Albania and Bulgaria which divided their parents.

Out To Lunch woke with a start. Where the fuck was he? Aha, now he remembered, he'd been flown out from Gatwick to Macedonia to help Sezgin Sputnik's absurdist campaign to align Punk nihilism with old-school Bolshevik principles of truth, justice and public libraries. The apartment he'd slept in was an Airbnb rented out by sons of worthy doctor parents, now dead, who'd taken seriously Tito's campaign to bring modern medicine to the peasants in the mountains. Wooden busts of Marx and Lenin still stood proud on the shelves of the flat's lobby. Attachment to the Communist ideal, a mere shrine to the long-gone parents, or postmodern irony? OTL couldn't tell. All three, probably ...

Sezgin's talk at the Dunya Project – a venue named after the first female partisan to be killed by the Nazis – had happened the previous evening. Dapper in his leather jacket and drainpipe jeans, Sezgin had traced the anti-art energies of Punk to Situationist critique – an aspect lost in the UK music industry's version, to the extent that London's tourist rag *Time Out* could actually use a Jamie Reid graphic to congratulate the Queen on her Platinum Jubilee in 2022. Sezgin's incisive, archive-fuelled intellectualism went down a storm with the crowd. For OTL, Punk signified packed gigs in sweaty basements, but what a refreshing change to hear its virtues sung in a medieval courtyard scented by blossoms of ohrid trees and juniper shrubs! The local Professor of Art, miffed to be lectured on a movement he only remembered from his teenage years, asked: "But where is punk now?" He didn't know Disease, the scathing and insupportable punks from Pločnik – the south Serbian town responsible for injecting copper into the veins of the Classical world – had just played a superb community fest of Folk, Rap and children's patriotic songs around the corner. T-shirts advertising Criminal Records, the shop run by Dean of Bad Sam, the UK's finest punk outfit, were on show. OTL's celebration of Punk as an instant anti-commercial international proletarian revolution – now! – became a scathing and insupportable put-down of Herr Doktor Prof, and drew cheers from the crowd; he was mobbed by groupies and plied with beers and raki.

OTL woke from this narcissistic reverie, seized his watch ... and realised he had half an hour before his rendezvous with Sezgin and his faithful companion Tevfik ... so he had a quick wank, imagining being force-fed

London gin as the Queen had her ladies-in-waiting paddle his skinny punk ass with bundles of ohrid twigs, and Skopje's finest groupies giggled and clapped applause.

Libido temporarily relieved, OTL performed his morning ablutions with a spirited spring in his step. Down the sticker-bespattered, rusty, clanking elevator and out into the sunshine. He made straight for Tito's bridge, ignoring the antique stone bridge (blocked for a cosmetics ad photo shoot), and disdaining the new art bridge, another outburst of nightclub trophy kitsch as nightmarish as the gigantesque oversized hobbyhorse Alexander. Instead of pompously detailing 'national' heroes – nation as ever a source of squabble in this part of the world, as all over the globe – Tito's bridge sported bronze plaques which conjured the spirit of popular carnival, with strummed ciftelis and blaring pipes. OTL could swear he heard music and shuffling feet as he crossed to the other side.

"Sezgin! Tevfik! How was your visit to the National Archive?"

"Terrible. All that interests them there is whether you support Albania or Bulgaria in the FIFA World Cup. If you're from Kosovo, you're a pathetic irrelevance. We were blocked every bit of the way, despite our pleading that Haxhi Ymer Lutfi Paçarizi's poems undermine the ideological apparatus of the US War on Islam and reveal the true pumping heart of popular religion as revolutionary Bolshevism!"

"It seems you've discovered a local Bishop William Montgomery Brown there," Out To Lunch shot back, "another revolutionary whose works have been buried by both sides, by a Church of America who suppress him as heretic and Satanist, and by the mandarins of academic Marxism, who abhor anything which upsets their glass-bead game and talks in a manner the masses can understand, i.e. using the poetry of religion, before it was relegated to the sidelines by the instrumental reason of Descartes and Newton."

"Right on! Right on!" – invoking the sacred words of the Civil Rights Movement, Martin Luther King's mobilisation of religious subjectivity for mass struggle, a cry communicated to global consumers by pop music – Sezgin and Tevfik began a *danse macabre* of Punk nihilism down the bank of the Vardar, a dance which somehow also evoked the spirit of Italian villagers hauling a wooden statue of the Virgin Mary up a mountain during some local festival of wine, song and Dionysian debauch.

"You see, a wooden bust in my Airbnb made me think of Lenin, and how he fits into my new, positive view of the secret heart of religion. Of course, he *opposed* religion. *Materialism and Empirio-Criticism* is not a cancellation of the ideas of Ernst Mach – I agree with the scientist guy I met on a train going to the Zappanale music festival in Mecklenburg-Vorpommern, that Stalin's treatment of *Materialism and Empirio-Criticism* as a physics manual set back Soviet science by decades and probably caused the collapse of Official Communism in 1989 – but ..." here OTL went back to the first part of his sentence by twirling his fingers in the air, a gesture borrowed from J. H. Prynne. It might have been interpreted as a dig at Boris Kremenliev, whose awful statue they were passing, since OTL profoundly disagreed with his ethno-musicology, and preferred Harry Halbreich's argument that east-of-Vienna harmonising most logically culminates in the insupportable noise compositions of Ana Maria-Avram and Iancu Dumitrescu, "... but, in fact, Lenin was criticising *religious uses* of physics in the Culture Wars, rather than Ernst Mach directly."

"That reminds me of Hannes Alfven criticising Big Bang cosmology! Science becomes myth ..." said Tevfik brightly.

"Precisely, my dear Tevfik!" said OTL, and skipped a caper down the street.

"But what of Lenin's critique of religion, as it was used by the Stalinists to suppress local customs and rites throughout the U. S. S. R.?" said Sezgin in the stern manner to which his friends – and enemies – have become accustomed.

"Yeah, and what about that group called Anarchists for Lenin you wanted to found in Istanbul when you were high on raki last night? And Esther Leslie's grandpa Charlie Lahr who ran anarchist bookshops, but joined the CPGB in 1919? And how Guy Debord's wrong line on Lenin corrupted Punk? And why Rab-Rab's *Coiled Verbal Spring* by Mayakovsky, Shklovsky and co. proves that the Real Lenin was nothing like Stalin's travesty? What about Lenin's notes on Hegel in Volume 38 of the *Collected Works*? And you haven't even mentioned Trotsky!" cried Tevfik in a high-pitched semi-modulated quaver.

"Well, to answer all *that* I need rather more space than that allowed me in this contribution to our comrades' 100 Years of Lenin volume! Would Rab-Rab like to publish a novel in this vein, by any chance? Could be a best-seller like Robert Kurvitz's *Disco Elysium!*"

With that, the three musketeers of *Le Leninisme Nouveau* broke ranks and jumped in the Vardar, which at that time of year only reached their kneecaps. Its cold mountain stream hit their nerves like that bracing tonic called Truth.

"Down with the pomp of monuments!" quoth OTL, "Long live the dialectic of conversation, friendship and good times!!!"

Ben Watson used to write about music – books on Frank Zappa, Valentin Volosinov and Derek Bailey – but instead of writing one on Johnny "Guitar" Watson, decided to abandon the reading world and formed a band called AMM All-Stars to undermine a toppling music industry by releasing two albums a week.

19. Pupils at the Same School, Enemies in 1917: Lenin, the Hereditary Nobleman and Unsuccessful Advocate, and Kerensky, the Successful Advocate

Bill Bowring

From 1879 to 1887 Lenin (born in 1870) was a student at the Simbirsk Classical Gymnasium for Boys, founded in 1809. The headteacher from 1879 until 1889 was Fyodor M. Kerensky, the father of Alexander F. Kerensky, Lenin's enemy in 1917. Lenin and Kerensky were briefly pupils at the same school. Lenin's father was Kerensky's father's boss, and the two families were close friends. Kerensky, 11 years Lenin's junior, lived much longer than Lenin, 1881 to 1970. My mother attended his lectures at Boulder, Colorado, USA.

Simbirsk was renamed Ulyanovsk in 1924. As it happens, my partner, Olga was born in Ulyanovsk and was a student at the very same Gymnasium No. 1 – by then it was co-educational – from 1984 to 1990, in the Soviet period.

Lenin

Lenin had a strong multi-ethnic heritage. Lenin's mother's family name was Blank, and she was of Swedish, German and Jewish heritage. Her father was a Jew who converted to Orthodoxy. Lenin's father, Ilya N. Ulyanov (1831 to 1886), was of (baptised) Kalmyk ancestry. Kalmyks are Buddhist and have their own ethnic republic, Kalmykia, in the Russia Federation. The Kalmyk are a branch of the Oirat Mongols. Hence Lenin's distinctively oriental appearance.

Lenin's mother and father came from the Tatar city of Astrakhan on the Caspian Sea coast. His father received a *Kandidat Nauk* (PhD) degree from Kazan University's Physics and Mathematics Faculty, and taught in secondary schools in Penza and Nizhni Novgorod. In 1869 he was appointed Inspector of State Schools in Simbirsk Gubernia, and in 1874 Director of State Schools. At that time there were 462 state schools with around 10,000 pupils in Simbirsk Gubernia.

In 1877 Lenin's father received the 'chin' (rank) of Active State Counsellor (IV class on the Table of Ranks), the equivalent of a Major-General in the Army, which from 1856 gave the right to hereditary nobility. This was for him, his wife, and all children born after the date of receipt of the rank. That is, his youngest daughter Maria, like all his children, a revolutionary. In January 1882 he was awarded the Order of Saint Vladimir Third Class, and as a result, the hereditary nobility was communicated to all his children, regardless of the date of birth (both after and before the award), that is, including his son Vladimir.

So Lenin was a hereditary nobleman, and this was inscribed on his passport.

In 1887 Lenin graduated from the Gymnasium with a gold medal, for special success in theology, Latin and literature. Against the advice of Fyodor Kerensky, he entered the Law Faculty of the Imperial Kazan University (Kazan is now the capital of the (ethnic) Republic of Tatarstan). I have been shown the seat where he sat and attended lectures.

1887 was also the year in which Lenin's older brother, Alexander, was executed as a member of the Narodnaya Volya (People's Will) conspiracy to assassinate Tsar Alexander III. Lenin became a member of the illegal Narodnaya Volya student circle at Kazan, and after three months at the University was expelled for participating in student riots. In 1888 he was permitted to return to Kazan from a short exile.

In 1890, the authorities relented and allowed him to study externally for the law exams. In November 1891, Lenin passed the external exams for the law faculty of the Imperial St. Petersburg University. He became an *advokat* (barrister).

In 1892-1893, Lenin worked as an assistant to the Samara advocate A.N. Hardin, taking mostly criminal cases, as a 'state defender.' He represented clients in sixteen criminal cases, in which his clients were acquitted in five, and four civil cases, two of which he won. He was not very good at it.

In 1893, Lenin arrived in St. Petersburg, where, on the recommendation of Hardin, he got a job as an assistant to the advocate (barrister) M. F. Volkenshtein. His revolutionary activity became more and more intense, and in May 1895 he left Russia. That was the end of his legal career.

Kerensky

Kerensky, from a family of priests, followed a rather different path. In May 1889, his father was appointed chief inspector of schools in the Turkestan region and moved to Tashkent with his family. His father achieved the same rank and status as Lenin's father, but too late for Kerensky also to become a nobleman. Kerensky studied at the Tashkent Men's Gymnasium. In 1899, he graduated with a gold medal and entered the Faculty of History and Philology of Imperial St. Petersburg University, and then transferred to the Faculty of Law.

In October 1906, after the 1905 Revolution, at the request of the advocate Nikolai D. Sokolov, Kerensky began his career as a political defence lawyer, in a lawsuit in Reval (now Tallinn). He defended peasants who plundered the estates of the Baltic barons, and participated in a number of major political trials.

On 22 December 1909, having worked as an assistant, he became an Advocate (barrister) in St. Petersburg. In 1910, he was the main defence advocate at the trial of the Turkestan organisation of Socialist Revolutionaries (he was a member of that party) accused of anti-government armed actions. The trial went well, Kerensky managed to prevent the imposition of death sentences.

In early 1912, he defended members of the Armenian Revolutionary Federation (Dashnaktsutyun) party at their trial in St. Petersburg. In 1912, he participated in a public commission to investigate the execution of workers at the Lena gold mines. He spoke in support of Menahem Mendel Beilis, a Russian Jew accused of ritual murder in Kyiv. As a result, in 1914, in the 'case of 25 lawyers' for insulting the Kyiv Court of Justice, he was sentenced to 8 months in prison. However, as an acting parliamentary Deputy, Kerensky enjoyed immunity, which was not lifted by the State Duma. On appeal, the imprisonment was replaced by a ban on practising law for 8 months.

Kerensky and Lenin
And he became the head of the Provisional Government, and Lenin of the Bolshevik Party.

Bill Bowring is a convinced Leninist, who has been visiting Russia since 1983, including Lenin's school in Ulyanovsk and university in Kazan, and his place of exile in Siberia. Bill is a law teacher at Birkbeck College and a practising barrister.

20. Lenin, the (un)making of a critical legal theorist

Camila Vergara

Before he became a lawyer in 1891, in his late teenage years, Lenin was first passionate about revolutionary populism. He became enamoured by the revolutionary fervour of Nicolay Chernyshevsky and his socialist utopian novel *What Is to Be Done?* The first time Lenin read the novel, which was one of his brother Alexander's favourite books, was in July 1887, three months after Alexander was executed for participating in a conspiracy to throw bombs at the Tsar.[1] Like his brother, Lenin became immediately captivated by Chernyshevsky's revolutionary vision of the world and its heroes. Then, after moving to Kazan in the fall of 1888, he was first introduced to Marx's *Das Kapital* and Plekhanov's criticism of populism in *Our Difference*.[2]

It was after this profound political and intellectual awakening prompted by revolutionary populism and Marxism, that Lenin began studying law, first at the University of Kazan and then, after his expulsion for revolutionary activities, independently for external examinations at the University of St. Petersburg. Though he passed these exams in 1891, achieving the best results of that year, and began working as an assistant barrister shortly after, Lenin developed a critical approach not only to authority and legality but also toward his fellow lawyers, whom he considered to be "born bearers of the ideas of bourgeois society"[3] and towards "bureaucratic judges who are themselves not far removed from police sergeants."[4] From this critical position, in the following years, Lenin elaborated first his opposition to populism and then his critique of law.[5]

After founding in 1893 a Marxist reading and discussion circle in Samara, Lenin published *What the "Friends of the People" Are and How They Fight the Social-Democrats*, in which he attacked "legal populism" and its focus on the "small producer" because it ignored the materialist method and therefore attributed "the cause of exploitation to things lying outside production relations."[6] *Narodnik* ideology did not seek to abolish the system of private property, but merely to correct "its various imperfections," promoting reformist policies sponsoring common land tenure and land redistribution, tax reform, and access to cheap credit and subsidies for farmers. This focus on the immediate welfare of the people made populism

---

1 Valentinov, Nikolai (1969), *The Early Years of Lenin*. Ann Arbor. University of Michigan, 60.
2 Ibid: 141-45.
3 Ibid: 149.
4 Lenin, V.I. (1977), "Casual Notes, I. Beat – But Not to Death!" in *Collected Works Vol. 4*, Moscow: Progress Publishers, 390-391.
5 The influence his legal work had on Lenin's thinking remains largely unrecognized as researchers favor the sources that influenced his ideas on revolution. Harding's otherwise excellent *Lenin's Political Thought* does not even mention his time as a prosecutor.
6 Lenin, V.I. (1977), "What the 'Friends of the People' Are and How They Fight the Social-Democrats," in *Collected Works Vol. 1*, Moscow: Progress Publishers, 213.

unable to "see the wood for the trees," blind to how the organisation of the Russian economy turns "the peasant into a commodity producer, transforms him into a petty bourgeois, a petty isolated farmer producing for the market."[7] From this structural critique of reformism in the economy, Lenin then focused on developing a critique of legal reform.

The scepticism of the legal system that Lenin developed was informed by his brief experience as an assistant defence lawyer in the Samara circuit, where he worked on 18 minor cases of property claims and petty thefts.[8] Even if he managed to win punishment reductions for the peasants and workers he represented, this did not give Lenin renewed trust in the Tsarist legal system, which he saw as reproducing bourgeois society and enabling exploitation.

In 1893, after moving to St. Petersburg and continuing to practise law as an assistant attorney for renowned lawyer Mikhail Volkenshtein, he co-founded the League of Struggle for the Emancipation of the Working Class to debate with comrades about revolutionary populism, Marxism, and the political strategy going forward. He also wrote his first critical essay on legality, "Explanation of the Law on Fines Imposed on Factory Workers," published two years later. His analysis focused on the legalisation of fines in the aftermath of one of the largest worker unrests – a "terrific outbreak of some ten thousand workers" – that had taken place a decade earlier in the Nikolskoye Mill, where workers went on strike to protest the reduction of wages and the imposition of arbitrary fines.[9] Although the resolution of this conflict, which entailed the acquittal of 33 workers and new regulations, was seen as a legitimate "condemnation" not only of the owners of that particular mill but "of the old factory system as a whole," the law regulating the imposition of fines on workers meant for Lenin the legalisation of exploitation that further entrenched the dependence of workers on individual employers and the system of production as a whole.[10]

According to Lenin, the legal codification of labour relations that rest on unequal bargaining power brings about a new form of *public* exploitation, in which domination is exerted not only through the power of the employer, but also by the police, and the administrative and juridical branches of the State that act as enforcers of the law. Therefore, even provisions designed to improve working conditions and empower workers tend to maintain the subordination of workers to employers, and create other forms of dependence and servility, in addition to opportunities for political corruption. In the case of fines imposed on workers for absenteeism, for

---

7 Lenin, V.I. (1977), "The Economic Content of Narodism and the Criticism of it in Mr. Struve's Book," in *Collected Works Vol. 1*, Moscow: Progress Publishers, 341.
8 Loginov, Vladlen (2019), *Vladimir Lenin. How to Become a Leader*. London: Glagoslav, 323-327.
9 Lenin, V.I. (1972), "Explanation of the Law on Fines Imposed on Factory Workers," in *Collected Works Vol. 2*, Moscow: Progress Publishers, 36.
10 Ibid: 39. For labour laws in the 1880s and 1890s see Rimlinger, Gaston V. (1960), "Autocracy and the Factory Order in Early Russian Industrialization," *Journal of Economic History*, 20(1), 67-92; and Giffin, Frederick C. (1975), "The 'First Russian Labor Code': The Law of June 3, 1886," *Russian History*, 2(2), 83-100. For a deeper analysis of Lenin's critical legal theory see Vergara, Camila (2022), "Lenin and the Materialist Critique of Labor Law," in Alla Ivanchikova & Robert Maclean (eds.) *The Future of Lenin*, New York: SUNY Press.

example, the law, "instead of abolishing the workers' dependence on the employers," created a new dependence by establishing a fund for fines and a procedure for workers to "apply for grants to the employer."[11] This workaround not only validated arbitrary power, but also divided the workers, creating "the servile and the go-getter types."[12]

Lenin's sharp critique of the inherent limitation of laws that codify existing power relations was modified after the revolutionary rupture of 1917 and the coming into power of the Bolsheviks. Despite his early critical insights acquired in the intellectual struggle against the reformist agenda of "legal populism," as well as from his own experience with the legal system and his knowledge of the material conditions of workers,[13] once in power Lenin used the law for the revolutionary cause. He immediately adopted new labour provisions establishing the eight-hour working day and other watershed protections against exploitation, and in 1922 approved a new Labour Code, which incorporated labour rights and stronger protections, but within a capitalist logic, as evidenced by his temporary market-oriented New Economic Policy (NEP). Despite all the material gains that the new labour regulations meant for workers, they did not overturn the alienating capitalist idea of labour power as a resource for the production of commodities, nor renounce the existing legal disciplinary provisions guaranteeing production that Lenin had previously denounced as legalising exploitation. While disciplinary labour laws endured, the source of control gravitated towards the State, which eventually became the main owner and manager of the productive forces.

Confronted with a complex reality of counterrevolution and crisis, Lenin saw labour discipline as an absolute necessity for the survival of the Bolshevik project, and therefore charged the courts to "mercilessly punish" anyone violating labour discipline and hampering production.[14] This empowerment of judges to discipline workers who breached their contracts was seen as a justified means of achieving the goals of the revolutionary government. Abandoning the critical position from where he had developed his interpretation of legality, Lenin reimagined the courts as "an instrument *for inculcating discipline*"[15] in the workers, a function that would reach its maximal expression under Stalinism. Despite the abandonment of the NEP in 1928, workers remained subordinate to the producer-state and its juridical enforcers. When Russia entered the Second World War, quitting a job without a proper, pre-approved justification became a criminal offence.[16]

---

11 Lenin 2018: 57.
12 Ibid: 66.
13 See Harding, Neil (1977), *Lenin's Political Thought*. Chicago: Haymarket Books & Le Blanc, Paul (1993), *Lenin and the Revolutionary Party*. Chicago: Haymarket Books.
14 Burbank, Jane (1995), "Lenin and the Law in Revolutionary Russia," *Slavic Review*, 54(1), 40.
15 Lenin, V.I. (1972), "The Immediate Task of the Soviet Government," in *Collected Works Vol. 27*, Moscow: Progress Publishers.
16 For a fuller account of the contextual evolution of labour law and the complex coexistence of labour protections, social rights, and mandatory labour provisions in court cases see Hazard, John N. (1953), *Law and Social Change in the U.S.S.R.*, Toronto: Carswell Company Limited.

The USSR's path of top-down, accelerated modernisation came together with a rather uncritical use of the law and the courts to discipline workers into compliance. The revolutionary conjuncture allowed no time to reimagine proletarian law made democratically by the workers themselves and instead pushed Lenin to compromise and use legality to control the labour force. Even though this was not meant to undermine the freedom of workers, the forsaking of the *critique* of law in favour of the *use* of law certainly enabled the rather smooth transition from bourgeois to soviet legality. Tsarist laws were repurposed and the foundations of the commodity-producing society, and the subordinate position that workers have in it, were allowed to endure, despite all efforts to the contrary. In sum, Lenin was unable to fully address the entanglement of legal, political, and economic structures, and therefore to reimagine the rule of law in the revolutionary struggle for emancipation. Truly proletarian law remains thus an aspiration.

Dr. Camila Vergara is a Senior Lecturer at the University of Essex Business School and the author of Systemic Corruption. Constitutional Ideas for an Anti-Oligarchic Republic *(Princeton University Press 2020).*

21. A Feminist-Socialist View of Lenin and the Soviet Revolution from the Río de la Plata

María Cecilia Espasandín Cárdenas

On May 24, 1916, Alicia Moreau, Argentine *feminista* and *socialista*, wrote from Buenos Aires to her friend Paulina Luisi: "Let's talk about something worthwhile. What can you tell me about the Russian Revolution? What an admirable movement. It is the beginning of a new era."[1]

I am moved by Moreau's prescient *entusiasmo* for the idea that another era of humanity would open. Reviving this sense of the socialist promise, still unfulfilled, is something essential to me. Even after all the failures and defeats of the socialist attempts in the 20th century, *pesimismo* is a luxury that we cannot afford, especially living in one of the most unequal continents in the world.

Moreau's letter reached Paulina Luisi, one of the leaders of the Uruguayan feminist movement. In 1908, Luisi had become the first woman in Uruguay to obtain the title of Doctor of Medicine. With her Argentine friend she shared a passion for medicine, feminism and socialism.

The story of the socialist feminists of the Río de la Plata evoked in me the name of Lenin because of the attention he paid to the question of female emancipation. Thanks to an edition of Lenin's articles and speeches on this issue, with a preface written by his wife, *la educadora* Nadezhda Krupskaya, I began to familiarise myself with some of his ideas on the matter. As Krupskaya says, it is not a question of knowing only what Lenin said, but of his entire activity, especially after the Revolution. The new Soviet state inaugurated: the right to divorce (1917), the new family code establishing legal equality between the sexes (1918), the legalisation of abortion (1920), and the criminalisation of brothel keeping and pimping to eradicate prostitution (1922), among other measures. All of these were also battlefronts of the first socialist feminists of the Río de la Plata (and some continue to be so: consider that the abortion law was approved in Uruguay only in 2012 and still provokes strong reactions).

In fact, in 1919, in the aftermath of WWI, Lenin denounced "the crudeness of the Americans' rapacious imperialism ... seen from the fact that American agents are buying white slaves, women and girls, and shipping them to America for the development of prostitution. Just think, free, cultured America supplying white slaves for brothels!" - Paulina Luisi participated in the recently founded International Abolitionist Federation, Argentine-Uruguayan section. Together with Alicia Moreau, they led campaigns against the regulation of prostitution and in favour of a new moral culture and sexual education.

---

1 Moreau, Alicia (1916), *Correspondencia a Paulina Luisi (unpublished)*. Montevideo: Carpeta M del Fondo Paulina Luisi del Archivo Literario de la Biblioteca Nacional del Uruguay.

Both women shared the socialist objective but had more affinity with the reformist wing of the international socialist movement that Lenin so derided. In her own words, Paulina Luisi defended *"un socialismo evolutivo."*[2] She thought that a comprehensive democracy could be implemented through gradual social reforms within the capitalist economy. In contrast, Lenin was a vocal critic of social democratic reformism, even with regard to the emancipation of women. In most of his speeches, he insisted that the legal rights won would not be enough to achieve actual equality between the sexes. Democratic reforms had to be articulated with the social revolution. "Equality before the law is not necessarily equality in fact," he said in 1920.[3]

These ideas remain fully valid today. In our region – and in light of the recent experiences of progressive governments in the *Cono Sur* – Lenin's criticism is very useful in elucidating the limits of reformist politics and recovering the revolutionary perspective.

In the case of Uruguay, the Frente Amplio governments (2005-2019) passed a raft of progressive gender legislation, including laws on equal rights and opportunities, and same-sex marriage. There was also important progress made in terms of income distribution; the number of people living in poverty in 2017 was a quarter of what it was in 2006. However, it cannot be ignored that social inequality continued unabated, with the connivance of the State. For instance, profound gender gaps persist in all spheres of society, the high prevalence of gender-based violence being the most brutal expression of this. Therefore, it is vital to identify the limits of reformist policies, even if it is often very hard for us on the left to criticise the left! (especially under the current right-wing, reactionary government). In this, we also learn from Lenin and his radical criticism of social democracy.

That is to say, linking democratic demands, of all kinds, with the revolutionary perspective, as Lenin urged, continues to be a fruitful instruction. In fact, the articulations between *marxismos* and *feminismos* – honed by the first *rioplatense* women socialists – are today part and parcel of the theoretical and political paths travelled by a growing number in the feminist movement. "Feminist struggle against hunger and oppression" and "Against the pillage of the environment, our territories and our lives, we weave care, enjoyment and rebellion" were two of the main slogans of March 8, 2023 in Uruguay.

That said, part of Lenin's legacy was also to expose imperialist plunder. In Lenin's as in our times, capitalism remains "a world system of colonial oppression and of the financial strangulation of the overwhelming majority of the population of the world by a handful of 'advanced' countries."[4] His work showed that the competition between capitalist groups, for the conquest of

---

[2] Luisi, Paulina (2015), *Bajo el signo de Marte. España. Homenaje a las Democracias Mártires*. Montevideo: Biblioteca Nacional de Uruguay, 89.
[3] Lenin, V. I. (1974), "To the Working Women," in *Collected Works Vol. 30*, Moscow: Progress Publishers, 371.
[4] Lenin V.I. (1974), "Imperialism, the Highest Stage of Capitalism," in *Collected Works Vol. 22*, Moscow: Progress Publishers, 191.

markets, is closely linked to the war between the dominant States, for the territorial conquest of the world. Furthermore, he revealed the political consequences of these processes for the international labour movement. He exposed the uncomfortable reality of the emergence of privileged categories of workers, who benefit from the colonial policy – blatantly or covertly – of their imperialist State. It is a lucid analysis of the fragmentation of the working class, as well as of the material foundations of reformist ideologies. How can we think the revolution in internationalist terms without ignoring the multiple differences within the working class (differences that translate into privileges according to sex, nation, ethnicity, etc.)?

The history of Uruguay – *colonia española, portuguesa, semicolonia británica, norteamericana* – shows the threads of dependency that are woven at the expense of the working class of the southern hemisphere. Today, when the legal working week in Uruguay is 48 hours (in industry and agriculture) and the retirement age has just been raised by five years (to 65), one wonders how many more working hours can be squeezed out of our exhausted bodies, just to further enrich global capital. Then again, we already know that many more hours are possible, we only need consider so-called non-productive work – so essential for capitalist accumulation – such as domestic and care work, mostly performed by women.

To conclude, in the current world situation, when the capital system devours us, cancels our ability to consciously control our own social reproduction, destroys our planet, reduces a large part of the world's workforce to precarious living conditions – and all of this is the result of human actions and paradoxically escapes their/our control – now more than ever the unity of the working class becomes imperative. How does the current international feminist wave move this path forward? Which aspects of the capitalist social order does it call into question? What emergency brakes are needed? The challenges of the present are best faced with the memory of the past. Going through the history of the "admirable socialist movements," to assess their possibilities and limits – particularly *la revolución soviética* – appears to me to be a necessary task to think "beyond capital," to borrow István Mészáros' expression, in order to one day be able to talk again "about something worthwhile, the beginning of a new era."

María Cecilia Espasandín Cárdenas is a social worker, PhD in Social Sciences and professor at the Faculty of Social Sciences of the Universidad de la República, Uruguay.

Translated from the Uruguayan Spanish by hjje.

22. Holiday Haunts for Progressive Travellers. Lenin's Guide to Europe

Chris Read

Editors 2024: Exciting news. We are delighted to be the first to republish a recently discovered item from the *Sunday Progressive Times* colour supplement thought to have been written in August 1916 and translated for us from the spirit world by Chris Read.

...

Original Editor of the *Sunday Progressive Times*: We are proud to present the latest in our series of 'Favourite European Haunts.' This week Vladimir Ilyich Lenin, the well-known but for many of us rather quarrelsome representative of our Russian sisters and brothers, will be sharing his thoughts from his always original and quirky perspective. Sick!

...

People are always asking me 'Vladimir Ilyich, where is your favourite place in Europe?' This is, of course, a ridiculously diversionary and irredeemably petty-bourgeois question. Are the naïve fools who ask it not smart enough to realise that the whole continent, even before the present horrific war, reeked of the bloody profits of imperialism and was no place for a socialist to enjoy themselves? However, setting that aside I thought I might be able to make some suggestions for true comrades who will not give up on the mighty proletarian struggle.

In that spirit I thought that I would begin with places to avoid. First and foremost, if you enjoy eating, keep well away from London. Fried skate's wings, jellied eels and whatever the hell oxtail really is should be avoided at all costs. The only place that comes anywhere near on the scale of gastronomic ghastliness is the so-called sanatorium in the lower reaches of the mountains of Tschudiwiese near Flums in Switzerland where you will be served an unrelenting diet of goat's milk. Nadya and I only go there because it is cheap (I wonder why?) and, since Mum died, we have been a bit short of the readies since she can't pass on Dad's pension anymore. I recall, on one occasion we were there, we were so pleased to see mushrooms growing in the woods as we left that we spent so much time picking them, despite the pouring rain. We missed our train back to the awfulness of Zurich and had to wait two hours for the next one.

However, I have to admit, the Swiss Alps are magnificent. In 1904 or 1905, can't recall exactly which, I spent so much time walking the trails with Sasha Bogdanov and later with other comrades such as Angelica Balabanoff, admiring the snowy glaciers, getting lost in the beautifully aromatic pinewoods, lying in sunny meadows and, best of all, reaching the highest peaks and looking down on the rest of humanity, that I could almost forget the entire existence of the snivelling Menshevik traitors and their Economist hangers on. Ah! Happy days! Until, of course, Bogdanov and Balabanoff showed themselves in their true colours. But the mountains and forests and lakes were restorative.

Indeed, Nadya is telling me I should mention our idyll in Siberia, the only place, she says, where we were really happy. Shushenskoye! Even the name was soothing! The glistening snow, the frozen streams, the jingle of icicles in my beard in winter, the massive outburst of flowers and leaves in spring, the plentiful duck to hunt and eat in summer and not a single Bernsteinian revisionist for 500 versts in any direction. Bliss indeed, spending the long cold months at my desk writing statistic-packed, gripping page-turners like *The Development of Capitalism in Russia* and articles on the importance of liberating women from domestic tasks and treating them with respect. Meanwhile, Nadya would sit in the corner, deal with my correspondence and edit my manuscripts, as the clumsy girl from the village, who came in and did for us, kept the fire blazing, did our shopping, cooked our meals, looked after our laundry, took items to the post and kept the izba clean. What's not to like? However, I had to point out to Nadya, as she seemed to have forgotten, that Siberia is not actually in Europe so didn't qualify.

Cities were another matter. London, Brussels, Berlin, Munich, Vienna, Geneva, Zurich, Stockholm, Paris. You never knew when a lily-livered Menshevik renegade might turn up round the next corner. The most ferocious arguments could ensue, and I would be wired for a week. So much so that twice I bumped into trams, and once I was knocked off my bike in Paris by an English milord in a Rolls Royce. Thankfully Nadya was able to patch me up, and soothe me, not with her awful cooking, but by taking rides and walks in the Parisian parks and suburban woods or admiring Sarah Bernhardt at the theatre (as long as it was not some mawkishly menshevising melodrama). My favourite city? I detested most of them, but some had their advantages. Above all, libraries. I have to admit that here, London with its magnificent reading room, unquestionably occupied first place. If you arrived early enough you might even have the privilege of sitting in Karl Marx' favourite seat, despite competition from local graduate students of the London School of so-called Economics set up by those renegade British and Irish compromisers the Fabian Society of George Bernard Shaw and the pusillanimous Webbs. Why call a movement after a Roman general famous for avoiding battle? Not my style! Not going to rename the Bolsheviks as the Kutuzov Society are we! The only other thing London is good for is rides on the upper deck of the omnibuses. For pennies, one can travel from the bourgeois enclaves of Mayfair and Bloomsbury to the working-class worlds of Clerkenwell and Seven Dials. Two nations! An education in class politics in half an hour! Not much else to recommend London! Apart from the rule of law. And a free press. And freedom of speech. And freedom of assembly. OK, apart from law, a free press, free speech, and freedom of assembly what has London done for us! What! Oh yes, after the perfidious Belgians ratted us out to the Okhrana we were able to cross the Channel to hold our Second Congress there under police protection from Russian spies so we could whip our opponents' sorry Menshevik asses.

There are so many wonderful European holiday haunts which I can wholeheartedly recommend. The amazing pink granite coast of North Brittany. The sands of Arcachon and the French west coast. The desolate beauty of the Baltic. The beer gardens of Germany where Nadya and I could sip a superb Weissbier and watch the serried ranks of militant proletarians marching by on their festive days. Nadya thought that like Lev Davidovich, we should be joining in with foreign workers' movements, but what's the point? The European workers are all hopelessly infected by the superprofits of imperialism and turn into bourgeois lackeys at the first sign of confrontation. So sad! Thank God, I mean thank heaven, I mean thank goodness for the tough, as the yet unformed, backward working class of Russia. There one might have at least a little hope that they could be moulded into something worthwhile, that could change history. I feel a party coming on!

Such are my favourite European haunts but don't forget, comrades, the only thing haunting Europe that really matters is the spectre of communism!

Chris Read is the author of many items on Russian social history and culture including The Russian Intelligentsia *(Bloomsbury) and* Lenin Lives? *(OUP) published in early 2024.*

Artist: Yevgeniy Fiks

23. Lenin and Black Power

Christian Høgsbjerg

After Lenin's death in 1924, one of the more remarkable tributes he received was from the Jamaican Pan-Africanist Marcus Garvey, leader of the mass black organisation, the Universal Negro Improvement Association. The UNIA, with its 700 branches in the United States alone, demanded 'Africa for the Africans' at a time when almost all of that continent was under European colonial domination, and so could be said to be the world's biggest ever Black Power movement, even though 'Black Power' as a slogan would not be coined until the 1960s by Stokely Carmichael. On 27 January 1924, Garvey felt moved to honour Lenin in a speech in New York:

> One of Russia's greatest men, one of the world's greatest characters, and probably the greatest man in the world between 1917 and 1924, when he breathed his last and took his flight from this world [...] We as Negroes mourn for Lenin because Russia promised great hope not only for Negroes but to the weaker people of the world.[1]

In other words, Lenin was truly himself a "tribune of the people [...] able to react to every manifestation of tyranny and oppression, no matter where it appears, no matter what stratum or class of the people it affects."[2] As such, he had a special appreciation of the racism suffered by black Americans in the Jim Crow United States, as well as their rich tradition of resistance and revolt. As Matthieu Renault has noted in a recent essay:

> Lenin learned of racial oppression in the United States at a young age. His favourite childhood book was none other than Harriet Beecher Stowe's *Uncle Tom's Cabin* [...] In 1913, he wrote an article titled, 'Russians and Negroes' in which he emphasises that "the emancipation of the American slaves took place in a less 'reformative' manner than that of the Russian slaves' and that "the Russians still show *many more* traces of slavery than the Negroes." However ... the "position of the Negroes in America," "unworthy of a civilised country," are proofs that "capitalism *cannot* give either *complete* emancipation or even complete equality." And in conclusion, he writes: "Shame on America for the plight of the Negroes!"[3]

Consequently, after the revolution, Lenin and other leading Bolsheviks, such as Trotsky, would champion the cause of black liberation.[4] We get a glimpse

---

[1] Hill, Robert A. (ed.) (1987), *The Marcus Garvey and Universal Negro Improvement Association Papers*, Vol. 5. Berkeley: University of California Press, 549 & 551.
[2] Lenin, V. I. (1977), "What is to be done?," in *Collected Works Vol. 5*, Moscow: Progress Publishers, 423.
[3] Renault, Matthieu (2021), "From Russian colonies to black America ... and back: Lenin and Langston Hughes" in David Featherstone and Christian Høgsbjerg (eds.), *The Red and the Black: The Russian Revolution and the Black Atlantic*. Manchester: Manchester University Press, 88.
[4] For more on Trotsky and race see Høgsbjerg, Christian (2009), "The Prophet and Black Power: Trotsky on race in the US," *International Socialism*, 121.

of the inspirational and transformational nature of the Russian Revolution on the African diaspora and the Black Atlantic from the following story relating to Emma Harris, a black American woman born in Georgia in 1871. Harris had decided to stay after touring Russia in the early 1900s, establishing her reputation as a singer and actress and becoming Russia's first black film star. Later Harris adapted to the revolution of 1917, serving with the Soviet Red Cross during the Russian Civil War and staying in the Soviet Union for twenty years until she returned to the United States in 1933 shortly before her death in 1940.[5]

In March 1918, Harris attended a huge rally in Red Square in Moscow that was addressed by Lenin. According to the journalist Theodore Postan,

> Lenin was explaining the meaning of the Bolshevik cause when he spied a smiling, middle-aged Negro woman in the forefront of the huge gathering. Extending his right hand in a characteristic gesture, he spoke directly to her: "The ideal of Communism," he said, "is to open the road for all the downtrodden races of the world. For you, comrade, especially, as we regard your race the most downtrodden in the world. We want you to feel when you come to Russia that you are a human being. The Red Army is ready to give its life at any time for all downtrodden races." Her neighbours hoisted Emma Harris to their shoulders and bore her triumphantly through the cheering throng...[6]

One year later, in March 1919, Lenin and the Bolsheviks attempted to put the theory of 'world revolution' into practice by forming the Third (Communist) International. Lenin played a leading role in ensuring national liberation movements in the colonies were seen as of central strategic importance. Shortly after, in July 1919, the US-based Jamaican black socialist Wilfred A. Domingo, writing in *The Messenger*, a Black revolutionary socialist magazine, declared that "Socialism" was "the Negro's Hope." Domingo – fittingly – also paid tribute to Lenin as a "tribune of the oppressed":

> The foremost exponents of Socialism ... are characterised by the broadness of their vision towards all oppressed humanity. It was the Socialist Vandevelde of Belgium, who protested against the Congo atrocities practised upon Negroes; it was the late Keir Hardie and Philip Snowden of England, who condemned British rule in Egypt ... today it is the revolutionary Socialist, Lenin, who analysed the infamous League of Nations and exposed its true character; it is he as leader of the Communist Congress at Moscow, who sent out the proclamation: "Slaves of the colonies in Africa and Asia! The hour of the proletarian dictatorship will be the hour of your release!"[7]

Tragically, with the failure of the Russian Revolution to spread to the West, the 'proletarian dictatorship' ultimately spiralled into counter-revolution amid the rise of a bureaucratic state-capitalist dictatorship under Stalin.

---

5 On Harris, see Tchijevsky, Ivan (2023), "Emma Harris (1871-1940)," *Black Past*.
6 Quoted in Featherstone and Høgsbjerg 2021: 7.
7 W.A. Domingo, quoted in Bergin, Cathy (ed.) (2016), *African American Anti-Colonial Thought, 1917-1937*. Edinburgh: Edinburgh University Press, 30.

Nonetheless, many Black activists still drew inspiration from the Soviet experience throughout the twentieth century, while Lenin's linking of the class struggle against exploitation to the wider struggle against oppression retains its relevance in the age of Black Lives Matter. As a result of what Lenin and the Bolsheviks managed to achieve, October 1917 will remain a resource of hope for those fighting racism and imperialism. The final word here might go to Nina Simone: "We never talked about men or clothes. It was always Marx, Lenin, and revolution – real girls' talk."[8]

Christian Høgsbjerg teaches in the School of Humanities and Social Science at the University of Brighton and is co-editor of The Red and the Black: The Russian Revolution and the Black Atlantic.

---

[8] See Taylor-Stone, Chardine (2021), "Nina Simone Was a Radical," *Jacobin*.

24. Lenin Met Makhno (Or Did He?)

Colin Darch

We think we know quite a lot about Vladimir Il'ich, who has now been dead for a hundred years. It used to be estimated that the special archive in the long defunct Institute of Marxism-Leninism (IML) in Moscow housed at least 25,000 documents either by him or addressed to him. In the 1920s there were appeals in the Soviet Union for anybody who had even a scrap of paper with his writing on it, to hand it over for preservation. The fifth (and probably the last) edition[1] of Lenin's *Collected Works* (in Russian, *Polnoe sobranie sochinenii*) was published between 1958 and 1965 in print runs of hundreds of thousands of copies and consists of 55 volumes containing several thousand documents.

Add to this the forty or so collections of ephemera in the 'Lenin Miscellany' (*Leninskii Sbornik*), which continued to appear until at least 1985.[2] If you want to know where Lenin was, and who he was talking to on any particular day, you can consult the Lenin Biographical Chronology (*Biograficheskaia Khronika*) in twelve volumes, compiled by Georgii Golikov and his team in 1970-1982. Plus, there are uncounted numbers of memoirs by people who knew him – Maxim Gorky, Krupskaya and so on – including, for example, the ten volumes of the IML's 'Memories of Vladimir Il'ich Lenin' (*Vospominaniia o Vladimire Il'iche Lenine*) published in the late 1980s.[3]

And yet, despite the pages and pages and pages of writings that have been published – books, pamphlets, letters, telegrams, essays, even the lovingly deciphered notes scribbled in the margins of other people's books – as well as the masses of materials by and about him in the now comparatively open Russian archives, there are still many silences, as well as some deliberate silencing – and not all of it by Soviet ideologues. In 1996 Harvard professor Richard Pipes edited a provocatively titled volume, *The Unknown Lenin: From the Secret Archives*, which was criticised at the time of its publication for sloppy editing, missing bits of text, and Pipes' desire to show Lenin as a self-righteous, cynical, aggressive misanthrope. Gorbachev himself reportedly commented, "Ah well, no doubt Mr Pipes selected just the right documents to make Lenin look terrible."

Of course, we can now see much of this as Cold War posturing – hagiography or demonisation –, neither of which help us much as historians and activists to evaluate Lenin's legacy in useful ways for present times. So, from the midst of all this fascinatingly messy detail, let's rather look at one

---

[1] In 1990, shortly before it was closed down, the IML had announced plans for an enlarged sixth edition.
[2] The IML also announced plans for a 41st volume of *Leninskii Sbornik* in 1990, but as far as I know it never appeared.
[3] Not such a remote possibility after all – when I worked in Ethiopia in the 1970s, I got to know well Richard Pankhurst, whose suffragette mother Sylvia had been a friend of Lenin's and corresponded with him.

brief moment in Lenin's life, *which may or may not have actually happened*, as an example of how much of what we know is actually what we surmise.

In mid-1918 the 30-year-old anarchist Nestor Ivanovich Makhno – then still unknown – fled the German and Austro-Hungarian occupation of Ukraine and ended up in Moscow. Probably sometime between 14 and 29 June, he seems to have gone to the Kremlin – a large walled complex rather than a single building – because he wanted (according to his own later testimony) to talk to the Bolshevik leadership, but more plausibly because he wanted to find somebody who could allot him free lodgings. After encountering various secretaries and receptionists, he ended up, astonishingly, in the offices of Yakov Sverdlov (1885-1919), chair of the All-Russian Central Executive Committee, an extremely senior position. Access to the top leadership was, evidently, still quite easy and informal. Sverdlov was a young man like Makhno, only 33 years old – Lenin at this time was in his late forties and was nicknamed *Starik* (the Old Man). According to the published narrative, after Sverdlov had pumped his visitor for first-hand intelligence about what was happening in Ukraine, he handed Makhno a pass and told him to come back the next afternoon, to talk directly to Lenin.

The next day the two of them went to Lenin's office together. In a wide-ranging conversation, at a certain moment, Lenin is supposed to have remarked:

> I consider you, comrade, to be a man of realism towards the hot topics of our times. If at least a third of the anarchist-communists in Russia were like you, then we communists would be ready to work together with you – on certain terms – towards the free organisation of producers.

At that point, Makhno writes, "I felt rising up in me a profound feeling of respect for Lenin." Given the fierce (and understandable) hostility in Makhno's later writings from exile, this comment is a testament both to Lenin's personal magnetism and to Makhno's emotional honesty.

The central problem with this whole story is, of course, its provenance – we have *only Makhno's own account* of the meetings with Sverdlov and Lenin, in two chapters of the second volume of his memoirs, *Under the blows of the counterrevolution* (*Pod udarami kontrrevoliutsii*). There is no mention of any meeting with a young Ukrainian revolutionary in Golikov's biographical chronology; no scribbled note by Lenin about Makhno has yet come to light in any obscure archival file. Besides, Makhno's book was published in Paris *after his death*, edited by Volin (Vsevolod Mikhailovich Eikhenbaum, 1882-1945), an intellectual and fellow anarchist with whom Makhno had an often stormy relationship, both during the revolution and afterwards in exile,[4] where they traded both insults and polemics. Volin calls the manuscript "notes" and describes his task as "imparting a minimally

---

[4] Makhno's army helped the Bolsheviks drive the Whites out of Crimea in 1920 but was then outlawed and eventually driven across the border into Romania. Makhno died in exile in Paris in 1934.

literary form to [them]." Patronisingly, he comments that Makhno's theoretical passages are "syntactically illiterate." Certainly, the articles that Makhno wrote in exile for the anarchist journal *Delo Truda* were muddled and needed extensive rewriting.

So, we have a participant account of a meeting, written from memory and then re-edited by an ideological opponent nearly twenty years after the event, in which Lenin allegedly expresses a vague willingness to cooperate with anarchist groups, not just militarily, but in the sphere of production. In 1917 and 1918 Lenin was writing fierce polemics against anarchists and anarchist ideas in such works as *The State and Revolution* and *The Immediate Tasks of the Soviet Government*, but to Makhno, a self-declared anarchist, he is conciliatory. Is there, consequently, any reason to trust this unsupported story and to accept the positions that it attributes to Lenin? Well, perhaps. Trotsky himself wrote, decades later and also in an unfinished manuscript, that

> Lenin and I seriously considered at one time allotting certain territories to the anarchists, naturally with the consent of the local population, and letting them carry on their experiment of a stateless social order there…

Even so, this is still a shaky foundation for the hypothesis that Lenin the pragmatist was open to the idea of cooperation with anarchists. Nevertheless, given the determinism of much current historiography of the 'Russian' revolution(s), which discounts the idea that Lenin and the Bolsheviks were struggling for a better world, and argues that the slide into totalitarianism was always inevitable, the story perhaps serves to remind us of the multiple possibilities that existed at any given moment in the tumultuous years of Great October.

Since the 1970s Colin Darch has survived interesting times in five African countries and South America; his book on Makhno was published in 2020.

25. Lenin: Building Hope

Constantino Bértolo

Not in brooding introspection
Bowed beneath a yoke of pain,
So that yearning, dream and action
Unfulfilled to us remain.
(Karl Marx)

The attacks on the work and figure of Lenin have one of their most outstanding points of support in the alleged coldness, theoretical and human, of the author of *The State and Revolution*, *What is to be done?* and *Materialism and Empirio-criticism*. This interested image has been transferred with particular insistence towards the interpretations of his character and temperament, giving rise to a portrait in which his desire for coherence has been translated as intolerance, his intellectual rigour as inclemency and his revolutionary will as 'Asian' hardness. A type of revived Ivan the Terrible full of theoretical intransigence, political resentment and cruel fanaticism. Manifestly, Lenin was very far from that bourgeois humanism with which Menshevik reformism fed, with the best of intentions and good manners, its revolutionary lethargy. Yet, this interpretation of his character could be found even among his own ranks, misinterpreting, for example, his "April Theses" as the adventurous result of his alleged impatience, anxiety and hasty judgment.

Among his biographers, whenever referring to the conviction and death of Lenin's brother Aleksandr, not one acknowledges the possibility of the personal pain that the event undoubtedly caused him. Rather, they take advantage of this episode to find in the execution the origin of the pathological hatred and thirst for revenge that would explain his tenacious fight against tsarism. No one among them – we are talking about the countless injurious portraits that have been made of him in anti-communist historiography – cares to even consider the expressions of warmth and human quality that can be seen in his relationship with Nadezhda Krupskaya while, at the same time, they never fail to emphasise, again and again, without any proof, the murky suspicions vis-à-vis his alleged relations with the revolutionary Inessa Armand.

Not that there is anything strange about this whole intrigue. In the end, the class enemy always resorts to every weapon and resource at his disposal, no matter how immoral or vile, when it comes to tarnishing the acts and ideas of those who, like Lenin, embody and represent what they most fear: the Revolution, that is, the loss of their economic, cultural, political and – last but not least – moral dominance, since let us not forget that every revolution also involves a radical ethical change in the scale of values. Based on lies and silences, reactionary thought thus gradually constructed the profile of that monstrous Lenin that is still widely adhered to today, because everything that is not convenient for the dissemination of this image of the cold, anti-human and cruel Lenin continues to be avoided or concealed. *Al enemigo, ni agua.* To the enemy, not even a glass of water. It is hence no coincidence that the Spanish writer Antonio Muñoz Molina, commenting on the recent Spanish-language edition of *Lenin, The Dictator* by Victor Sebestyen, insists that "Lenin's obsession was not social justice or equality, but absolute political power," or that Federico Jimenez Losantos, in his commercially successful book, *Memoria del Comunismo – De Lenin a Podemos*, did not hesitate to describe him as a "cold-blooded illusionist who respects neither the honour nor the life of the proletariat."

Perhaps that is why such little attention has been paid to the Lenin who, against this image of rough and ruthless coldness, provides a vision of the revolutionary tasks in which aspects and concepts are present that can be identified and found within that very humanist tradition that the sanctimonious bourgeoisie accepts, approves of and acclaims. The right to dream, for example. The act of dreaming, which for them, at once so enlightened and ignorant, implies the exact opposite of that rude and soulless materialism typical of Marxism and Marxists. It is precisely in the final pages of *What is to be Done?*, the book that for the bourgeois intellectual embodies the peak of Leninist dogmatism, where, with the sarcasm that so characterises his style whenever he enters into controversy with others, Lenin deals in an outstanding manner, via the hand of Pisarev, with the question of dreaming in the revolutionary tradition:

> "We should dream!" I wrote these words and became alarmed. I imagined myself sitting at a "unity conference" and opposite me were the *Rabocheye Dyelo* editors and contributors. Comrade Martynov rises and, turning to me, says sternly: "Permit me to ask you, has an autonomous editorial board the right to dream without first soliciting the opinion of the Party committees?" He is followed by Comrade Krichevsky, who (philosophically deepening Comrade Martynov, who long ago rendered Comrade Plekhanov more profound) continues even more sternly: "I go further. I ask, has a Marxist any right at all to dream, knowing that according to Marx, mankind always sets itself the tasks it can solve and that tactics is a process of the growth of Party tasks which grow together with the Party?"
>
> The very thought of these stern questions sends a cold shiver down my spine and makes me wish for nothing but a place to hide in. I shall try to hide behind the back of Pisarev.
>
> "There are rifts and rifts," wrote Pisarev of the rift between dreams and reality. "My dream may run ahead of the natural march of events or may fly off at a tangent in a direction in which no natural march of events will ever proceed. In the first case my dream will not cause any harm; it may even support and augment the energy of the working men.... There is nothing in such dreams that would distort or paralyse labour-power. On the contrary, if man were completely deprived of the ability to dream in this way, if he could not from time to time run ahead and mentally conceive, in an entire and completed picture, the product to which his hands are only just beginning to lend shape, then I cannot at all imagine what stimulus there would be to

induce man to undertake and complete extensive and strenuous work in the sphere of art, science, and practical endeavour... The rift between dreams and reality causes no harm if only the person dreaming believes seriously in his dream, if he attentively observes life, compares his observations with his castles in the air, and if, generally speaking, he works conscientiously for the achievement of his fantasies. If there is some connection between dreams and life then all is well."

Of this kind of dreaming there is unfortunately too little in our movement. And the people most responsible for this are those who boast of their sober views, their "closeness" to the "concrete," the representatives of legal criticism and of illegal "tail-ism."

Here, dreaming is no longer a right but a revolutionary demand, understood as an indispensable aspect of the 'crazy' art and work of revolution. Not the pleasant bourgeois dreaming of castles in the air and vague, vain fantasies, but the "concrete analysis of the concrete situation" hand in hand with dreaming as a subjective force and condition. A few years later, Ernst Bloch, author of *The Principle of Hope*, would not hesitate to rescue these thoughts of Lenin, affirming that, "Objectivist idolatry of the objectively possible [...] waits winking until the economic conditions for socialism have become completely ripe, so to speak. But they are never completely ripe or so perfect that they are in no need of a will to action and an anticipatory dream in the subjective factor of this will. Lenin, as is well known, did not wait until the conditions everywhere in Russia gave leave for socialism, in a comfortably distant age of his children's children."

Sometimes, in situations when the Revolution seems all but impossible, it is necessary to imagine it as a dream that should not catch us sleeping. The Revolution as hope – argued for, built, and won.

Constantino Bértolo (Navia de Suarna, Spain, 1946), is a critic, publisher and author, among other books, of Lenin, el revolucionario que no sabía demasiado *(Los Libros de la Catarata, 2012).*

Translated from the Spanish by hjje.

26. Lenin on Women's Emancipation and Sexuality

Daria Dyakonova

Vladimir Lenin, like many communists of his time, was a champion of women's emancipation, which he linked to the revolutionary socialist transformation of societies. "Wherever there is capitalism, wherever there is private property in land and factories, wherever the power of capital is preserved," he argued, "the men retain their privileges." Women, moreover, Lenin contended, faced double or triple slavery as "all housework was left to them."

After the revolution, Lenin in collaboration with Communist revolutionary women in Russia – Alexandra Kollontai, Inessa Armand, Nadezhda Krupskaya, among many others – promoted the liberation of women in the new Soviet state, in the family, at work and in the political sphere. He also greeted the foundation in 1920 of the international Communist Women's Movement (CWM) as an auxiliary organisation of the Communist International (Comintern). The CWM organised internationally coordinated campaigns that aimed to achieve complete gender equality in both legal and practical aspects. They pushed for the full inclusion of women in political, economic, and social spheres, as well as the provision of free education and healthcare for women. The movement also called for social policies to alleviate the responsibilities of housework and childcare, along with the right for women to have control over their reproductive choices. These demands were quite radical and ahead of their time and today, over one hundred years later, continue to be unmet in numerous societies worldwide.

Lenin supported communist women in this endeavour, both in Soviet Russia and within the Comintern. For instance, the 1918 Soviet family legislation, encouraged by Lenin, enhanced women's position in the family. The new code prescribed the equality of spouses, secular marriage and divorce initiated by either one of the parties and equality of children before the law (independently of the marital status of parents). Lenin was also adept at gender equality within the communist movement itself, whether in the CPSU or the national sections of the Comintern and its central apparatus. Unfortunately, not all communist men shared Lenin's zeal. According to Clara Zetkin, editor of the CWM's journal *Die Kommunistische Fraueninternationale*, many communist men "overtly or covertly" resisted a women's agenda, separate organisation and/or organising among women, seeing it as challenging class-based activism as well as party and Comintern unity. This attitude was arguably "inherited" from the earlier social-democratic movement, with its history of banal sexism and gender prejudice. By way of example, at the First Women's Conference of the Communist Party of France held in Marseilles in December 1921, French communist women argued that by their reluctance to actively support a women's agenda male comrades pushed revolutionary women out of the Communist movement into the arms of liberal feminism. Lenin himself was aware of sexism within the communist movement. Italian Communist leader Camilla Ravera recalled Lenin's biting comments on the issue of women's emancipation and the attitude of male comrades: "'on the women's question,' Lenin told her once, 'scratch a communist and there, too, you'll find a reactionary.'"

Male Communist resistance notwithstanding, Communist Women continued to advocate for the elimination of unfair sex-related double standards. Among the leading figures of the movement, Alexandra Kollontai, who in 1917 was named Commissar for Social Affairs within the Soviet government, thus becoming the first woman minister in history, wrote a number of works on reproductive rights, motherhood, and sexuality. An advocate of the women's right to abortion, she however saw it as a temporary measure and promoted larger responsibility of the state in support of motherhood and the upbringing of children. The CWM adhered to these ideas and advocated the socialisation of childcare through the creation of public institutions (daycares, nurseries, milk kitchens, canteens, etc.) in all countries where the movement was active. Communist Women also fought for increased support of mothers through labour legislation, the introduction of paid maternal leave and benefits for children and families around the world.

In addition, Kollontai was interested in other aspects of sexuality such as non-exclusive love. In 1919, she published *The New Morality and the Working Class*, a 60-page pamphlet that delved into the relationship between socialism, women's emancipation and sexual liberation. Kollontai argued that in the new proletarian society, the concept of love had to undergo a profound transformation. She maintained that in previous social systems – clan, tribal, feudal, and bourgeois – love was used primarily as a tool for the subjugation of women. Proletarian love, by contrast, was a feeling based on understanding between comrades, "the great new psychological force of comradely solidarity," which could take on multiple forms: friendship, passionate love, or intellectual love. This vision implied diverse loves for equally diverse people. In 1923, in an article entitled "Make way for winged Eros!" Kollontai defined the new type as "the many-faceted love experience of love-comradeship" based on three principles: "equality in relationships," "mutual recognition of the right of the other," and "comradely sensitivity, the ability to listen and understand the soul of the loved person (bourgeois culture demanded this only from the woman)." Kollontai was, however, far from defending limitless promiscuity and instead advocated love that brought together physical and spiritual elements.

Yet, despite her nuanced position on sexuality, Kollontai's ideas aroused criticism within the Women's Department (or Zhenotdel) of the CPSU as some of her collaborators saw the concept of non-exclusive love as necessarily implying cohabitation with several partners. One of Kollontai's colleagues, Polina Vinogradskaya, regarded Kollontai's "moral philosophising" on love as superficial and in any case untimely in the post-World War I (and post-Civil War) Soviet Union, where economic problems and the lack of employment of women, as well as the problems of child abandonment and prostitution, were to be placed at the centre of intellectual debates. According to Vinogradskaya, cohabitation with several partners – instead of leading to an "intensification of proletarian strength" – risked consuming all the energy of the people concerned, which they could otherwise put to the service of the party and society. The non-exclusive love concept, however, became quite popular among the urban youth, including members of the Soviet Young Communist League (Komsomol), and was understood primarily in terms of sexual intercourse liberation. These developments led Sara Ravich, an activist of the CWM, to criticise in 1921, in the monthly magazine of the Zhenotdel, *Kommunistka*, the "unimaginable bacchanal" which took place in Soviet Russia, where free love was understood by many young people as "free debauchery."

Interestingly, Lenin had his own views on these ideas and practices, which he shared in 1920 in a conversation with Clara Zetkin. Lenin mentioned that he was not adept at the "so-called 'new sexual life' of young people, and often adults" which seemed purely bourgeois to him, "a kind of good bourgeois house of tolerance." He argued that the liberation of sexual desires was "neither new nor communist," contending nevertheless that Communism did not imply asceticism either. "Communism will bring," Vladimir Lenin maintained, "the joy of living, and the power of life and of fulfilled love life will help this. In my opinion, the hypertrophy currently widespread in sexual matters does not give joy or strength to life, but on the contrary deprives it of it."

Although Lenin's attitude towards sexual freedom was more cautious than Kollontai's, both seem to have shared the reflection on the importance of the "Wings of Eros" that described love in the new socialist state as a harmonious combination of emotional and sexual involvement. In any case, Lenin opposed the double standards or double morality for men and women that bourgeois societies had imposed on the latter. He was a relentless fighter for the emancipation of women from both capitalist subjugation and "kitchen slavery," through a revolutionary transformation of societies that would inevitably empower women in all spheres of life.

Dr. Daria Dyakonova is a Marxist historian and has written about Young Communists and Communist Women of the interwar period.

27. Richter and Gus

David McIlwraith

It wasn't because he feared the British police that Dr. Jacob Richter varied the streets he walked each morning between Holford Square and the Museum. In fact, his few acquaintances had assured him that the English were quite tolerant of continental radicals, since it wasn't King Edward's head they were after. No, it was rather that he had begun to take a liking to London, and enjoyed walking the streets of Clerkenwell and Bloomsbury, admiring the squares and gardens and tidy Georgian homes. Of course, the delights of his many outings did not dissuade him from his conviction that the country was the dean of modern imperialism and its bankers the rapacious guardians of global capital. But England had London and London had the Reading Room at the British Museum.

"Good day, Gus," Dr. Richter said to the porter sitting on a stool just inside the Reading Room door. "And a very good day to you, Dr. Richter. Lovely day if you're a duck." A smiling Augustus Cole stood and gestured into the great domed room. "You'll be 'appy to know your preferred desk is vacant." "Excellent," said Richter, clapping the porter's shoulder as he passed him by. He stopped to look up at the gleaming windowed dome before going to his desk.

Augustus Cole had no reason to vary the streets he walked from Camden Town to the Museum and paid little attention to parks and squares he'd seen hundreds of times. With commendable regularity, he would leave the flat he shared with his wife and three daughters above a tobacconist on Camden High Street, umbrella in his right hand and lunch in his left. He walked briskly and always arrived on time. Among the dozen porters who worked in the Reading Room, Gus was a favourite with the patrons, a friendly fellow, well-liked by all during the thirteen years he'd worked there. But Jacob Richter was the only reader he'd spoken to outside the sanctum. It happened by accident. After closing one day, they found themselves walking together for part of their respective journeys home. Gus did the talking, mostly about London, as the doctor preferred to listen.

Richter's principal frustration in the early days of his stay was his struggle with the English language. Before arriving in the city, he had somehow convinced himself that he could both understand and speak the tongue, a sorely misguided conviction. Within a week he had arranged English tutoring for both himself and his wife Nadya, from an aspiring poet willing to come to their flat. The tutor came on Wednesday mornings, which explained Richter's later-than-usual arrival at the Museum on this particularly drizzly Wednesday.

As it happened, the Reading Room porter and the doctor shared something akin to political views. Augustus Cole had become an admirer of the socialist poet and artist William Morris. He began to seek out public gatherings where the poet spoke of socialism to small groups in the streets.

Jacob Richter was a student of the writings of Karl Marx. Occasionally he even allowed himself the pleasure of acknowledging he was working in the same room where Marx wrote *Das Kapital*. Richter was also a student of London, riding atop the omnibuses studying what he called the two nations, the obscene wealth of Kensington and the brutal poverty of Whitechapel. The doctor had let people believe that like Marx, he was also German. Richter was the name he'd given the British Museum when he applied for a Reading Room ticket, and it was the name by which he was known to the porters there. After agents of the Czar had traced him to Germany, forcing his move to London, yet another pseudonym seemed a prudent option.

When Gus noticed books by Marx and other political writers on Richter's request slips, he considered raising the subject with him, but porters were not permitted to 'bother' the readers. On this wet Wednesday though, as he finished storing the trolleys at closing, he noticed Richter leaving at the same time. On a whim, he suggested they go for a pint at a pub on their shared walking route. Dr. Richter hesitated. His limited social life in London thus far had been lived principally among Russian-speaking emigres in Spitalfields and Whitechapel. But just that very morning his tutor had advised him to seek out conversations with English speakers. Surprising even himself, he accepted Gus's invitation.

They walked out through the colonnade, along Great Russell Street and up Southampton Row, Gus talking the whole way. He spoke about his years at the Museum, and named notables to whom he had delivered books, including Mark Twain and Bernard Shaw, neither of whom were known to Richter. He talked of his daughters, the eldest of whom dreamed of studying at University College now that women were being admitted. As they reached Russell Square and came within sight of the arches of the opulent Hotel Russell, a coal wagon came out from Guilford Street, turning toward Woburn Place. Halfway through the turn, the lone horse collapsed onto the rain-soaked cobblestones glistening in the hotel's new electric lights.

Richter and Gus saw the horse go down and the driver jumps off the wagon. A doorman standing on the hotel steps hurried over to have a closer look. As Gus and Richter approached the wagon they found the driver, a lad about fifteen, black with coal dust, sitting on the road next to the horse, its head in his lap. The doorman leaned into the two men. "The old nag's dead," he said. The young driver was whispering the horse's name – "Rosie. Rosie." The doorman laughed. "How many dying nags in London are called Rosie?" Gus gave him a withering look and walked to the boy, put a hand on his shoulder and said, "It's alright lad, she didn't suffer as she died. Which is more than you can say for how she lived." He put a hand under the boy's arm, lifted him up and helped him to sit on the steps. "I'll be sacked for this," the boy said. "Don't be daft," said Gus, "it's not your fault Rosie's gone. She's been pulling overloaded coal wagons since before you were born. Who you working for lad?" The boy named a company on the canal near King's Cross.

The doorman pushed by Gus to speak to the boy. "Time to move the horse meat lad. This is a better sort of hotel. The guests won't get their carriages through." Jacob Richter stepped in beside him and said, "Then they will walk." Gus smiled and told the doorman to "telegraph the company up at the coal drops and have them send an empty wagon." He gave the lad a penny for an ice cream from the 'okey pokey' man in the Square, "but mind they use a wafer cone," he said. Then Gus and Richter walked around the corner to the pub. They found a table from which Richter could see each person who entered. It was still his habit to be wary. Gus grabbed two pints at the bar and after a couple of quaffs began to laugh as he repeated Richter's accented words. "Den dey vill valk." Richter interrupted, apologising for his English. "No, your English was fine," said Gus. "I was laughing at the way you took that bugger to task for his treatment of that poor lad. I think you're a good man, Dr. Richter." The doctor sighed. "I am not sure I am a good man. I believe I am a man who will get things done. It will be for history to decide if the things I will do are good." "Well, you spoke up for that boy. That was good. I felt badly for him."

The doctor sipped his ale and looked at Gus for a few seconds. "You are a kind man, Augustus, a compassionate man. But you must learn that as often as not, compassion will kill the revolution." "I didn't know we were talking about revolution." "We are always talking about revolution." Gus smiled at Richter and said, "So you do have an interest in politics?" "I believe you could say so," Richter replied. Gus said, "I could see from the books you requested." "Ah, I understand. Well, well. Now I should be going. Tea will be waiting." Gus stood and said he must also be on his way home. At the street corner, they shook hands. "Good night, Dr. Richter." The doctor did not reply, nor did he let go of Gus's hand. He paused for a moment, then said, "I have never been a doctor, my friend. And my name is Vladimir Ulyanov." Without a pause, Gus replied, "Righty-ho then, good night, Vladimir Ulyanov."

David McIlwraith is a Canadian writer and filmmaker. His short story, The Stone Bench, *about Antonio Gramsci's final days, was short-listed for The Commonwealth Prize.*

28. Lenin, Psychoanalysis and Free Love

David Pavón-Cuéllar

Lenin and Freud are emblematic figures of the first half of the 20th century. Both lived in Europe at the same time, scandalised the bourgeoisie, criticised the dominant ideology and were considered a threat to religion, morality and society. Their books were banned from conservative homes and burned on Nazi bonfires.

Lenin and Freud did not know each other personally, but they had acquaintances in common. A youthful friend of Freud, Liverij Darkschewitsch, was Lenin's doctor. A socialist comrade of Lenin, Victor Adler, sold his house in Vienna to Freud, who had been his childhood friend.

Freud and Lenin watched each other from a distance. The former showed scepticism towards what he described as "the Bolsheviks' illusions." The latter has often been perceived as hostile to psychoanalysis, but... is this perception correct? Experts Martin Miller and Christfried Tögel think that Lenin's hostility was only directed at certain uses of Freudian doctrine, but not against psychoanalysis as such. Criticising these authors, Jacquy Chemouni is convinced that Lenin was indeed hostile to psychoanalysis.

Chemouni's conviction is based on Lenin's only known explicit statement about Freud, which was expressed to Clara Zetkin during an interview in 1920. In this interview, Lenin regrets that certain communist women are concerned above all with sexual issues under the guidance of a pamphlet with psychoanalytic references. Lenin adds that Freud's theory is "a fad" and reveals his distrust in sexual theories that "exuberantly sprout from the dunghill of bourgeois society." Such theories were for Lenin a typically bourgeois form of "navel-gazing." His conclusion is that we should stop imagining that the social problem is "a part, an appendage to the sexual problem."

As is well known, Freud places sexuality at the origin, background and foundation of society. He thus deserves Lenin's criticism. This criticism, however, seems to be directed not at psychoanalysis per se, but at the way in which various theories, including the Freudian one, overstress sexual, personal and individual issues at the expense of social matters.

Curiously, Lenin criticised the "superabundance of sex theories" in the autumn of 1920, precisely in the days in which he learned of the death of his beloved friend Inessa Armand, a death that left him devastated and from which he never recovered, according to Aleksandra Kollontai. The coincidence in time is intriguing because of everything that existed between Lenin and Armand, not only their passionate bond, but also the revealing contradiction between their respective ideas about the liberation of women. This contradiction can be appreciated in two letters dated 1915 in which Lenin advises Armand to suppress the demand for "free love" in a pamphlet for working-class women.

In his first letter, Lenin rejects free love because he considers that it is usually understood in a bourgeois way as "freedom of adultery" and from "procreation" and "seriousness in love." Instead, he advocates a liberation of women from material concerns, social and religious prejudices, male prohibitions and "the fetters of the law." What Lenin defends corresponds to what was earlier claimed by August Bebel in his 1879 *Woman and Socialism*, which Lenin would praise for its "gripping agitation full of attacks on bourgeois society" in his interview with Zetkin, contrasting it with the sexual exaggerations in texts of psychoanalytic inspiration.

The 1920 interview and the 1915 letters thus seem to display two different conceptions of women's emancipation. On the one hand, there is the bourgeois conception that is incompatible with Marxism, usually invokes Freud, overestimates the sexual factor, and claims a free love associated with adultery and a sexuality without procreation. On the other hand, there is the proletarian conception, guided by Bebel, that demands a liberation of women from the socioeconomic base and the legal, political and ideological-religious superstructure.

Lenin's distinction was rejected by Armand. While we do not know her exact responses, we can infer them from other texts and from Lenin's second letter. This letter in fact cites some passages from Armand, among them the following that takes on additional meaning in light of the bond between the writer and the recipient: "passionate fleeting relationships" are "more poetic and cleaner" than "kisses without love" from the spouses. Love is what is important for Armand, who seems to give no importance to the "adultery" that Lenin associated with the "bourgeois demand" of free love.

In fact, there are no bourgeois and proletarian conceptions for Armand, but rather a single free love that would liberate itself from a certain subjective cultural morality and not only the objective socioeconomic, legal and ideological chains inherent to class society. For Lenin, on the contrary, "the thing is the objective logic of class relations in affairs of love", and for this reason, he reproaches Armand for persisting in "subjectively" understanding free love and for "refuting and demolishing" him, Lenin, as a subject. This response from Lenin is fascinating, not only because of his relationship with Armand, but because the reformulation of the conflict between the two as a contradiction between objectivity and subjectivity is closely related to Lenin's general thought.

In *Materialism and Empirio-criticism*, for example, Lenin defends objective knowledge understood as a faithful reflection of reality. This objectivist realism, however, is invalidated both by Leninist dialectical materialism, which goes beyond the subjectivism/objectivism dichotomy, and by the derived political choices against the realist-objectivist orientations of opportunism, reformism and revisionism. Instead of adapting to the supposed objective reality by taking advantage of opportunities, making reforms and revising Marxism, Lenin opted for the subject of the revolution that demonstrates the truth of Marx despite adverse 'objective' circumstances such as the insufficient historical-economic development of Russia.

Lenin's revolutionary achievements connect the subjective with the objective in a way that proves Armand right, but also Lenin and above all the links between them and the other communists who made the revolution. These links also demonstrate the truth of what Armand stated by confirming the power and political importance of sexual bonds independent of existing social relations, since it is evident that the profound revolutionary transformation of Russian society would not have been possible if the Bolsheviks had established among themselves only those social relations sanctioned, institutionalised and predetermined by that society. On the contrary, it was necessary to establish other kinds of relations, "more poetic and cleaner" like those imagined by Armand, previously impossible relations like the 'sexual links' in Freud.

Here we must understand that in Freud, sexual links cannot be reduced only to genital intercourse, but are what internally animates what is alive in society, culture and history. They are what unfolds in comradeship, revolutionary struggle and the various prefigurations of communism. It is here that sexuality was discerned by Armand, Kollontai and other female companions of Lenin in that great sublimated realisation of free love that was the revolutionary movement of 1917.

The free love aspired to by Armand could only be realised through a Revolution as transcendent as the October Revolution, led by Lenin. He may not have been clear about everything he was helping to make possible, but the important thing is that he helped make it possible. The Bolshevik Revolution was also a revolution against patriarchy and not only because of its radical reforms in favour of women.

David Pavón-Cuéllar is a Mexican Marxist philosopher, a critical psychologist and Professor of Psychology at the Universidad Michoacana de San Nicolás de Hidalgo, in Morelia, Michoacán, Mexico.

Artist: Unknown

29. Lenin's Enduring Influence on the Struggle against Imperialism in Africa

Demba Moussa Dembélé

Lenin's brilliant pamphlet on imperialism has become a classic that has influenced the thinking of political and social forces fighting foreign domination around the world. In particular, it has had a profound resonance for African revolutionary and anti-imperialist movements in their struggle against imperialism and neocolonialism.

According to Lenin, the deep transformation of late 19th-century capitalism, from free competition to monopoly capitalism, inaugurated the era of imperialism. This opened a period of intense colonial conquests: "For England, the period of prodigious accentuation of colonial conquests is between 1860 and 1890, and it is even more intense during the last twenty years of the 19th century. For France and Germany, it is particularly these twenty years that count the most."

This translated into the scramble for the control of non-European countries and the plunder of their resources. It was within that general context that the infamous Berlin Conference of 1884-1885 took place. During the conference, European imperialist powers carved up Africa into spheres of influence, which sealed its fate until today. Indeed, Africa paid a heavy price to the birth and expansion of capitalism and to the rise of European imperialism.

This was clearly shown in Walter Rodney's seminal 1972 book, *How Europe Underdeveloped Africa*. A native of Guyana, Rodney was a staunch Pan-Africanist. He lived and taught in Tanzania for several years in the 1960s and 70s, a period of great revolutionary debates on the way forward for Africa's development. Analysing the continent's "backwardness" from a Marxist perspective and calling Lenin "prophetic" for his analysis of monopoly capital, Rodney argued that the destruction of Africa's social structures by European invaders and the plunder of its resources – gold, diamonds, silver and many others – contributed decisively to the (industrial) development of Europe and the concomitant underdevelopment of Africa. "From the very beginning of the Scramble for Africa, huge fortunes were made from gold and diamonds in Southern Africa by people like Cecil Rhodes..." Besides, several European cities, banks and companies could not have been built without the resources from the slave trade, cities like Bordeaux, Nantes and Liverpool, and companies like the British Barclays Bank and the Insurance Company Lloyds.

In other words, late 19th-century colonisation opened a new phase in the development of capitalism. According to Lenin, "the fiercer the competition and the scramble for raw materials in the world, the more brutal is the struggle for the possession of colonies."

The legacy of this brutal colonisation was later analysed by Ghanaian President Kwame Nkrumah, one of the leading figures in the Pan-Africanist movement and a fierce opponent of imperialism and neocolonialism in Africa. In his 1965 book, *Neo-Colonialism, the Last Stage of Imperialism,* named after Lenin's 1917 pamphlet, he argued that since direct colonial rule had become more difficult after the wave of independence in Africa, former colonial powers now used an indirect control of "neocolonialism" to continue their domination and exploitation of the continent. He claimed that Africa's balkanisation – its division into small, weak states with weak governments and institutions – had made it easy prey for imperialist powers to impose their will on African countries. By way of example, President Nkrumah listed dozens of Western companies and banks controlling African economies in formally 'independent' countries.

Following Lenin's affirmation that imperialism used all possible means of "camouflage of its real nature," President Nkrumah went on to emphasise that neocolonialism had not only economic and financial but also cultural and religious dimensions, using new instruments of influence and control like mass media, advertising and the "neocolonialist trap" of "multilateral aid." In recent decades, we can add to this the emergence of Western(-backed) 'humanitarian' NGOs promoting 'anti-corruption,' 'democracy' and 'human rights,' all of which contribute to maintaining Western domination and exploitation.

Indeed, the ideology of European 'superiority,' inherited from the times of slavery, was one of the driving forces behind the colonisation of Africa. Walter Rodney observes that "all Europeans had derived ideas of racial and cultural superiority between the fifteenth and nineteenth centuries, while engaged in genocide and enslavement of non-white peoples."

However, even if cultural factors are undoubtedly important aspects of imperialism, it remains first and foremost an economic phenomenon, characterised by the reign of monopolies, "for the partition of the world and the right to rule over other countries," according to Lenin and cited by Nkrumah.

Building on and "benefitting from the lead of Lenin in this field," in his *Ending the Crisis of Capitalism or Ending Capitalism?* Samir Amin argues that historical capitalism evolved through the "permanent dispossession" of the dominated countries of the Periphery. In the second half of the 20th century and the beginning of the 21st, the concentration of capital has accelerated in ways "unprecedented compared with previous stages of capitalism's history."

Concretely, US imperialism, in close alliance with Japan and the European Union, is at the head of what Amin calls the "collective imperialism of the Triad." In his view, this Triad is a response to growing challenges to Western imperialism's economic, political and military hegemony vis-à-vis the rising powers from the Global South. In the face of these challenges, western imperialist countries tend to tone down their rivalry and form a front against what is perceived as a threat to their economic, financial and political hegemony.

What's more, in its confrontation with rivals and enemies, the Triad has a number of "common instruments" aimed at protecting its interests around the world, such as the IMF, the World Bank, the WTO and the OECD. The military instruments of the Triad, on the other hand, are mainly the Armed Forces of the United States and their "subordinated allies of NATO." Yet, according to Amin, "the model of globalisation that is currently in place is vulnerable." He thus calls for a "second wave of victorious struggles for the emancipation of workers and peoples," based on a "renewal of a creative Marxism," to make historical capitalism a "short parenthesis in history."

In conclusion, Lenin's insights on imperialism have inspired analysis of foreign domination and imperialism in Africa and the Global South for many decades. In contemporary Africa, there is a new generation of anti-imperialist movements and organisations whose agenda is to rid the continent of foreign domination in all areas: political, economic, military and cultural. The issue of sovereignty is once again on top of their agenda. In West Africa, a new anti-imperialist wind is blowing. Inspired by the ideas of Kwame Nkrumah, Samir Amin, and the example of Thomas Sankara, the murdered charismatic revolutionary from Burkina Faso and an avowed admirer of Lenin, young military leaders, allied with progressive political and social forces, are leading their countries in the renewed struggle against imperialism under the banner of patriotism and sovereignty. This is illustrated by the recent closing of French military bases in Burkina Faso, Mali and Niger, and the more general revival of the Pan-Africanist spirit. These examples are giving renewed optimism to progressive and anti-imperialist forces in their struggle for the second Liberation of Africa.

Demba Moussa Dembélé is an economist and researcher from Senegal.

30. How the Soviet Union Saved the Caribbean Without Colonisation

Earl Bousquet

I grew up near the seaside at Hospital Road in Castries, Saint Lucia's capital, in the 1960s, hearing my father, Charles Victor Emmanuel Bousquet, proudly discuss his experiences as a British Merchant Navy seaman during World War II. He'd sailed the seas on the 'cable ships' that laid cables for the first telephone lines in the British West Indies, and one of his favourite quotes was: "If not for the Russians, we'd be speaking German."

It wasn't until the mid-70s that I came to understand what he meant: that if not for the Soviet fleet of submarines tracing and chasing the German U-Boats operating out of the neighbouring French colony of Martinique, his and other non-combatant ships operating in and out of Saint Lucia could have been among the many torpedoed by the Nazi submarines.

France's Vichy regime collaborated with Hitler and allowed the German 'subs' to hunt and haunt British and other Allied forces in the West Indian (Caribbean) islands on this side of the Atlantic. Indeed, two ships, the 'Lady Nelson' and the 'Umtata', were torpedoed in the Castries Harbour during the war – less than 200 yards from our home – by a Martinique-based German 'U-Boat' that silently entered, hit the two payloads – and left.

In other words, what my four-times-decorated sailor father was saying in the 60s was that while the Cold War culture had sold the Soviet Union and Russians as 'Reds' and Bad Guys, he (and the many others who lived the truth) were very much aware of and grateful to the Union of Soviet Socialist Republics (USSR) for its role in patrolling Caribbean waters and taking the underwater fight to the German Nazis, protecting him and other British subjects left to largely fend for themselves while the US, UK and allies concentrated on protecting Europe.

My dad was a bosun and one of his (still very rare) feats was to have four brothers (Charles and his three siblings Allan, Joseph and Leo) on the same ship ('Norseman,' if my memory still works). He always felt he owed his and his brothers' lives to "the Russians." But when he discovered I was interested in the role the USSR played in the West Indies, he evaded what he called "the politics," saying only, "The Russians were brilliant military strategists, but in the end they lost more lives than the British and the Americans in the war." And he was also the first to tell me: "It was the Russians who chased Adolf Hitler out of Germany."

But Charles wouldn't discuss Russian leader Vladimir Lenin, simply saying, "That was before my time." Indeed, when the Russian Revolution triumphed in 1917, he was only 12 years old in the West Coast town of Soufriere (the island's first colonial capital), swimming, fishing, cleaning fish – and growing up under the Union Jack (the British flag).

I got the same brush-off reaction from my Rastafarian brethren on the block in Grass Street, Castries, when Ethiopia's Emperor Haile Selassie was overthrown in June 1974 through an army coup led by pro-socialist Col. Haile Mengistu Mariam. At the time, the likes of myself and Comrade Lawrence Poyotte wore Rastafarian dreadlocks and, together with our Rasta Brethren, were trying to organise the movement against the growing police persecution and prosecution, and the gross human rights violations, in the period leading to and immediately after independence in 1979. We didn't try to win the Brethren over to Mengistu, but simply explained to those who'd listen that, in our considered political view, 'Socialism is better than Feudalism' for Ethiopia's future. Those opposed to Mengistu argued on the basis of Theocracy, we on the basis of Class Struggle; they defended 'The Emperor' and we 'The Masses'.

We hadn't yet established the Workers Revolutionary Movement (WRM) that a few years later began the local charge for alternative political thought and action in the late colonial and immediate pre-independence era, when the Caribbean was embracing the Black Power movement and younger minds were open to wider historical world views and new ideas like Marxism-Leninism. Just as the Fabian Socialists in the UK and Europe and their followers in the West Indian Labour Movement were branded 'communists' during the early Cold War, the WRM was also dubbed 'communist' by the colonially educated ruling class, while the Rastas called Lawrence and me 'Communist Ras.'

We stumped the more vociferous arch-critics in the wider Black Power movement who loudly claimed 'Lenin is not relevant to the Caribbean' by producing a copy of Marcus Garvey's 1917 letter to Lenin in the Rasta movement's newspaper *Calling Rastafari*, in which 'The Mosiah' expressed the support of the Jamaican and West Indian working class for the Russian Revolution he led with the Russian Social Democratic Labour Party (RSDLP-Bolsheviks).

Indeed, it wasn't known back then (and still largely now in the Caribbean) that there was an element of Black Attraction to the Russian Revolution because of what it meant for the political struggle of the working class at the start of the 20th century. Not only did the likes of Black American singer Paul Robeson win the hearts of Russian and Soviet citizens with his Negro Spirituals, but many others actually moved to and settled in Russia, attracted by what Lenin and the RSDLP(B) were doing to unite the scores of related republics held in divisive feudal grip by czars and family dynasties supposedly born to rule – in the same way that the British national anthem 'God Save The Queen' taught us (in the Caribbean and then British Commonwealth) that the Royal Family at Buckingham Palace was 'Born to reign over us...'

The WRM, like other leftist groupings grappling with Lenin's ideas, had ties with Grenada's Organisation for Revolutionary Education and Liberation (OREL) and the New Jewel Movement (NJM), led by Maurice Bishop, Bernard Coard and others, in what was to become the first genuine socialist revolution in the English-speaking Caribbean, lasting just over four-and-a-half years (March 1979 to October 1983).

I served as a journalist in Grenada for almost two years during the Revolution, when and where texts by Lenin like *What is to be Done?*, "Where to Begin" and *"Left-Wing" Communism – An Infantile Disorder* featured prominently in weekly NJM Political Education classes. The Revolution ultimately committed suicide and died with Maurice Bishop on October 19, 1983 – followed by the US-led invasion to 'restore democracy,' yet it left a lifelong record of achievements that still live on in Grenada.

Today, just over a century after Lenin died, contemporary Caribbean radical socialists of the 70s and 80s – like current Saint Vincent and the Grenadines Prime Minister Dr Ralph Gonsalves and Guyana's ex-President Donald Ramotar, ex-Guyana Foreign Affairs Minister Clement Rohee and ex-University of the West Indies (UWI) lecturer in Political Science and Leader of the Workers Party of Jamaica (WPJ) Dr. Trevor Munroe, and many more – have shown, in and out of office, that once local peculiarities are considered and necessary adjustments made, Lenin and Marx's political ideas and prescriptions can still be creatively applied in the search for home-grown solutions to today's Caribbean realities.

And like my dad, four-star-sailor C.V.E. Bousquet, they too will not deny the crucial role played by 'the Russians' in saving the Caribbean from Nazi Occupation during World War II, after it was left largely unprotected by the British and Allied colonial forces. Thanks to Lenin's political leadership and the creation of the USSR, West Indians didn't ever have to forcibly learn to speak German, but they didn't have to learn Russian either.

And that's the Bottom Line.

Earl Bousquet is a veteran Caribbean journalist specialising in global geopolitical affairs and their impact on the Caribbean and Latin America.

31. Reclaiming Lenin in Iran: Challenging Male Dominance in the Revolutionary Movement

Elsaa and La'al

Writing about Lenin is by no means an easy task, especially if you aim to speak of him from the perspective of an Iranian Marxist woman and reclaim a version of his thought and methods in the current era, profoundly marked by the Woman, Life, Freedom movement and the violent response to it by the Iranian regime. The difficulty in writing about him is not only because of the more general challenge of writing about 'great leaders,' so proficient in profound analysis and strategic thinking but also because remembering Lenin inevitably reminds us of the countless Iranian male figures, calling themselves Leninists, who have dominated various leftist groups and parties in Iran and later in exile, both before and after the 1979 revolution. These male figures stood, and continue to stand, at the height of their respective party or group, claiming all power and control. These are men who believe that they alone possess a revolutionary instinct, knowing better than anyone else the current political strategy of the party: where to compromise, how to employ new tactics, and where to launch an attack.

As we remember these male figures, their faces and voices become clearer. They firmly assert that they are the embodiment of Lenin himself and that only they and their male comrades can interpret what Lenin said. Writing about him is not easy because many of these male figures in fact hide behind Lenin. Behind his name. Behind his picture. Behind his theory. Behind his supposed understanding and worldview, which does not envision a leading role for anyone who is not male. For these men, the only reason for the presence of women in parties is that women make up half of the population, and they thus need women for *their* revolution.

Writing about Lenin is difficult because it cannot conceal the memories of the innumerable injustices that have occurred throughout the years against women and Queer people in Iran. We cannot forget the oppressions, tortures, wounds, and numerous deaths suffered in so many battles. We remember the 1979 Revolution and the many brave women who had fought against the Pahlavi regime for years, and who then became the first protesters against the new Islamic Republic and their attempts to turn back the clock on women's emancipation, facing male figures who downplayed the issue. We remember the Green Movement in 2009, where people took to the streets to demand their stolen vote, and many of these male figures ended up abandoning the movement, deeming it too middle-class and reformist. We remember the Bloody November 2019 protests, where people on the streets, including many women, were killed for demanding basic life needs, and these very same male figures tried to gain credibility and prestige by using the name of the subalterns for themselves. Today, we remember the Woman,

Life, Freedom movement, and the repeated justifications of these male figures who once again consider the fight against the mandatory hijab a marginal issue. For these 'Leninist' men, the issue of the hijab, and women's and Queer people's questions in general, are considered separate from working-class concerns, at best a problem of 'the other,' but in no way related to the struggle for socialism.

In short, writing about Lenin is difficult because it requires us to remember several decades of wounds inflicted by 'great' men who claim(ed) to be followers of Lenin and who yesterday as today – instead of fighting together with us against all forms of oppression and exploitation – cling to the false notion that feminists only focus on women's issues, thereby deliberately ignoring and rendering invisible the countless feminists who actively advocate and struggle for the establishment of revolutionary *Shooras* (councils) and indeed a future Communist society.

But ...

Writing about Lenin becomes possible when we remember that he was never like these men! While not forgetting Lenin's masculine, patriarchal language of command and prohibition, his speaking from a position of the enlightened Marxist vanguard who knows the method of revolution and thus aims to guide everyone in that direction, and the fact that all too few women were in positions of power and influence during and after the October revolution, nevertheless his sustained collaboration with and support of Marxist-feminists and his emphasis on the crucial importance of women's emancipation led to multiple achievements, including legal equality, the Family Law of 1918, increased access to education and employment, the socialisation of childcare and the legalisation of abortion.

Writing about Lenin becomes possible when considering Lenin's method as a dynamic approach recognising existing social forces and the linkages between them, i.e. that which has always stood against the captive minds of those who adhere to and insist on linear thinking. Inviting this Lenin into contemporary Iran, we could gain a comprehensive understanding and perhaps strengthening of the Woman, Life, Freedom movement and its connection with other progressive movements in the Middle East and the world, as it would become possible to perceive class not as a singular entity but as a relational concept.

Writing about Lenin becomes possible, and perhaps even necessary, when highlighting the immanent potential for change in every aspect. All of us – men, women, Queers and... – can and must recognise that revolutionary change happens at different speeds, levels and through various means. Identifying the moments when these potentials become prominent, in turn, can lead us to understanding and acting upon the "concrete analysis of the concrete situation" and beyond.

Elsaa is a militant woman living in Iran, a companion of the subalterns, and a storyteller of the tales of the oppressed. La'al is a militant woman born in Iran who tries to shout out contradictions and never be silent.

32. Snapshot of the Statues

Esther Leslie

They took down the Lenin statue in 2014. They took down something like themselves but distorted. Magic mirror Lenin, dark, granite grimace, outside the Kryvyi Rih steelworks of the world's largest steelmaker ArcelorMittal, the descendant of Kryvorizhstal, founded in 1934. *They* were not the steelworkers, but the company, because it was anyway just a matter of time before the protestors, who had made a president flee to Russia, would topple it, smash it apart on the steelworks' hard ground. The Luxembourg company's intervention was an effort to seize control of history, to author it or at least not be authored by it. A reason for removal was given: "in order to ensure the safety of our employees and protect the company's buildings." The block needed to be removed in an orderly fashion, winched out of place, just as it had been winched into place, the removal action a kind of winding time backwards so that it may go forwards otherwise as if the whole intervening period had never happened. Lenin's statue, lifted off, like Tsar Alexander III, in S.M. Eisenstein's *October* film. Here a statue that represents the dead Tsar sat on a throne, holding the baubles of power, is assaulted by the revolutionary crowds, only then to dismantle itself, like something rotten falling apart. Later in the film this segment is played backwards, signalling a reversal of history, the re-installation of oppression by a government betraying the revolution. The fate of the statue in both cases plays to the camera, sliding backwards and forwards on the axis of spectacular history, in an effort to comment on and control the historical process. Eisenstein, it should be noted, did not aim for documentary truth, but some other kind of truth: the portrayed statue stood in Moscow, not Petrograd, the site of the film's revolutionary action, and it was dismantled not before May 1918. Eisenstein's seated Tsar was only a papier-mâché replica. In some way or another, statues always lie.

Through statues, Stalinism came to colonise memory and the present. The statue's primal form was the embalmed Lenin, put on show from 1924, first in a wooden tomb, later within marble, porphyry, granite and labradorite. He was held there like a religious icon, his death and decay a glaring analogue of the putrescence of revolution. Versions of Lenin were rigidified afterwards as statues, lording over every city, town and village in the Soviet Union, and then beyond into the satellite states. Shiny metallic or sleek granite forms of Lenin blotted out the sunlight of the revolution, and certainly, even if the pose was dynamic and future-pointing, did nothing to ensure the revolution had a future. The greatest one of all was never built – the Palace of the Soviets, designed in the 1930s, once 'soviet' meant only bureaucracy and 'palace' was a name for monumental historicism. Someone planned a nightmare wedding cake of columned cylinders topped by a skyscraper pedestal atop which loomed a 100-metre Lenin.

Big Stalinist statues of Lenin should have no tears shed for them. Nor should their removal, but something to do with lost possibilities in history aches when I watch them go or crumble. I feel as if I was there when Nikolai Tomsky's statue of Lenin in East Berlin's Friedrichshain was hoisted up and away into the clouds in 1991-2, but I think I just saw a photograph or film footage of the event – not to mention the scene in *Goodbye Lenin*, where (a fake version of) this Lenin hangs from a helicopter, against the bright clouds of an Ikea'd Germany, in the act of removal, his stiff arm a final valediction. But there was no event, and it was not actually lifted away, but dismantled over a period of months, fragmented into 129 pieces and buried in the woods. This event of removal seems to hold the power of a fantastic projection that binds us into the power of its articulation, just as had Eisenstein's filmic rendition of the mutiny on the Battleship Potemkin: so many claimed to have cowered under the tarpaulin, but, in truth, they had only seen this event in a film and the event did not take place. Statues, films, fake statues in fake films: efforts to shape memory. Even in their removal, these things, these monster forms, crush the self, the true collective, and any capacity for reliable witnessing, because that is what they were made for all along.

The statues lie and take us over. Mayakovsky hated the portrayal of Lenin in Eisenstein's *October*. He thought the actor looked only like Lenin's statue. How to embody Lenin in life? He wrote a polemic in LEF in 1924 titled, "Don't Merchandise Lenin!" In response to advertisements in the Soviet press for busts in plaster, patinised, bronze, marble and granite, life-sized and double-sized, he writes a poem-manifesto insisting on life – the life of the idea, of memory – and railing, as had, he noted, the workers of the Kazan Railroad, against icons in their midst, against keeping alive a memory in the form of a statue:

> We insist
> Don't crank out Lenins
> Don't print his likenesses on posters, oilcloths, plates and mugs
> And cigarette cases.
> Don't embronze Lenin
> Don't take away his living gait and human traits,
> Which he was able to preserve as he guided history.
> Lenin is still our contemporary.
> He is among the living.
> We need him alive, not dead.

Lenin is dead if he is kept alive, as icon, as waxwork, as relic, as remainder. He is in life if he is, or his ideas and actions are, in the world, in those who follow. It is action not image – a walking spirit taken up in the many, not a ghostly afterimage on celluloid or stone – that makes up the spectre stalking the world.

Trotsky, forced into exile, took with him a handful of photographs of Lenin – he describes them in his *Notebooks* of the 1930s. The photographs are an aide-memoire, but they also reveal to him something of the direction of history, the time on the revolution's clock in the moment of the photograph's capture. Serial portraits reveal the truth of history – and of the historical actor – as contingent, shifting, always in motion, in flux, open and openable to various forces, not fixed and determined and understood only in one strict way forever more. The revolution is permanent, as it is temporary and contemporary. Rodchenko concurred:

> ... there is a file of photographs, and this file of snapshots allows no one to idealise or falsify Lenin. Everyone has seen this file of photographs, and as a matter of course, no one would allow artistic nonsense to be taken for the eternal Lenin.

It should be stated firmly that with the appearance of photographs, there can be no question of a single, immutable portrait. Moreover, a man is not just one sum total; he is many, and sometimes they are quite opposed. Rodchenko asked:

"Tell me frankly, what ought to remain of Lenin:

- an art bronze?
- oil portraits?
- etchings?
- water colours?
- his secretary's diary, his friends' memoirs?

Or

- a file of photographs taken of him at work and rest?
- archives of his books, writing pads, notebooks?
- shorthand reports, films, phonograph records?"

I don't think there's any choice."

Trotsky was in agreement, even if the single photograph could be retouched to cut him out and blurs in the record are introduced to segue Stalin into history and blur him into Lenin. Remaining still is a multiplicity of traces and efforts, partial glimpses, moments in time, half-completed attempts, negations, contradictions, self-criticisms, through which, after which, out of which hope that it would have been all so different might yet breathe.

Esther Leslie imbibed Lenin and Trotsky from her mother's breast (who in turn had suckled Anarchism from hers) and has spent a merry life trying to marry up these multifarious anti-traditions.

33. "Vilici": The Theoretician of Hegemony in Antonio Gramsci's Prison Notebooks

Fabio Frosini

It was only in 1917, when Lenin's name began to truly spread throughout the world, that it also became important to Antonio Gramsci. Articles such as *The Revolution Against "Capital"* (December 1917) can therefore be considered a first serious attempt to engage creatively with Lenin's thinking. But it was above all when Gramsci moved to Moscow in May 1922, as a delegate to the Comintern, that Lenin ceased to be for him a mere name, myth or a set of theses. In Soviet Russia, Gramsci came into personal contact with all the great Bolshevik leaders, including Lenin (the meeting took place in October 1922 and, according to Camilla Ravera, the main topics of discussion were the political situation in Italy and the need to build a broad front of revolutionary forces beyond the conflict between the political parties of the Left). Thus, the image of Lenin that Gramsci would later develop in the *Prison Notebooks* was decisively influenced by this stay in Moscow, at a moment when Lenin was arguably no longer interested in conducting fierce polemics on Marxist orthodoxy. Instead, as a state leader, and leaving behind any type of concern for strict ideological coherence, he was now trying to trace in concrete government action the specific features of a new and original conception of the State and revolutionary politics in the transition to socialism.

In the years when Gramsci was writing his *Prison Notebooks* (1929-1935), Lenin, like all the major leaders of the Third International and the USSR, was still too topical and compromising a reference to be made explicitly. Consequently, when mentioning Lenin, Gramsci uses only substitutes: first "Iliič," then "Ilici," and finally, "Vilici," thereby gradually deforming the patronymic, when not directly replacing it with a periphrasis such as "the greatest modern theoretician of the philosophy of praxis." Moreover, whenever speaking of the Bolshevik leader, Gramsci argues in a deliberately elusive manner. Beneath this veil, however, the meaning appears crystal clear: for Gramsci, Lenin is the one true, great continuator of Marx, though not in the by then canonical Marxist-Leninist sense, i.e. as a dialectical-materialist theorist, but rather as a *practical politician* and *political theorist*.

In this sense, in a passage of the *Notebooks*, Gramsci states that the canonical idea of condensing the originality of Marxism into *three sources and three component parts* (implicitly referring to Lenin's famous 1913 pamphlet) is wrong: "One widespread conception is that the philosophy of praxis [that is, Marxism] is a pure philosophy, the science of dialectics, the other parts of it being economics and politics, and it is therefore maintained that the doctrine is formed of three constituent parts, which are at the same time the consummation and the transcending of the highest level reached around 1848 by science in the most advanced countries of Europe: classical German philosophy, English classical economics and French political activity and science. This conception, which reflects rather a generic search for historical sources than a classification drawn from the heart of the doctrine itself, cannot be set up in opposition, as a definitive scheme, to some other definition of the doctrine which is closer to reality."[1]

This "other definition of the doctrine" is precisely, in Gramsci's intention, a reformulated "philosophy of praxis," to which Lenin the practical politician and political theorist decisively contributed, in that – Gramsci says – it was Lenin who coined the concept and produced "the fact of hegemony." Accordingly, in Gramsci's philosophy of praxis, politics, philosophy and economics are mutually translatable, and this fact, which implies the possibility that a politician's philosophy resides in his politics, also makes it possible to study hegemony as a *philosophical fact*. It is precisely in this light that Lenin repeatedly appears in the *Notebooks*: the concept (theory) and the fact (concrete realisation in a State apparatus) of hegemony is how Lenin creatively contributes to the development of Marxism: "by advancing political theory, he [Lenin] also advanced philosophy," and in this lies, for Gramsci, "Iliíč's greatest contribution to Marxist philosophy, to historical materialism, an original and creative contribution."[2] In the second version of this same text, Gramsci adds: "Iliíč advanced philosophy as philosophy in so far as he advanced political doctrine and practice. The realisation of a hegemonic apparatus, in so far as it creates a new ideological terrain, determines a reform of consciousness and of methods of knowledge: it is a fact of knowledge, a philosophical fact."[3]

The fact that Lenin set himself the task of developing "on the terrain of political struggle and organisation and with a political terminology, [...] in opposition to the various 'economist' tendencies [...] the front of cultural struggle, and constructed the doctrine of hegemony as a complement to the theory of the State-as-force, and as the present form of the Forty-Eightist [i.e. Marx and Engel's post-1848] doctrine of 'permanent revolution'"[4] implies his recognition of the gnoseological value of ideologies and the political function of "culture." The "realisation of a hegemonic apparatus," i.e. "realised hegemony [thus] means the real critique of a philosophy, its real dialectic."[5] Gramsci's appreciation of Lenin goes as far as to write that "the theorisation and realisation of hegemony by Ilici was also a great 'metaphysical' event."[6]

In Gramsci's view, Lenin felt the need to develop the notion of hegemony in order to reformulate the Marxist, Jacobine-inspired doctrine of "permanent revolution." This reformulation consisted in the necessity, set out by Lenin in 1921, to move from "war of manoeuvre" to "war of position,"

---

1 Gramsci, Antonio (1992), *Selections from the Prison Notebooks*. New York: International Publishers, 431.
2 Gramsci, Antonio (1996), *Prison Notebooks Vol. II*. New York: Columbia University Press, 188-89.
3 Gramsci 1992: 365-366.
4 Ibid: 56.
5 Gramsci, Antonio (2007), *Prison Notebooks Vol. III*. New York: Columbia University Press, 183.
6 Ibid: 187.

that is, to think of power no longer in terms of a decisive and unique frontal "assault," but as a "siege" in which all energies had to be mobilised, and for which it became therefore indispensable to gain the convinced support of the broad popular masses. This shift from "assault" to "siege" applied as much to the goal of maintaining power in Soviet Russia as to the goal of conquering it in Europe: consent, culture and, in the last instance, hegemony, became the terrain for the political struggle and the revolutionary process in the post-war period.

Yet, Lenin, Gramsci argues, did not have the time to further this formula in all its implications: "One should [...] bear in mind that Iliič could only have developed his formula on a theoretical level [anyway], whereas the fundamental task was a national one; in other words, it required a reconnaissance of the terrain and an identification of the elements of trench and fortress represented by the components of civil society, etc."[7] This "reconnaissance" is precisely what Gramsci intends to do in his *Notebooks*, i.e. an analysis of the history of bourgeois hegemony and its present structure, in order to understand the reasons for the defeat of revolutionary attempts in Western Europe after WWI. Nevertheless, he is convinced that the notion of hegemony, as sketched by Lenin in his last writings, is the clearest formulation of the need to move in this direction.

In sum, hegemony as both a theory and a practice of governance reflects the necessities of the dominant group that, having attained power in a particular territory, must cultivate a precise skillset and understanding – an "art and science of politics" – that cannot be reduced solely to the technique of domination, but has to include the task of mobilising, motivating and governing the people as a whole in an asymmetric relation of forces. Hence, the need to involve actively "infinite masses of people" in the construction and consolidation of a new kind of State power but also – and this is the most important lesson Gramsci draws from Lenin – to do de same when the objective is to overthrow it. To know that this active involvement was of vital importance for the survival and success of the Revolution – this is what in Gramsci's view makes the greatness of Lenin.

Fabio Frosini teaches philosophy at the University of Urbino (Italy). He has written extensively on the topics of Gramsci and Marxism, in addition to Early Modern philosophers.

---

7 Gramsci 1992: 238.

34. Lenin's Vanguardist Party: Reflections on the Nigerian Revolution

Femi Aborisade

Karl Marx, it was, who said "the philosophers have only interpreted the world, in various ways. The point, however, is to change it."

In Nigeria, whereas the objective conditions for revolutionary rupture of society are overripe, the subjective factor, the organisational leadership for change, is extremely weak. Therefore, Marxists of different variants, as well as 'ordinary people,' are concerned with how to build the type of political organisation that would engender socialist transformation or a society that works for the downtrodden. Socialist-inclined organisations and 'parties' have striven to build (an) alternative political force(s). An overwhelming majority of these organisations formed The Peoples Alternative Political Movement (TPAPM) in 2021. The vision of TPAPM collapsed as it could not formally register a party to participate in the 2023 general elections due to its inability to build a strong social base of support. Component organisations were also divided on whether or not to join or collaborate with the Labour Party (LP) formed by the unions. The LP is perceived not to be different from the bourgeois parties in terms of the programme and the opportunity provided for liberal capitalists to join and contest general elections on its platform. There is also an increasing loss of confidence in the capacity of the leadership of organised labour, particularly in the central trade unions, the Nigeria Labour Congress (NLC) and the Trade Union Congress (TUC), to consistently fight and inspire workers, as they are perceived to be acting more or less as representatives of the ruling class who have resolved to apply the brakes at every critical point requiring decisive class action.

The concern then is how do socialists and radical unionists organise to win political power. Some trends, represented by the Campaign for Socialist Transformation of Nigeria (CAST), argue that socialists should build political forces independent of the LP, on a clear socialist manifesto. Others argue that given the organisational weakness of socialist revolutionaries, joining or developing an orientation towards the LP, which has a larger base of support, is advisable, provided the LP expresses commitment to basic welfare issues touching on the day-to-day lives of the masses.

The question as to the way forward is hence urgent. The bourgeois ruling class cannot take society forward. There is an unprecedented deepening of poverty. The masses are yearning for action and looking up to organised labour. Pressure is continually on the leadership of organised labour to fight. But a certain pattern appears to have emerged that notices of the threat of action would be called off just when action ought to commence. On the industrial front, labour leadership appears to have fallen below the expectations of the masses. On the political front, Marxist revolutionaries have failed to politically organise the masses.

To Lenin, the task of overthrowing capitalism and engendering a socialist transformation of society requires the critical leadership of the most advanced communists, intellectuals and workers, constituting the revolutionary vanguard party of the working class. From the Leninist perspective, in the early 20th century as well as today, the vanguard party is therefore the main vehicle for effecting the move from the undesirable to the desirable state of life.

In the concept of the vanguard party, Lenin recognises the limitation of pure economism that characterises trade unionism. Without necessarily discounting the possibility of workers gaining socialist consciousness based on their experiences in the workplace, Lenin contends that workers can arrive at class political consciousness only from outside the sphere of the worker-employer economic relationship. In other words, workers can gain class political consciousness only from the context of the sphere of state-society relationships or the interrelationship between all classes, which includes experiences of employer-worker relationship. Restricted only to the latter, the worker is likely to gain only economist or trade unionist consciousness, at best.

Implicit in Lenin's vanguard party concept is an understanding that trade unions are primarily institutions set up for negotiations and bargaining with the employer class, which may, more often than not, involve concessions, principled and unprincipled. The current scenario in Nigeria is a case in point. On 2 October 2023, the NLC and TUC suspended for 30 days an indefinite strike action that would have commenced on 3 October 2023, without any major concession related to labour's key demands. Earlier, in August this year, the unions also suspended a nationwide action, just a few hours before a strike was to commence. There is therefore much scepticism about any idea that suggests reliance on the trade union structure as a means to challenge State power. Then again, historically, the only impactful challenge to capitalist state power has come through the unions, weak as they are. Without them, the Left, in Nigeria, is totally marginalised, organisationally.

Therefore, it is important to stress that the vanguard party concept should not be mistaken for sectarianism in which a few socialists, without roots in the working class, proclaim themselves as a revolutionary party that workers must join, as some organisations on the Nigerian Left have historically done. Rather, the idea of the vanguard party should today be understood as the leadership of socialist revolutionaries, that actively supports the practical, day-to-day struggles of all segments of the downtrodden, including the unions; that acts as the tribune of the oppressed, struggling against tyrannical policies of the State; that analyses and locates working-class struggles within a wider societal context; that provides the working class and the poor with socialist ideas that aid successful mass action from below, etc. That is to say, an organisation is neither socialist nor vanguard just because it names itself as such. It must, by its statements, analyses and activities, demonstrate that it is pro-active, advocating policies and measures that will put the working class and its allies in an improved economic and political situation.

For example, in the context of contemporary Nigeria in which the President once begged a US Court not to order the Chicago State University to release his academic records because releasing them would cause "severe and irreparable damage" to his political career, Left political 'vanguard' organisations ought to be at the forefront of campaigning for constitutional amendments to pass and enact a moral code of conduct for contestants for political offices. The expectation is that such a moral code of conduct would put working class candidates in a better position to contest and win elections, as more and more of wealthy candidates with skeletons in their cupboard may be excluded, by law, from the electoral process.

The Left in Nigeria should take interest in building the political organisations of the working people and participating in elections. The argument of some Left organisations today, suggesting that socialists should not participate in 'bourgeois' elections, is, in my opinion, a misconceived variant of anarchism.

The caution which the Leninist perspective offers is against what Marx and Engels called the "incurable disease of Parliamentary cretinism" (a misconception that a socialist society can be achieved solely by peaceful, parliamentary means as opposed to class struggle). What is important is that independent political action of the working class should not be constrained on account of participation in parliamentary elections or even electoral victories. In other words, participation in electoral politics should be subordinated to independent working class industrial and/or political actions led or supported by organisations of socialists and/or workers.

In sum, the crisis in society will eventually compel the masses to walk the road of revolution. Until then, socialists should find the way to the masses in their daily struggles, during or outside the period of parliamentary elections. Having said that, we should never nurture the misconception that a self-proclaimed 'socialist vanguard' party alone will carry out the revolution. History is made by the masses, not by the few. However, as Trotsky once put it, "a revolution takes place only when there is no other way out." Until that glorious moment comes, patiently harnessing political leadership among workers and the poor, with or without the top leadership of the unions, is the way forward in building the 'vanguard' party in the current phase of history.

Femi Aborisade, a former education officer of the Nigeria Labour Congress (NLC) in the early '80s, is a labour and human rights lawyer.

35. Back to Zimmerwald

Franco 'Bifo' Berardi

The outbreak of the European war in 1914 led to the scission of the Second International. The majority of the socialist organisations, particularly the German Social Democratic Party, accepted the idea that the homeland was to be defended. Many socialists turned interventionists and created nationalist parties, like Benito Mussolini in Italy. Some of them considered their homeland to be in danger due to the threat of external enemies, and saw it as their duty to put the Nation before the interests of a social class. Others, more realistically, identified the interests of the worker class with those of the nation, expecting that the victory of their country would bring prosperity to the proletariat. In the end, however, victory was an illusion, because the end of the first world war was simply the beginning of a catastrophic period of more violence and humiliation, a period that culminated in the second world war.

What is the homeland? Who are the enemies? By what criteria can we differentiate between the good guys (who resist) and the bad guys (who aggress)? These questions are being asked again, today, as actual war rages in Ukraine and the winds of war blow everywhere around the planet. Why should we defend borders? And what is the nation if not the imaginary entity whose borders are defined by war? Rightly, Russia is blamed for invading the Ukrainian territory on February 24, 2022; but the story did not begin there.

Before stating that Russia is the aggressor and Ukraine is the defender (of democracy), one should reflect on many factors: the systematic violation of the Minsk agreements brokered by Germany and France; the American push to expand NATO to the borders of the Russian Federation; the influence of Nazi organisations in the Ukrainian Army and in the Ukrainian state; and so on. At the same time, we should remember that the Ukrainian people have many historical reasons to demand independence from Russia, among them the violent repression of the Ukrainian republic established by the anarchist group of Nestor Makhno; the Holodomor, the mass famine provoked by the political choices of Stalin in the 1930s; the criminal silence of the Soviet authorities after the Chernobyl incident of 1986.

The knot, however, must be cut at the root: whatever its origin and motivations, war is the cruellest form of exploitation of human labour; it is the pursuit of profit by the means of violence, mass killing and extermination. War must be rejected because workers have nothing to gain from war but have everything to lose.

That is why in 1915 the left wing of the Socialist International decided to break ties with the German Social Democratic Party and other organisations who accepted the nationalist imperative in support of the war effort. The left wing of the International reasserted in a radical way the meaning of Internationalism: the working class has no nation, no national interest, and therefore the participation of workers in the war only means unmitigated exploitation, extreme suffering and, finally, impoverishment.

Those who refused to bend to this nationalist blackmail met in the Swiss village of Zimmerwald in 1915, giving birth to a new international organisation that eventually took the name of the Third International. One of the participants in the Zimmerwald Conference, Vladimir Lenin, went even further. Not only did he state that socialists must reject the patriotic calls, he also said that the war was an opportunity for revolutionaries, as the exploiters were obliged to give weapons to the workers, and the workers could turn those very weapons against their exploiters. In the words of Lenin:

> The European war, which the governments and the bourgeois parties of all countries have been preparing for decades, has broken out. The growth of armaments, the extreme intensification of the struggle for markets in the latest – the imperialist – stage of capitalist development in the advanced countries, and the dynastic interests of the more backward East-European monarchies were inevitably bound to bring about this war, and have done so. Seizure of territory and subjugation of other nations, the ruining of competing nations and the plunder of their wealth, distracting the attention of the working masses from the internal political crises in Russia, Germany, Britain and other countries, disuniting and nationalist stultification of the workers, and the extermination of their vanguard so as to weaken the revolutionary movement of the proletariat – these comprise the sole actual content, importance and significance of the present war. One group of belligerent nations is headed by the German bourgeoisie. It is hoodwinking the working class and the toiling masses by asserting that this is a war in defence of the fatherland, freedom and civilisation, for the liberation of the peoples oppressed by tsarism, and for the destruction of reactionary tsarism. In actual fact, however, this bourgeoisie, which servilely grovels to the Prussian Junkers, headed by Wilhelm II, has always been a most faithful ally of tsarism, and an enemy of the revolutionary movement of Russia's workers and peasants. In fact, whatever the outcome of the war, this bourgeoisie will together side with the Junkers, and exert every effort to support the tsarist monarchy against a revolution in Russia.[1]

One may repeat the words of Lenin today: the Euro-Americans are hoodwinking the working class, and public opinion at large, by asserting that this is a war in defence of democracy, for the liberation of the Ukrainian people from Russian domination. Meanwhile, Russia's leadership is hoodwinking its population, promising revenge against its Western enemies, who bear the historical blame for surrounding and threatening the Holy Land of Russian Christianity. To return to Lenin:

> The other group of belligerent nations is headed by the British and the French bourgeoisie, who are hoodwinking the working class and the toiling masses by asserting that they are waging a war for the defence of their countries, for freedom and civilisation and against German militarism and despotism. In actual fact, this bourgeoisie has long been spending thousands

---

1 Lenin, V.I. (1974), "The War and Russian Social-Democracy," in *Collected Works Vol. 21*, Moscow: Progress Publishers, 27-28.

of millions to hire the troops of Russian Tsarism, the most reactionary and barbarous monarchy in Europe, and prepare them for an attack on Germany.

Similarly today, the North Atlantic powers are trying to convince people that we must fight against the Russian fascists. In order to smash Russian fascism, however, we are supporting Ukrainian nationalism. Furthermore, the Western powers have contributed to the raise of nationalism in Russia by destroying the social welfare system of the Soviet years, thereby impoverishing the Russian population, provoking a wave of extreme humiliation that now forms the background of popular support for Putin. Then Lenin argues:

> In fact, the struggle of the British and the French bourgeoisie is aimed at the seizure of the German colonies, and the ruining of a rival nation, whose economic development has been more rapid. In pursuit of this noble aim, the 'advanced' 'democratic' nations are helping the savage tsarist regime to still more throttle Poland, the Ukraine, etc., and more thoroughly crush the revolution in Russia.

The US has pushed Russia and Ukraine to war and are now trying to extract a political and an economic dividend. It is far from certain that they will get what they want, but the US has already inflicted much damage: Germany is broken, the European Union as a whole has completely changed its tune, while nationalists are winning elections and turning the continent into something that resembles the Europe of 1941. The spectre of the past is returning: national war is yet gain on the continent's horizon. What to do in such a situation is totally unclear: political leadership can no longer be trusted, while the Left has proved to be a miserable failure. We can only preach desertion, and wait for the war to produce its inevitable effects.

Desertion traditionally refers to a refusal to kill and die in war. But I see much more in this concept. I see desertion, in the form of what US journalists call the Great Resignation, as the mass refusal of people to return to work after the Covid pandemic. I see desertion as a refusal of fake democracy: the level of electoral absenteeism recorded in the French elections of spring 2022 was unprecedented; the same was true of Italian local elections in June the same year. Finally, I see desertion as the growing refusal by the women of the world to generate more victims of the impending climate catastrophe, or more victims of the expanding world war: birth strike, self-termination of the human race.

Lenin invoked us to transform imperialist war into revolutionary civil war. Today, the term revolutionary civil war means little, and so let us reimagine this as desertion – the only means of escape when faced with the current disintegration of the social, political and environmental order.

Franco 'Bifo' Berardi was a militant of the leftist organization Potere Operaio, and founded the magazine A/traverso and the first free radio in Italy, Radio Alice. He is the author of And, phenomenology of the end.

36. How I Cooked Soup with Lenin

Frigga Haug

When I studied at the Free University of Berlin in the 1970s, Berlin was still a divided city, and for me, hungry for books and with little money, that meant frequently taking the train across the border into the GDR and buying as many books as I could carry, at an exchange rate of 1 to 6: first, Marx and Engels' *Works* and soon after Lenin's *Collected Works* in the brown leatherette edition. In this way Lenin moved in with me into my small flat long before I actually read him. A second detour was via Brecht, whose theatre at Friedrichstraße station invited people to experience his plays and read his writings at affordable prices. He wrote:

1) "Lenin once said that even a [female] cook should be able to rule the state," adding, "Of course, he had in mind a different state and a different cook," thus extending Lenin's sentence into a project of revolutionary learning: change of both the state and the individual. In *Me-Ti: Book of Interventions in the Flow of Things*, Brecht clarifies:

> Mi-en-leh [Lenin] said, every [female] cook ought to be able to govern the state. He was thinking of a change in the state as well as the cook. But you can also conclude from this that it's advantageous to arrange the state like a kitchen, but also the kitchen like a state.

Perhaps this was Brecht's advice for the politics of the GDR.

2) Lenin's famous 1917 text "Can the Bolsheviks retain state power?" affirms:

> We are not utopians. We know that an unskilled labourer or a cook cannot immediately get on with the job of state administration. In this we agree with the Cadets, with Breshkovskaya, and with Tsereteli. We differ, however, from these citizens in that we demand an immediate break with the prejudiced view that only the rich, or officials chosen from rich families, are capable of administering the state, of performing the ordinary, everyday work of administration. We demand that training in the work of state administration be conducted by class-conscious workers and soldiers and that this training be begun at once, i.e., that a beginning be made at once in training all the working people, all the poor, for this work.

Against the capitalists and landowners who, with the help of the likes of Plekhanov, Breshkovskaya, Tsereteli, Chernov and others, did everything in their power to slander the democratic republic and not hand over power to the Soviets, the "chief thing" is

> to imbue the oppressed and the working people with confidence in their own strength, to prove to them in practice that they can and must themselves ensure the proper, most strictly regulated and organised distribution of bread, all kinds of food, milk, clothing, housing, etc., in the interests of the poor.

Therefore, the most important thing, Lenin said, is to ensure that it

> will become possible for the millions, [to] begin to work for themselves and not for the capitalists, the gentry, the bureaucrats, and not out of fear of punishment.

3) On 19 November 1918 Lenin writes programmatically:

> The status of women up to now has been compared to that of a slave; women have been tied to the home, and only socialism can save them from this. They will only be completely emancipated when we change from small-scale individual farming to collective farming and collective working of the land.

4) In September 1919 he speaks at the Fourth Moscow City Conference of Non-Party Working Women about the "The Task of the Working Women's Movement in the Soviet Republic":

> Owing to her work in the house, the woman is still in a difficult position. To effect her complete emancipation and make her the equal of the man it is necessary for the national economy to be socialised and for women to participate in common productive labour. Then women will occupy the same position as men. [...] You all know that even when women have full rights, they still remain factually downtrodden because all housework is left to them. In most cases housework is the most unproductive, the most barbarous and the most arduous work a woman can do. It is exceptionally petty and does not include anything that would in any way promote the development of the woman. In pursuance of the socialist ideal we want to struggle for the full implementation of socialism, and here an extensive field of labour opens up before women. We are now making serious preparations to clear the ground for the building of socialism, but the building of socialism will begin only when we have achieved the complete equality of women and when we undertake the new work together with women who have been emancipated from that petty, stultifying, unproductive work. This is a job that will take us many, many years.

5) Two years later, in his speech "On International Working Women's Day" on 4 March 1921, Lenin announced the program for the movement:

> It is the chief task of the working women's movement to fight for economic and social equality, and not only formal equality, for women. The chief thing is to get women to take part in socially productive labour, to liberate them from "domestic slavery", to free them from their stupefying and humiliating subjugation to the eternal drudgery of the kitchen and the nursery. This struggle will be a long one, and it demands a radical reconstruction both of social technique and of morals. But it will end in the complete triumph of communism.

Who struggles?

6) Lenin says:

> We say that the emancipation of the workers must be effected by the workers themselves, and in exactly the same way the emancipation of working women is a matter for the working women themselves. The working women must themselves see to it that such institutions are developed, and this activity will bring about a complete change in their position as compared with what it was under the old, capitalist society.

In his *The Aesthetics of Resistance,* the Brechtian Peter Weiss paraphrases Lenin's passage: "Liberation cannot be handed to us, we have to conquer it ourselves. If we fail to conquer it ourselves, then it will have no consequences for us." Weiss' book had a profound impact on the West German left. In the Socialist Women's Association West Berlin, which I was part of, we adopted his instruction in our programmatic self-image. The political climate during the Cold War did not allow us to embrace Lenin directly; rather, we found our way to Lenin's project via Brecht.

7) In conclusion: The historical materialist Jürgen Stahl from Leipzig, who, as always when it comes to past socialism, helped me to secure the sources for this piece, writes:

> Dear Frigga, what moves me about the image of the [female] cook is the fact that Lenin is not calling on women in general to participate in social negotiations, but a figure who is commonly (made) invisible. It wasn't like it is today in Michelin-star kitchens, where the cooking is put on show. Instead, the [female] cook is a depersonalised something or somebody who works in the background. Through Lenin, she is brought out of the shadows into the light as a representative of the many activities that are indispensable in our common life [*Gemeinwesen*] and yet are not valued.

Almost all the changes aimed for in Lenin's dictum – democracy from below, the generalised learning of politics and economics, the socialisation of domestic labour – remained unrealised or got stuck halfway in the countries of the former Eastern bloc. Yet, in the face of a capitalism that continues to destroy life and resources, the Leninist notion of the [female] cook as ruler of the state keeps open the gateway to a liberated world.

Postscript: Lenin's surprising statement about the cook as the head of the state prompted me to write a short cultural study on the notion of the '[female] cook,' published in German in the Historical-Critical Dictionary of Marxism. There I also compiled all of Lenin's statements on the situation and prospects of female housework, in total 15 closely printed columns, as a basis for the development of a perspective, a utopia of domestic labour that is worth fighting for and must be won by those who do the work.

Frigga Haug, a lifelong Marxist feminist, is Professor Emerita in Sociology and Social Psychology, University for Economics and Politics, Hamburg.

Valentín Carmín is a visual artist and musician; his mother taught him to love plants and hate fascism; he complies.

37. Lenin's Vision: Awakening of the Masses to Socialist Future

Gal Kirn

I first encountered the name Lenin when I was 7 years old, in the early days of primary school in Ljubljana in what was then still the Socialist Federal Republic of Yugoslavia. For some, this might sound surprising, as those who entered the school at the time – mine was one of the last generations of pioneers in the late 1980s – would usually first meet the figure of Tito, either through poems or the photos on the walls of our classrooms. So, why Lenin? Well, because I visited the Prežihov Voranc school – named after one of Tito's rivals for the post of General Secretary of the CPY – in the centre of town and just across the street there was the large *Leninov Park*. The park was built after WWII on the grounds of destroyed buildings and soon became home to a beautiful array of trees. Children loved that park, it had space to run around in, there were many things to play with, and many old trees to protect us from both sun and rain. Then, in the early 1990s, with the destruction of socialist Yugoslavia, the ensuing inter-ethnic wars and the swift transition to capitalism, intense memory wars took place resulting in the destruction and removal of partisan and socialist monuments, the 'recycling' of now undesirable literature, the renaming of streets, squares and parks – in particular Leninov Park. In 1995 it was renamed Argentine Park, on the occasion of the erecting of a new monument – gifted by Argentina – of General San Martín, who successfully defeated the Spanish at the beginning of the 19th century. Due to intense public debate over both the country's socialist and also fascist past – local fascist collaborators had fled to Argentina after WWII – the statue was never erected, but the park's new name remained. *Lenin was no more* and for many outside observers, as well as the European political establishment, the little country of Slovenia that had escaped the most tragic aspects of war, soon became the success story of 'transition' to liberal democracy and a capitalist economy.

The success story, however, began to falter from at least 2012 onwards, with the far-reaching effects of persistent capitalist crisis in Slovenia, and more generally on the European periphery. As a matter of fact, across the world, multiple crises seem to have been proliferating and converging: political (the crisis of the left, but also of the extreme centre and the political establishment); economic (austerity and the dismantling of the welfare state); environmental (catastrophic droughts, floods and fires), as well as the crisis associated with an increasing normalisation of war. What Walter Benjamin once called the state of emergency is yet again becoming normalcy. Having said that, I do not believe that we can simply equate Benjamin's 1930s, which saw the advance of fascism culminating in WWII, with today's times. Rather, I would argue that the current world bears more resemblance with that before 1914, when superpowers amassed their military machines in order to fulfil age-old imperial dreams, while the working classes were sent to the trenches and their politics were betrayed by Social-Democratic parties across Europe, and in particular in Germany. At the time, an alternative response to imperialist war and the betrayal of antiwar and communist positions came from the politics of Lenin and the Bolsheviks, who politically awakened both those in the trenches and at home, in factories and on the barricades, the cumulative force of which eventually resulted in the October Revolution.

As such, I believe that the concept of awakening, as elaborated by Lars T. Lih in his "Lenin and The Great Awakening," can be very useful for understanding both Lenin's and our own political predicaments. Lih puts forward the interpretation that "awakening" can be regarded as a central political and rhetorical mechanism in Lenin's oeuvre and that he could hence be viewed as a "revolutionary preacher" rather than only as a theorist or a party organiser. He arrives at this conclusion given Lenin's trajectory evidenced by a long fidelity to the "Old Testament," i.e. the Communist Manifesto, and to the carrier of the "New Testament," that is, German Social Democracy.

Lenin's loyalty – and that of millions of workers and activists – to German Social Democracy was "true," however, only until the German Social Democrats' vote in favour of war credits in 1914. The event of the October Revolution, that is, the historical fact that it first happened and succeeded in a *non*-Western and economically 'backward' environment, consequently broke once and for all with the teleological view of the Second International, led by Western Social Democracy. The Second International had long preached that the communist revolution would first take place in the West and then spread out to the rest of the world. But as with any great political event, the timing and location of the revolution had a contingent character. This does not mean one should simply wait for the miraculous event to happen, but to actively organise and prepare and to engage with the unpredictability of any given political constellation. It also means that one cannot simply predict either the inevitability of the coming communism nor the impossibility of its advent. Lenin's legacy might be traced precisely in his agility and lucidity to discern where, when, how and in what form a social, cultural and political awakening by the dominated classes was due to happen.

This, in turn, was intimately linked to Lenin's political ability and that of the revolutionary organisation to attentively 'read' the changing situation, be prepared to organise within it, and dream and risk together with the masses. Lenin's *What Is to Be Done?* becomes very concrete when famously quoting Pisarev and his evaluation of the "rift between dreams and reality, the political role of dreams for communist organisation and the need to work conscientiously for the achievement of [one's] fantasies." The need to dream but not without political efficacy is thus something inscribed in Lenin's political bequest, shaking the linearity between the 'Old' and 'New' Testaments,' that is the path that the Party (and the intellectual) commonly adopts in its 'correct' reading of a sacred text. As all major revolutions of the twentieth century demonstrated, there are certain theoretical and practical problems that can only be solved by political activity. This is how we can understand Lenin's maxim that he announces to all revolutionary leaders, who need to answer the call "from the spontaneously awakening masses" and whose "sparkling energy is answered and supported by the energy of the revolutionary class."

The historical task of the revolutionary organisation does therefore not consist in somehow magically awakening (dead) labour and the sleeping masses into a revolutionary class, but to *detect and to participate in* the process of their awakening. This rousing of expectations of revolution is related to its point of departure in a paradoxical maxim that is condensed in the need to continue revolutionary dreaming, while at the same time awakening from the death/sleep/dream.

Then again, Lenin was also a pragmatic and able organiser who saw that the Communist project needed a concrete program. Thus, a strong formula was created that brought together electrification (NEP and the building of crucial infrastructure), cinefication (film became the most important art medium to awaken the masses), and the rule of the soviets (as the most fundamental popular form of democracy and workers' rule).

Applying this Leninist pragmatism to the current situation – despite the thickly layered streams of fake news and neoliberal, greenwashed establishment dreams with which we are constantly bombarded – the left, or those of us who still feel inspired by Lenin, must not be put to sleep. We must neither capitulate to the retrotopias of old growth models, nor stop dreaming merely in order to defend the little that has remained of the welfare state. On the contrary, the time has come for the left to yet again take more ambitious steps, both in terms of daring to dream and to organise practically and in a revolutionary, internationalist way, in order for the gates of a new "communist horizon" to open, informed by a postgrowth, ecological and peace-centred orientation and the democratic planning of production and distribution. In light of the historical erasure of the revolutionary tradition, in the former Yugoslavia and beyond, our task is to awaken, be in solidarity with and reanimate past struggles, learn from the defeats of the oppressed and take inspiration from such lucid revolutionary figures and spaces as Vladimir Ilych Lenin and Leninov Park.

Gal Kirn is a political and cultural theorist at the Faculty of Arts in Ljubljana. He has published on socialist and partisan history, for instance, his recent monographies Partisan Counter-Archive *(2020, De Gruyter) and* Partisan Ruptures *(2019, Pluto Press).*

38. Lenin, Partisan of the Conjuncture

Gavin Walker

To consider the actuality of Lenin today is also to consider Lenin's *inactuality*, in the terms of Sylvain Lazarus, who has long attempted to derive a distinct and generic "mode of politics" that characterises Lenin's thought. Lenin's *inactuality* is a given: the social and theoretical basis of the Russian situation of the early twentieth century is not ours. We could even follow Lazarus further and declare that "the Leninist sequence has been fully saturated by the twentieth century and is now closed. The Leninist form is a *historical mode of politics*." But in this attempt to think of a renewed generality for Lenin's thought, we run up against the actuality of this very inactuality, the historical genericization of Lenin as a thinker, no longer solely tied to the October Revolution and its highly specific politics of the global moment. At that point – to paraphrase here both the conclusions of Lazarus, but also Etienne Balibar, not to mention the 'King Hamlet' of 1968 himself, Robert Linhart – Lenin becomes a master thinker not only of *his* conjuncture, but of recurrent political concepts in general: of self-determination, of partisanship or the partisan, and above all else of a conception and practice of political thought that is itself *conjunctural*, and never 'normative.'

We can gain certain clues to this understanding from an old text of Lenin, "The Socialist Party and Non-Party Revolutionism," originally published in *Novaya Zhizn* in November and December 1905. The text emerged at a time of intense political turmoil, the mass strikes in St. Petersburg that preceded the revolutionary events of January, the mass repression directed against the workers' movement by the Tsar, and just on the eve of the final 1905 uprising in Moscow. In it, Lenin develops the concepts of "party-ness" (or "the party idea") and "non-party-ness" (*bespartiinost*), something deeply related to the concept of 'partisanship' and the figure of the 'partisan.'

Responding to the liberal critics of the time who reject the very concept of the party in order to ensure the revolution in process will not go beyond the bourgeois stage, Lenin sarcastically comments, "Simple democracy, ordinary bourgeois democracy, is taken as socialism and 'registered' as such. Everything seems to be 'non-party' (*bestpartiino*); everything seems to fuse into a single movement for 'liberation' (actually, a movement liberating the whole of bourgeois society); everything acquires a faint, a very faint tint of 'socialism'."[1] But Lenin's stern "realism" (never a *Realpolitik*, but ruthless insistence on the actual relations of power of the given situation) prevents him from agreeing with this "abstentionism":

---

1 Lenin, V.I. (1978), "The Socialist Party and Non-Party Revolutionism," in *Collected Works Vol. 10*, Moscow: Progress Publishers, 78.

> The non-party principle means indifference to the struggle of parties. But this indifference is not equivalent to neutrality, to abstention from the struggle, for in the class struggle there can be no neutrals; in capitalist society, it is impossible to "abstain" from taking part in the exchange of commodities or labour-power. And exchange inevitably gives rise to economic and then to political struggle. Hence, in practice, indifference to the struggle does not at all mean standing aloof from the struggle, abstaining from it, or being neutral. Indifference is tacit support of the strong, of those who rule.[2]

Indifference, in such a sense, is a refusal of the conjuncture, a refusal of situatedness, a refusal to acknowledge the stark choices that condition the immediate situation. In the most concrete sense, Lenin frames the problem concisely:

> Political unconcern is political satiety. A well-fed man is 'unconcerned with', 'indifferent to', a crust of bread; a hungry man, however, will always take a 'partisan' stand on the question of a crust of bread. A person's 'unconcern and indifference' with regard to a crust of bread does not mean he does not need bread, but that he is always sure of his bread, that he is never in want of bread and that he has firmly attached himself to the 'party' of the well-fed. The non-party principle [*bespartiinost'*] in bourgeois society is merely a hypocritical, disguised, passive expression of adherence to the party of the well-fed, of the rulers, of the exploiters.[3]

The concept here in Lenin of the basic *partisan* nature of politics is precisely related to the concept of the broader party emerging out of the soil of modern bourgeois society. What is this partisanship? What does it imply about the concept of 'party'?

The party-idea, in Lenin's terms, means that the denial that there is a choice to make is precisely the abstentionist position, the one that secretly-inevitably connects back to a certain opportunism, whether consciously or not. In Lenin's as in today's times, if the choice is between the people and the police, politics means choosing. You cannot uphold both sides – upholding both sides is precisely the false "non-choice" that liberal democracy makes, that the welfare state ideology enforces – i.e., "sure, we accept the exploitative nature of capitalism and the state, but we'll try to at least make it as friendly and painless as possible. The main thing is never to go to extremes, but to have a respectable dialogue." Never going to extremes means that the pinnacle of a possible politics in this framework is simply the upholding of the status quo, the already-existing situation. This ideology is the death of politics. It is exactly against this that Alain Badiou has emphasised the position *il vaut mieux un désastre qu'un désêtre*: better a disaster than a form of non-being. Better to struggle on a chance, on a wager,

---

2 Ibid: 79.
3 Ibid.

than to give up and accept the destitution of our social existence that 'impartiality' produces.

In our current moment, Marx has experienced a massive resurgence of popular relevance: the reality is that today even the seemingly 'apolitical' and those who uphold the dominant order recognise the self-limitations of capitalism, and in the general ideological field, few celebrate anymore the possibility of endless growth. The work of Marx provides us with clues to the Achilles' Heel of capitalism's aggregate reproduction but no certain roadmaps towards what a Marxist position within *politics* could look like: Lenin provides another orientation, in which the political, conjunctural element is raised to the central object of analysis.

This is why Lenin's famous dictum: "The doctrine of Marx is omnipotent because it is true" must be read today in relation to a conjunctural and partisan reading of the category of truth in Lenin. Truth is always directly political, always conjunctural – generating a new and decisive concept of the function of 'conjunctural truths.'

Lenin was notorious for his pithy expression of these conjunctural truths of politics, noting that the only true political criterion in the evaluation of any contemporary position was derived from adding to any sentence the phrase "For whom?" "To do what?" – in our current era, in which the national question has returned with a force, in which we are continually told that parliamentary democracy and the liberal-capitalist consensus are the only 'reasonable' options, the actuality of Lenin's thought could not be more conjuncturally relevant.

Gavin Walker is Professor of Comparative Literature at Cornell University, and the author/editor of many books including The Sublime Perversion of Capital *(Duke, 2016),* Marx et la politique du dehors *(Lux Éditeur, 2022),* The Red Years *(Verso, 2020), and* Foucault's Late Politics, *a special issue of South Atlantic Quarterly (Duke, Fall 2022).*

39. Lenin and the Weltgeist: A Philosophical Reflection

George Sotiropoulos

[T]he life of spirit is not a life that is fearing death and austerely saving itself from ruin; rather, it bears death calmly, and in death, it sustains itself. Spirit only wins its truth by finding its feet in its absolute disruption. Spirit is not this power which, as the positive, avoids looking at the negative, as is the case when we say of something that it is nothing, or that it is false, and then, being done with it, go off on our own way on to something else. No, spirit is this power only by looking the negative in the face and lingering with it. This lingering is the magical power that converts it into being. – This power is the same as what in the preceding was called the subject, which, by giving existence to determinateness in its own element, sublates abstract immediacy, or, is only existing immediacy, and, as a result, is itself the true substance, is being, or, is the immediacy which does not have mediation external to itself but is itself this mediation.[1]
(Hegel)

The story is known, even outside Hegelian circles. On October 13 1806, Napoleon was in the city of Jena, riding his horse, and a young philosopher who had just finished writing what was to become a classic of modern philosophy, *The Phenomenology of Spirit*, watched him from the window. The spectacle impressed our philosopher, Hegel, to such an extent that he would comment on it in a letter he sent to a friend, Niethammer: "I saw the Emperor – this spirit of the world – go out from the city to survey his reign; it is a truly wonderful sensation to see such an individual, who, concentrating on one point while seated on a horse, stretches over the world and dominates it."[2]

It is certainly possible to see here an ersatz mystery of incarnation, embedded whilst feeding the secular(?) theology of Reason that the philosopher was in the process of constructing. After all, Hegel has stated in seemingly clear words that Reason is God; so, given that *Geist* is the form Reason appears in-itself and for-itself, we are presented with a chain of identifications (Napoleon ↔ *Weltgeist* ↔ Reason ↔God) that, taken together, give to Hegel's statement to Niethammer a distinctly theological/religious aura. An aura, moreover, that seems to be fitting for the figure my essay focuses on, Lenin; has not the Russian revolutionary been virtually sacralised after his death? In which case, the following could be the critical point advanced here: in the Lenin Mausoleum lies the Hegelian world-spirit, leaving a world without spirit, hence without will and hope, to drift towards its apocalyptic doom.

Yet, while Hegel shows the truth *in* God, this was not the truth *of* God; it was of Reason, which once it has attained conceptual self-transparency need

---

1 Hegel, G.W.F. (2018), *The Phenomenology of Spirit*. Cambridge: Cambridge University Press, 21.
2 See Broussard, Nicholas (1995), "Napoleon, Hegelian Hero," *Napoleon.org*.

not put on theological garments. In these terms, the mystery of incarnation, as expressed in Napoleon's embodiment of the *Weltgeist*, is sublated by the manifestation of the triadic movement of the Concept, wherein the Universal becomes concrete through its individual instantiation(s). In place of a religious representation (Napoleon as a new Messiah), we are given a rational form for determining and comprehending the historical-cum-dialectical, hence, contradictory, actualisation of freedom. For the essential determination of Spirit, in Hegelian parlance, its *concept*, is freedom: the capacity to determine itself and hence to be its own explanation. Any being that partakes in Spirit partakes in freedom so the process of freedom's actualisation is necessarily a process of equality becoming actual. In other words, freedom, to be adequate to its concept, has equality as an intrinsic determination, for in every other case freedom becomes privilege. What would it mean in these terms to see Lenin as a hypostasis of the *Weltgeist*?

Once Spirit has attained self-consciousness it knows itself not as a Subject-Being upon whom History is grounded and predicates attributed, but as a becoming that finds in subjectivity one of its essential, immanent determinations. That is to say, Spirit, rather than a substantive Entity, is a universal structure of recognition. As such it posits a fundamental equality of being (History in all its multiplicity and diversity is the unravelling of Spirit) at the very same moment that it offers a criterion of differentiation; for at a given time, one political community may embody more clearly the Spirit in its true concept while another political community may react to its Idea, i.e. to the process wherein Spirit realises itself. Moreover, since both communities are objectifications of Spirit, the latter is in conflict with itself. This does not simply denote opposition to an Enemy, and the "fanatical hostility" that a new form "in its first manifestation displays toward the entrenched systematization of the older principle."[3] More dialectically, freedom necessarily has to pass through its Other, to alienate itself in order to actualise itself. This means that, in the process, the Spirit may lose itself and conform or even commit to its alienated form.

The Autocratic Empire of Russia was a form objectively blocking the realisation of Spirit, not simply formally, by its sheer presence, but energetically, as its pivotal role in crushing the 1848 revolutionary wave makes manifest. The prospect of a peaceful, gradual road to democracy (even in its bourgeois-capitalist form) is thus a retrogressive liberal fantasy, which reifies a historical moment of the Spirit as an evolutionary norm, blissfully forgetting the revolutionary origins of democracy even in liberal states. In fact, the resilience of Russian Autocracy to liberalisation, coupled with the intransigence to labour reform that capitalist modernisation in Russia required, opened a space for freedom and equality to assume a more radical form, which was in tune to the new idea that Spirit had posited for itself since the mid-19th century, i.e. *Socialism* or else the socialisation of freedom and equality as a necessary aspect of the Spirit's actuality.

---

3 Hegel, G.W.F. (2010), *The Science of Logic*. Cambridge: Cambridge University Press, 9.

From this perspective, Lenin in 1917, the Lenin of the *April Theses* and of *State and Revolution*, is a subjective expression of Spirit in all its creative and contradictory intensity: theoretical reflectivity and strategic thinking porous to rebellious pathos and self-organising energy, all coming together to turn desire for justice into political will. October and the creation of a Soviet Union of Socialist States marks a new chapter in history, the qualitative advance of Spirit to a new hypostasis. The advance would be as full of contradictions and uncertainty as the historical moment of its emergence. But we must not allow subsequent history to determine entirely our appreciation of a historical moment, as if events obey a strong causal mechanism. Lenin's ethos is a practical manifestation of how the "force of spirit is only as great as its expression, and its depth goes only as deep as it trusts itself to disperse itself and to lose itself in its explication of itself."[4] The Spirit is not advancing irrespective of, but through, the decisions, the risks and the leaps we are willing to take. In these terms, the Leninist ethos remains today as relevant as ever.

George Sotiropoulos writes on various aspects pertaining to political philosophy and is a member of the Void Network collective.

---

4 Hegel 2018: 8.

40. Consciously Revolutionary Workers Do Not Fall From Heaven

Gianni Del Panta

Intellectual encounters are often full of references to mentors, libraries, book presentations, lectures, university rooms, and the like. My first time with Vladimir Lenin was definitely not as grandiose. In the late 1990s, whilst I was turning into a carefree teenager, Renzo Ulivieri was the coach of FC Bologna – a medium-level football team in the Italian first division. Not particularly visionary and innovative, Ulivieri was first and foremost known for a bust of Lenin that he proudly claimed to have on his desk – likely a legacy of the cultural hegemony that the Stalinized Italian Communist Party had had on vast sectors of local leftists in the 70s and 80s. At the time of my adolescence, Bologna's by far most famous player was Roberto Baggio, one of the most talented number 10s in the history of Italian football. The relationship between the two men was full of contrasts, up to the point where Ulivieri went so far as to sideling Baggio for 'tactical reasons' in a match against Juventus. My father, who loved Baggio's flair and genius on the pitch, took a position against Ulivieri. He worked as an electrician at the local public transport company in Florence where we lived, was unionised in the largest and previously Communist-linked trade union CGIL, and stood for labour rights and the welfare state. A few years later, I learned to call him a social democrat, but for the moment he was simply my father. The argument that he proposed against Ulivieri linked the bust of Lenin to the supposed obtuseness and ideological fervour of any communist. This was how I first learned about the existence of a Russian revolutionary named Vladimir Lenin. It took me many years to move beyond bourgeois- and fatherly-infused stereotypical representations of Lenin and Leninism, not only thanks to first-hand readings of 'classic' texts, such as *What Is to Be Done?* and *State and Revolution*, but also as the product of the understanding of the inner dynamics of the 1917 Russian Revolution that authors such as Alexander Rabinowitch, John Reed and Leon Trotsky provided me with.

More recently, there has been a single Lenin statement that I have started to see as particularly valuable for today's times. It is true that there are many reasons not to attempt to focus on any one sentence that Lenin pronounced or wrote. On the one hand, it is very difficult to find any of his speeches or writings that were not profoundly shaped by the audience addressed, the issues at play, and the internal or external opposition that he intended to overcome. On the other, there is a well-established and depressing tradition that relies on Lenin's single and decontextualised quotations to support views and actions that are all but Leninist. The main culprit here is definitely Stalinism, but many others have since followed in its footsteps. In any case, the statement that I have in mind does not concern a specific and transitory aspect, but could actually be considered as one of the crucial axes of Lenin's entire thought. As such, it epitomises what could be regarded as a distinctively Bolshevik point of view of politics.

I am talking about Lenin's closing speech at the 11th Congress of the Russian Communist Party, held in the spring of 1922, where he vehemently argued against Left Communist Evgenij Preobrazhensky who proposed a scholastic understanding of state capitalism, overlooking the context in which economic policies were carried out in Soviet Russia at the time. In particular, Lenin pointed to the organic bonds that linked together political and organisational aspects. In his own words, "political questions cannot be mechanically separated from organization questions." This is a statement I have constantly referred to in recent years, especially in the context of my studies on revolutionary movements in North Africa and the mass protests that shook the region, and many other parts of the world, throughout the 2010s. As various datasets have shown, this was one of the most turbulent decades in human history, and while whether it can aptly be called a revolutionary period is debatable, the extraordinary propensity of the masses to take to the streets is simply a fact. Two other elements are similarly difficult to contest. First, the clear lack of any significant political and social transformation. Secondly, in none of the mass movements was there a distinguishable hegemonic role of the working class. I see these two aspects as intimately connected. The issue that I am addressing here concerns, however, the working class per se.

Though it would be incorrect to overlook the key role that workers played in many of the mass mobilisations of the 2010s, especially in countries like Egypt, Tunisia, and Algeria, the working class as such remained at best a junior partner in broad political convergences under the leadership of the middle classes and their liberal or mildly leftist, neo-reformist parties. As a consequence, workers never truly led these mass movements. In the view of scholars such as Donatella Di Cesare and Asef Bayat, this is no accident. Rather, it represents an enduring feature of mass mobilisations in the 21st century, when the beating heart of radical movements has largely moved away from the occupation of workplaces and the emergence of radical democratic experiments of self-management towards everyday forms of resistance symbolised by the occupation of central squares. While I accept their analyses as largely accurate, what I strongly reject is the conclusion they reach: that as a result of neoliberalism – both as a set of economic policies and an art of government that shapes behaviours and subjectivities – the working class is no longer a revolutionary class because it lacks the numerical concentration and/or the representation of itself as a universal and liberating class that it once had. In such an understanding, there is no space at all for the capacity of the working class to acquire class consciousness through struggle or for the action of a revolutionary party. In fact, the notion of revolution itself becomes obsolete.

For me, this view represents an example of Lenin's observation about the mechanical separation between politics and organisation. The emergence and development of a revolutionary situation is not merely a product of a set of objective and immutable conditions that follow directly from the specific mode of exploitation. Rather, by creating a working-class revolutionary party that constantly educates its members, revolutionaries concretely influence the unfolding of events and, in so doing, contribute to shaping the political environment in which they operate. The latter does not exist in a vacuum but is shaped by those class and political struggles that a genuinely revolutionary party must wage in order to support, influence and lead. What is more, as a result of the ideological domination of the bourgeoisie and due to their specific position within capitalism, workers might be able to collectively challenge some particularly damaging aspects of the system, but in general, they tend to accept and naturalise it. As October 1917 showed, and it remains valid today, this kind of reformist, economist working-class consciousness can only be challenged if a revolutionary party intervenes to win the mass of workers over to their ranks, especially in phases of extended mobilisation, and consequently changes the very course and development of the revolutionary process. In other words, consciously revolutionary workers do not fall from heaven, but ever larger sections of the working class might become so in the course of the revolution. It is precisely in this sense that the issues of the nature of the revolutionary process and the problems of organisations are bound up in a dialectic and inseparable unity.

Returning to North Africa, in basically all the great mass movements of the last decade, (strong) revolutionary parties were lacking. I contend that this has significantly limited the capacity of the working class to emerge as the hegemonic actor capable of creating the political form of its social and human emancipation. This incapacity – by no means only a North African phenomenon – could be alleviated by some of Lenin's insights. His bust, however, and the Stalinist Lenin cult it represents only merits the dustbin.

Gianni Del Panta is Junior Assistant Professor at the University of Pavia and editor of the magazine Egemonia. *His main research interests focus on political regime, revolution and labour movements.*

41. One of the Creators of the 20th Century

Göran Therborn

Lenin was one of the creators of the 20th century. Without his insistence and leadership, the Russian Revolution would not have taken place. And without it, the Chinese Revolution would not have happened. The ensuing Soviet Union then played a major world role in the century, and the horrors of Stalinism cannot be ascribed to Lenin. The USSR was decisive for the defeat of Nazi Germany. It was an important support of the decolonisation process, particularly in Africa. Its challenge to US world domination shortened the civil rights struggles of African Americans in the USA, struggles for the right to go to school, for equal access to facilities, services, and public space, for the right to vote. Racist resistance was ferocious, and without Cold War competition, President Eisenhower, by no means a committed anti-racist, would never have sent federal troops to protect the first token Black children going to school from the White mobs of the Southern states. Also, without the Soviet Union, the Cuban Revolution would have been liquidated. Social protection and labour rights in Western Europe would have been fewer and slower without bourgeois fears of Communism and the USSR. The Soviet bloc in the United Nations was behind the UN's tremendously successful and globally inspiring 1975 World Conference on Women in Mexico.

In short, the Russian October Revolution was a pivotal moment in world history. Lenin was the single Russian political leader who grasped the socially explosive potential of the breakdown of the Tsarist empire under the impact of a hopeless war, and who understood the radicalisation dynamic of the popular masses, which not only swelled the number of Bolshevik supporters and members, but which also overtook the Bolshevik party itself. The revolutionary process was much larger than Lenin, and his role in it had two sides.

One was the perspicacious, daring, insistent leader and shrewd insurrectionist tactician, the other was an intolerant and ruthless sectarian who failed to respond to the wide surge of anti-bourgeois class consciousness and of socialist enthusiasm. This second side of Lenin was hardly a unique personality trait, the Russian revolutionary intelligentsia was notoriously quarrelsome and allergic to compromise. Upon pressure from non-partisan working class organisations – soviets and trade unions – negotiations to form a coalition government were started, with the Socialist-Revolutionaries (SR) and the Mensheviks. They soon ended, because the first demand of the SR and Mensheviks was that such a government should not include Lenin and Trotsky.[1] The ferocity of the war of counterrevolution and foreign intervention, in which right-wing SRs sometimes participated, had a brutalising impact on all sides, including Lenin.

---

[1] The Left SRs did finally enter into a coalition government with Lenin and the Bolsheviks, but they withdrew in July 1918 in protest against the peace with Germany and authorised the assassination of the German ambassador.

Then again, Lenin was much more than the leader of a successful insurrection. He was also a brilliant political analyst and a broad-minded progressive politician. He was a staunch internationalist, who in 1914 almost alone among Social Democratic leaders refused to rally behind their national belligerent governments and support the slaughter of World War I. As a revolutionary of a multi-national state, he propagated national self-determination, explicitly including a nation's right to secession. In power, he granted that right to Finland in December 1917. As an internationalist he was a scathing critic of Russian chauvinism: "I declare war to the death on Great Russian chauvinism," he wrote to the Politburo in October 1922.

He had an anti-imperialist geopolitical vision virtually unique among working-class leaders of his generation. One example is a piece he wrote for *Pravda* in 1913, in the wake of the Chinese Republican revolution, under the title "Backward Europe and Advanced Asia": "Everywhere in Asia a mighty democratic movement is growing, spreading and gaining strength. ... And 'advanced' Europe? It is plundering China and helping the foes of democracy, the foes of liberty in China!" (This refers to a profitable loan which European powers were about to give the aspiring Chinese dictator Yuan Shikai, soon to take power.)

What's more, Lenin, the Russian Revolution, and the Comintern connected the revolutionary European labour movement to global anti-imperialist movements, primarily in Asia. Its first public manifestation was the Congress of the Peoples of the East in Baku in September 1920 at the call of the Comintern. About a year earlier, in an address to the Second All-Russian Congress of Communist Organisations of Peoples of the East, Lenin laid out the 20th-century struggles for socialism: "Hence [because of imperialist interventions] the socialist revolution will not be solely, or even chiefly, a struggle of the revolutionary proletarians in each country against their bourgeoisie. No, it will be a struggle of all the colonies and countries oppressed by imperialism, of all dependent countries against international imperialism."

Finally, feminism had a legitimate place in Marxist theory, laid out by Engels and August Bebel, but was usually shoved aside in labour movement practice. Lenin, on the other hand, was the first labour leader who left a practical Feminist footprint. He appointed the Feminist Alexandra Kollontai 'People's Commissar' for Welfare, and before the end of 1917, his government had decreed an equal conception of marriage, the first in the world together with the Scandinavian countries: the right to divorce; day-care for working women; and equal political rights for women, well before the female right to vote had been granted in leading capitalist countries. However, Lenin did not stop there. "Notwithstanding all the liberating laws that have been passed, woman continues to be a domestic slave ... Do we in practice devote sufficient attention to this question ...? Of course not."

Lenin is a towering figure of modern history, one of the creators of the progressive side of the conflict-ridden and violent 20th century.

Göran Therborn is a Swedish intellectual, a frequent contributor to the New Left Review, and professor emeritus of sociology at the University of Cambridge.

42. The Mass Psychology of the Renunciation of Lenin

Gordana Jovanović

A hundred years after Lenin's death we live under a regime often described as globalisation. This seemingly descriptive term, pointing at global processes that allegedly unite people worldwide, hides the repressive origin, character and objectives of globalisation and consequently leaves many forms of inequality, exclusion and suppression unnamed. Globalisation means the imposition of the capitalist order by military, economical, ideological, scientific and cultural means. It also includes the appropriation of former and emerging critical or alternative agendas for the purpose of the reproduction, advancement and legitimisation of the capitalist system.

Under the regime of globalisation, discourses on differences and multi-perspectives are flourishing, in scientific and the broader socio-cultural sphere. This might seem to be a contradiction possibly questioning the very unifying objectives of globalisation. However, in reality, only differences that do not aim at transcending the capitalist system as such are on the approved agenda. Similarly, there are critical voices in the social and human sciences on the effects of so-called othering – in terms of discriminating, repressing and/or excluding other genders, races, cultures, sexual and political orientations. But again, even these forms of othering can at best be critiqued only inside the very capitalist system that generates them in the first place.

In this sense, I argue that the most comprehensive, radical and repressive type of othering today is the capitalist othering of socialism. Socialism is the big 'other' of capitalism – and vice versa, and the othering of socialism is thus pursued by all means, as under the present regime othering seems not just a desirable act, but a kind of socio-political necessity.

It is within this dominant contemporary discursive and socio-political framework that I place what may be called the mass psychology of the renunciation of Lenin. The term 'Lenin' here stands in for socialist revolution, i.e. for the necessity to build a new society based on structures and values fundamentally opposed to capitalism. Consequently, the repression and renunciation of Lenin means the repudiation of the very idea that an alternative to capitalism is needed, and retrospectively the denial and/or total delegitimization of the historical attempt to build such a society, led first by the actual Vladimir Ilyich Lenin.

The phenomenology of the renunciation of Lenin, i.e. of socialism, includes a variety of forms and is nurtured by different historical and contemporary sources. For instance, the association of socialism with the 'East' – despite its origin in Western European thought – allows for the mobilisation of the historically rooted Western European construction of Eastern Europe as an alien, backward, un(der)developed place, which nevertheless constitutes a source of threat.[1] Even though such a construction of Eastern Europe, as a product of the self-declared enlightened West, preceded the socialist revolution, I believe that it is still a vital source of delegitimization of anything associated with the East, including socialism.

It seems reasonable to assume, in such processes of cultural denial and political rejection of the other, accompanied by intense hostile emotions, that a defence mechanism of projection is at work – i.e. that all the negative attributes, strongly associated with a past believed to be long overcome by the enlightened West, are projected onto others, who by their very nature are incapable to embark on the path of 'civilisation.'

And it was precisely on that vast, constantly vilified 'Eastern' territory that a unique historical event happened, a radical break with the past socio-political system and a project for the future, which included basic civilisational progress in terms of the material conditions of life, but went far beyond it by building new institutions and cultivating values incompatible with capitalism, in particular the expropriation of private property of the means of production.

The Western discursive and political agenda at the very beginning of the transformation of the medieval feudal system into the capitalist social order inaugurated private property as the core structure in society. Concretely, people like John Locke argued that by the acquisition of private property man follows the command of God. The main goal of state organisation, i.e. government, is hence the protection of private property and consequently, any intervention into the structure of such a sacred 'natural' status equals an act against this nature. The first socialist revolution led by Lenin aimed indeed at radically questioning and dismantling the naturalised structure of private property. While liberalism associated private property with freedom, Marxist accounts revealed its other, repressive and discriminatory functions in the form of the exploitation of the majority by a minority and the constant (re-)production of social injustice.

Beyond the widespread critique and rejection of Marxist theory in general both historically and today, Lenin is exposed to additional hostilities precisely because of his practical-political achievements. Scholars have incessantly looked for possible 'dark sides' in his biography, and despite the fact that the attempt to discredit such an epochal socio-political turn as the October revolution by reference to individual psychological traits is certainly a deliberate theoretical fallacy, it nevertheless serves the political agenda of discrediting socialism by all means. As a matter of fact, a whole arsenal of mechanisms – military, economic, political, ideological, cultural, but also psychological (the latter well explored by people like Wilhelm Reich and Herbert Marcuse) – are available and have been used to secure the omnipresence of capitalism and in the process suppress all ideas, and even memories, of previous attempts aimed at building an alternative.

---

1 See Wolff, Larry (1994), *Inventing Eastern Europe. The Map of Civilization on the Mind of Enlightenment*. Stanford: Stanford University Press.

The destiny of socialist Yugoslavia, the country I was born into, is a telling example. Neither the country nor its name exists any longer – except in the strange expression 'the former Yugoslavia,' which sends in fact a double message of non-existence. As is well known, Yugoslavia was brutally destroyed in a bloody civil war, substantially supported – and not only by soft means – by foreign and domestic antisocialist forces, which nurtured hostile attitudes against anything associated with socialism, even among those who in fact experienced unprecedented personal and national progress while living in socialist Yugoslavia. Exactly such experiences, backed by evidence of the improvement of objective living conditions, continue to be repressed today, thereby leading to a scenario where the majority of people choose the socio-political option that necessarily entails their own exploitation and discrimination.

Perhaps this could be considered a peculiar type of defence mechanism operating to expel good experiences from the socialist past in order to comply with the present hegemonic capitalist discourse, which aims at retrospectively constructing the socialist past in accordance with the dominant capitalist present.[2] Thus, historical regression – a return back to capitalism – is to be understood as liberation and progress, while any reference to a better socialist past, when not directly suppressed, is once again discredited as a sign of backwardness, or even as a new proof of the everlasting toxic power of socialist propaganda. In its contemporary enlightening drive, the West, represented by the EU, has hence gone as far as officially promoting the identification of socialism with fascism, in psychoanalytical terms possibly (once again) projecting their own guilt about their complicity with fascism onto the big socialist 'other' that actually fought and finally defeated it.

In other words, people having their own, positive life experiences of socialism are told by dominant discourses what kind of experiences they are supposed to have had and how they should think and feel about them. Those who are not ready to comply are excluded, discredited and pathologised as unable to adapt, obsessed with the past, wrongly committed to the false side of history, etc. Finally, any symbolic traces of the socialist past – i.e. anything named after Lenin or Marx – had and have to be erased in order to remove any material or symbolic base to remember that a socialist system did in fact once exist.

In conclusion, the imperial project of capitalism continues to devastate societies, nature, human lives and even individual and collective memories of the revolutionary attempts to build a more just world. Therefore, to remember Lenin in 2024 is not just a tribute to the past, but a vow to an urgently needed different future.

Gordana Jovanović, Professor of Psychology, is an independent academic in Belgrade, Serbia.

---

[2] See Jovanović, Gordana (2023), "(Childhood) Memories at the Intersection of Coloniality and Decoloniality," *Human Arenas*. Available online.

43. A Century of Lenin in Tunisia (1924-2024)

Habib Kazdaghli

The name Lenin was very popular in Tunisia for a long time, not because of ideological adherence – even though a fringe of the Tunisian elite had supported the Bolshevik revolution and rallied to Lenin's ideas by creating the first communist nucleus in March 1921 – but above all because for a long time the headquarters of the Tunisian Football Federation were located in *Rue Lénine*, right in the centre of Tunis. The Federation's headquarters was a place of incessant activity: it was the usual meeting place for club officials from this most popular of sports throughout the country, who went there to deal with administrative matters relating to the management of their clubs or to hold meetings. The headquarters were also used at times as a sales point for stadium tickets for selected important matches. Tens of thousands of Tunisians went *to Rue Lénine* to buy their tickets! Also, by providing the address of the Football Federation, announcements of these sales in the media helped to make the use of Lenin's name even more familiar.

But how did the naming of a street in Tunis after Lenin come about? Well, unsurprisingly, there's a whole history to it, with its own symbolism and political reasons.

It was Habib Bourguiba (1903-2000), the first president of independent Tunisia, who made the decision in the early 1960s. In fact, he felt the need to justify publicly this truly unexpected choice by a President known for his proximity to the USA. Comparing himself to the great men of the twentieth century, Bourguiba said that it was a way of paying tribute to this outstanding leader who, like him, had devoted his whole life struggling to ensure the best possible destiny for his country and that it was not up to him to "contest the right of any people to install a communist regime in their own country if they so wished. But we do not want it for ourselves."

The fact remains, however, that it was the communist militants of Tunisia who were the first to popularise the name of Lenin and the crucial role he played for his country, in the process explaining how his life and ideas could have meaning for Tunisia, which was at the time under the yoke of French colonisation.

In the mid-1980s, when I was in the middle of preparing my doctoral thesis on the history of the Tunisian Communist Party, I told an old Communist activist, Léon Zana, of my intention to go to Moscow for archival research. He insisted that I check whether the Kairouan carpet that Tahar Boudemgha, a young postal worker and the first Tunisian communist to attend a Comintern congress, gave to Lenin as a gift from Tunisia (on the occasion of the Fourth Congress of the Communist International in December 1922) was in fact on display in the Central Museum of the Revolution. Zana told me that, in his day, it was said that following the Tunisian delegate's speech, in which he had severely criticised what he had described as the "pseudo-communists of the [Algerian] Sidi bel Abbès section," Lenin expressed his esteem for him by offering him his coat.

In more general terms, for decades the dates of Lenin's birth and death were celebrated by communist newspapers in Tunisia. At each of these commemorations, photos of Lenin adorned the front pages of the various newspapers that highlighted the anniversaries: *L'Avenir social, L'Avenir de la Tunisie, Liberté, La Voix du peuple, L'ami du peuple, Espoir, Attariq al Jadid* ("New Path") and others. For example, the front page of the Communist weekly *Liberté* (22-28 April 1955) ran the headline "Lenin was born 85 years ago," and wrote: "This anniversary is dear to the hearts of all those who fight for a better world free from exploitation and oppression, a truly free and peaceful world." At the end of the article, the author reminds us that although "Lenin has been dead for thirty-one years, Leninism is more alive than ever. It lives on in half of humanity, forever freed from imperialism."

The tradition of commemorating Lenin's birth continued after Tunisia gained independence in March 1956. By way of example, in April 1970, *Espoir*, the underground journal of Tunisian communist students (the PCT was banned in January 1963), published a special issue devoted to the centenary of Lenin's birth, in which most of the articles focused on his work, his career and his merits not only for Russia but also for Tunisia. In particular, it stated that: "Lenin's theoretical legacy is of inestimable richness and value. It constitutes a precious guide and an inexhaustible source of inspiration for all those who work for the interests of their people, for any national-democratic or social revolution. The Tunisian progressive forces, and above all the communists, join in this celebration with ardour and enthusiasm." The article goes on to regret that this commemoration could not take place with much fanfare in Tunisia because of the anti-democratic atmosphere prevailing in the country, due to which "progressive forces have been systematically deprived of any legal opportunity to express themselves, following the banning of the Tunisian Communist Party and left-wing newspapers." The author added: "Despite these conditions, we are making our contribution to the celebration of the centenary of the great Lenin."

Fast forward to the 1990s and the current times. After its return to legality, and in the context of the fall of the Berlin Wall, the PCT was transformed in 1993 into a broader centre-left party, the Ettajdid (Renewal) Movement, which no longer made any reference to Leninism in its statutes. The new party did, however, continue to regularly celebrate Lenin's birthday in its newspaper, *Attariq al Jadid*.

Also, in the aftermath of the 2011 Tunisian revolution, some radical leftist groups, no doubt likening the revolution to the "bourgeois revolution" of February 1917 in Russia and inspired by Lenin's famous slogan "All power to the Soviets," called for the revolution to be accelerated and radicalised, and for the constitution to be abolished. They were convinced that they would win a majority in a future constituent assembly. Unfortunately, in the 2011 elections, the Islamist Ennahda movement came out on top. Lately, and in particular since 2019, when Kais Saied became President of the Republic of Tunisia, Lenin's name has been making an unexpected comeback in the media. Ridha Chiheb Mekki, nicknamed "Ridha Lénine" since his radical left student days, suddenly appeared on the political scene as a close friend of Saied's and a member of his election campaign. With the election won, "Ridha Lénine" is now part of Saied's inner circle.

In conclusion, we can affirm that, in various forms corresponding to changing needs and contexts, the name of Vladimir Ilyich Ulyanov has not been forgotten, but continues to be relevant to the Tunisian intellectual, activist and popular imagination and practice. Since his death in January 1924 until today, Lenin has thus, through his ongoing presence in the public space, accompanied Tunisia on a one-hundred-year journey.

Habib Kazdaghli is an historian and former Dean of the Faculty of Arts at the University of Manouba in Tunisia. His research focuses on the history of communism and the history of religious minorities in contemporary Tunisia.

Translated from the French by the editors.

Laya Hooshyari, a Marxist-feminist activist and researcher, lacks formal art education but finds painting Lenin a means of reconciling with his ideas.

44. Lenin's Battles

Helena Sheehan

When we looked across the bay from Napoli
To the island of Capri,
I said to my son "Lenin and Gorky once played chess there"
And he asked "Who won?"

I didn't know who won,
Nor did I care really.
What interested me were Lenin's bigger battles.
I was invariably, although not uncritically, on his side.

Of course, one hundred percent
When it was reds versus whites.
Capitalism versus socialism:
That was the biggest battle.

Within the movement for socialism,
He pitched up on every difficult division,
Displaying the breadth and depth of his thinking.
In his émigré life, he weighed in on every matter firing up the Socialist International:
Strategies, tactics, funds, publications, personalities, congresses, manifestos, splits.
Taking stands on the big debates:
Evolutionary versus revolutionary paths to socialism,
Empirio-criticism versus realism and materialism,
National interests versus proletarian internationalism,
When war engulfed the continent and shattered the International.

When Russia rose up in revolution,
Lenin stood at the helm,
Steering the state through many storms in uncharted seas.
When the very existence of the worker's state was still at stake,
When he had to deal with military tactics, industrial and agricultural production, governance structures, factional fighting,
He nevertheless addressed matters of gender, morality, culture, even philosophy of science.
Mastering multitudinous details and monumental tasks,
Exploring the most searching questions,
Intervening in the most fraught debates
And there were debates about almost everything in those years.

In the battles of my own generation,
When we beheld the world we inherited
And found it so corrupted by capital
That it was hard to resist the impulse to renounce it all,
I thought of those first years of Soviet power,
When Proletkult issued a clarion call to obliterate the old
And start again at zero.
Lenin forged a path of radical re-appropriation,
Neither uncritical assimilation nor nihilistic rejection,
Of the best achievements of the labour of the past
In philosophy, science, technology, art,
To build the socialism of the future.

I saw him once, but he was so still,
Embalmed and entombed.
I had to struggle
To re-imagine him in the heat of battle.

I was never one of those who had to justify every stance
With a quote from Lenin.
At meetings of my vanguard party,
I had to bite my tongue
When I heard those baby bolsheviks
Leaping from quoting him
To listing those they would send to labour camps,
When I knew they wouldn't even
Turn up to man the literature table the next day.

So much water under so many bridges,
So much blood, so much sweat, so many tears
Have flowed between those times and ours.
After magnificent victory,
Such spectacular defeat.

Still the old debates keep percolating
With new nuances:
Evolution versus revolution.
Idealism versus materialism.
We still wrestle with the whole cluster of issues
Dealing with the political, cultural and intellectual inheritance of the past,
Constantly retelling, reinterpreting, reintegrating it all
For our own times.

Lenin's voice still echoes in these debates.
So many books published between his time and ours

Are long forgotten.
Whereas Lenin's books, in many editions, translated into many languages,
Are still discussed and debated.
Recently Lenin trended on twitter (x)
When his image on a poster at a protest
Provoked a politician to write an opinion column
Preaching that Lenin was no model for today.
The protestors thought otherwise.

So many statues of Lenin were erected
On that terrain where Soviet power
Remade the world,
Lifting masses from darkness, poverty, illiteracy
All the way into space.
Perhaps there were too many of those statues
For a movement that rejected the great man theory of history.
Yet I was still sorry to see so many of them fall,
Rejecting the forces of history that he and we embodied.
Now in some of those spaces
Lenin's books are banned,
As are all symbols of the socialism
So many strove so zealously to build.

On my garden wall in Ireland is a head of Lenin
Once hung in a regional party headquarters in Ukraine.
I ordered it on etsy.com.
While I am glad that it is no longer
Gathering dust in a rural antique shop,
I am sad that it is no longer
Where it was meant to be.

Why are they still so afraid
Of what they have declared to be dead?

Years ago there was a poster in my flat
Portraying Lenin with his great coat
Swept up in the wind of history
Proclaiming that
"Lenin lived. Lenin lives. Lenin will live."
It seems to be so,
Even if always embattled.

Helena Sheehan is an academic, author and activist. Latest books: Navigating the Zeitgeist *(2019) and* Until We Fall *(2023).*

45. Between the Poetry of Revolution and the Prose of State Formation: Lenin in Memoriam

Himani Bannerji

History moves on galloping horses

Left

Left

Left

(V. Mayakovsky)

Vladimir Ilyich Ulyanov, a.k.a. Lenin, has not had his due as a social critic and political philosopher for a long time. The cold war, capitalism's naturalisation, and the appropriation of his ideas by political parties have put paid to that. But he is resonating strongly again for understanding capital's contemporary crises hurtling the world into wars, climate and other catastrophes.

Lenin's point of departure was Marx. He and the Bolsheviks tried to realise Marx's exhortation to change the world and not merely interpret it. Following *The Communist Manifesto*, they embarked on a project of conscious history-making based on 'open' and 'hidden' class struggles. The subsequent development of the Soviet Union was not merely an unfolding of Lenin's ideas. He died in 1924, his political life cut short by Fanny Kaplan's assassination attempt (1918).[1] Nonetheless, his insights taught us that the communist revolution is a social process and not an event, a vital lesson for studying the course of modern history.[2]

Lenin's inheritance from Marx confronts him with the task of actualising a revolutionary state based on the conscious agency of the proletariat. In so doing, socio-historical determination was central for both Lenin and Marx. They were deeply concerned with the vital roles of history, class and culture on the course of the revolution. Lenin learned from Marx and Engels that liberalism's political imaginary of unfettered individual freedom was illusory and counterproductive to a collectivist cause and that the imperatives of communist revolution lay in material grounds. In his own manifesto, *The State and Revolution,* Lenin excoriated current pseudo-socialist and populist ideologies of Russian politics – of the Narodniks, Mensheviks and Kautsky, to name but a few. Like Marx, he saw the state as a vital institution for communist construction and its formative relation with civil society. The state, therefore, had to be both socially immanent and politically transcendent. But here, significantly, Lenin parted company with Marx. For him the state was eventually to overdetermine society, while for Marx the state was distinct from society and temporary. Marx privileged society over the state and envisioned its ultimate submergence in the former. Lenin

---

1 A situation reminiscent of Jean-Paul Marat's assassination by Charlotte Corday.
2 A piece of wisdom we also find in Frantz Fanon's *The Wretched of the Earth.*

generally conflated them, and society was brought into the orbit of a vanguard state.

This difference between them had decisive consequences for the future of communism in democratic or authoritarian directions. Through democratic centralism, the Bolsheviks tried to negotiate between the dictatorship of the proletariat and the relinquishing of its role as a ruling class. However, Marx and Lenin agreed on the necessity of a state formation adequate to the tasks of building communism, and both knew that this state would not be born fully armed like Athena from the heads of theoretical heroes and ideologues. Rather, it would be shaped over time, expressing evolving class relations, meeting new social needs, and internal and external challenges. This was a daunting task because such a state of a non-propertied people had never existed, nor had the idea of a state which would be complicit in its own 'withering away.' Bourgeois revolutions could clearly not provide a positive example. Also, important for both as the Paris Commune was, it was short-lived and only an embryonic form of communist governance.

Lenin's major contribution to understanding the transition from Tsarist capitalism to communism was an astute critique of various guises of liberal democracy and its creeping influence on left thinking. He thus steered a fine line between petty-bourgeois Menshevik social democracy and a constant threat of autocracy of a growing bureaucratic state. It is a pity that his criticism of liberalism has been so neglected up to our time. Instead, many of its so-called left critics have made a reactionary turn through Carl Schmidt. Lenin exposed the fascism latent within the capitalist state, which becomes blatant during capital's crises, for example in the imperialist rivalry of the First World War and its aftermath. But beyond a critique of liberalism, he engaged in the praxis of communist revolution. When history confronted them with a situation of *hic Rhodus, hic salta,* Lenin and the Bolsheviks made their jump in 1917, precipitating the world-historical task of creating a true democracy, the rule of the majority. Besieged on all sides and riven with disagreements inside the party, they groped towards the ideal of a communist state and society.

Lenin's own political activity ended during the interregnum of the crumbling of the old state and the inadequate development of the new. Immediate tasks of reconstruction forced him to advise pragmatism, as shown in his last letters and writings. The threat of counter-revolution led him to compromise many of his old and bold ideas. Under the circumstances, the institutions of the old state and its semi-bourgeois economy could not be immediately dispensed with, and the New Economic Policy (NEP) emerged. Lenin was very critical of the proliferation of bureaucracy, which had the potential for incompetence, corruption and becoming a class of its own. Since both old and new class relations were active, ruthless criticism of all things existing had to include the new experiments as well. Marx's lusty idea of smashing the state and Engels' idea of its withering away were now a distant dream. The most urgent task for the Bolsheviks was establishing Marx's notion of the dictatorship of the proletariat as a transitional period. In this situation, the coercive aspect of the new state overshadowed the consensual. Thwarted expectations, conflicts of interest, and old and new class struggles abounded. The barriers between mental and manual labour vital for a communist society were only partially broken.

Pervasive revolutionary aspirations released dreams and desires; futurism, Vertov and Mayakovsky appeared. The poetry of this revolution, as Marx said, was drawn from the future rather than the past. In spite of the experience of Bloody Sunday (1905), euphoria filled the air. Cries for freedom, for a just society, for the fulfilment of all human capacities formed the vast river of awakened Russian consciousness. 1917 was marked with red on the world's calendar, but eventually, recognition of the revolution's shortcomings also dawned. The socialist mode of production and political subjectivities and agencies were yet to be fully elaborated. At its inception anywhere communism lacks a guarantee, its creative path is unmapped. Passionate revolutionary eagerness was accompanied by echoes of disappointment and vicissitudes of state formation. The interregnum had no fixed timeline. Nonetheless, Lenin himself retained a visionary determination to forge the path to communism. For him, there was no shadow between the promise and realisation of revolution.

In capital's present neoliberal phase, in which imperialism is fully manifest, export of capital matched by territorial annexations, Lenin's political thought is crucial for us. It simultaneously validates communism and warns us about the dangers of cultural, nationalist decolonisation disconnected from capital. Like Marx, Lenin tried to forestall the return of the old forces in venerable religious or new liberal masks to continue the filthy business of domination and exploitation. He was the first to ponder how to steer communism's course between the *Scylla* of counter-revolution and the *Charybdis* of ultra-left infantilism. In fact, Lenin waxed poetic on the utopian vision of a stateless society in *State and Revolution*. Enthusiastic about art and literature that flowered around the revolution, he was a nuanced realist who persistently negated the hopelessness and cynicism that facilitates capital's triumph. Especially today, as we face the terrors of settler colonialism, occupation and global imperialism, Lenin gives us hope for a new beginning. For this hope Pablo Neruda in his "Ode to Lenin" thanks him, Turkish poet Nazim Hikmet eulogises him in the "The death of Lenin," and Aram Khachaturian composes music. We neglect Lenin's voice at our own peril.

Himani Bannerji is Professor Emerita at York University in Canada, and among her many publications is The Ideological Condition: Selected Essays on History, Race and Gender *(Haymarket 2021).*

46. I Do Not Know

Ian H. Birchall

On 13 November 1922 Lenin addressed the Fourth Congress of the Communist International, his health broken by five years of steering the new revolutionary society through internal contradictions and foreign invasion. Alfred Rosmer, a French Communist, recalled the scene: "Lenin... was deeply marked by paralysis. His features remained fixed and he walked like a robot. His usual simple, rapid, self-confident speech had given way to a halting, hesitant delivery."[1]

At the beginning of his address, the delegates hailed Lenin's achievements: "Comrade Lenin is met with stormy, prolonged applause and a general ovation. All rise and join in singing 'The Internationale'."[2] How closely they were listening is another story. Lenin had spent his life writing polemics against political opponents. This last speech to the International was a polemic, which must be understood in the context of developments in the Soviet leadership.

He began by defending the New Economic Policy, a short-term retreat which restored some private ownership. Then he turned to the international movement. The Communist International had been founded in 1919; the Bolsheviks realised that the Russian Revolution could survive only by spreading rapidly to other countries. As Lenin put it in December 1917, "the socialist revolution that has begun in Russia is, therefore, only the beginning of the world socialist revolution."[3] While Lenin lived there was no talk of "socialism in one country."

On the contrary, for millions of working people, the Revolution in Russia had represented hope of an alternative to the barbarous system that had dragged the world into four years of war. Leaders like Churchill and Clemenceau feared that hope and were determined to destroy it. The 'civil war' in Russia was in fact an invasion by foreign armies.

But how that hope could be transformed into a spreading of the revolution remained an open question. In 1920 Lenin had clashed with Zinoviev, president of the International, who ranted at foreign anarchists and syndicalists about the necessity for the revolutionary party. Lenin, on the other hand, adopted a much more conciliatory approach, arguing that the syndicalist idea of an "organised minority" of the most militant workers and the Bolshevik idea of the party were the same thing.[4]

---

1 Rosmer, Alfred (2016), *Lenin's Moscow*. Chicago: Haymarket Books, 175.
2 Lenin, V.I. (1973), "Fourth Congress of the Communist International," in *Collected Works Vol. 33*, Moscow: Progress Publishers, 418.
3 Lenin, V.I. (1977), "For Bread and Peace," in *Collected Works Vol. 26*, Moscow: Progress Publishers, 386.
4 Lenin, V.I. (1974), "The Second Congress of the Communist International," in *Collected Works Vol. 31*, Moscow: Progress Publishers, 235.

Now in 1922 Zinoviev was aiming, in Rosmer's words, to impose the "mechanical and slavish imitation of Russian methods" in the name of so-called "Bolshevisation."[5] After Lenin's death the term 'Leninism' would be rapidly promoted by Zinoviev and Stalin, in a series of lectures called *Foundations of Leninism* (1924). For Stalin Leninism was "not merely a Russian, but an international phenomenon rooted in the whole of international development."[6] But would Lenin have called himself a Leninist? I doubt it. Kamenev, who edited the first edition of Lenin's *Collected Works*, reported that Lenin opposed the project, believing there was no point collecting obscure writings from the past.[7]

In any case, Lenin was aware of the ideas Zinoviev and Stalin were developing, and sought, in what turned out to be his farewell speech, to warn against them. Lenin had certainly devoted a great deal of thought to the question of party organisation. Whether there is any such thing as the 'Leninist party,' however, is another matter. In fact, the form of party organisation advocated by Lenin varied enormously according to circumstances; his greatness lay not in spinning organisational recipes out of his skull, but in his ability to learn from the experience of the working class. Two examples: In 1905 striking workers invented *soviets*; Lenin, after initial hesitation, recognised their importance. In 1917 Lenin observed the revival of *soviets* and revised his previous strategy. In my view, historians like Lars T. Lih who stress Lenin's consistency underestimate his ability to learn from the class.[8]

Having said that, Lenin's achievement lay not so much in his arguments on organisation as in his restatement and development of the Marxist tradition on workers' democracy. His most important work was *State and Revolution*, which undermined the claim that socialism can be identified with state control of the economy: "So long as the state exists there is no freedom. When there is freedom, there will be no state."[9] Also, for Lenin revolution came down to the self-activity of workers. "To be successful, revolutionary insurrection must rely not upon conspiracy and not upon a party, but upon the advanced class."[10]

Speaking of reliance, many of Lenin's admirers claim that the whole revolution would have been inconceivable without him. They fail to note the weakness of a revolution that depends on a single individual. (It was a point well understood by those who murdered Rosa Luxemburg.) In reality, the Bolshevik Party was not built by Lenin alone; thousands of individuals played their part. As Victor Serge, who knew Lenin well, recalled, he was part of a

---

5 Rosmer 2016: 219.
6 See Stalin, J.V. (1924), *The Foundations of Leninism*. Marxists Internet Archive.
7 See Serge, Victor (1925), "Lenin in 1917," *Marxists Internet Archive*.
8 See Lih, Lars T. (2008), *Lenin Rediscovered: What Is to Be Done? in Context*. Chicago: Haymarket Books.
9 Lenin, V.I. (1974), "The State and Revolution," in *Collected Works Vol. 25*, Moscow: Progress Publishers, 473.
10 Lenin, V.I. (1977), "Marxism and Insurrection," in *Collected Works Vol. 26*, Moscow: Progress Publishers, 22.

collective leadership: "Lenin, Trotsky, Karl Radek, and Bukharin had ... become the brains of the Revolution. ... they understood one another so well, by the merest hints, that they seemed to think collectively."[11] Furthermore, Lenin depended on people like Shlyapnikov, who travelled to and from Russia during World War I, to get an understanding of what was happening there.

Returning to Lenin's farewell speech and the question of the "mechanical and slavish imitation of Russian methods," he urged those who sympathised with the Russian Revolution to "assimilate part of the Russian experience. Just how that will be done, I do not know. ... the most important thing in the period we are now entering is to study." "I do not know" is pure Lenin. Neither Zinoviev nor Stalin could have said it; they thought they knew it all.

Much has changed since Lenin's death, but yesterday as today there are no 'Leninist' formulae to know, copy and solve our problems. If another revolutionary social transformation comes (and otherwise climate change will kill us all) it will be very different from 1917. In Victor Serge's words, the workers of 1917 were "infinitely different from us, infinitely like us."[12] But in his understanding of the state and of the need to learn from working-class creativity, Lenin still has much to teach us.

Ian Birchall (he/him) is a writer and translator living in London, committed to socialism from below.

---

11 Serge, Victor (2002), *Memoirs of a Revolutionary*. Iowa City: University of Iowa Press, 135.
12 Serge, Victor (2014), *Birth of our Power*. Oakland: PM Press, 63.

47. Lenin's Dream

Ian Parker

Trotsky, during his time of exile before his death at the hands of Stalin's henchman, and when he was suffering from severe migraines and other illnesses, had a dream about Lenin. In the dream, Lenin, who was long dead, was talking to Trotsky and did not know that he was dead. That dream is susceptible to many psychoanalytic interpretations, ranging from wish fulfilment, that the indomitable spirit of Lenin and the revolution was still alive, to an appeal to a father figure, father of revolution. Trotsky himself may have been willing to offer his own interpretations, the only interpretations that count in psychoanalysis, those given by the analysand themselves rather than by the analyst, still less by a psychoanalyst many years later attempting a form of speculative wild analysis.

Trotsky was himself sympathetic to psychoanalysis, defending the approach against the Stalinist crackdown on what was accused of being a bourgeois degenerate non-science, and sending his own daughter Zina to a psychoanalyst in Berlin (a choice explored in the 1985 film *Zina*). Lenin, on the other hand, was a more hard-headed character, and most of the time held to a strict and rather reductive 'materialist' approach to culture and subjectivity, and, sad to say, Lenin's own comments about sexuality were somewhat prudish, including some rather reactionary comments about not wanting to have sex with a woman who was already, in some sense, spoiled by previous encounters.

A wild analytic interpretation of Lenin's own resistance to embracing the forms of sexual revolution that must necessarily accompany social revolution, and to psychoanalysis as such, might be that Lenin repressed his own sexual urges and then sublimated or redirected them into political activity. It is that kind of approach that also suffuses popular culture and then appears in crass representations of revolution as some kind of orgasmic rebellion and release of instinctual energies; one thinks here of the portrayal of the October Revolution in the 1981 film *Reds,* in which Warren Beatty's character reaching sexual climax is intercut with scenes of the Bolsheviks seizing power. We would also see that link re-enacted in Situationist posters – and, yes, I had one up on my wall as a student – that proclaimed, "The more I make love the more I want to make revolution, the more I make revolution the more I want to make love."

This quasi-psychoanalytic image of revolution – in my view now, as a practising psychoanalyst, a fake psychoanalytic image of revolution – then haunts many of the failed attempts to connect psychoanalysis and Marxism, to connect psychoanalysis with Lenin. It feeds a caricature of Marxism that aims for immediate instantaneous world revolution and, worse, an image of revolution as wiping away the past and starting from 'year zero' (the worst case of which was that brutally implemented by Pol Pot). It is this kind of apocalyptic image of revolution that we find in Slavoj Žižek's sub-Maoist and implicitly Christian view of revolution and, not incidentally, of psychoanalysis itself.

We should note that this apocalyptic image of revolution is light years away from Trotsky's account of the careful work of building alliances and 'transitional methods' which led people from their experience of oppression to collective activity preparing for taking power, an account that is, by the way, congruent with later socialist feminist arguments that we need to 'prefigure' the kind of society we want to build in the kind of political activity we engage in now. That mistaken image of revolution is also not actually Leninist; remember Lenin's call to the masses storming the Winter Palace in St. Petersburg: "Save the paintings!" For Lenin, revolution was a process concerned as much with building on the achievements of civilisation as with abolishing capitalism.

In a word, Lenin's revolutionary Marxism was underpinned by the Hegelian concept of 'sublation,' a concept translated from the original German *Aufhebung* and taken up by Marx to describe the dialectical process through which objects of critique are both abolished and preserved, simultaneously negated and improved upon. The point of this journey from the many failed encounters between Marxism and psychoanalysis to Lenin and revolution is that this is where Lenin's revolutionary Marxism – despite Lenin's own apparent personal distaste for Freudian theory – does actually connect with psychoanalytic conceptions. That is, a concern with how the past bears on the present, and cannot be wiped away, but must instead be 'worked through,' and with how what is 'repressed' can actually become a function of power rather than always bubbling away under the surface.

There is a caricature of Lenin and Marxism that was maintained by the Stalinist bureaucracy which reduced dialectics to a crude sequence of 'thesis – antithesis – synthesis' (a representation of dialectics that is also unfortunately present in some of Trotsky's writings). This caricature needs to suppress – we might also say 'repress' – what Lenin found in his reading of Hegel in the crucial few years he spent in exile just before the October Revolution. It was there that he encountered the importance of revolution as dialectical rupture, one that breaks from the past but also saves and repeats its most valuable elements in a new context, and the importance of revolution as something that is not imposed from the above but built by the masses in their own collective self-activity.

That Leninist reading of Hegel needs to be remembered now by psychoanalysts who wish to connect their own practice with Marxism. It gave us the political analysis that is to be found in Lenin's *State and Revolution,* which is about self-organisation of the working class against the capitalist state and, for that matter, against any state apparatus, and in Lenin's *Imperialism, the Highest Stage of Capitalism,* in which Lenin championed the rights of colonised nations to self-determination. This was a political imperative that has now, as Žižek rightly points out, led to Putin blaming Lenin for present-day Ukrainian struggles for independence, for their very existence as a separate nation.

At the heart of this is Lenin's dream – something he was an active participant in mapping out and building with others – that we together can engage in a dialectical revolutionary process of self-understanding and societal progress. We don't need to 'interpret' Lenin's life in order to bring this to the fore, but rather to think in Hegelian terms, and psychoanalytically, about how to make sense of the past in order move into the future.

Ian Parker is a revolutionary Marxist and psychoanalyst in Manchester in the north of England.

48. Lenin and Nyerere – A Conversation in the Heavens

Issa Shivji

Lenin opened the window of his ramshackle apartment, a wave of heat fiercely rushed in from the hellish flames surrounding him. Across the inferno, Nyerere kneeled in solace and solitude on the other side of a deep valley in heavenly bliss, surrounded by plush vegetation. Nyerere fixed his kneeler and rested his arms on a pew in a state of intense prayer (or sleep).

Lenin *(waving at Nyerere)*: Hello, Julius. You are in the same pose as when I last saw you.

Nyerere *(waking from his slumber)*: Good to see you again, Ilyich. Yes, I have been praying. It is the conditionality which comes with my Sainthood.

Lenin *(grinning)*: Like the IMF conditionalities that you fought so hard, back home!

Nyerere *(smiling wryly)*: I expected an atheist to say that! But comrade, how are you managing to breathe in the midst of this hellish smoke?

Lenin: My Chinese comrades have sent a plethora of locally manufactured heaven-like fans. Et tu? How are you managing the heavenly cool? You are from the tropics, Julius!

Nyerere *(flashing his coat)*: See my heavy wool coat, with the pan-African red, black and green stripes, ordered all the way from Moscow's Marks and Spencer.

Lenin: Ha! Proletarian internationalism!

Nyerere: African *Ujamaaism* (socialism), old friend.

Lenin *(after a deep breath)*: By the way, Julius, whatever happened to your socialist project?

Nyerere *(sadly)*: The same that happened to yours. Misguided workers, backward peasantry, a bureaucratic state and of course neo-colonial intrigues. On top of it all, I also had my Yeltsins and Gorbachevs.

Lenin: I warned my party of all that from my deathbed. I guess you were not familiar with my writings. They were too Marxist for you.

Nyerere: Truth be told, I was quite fond of your writings, Ilyich, unlike Marx's, but I never came across your *(with a sardonic smile)* "Letters from the deathbed." I did read your "Letters from afar," which I often used, without acknowledgement of course *(bursts out laughing)*.

Lenin: For your benefit, ndugu, I'll set aside modesty and quote from what I told my party *(shuffles through a bundle of papers)*. You see, they buried my archives with me hoping to museumise my thoughts, just as they iconised me.

Here it is! Here it is! *(quotes)*

Our state apparatus is so deplorable, not to say wretched, that we must first think very carefully how to combat its defects, bearing in mind that these defects are rooted in the past, which although it has been overthrown, has not yet been overcome, has not yet reached the stage of culture, that has receded into the distant past.

... ...

The most harmful thing here would be haste. The most harmful thing would be to rely on the assumption that we know at least something, or that we have any considerable number of elements necessary for the building of a really new state apparatus, one really worthy to be called socialist, Soviet, etc.

... ...

In order to renovate our state apparatus, we must at all costs set out, first, to learn, secondly, to learn, and thirdly to learn, and then see to it that learning shall not remain a dead letter ... that learning shall really become part of our very being, that it shall actually and fully become a constituent element of our social life.

Lenin: I see you are amused.

Nyerere: No insult intended, Ilyich. The excerpt you read from your "Letter from the deathbed" reminds me of a story I once told my party.
Unfortunately, I don't have my archives with me. You see, comrade, my people don't believe in keeping archives, in preserving documents. We stamp all our government documents 'confidential,' 'top secret.' My people even invented a pun to mock the government – they'd pronounce *serikali* (government) *siri kali* (top secret). I'm told my personal assistant Joan Wicken, a British Fabian of long standing...

Lenin *(butts in)*: Yes, and some of her Fabianism rubbed off on you!

Nyerere *(annoyed)*: I'll let it go ... ...Where was I before your rude interruption...? Yes, she transcribed all the long conversations I used to have with her every evening and deposited them in some British library, imposing a thirty-year embargo! Even I cannot access it. The other day I asked our BibliothecaCaelum – *(tauntingly)* haha! I know you don't have one – to get me something but they couldn't.

Anyway, the story goes something like this. In a certain country a beautiful princess living on the summit of a mountain had announced that she'd marry the young man who could climb the mountain to the summit. Many a young man tried, but as soon as he began to climb, he'd start hearing fierce noises from all around, threatening death. The noises became more and more unbearable the higher he went. Not being able to tolerate this, the young man would look back. As soon as he did so, he would turn into stone.

I told my party that we had declared socialism and I was not prepared to look back. I didn't want to become a stone.

Later I came across your "On Ascending a High Mountain," somewhat similar to the story I narrated to my party. A man is ascending a very steep, unexplored mountain. He succeeds in coming very close to the summit but fails to reach it. He decides to descend but the descent is painful. "The voices from below ring with malicious joy. They do not conceal it; they chuckle gleefully and shout: 'He'll fall in a minute! Serve him right, the lunatic!'" Some of my detractors nicknamed me Mussa (Moses), the one that failed miserably to lead his people to the promised land and deserved to be abandoned! Maybe I should have beaten a retreat to find a "safe detour by which one can ascend more boldly, more quickly and more directly to the summit." But where was the time, Ilyich? The Shylocks, the IMFs of that world, were after their pound of flesh.

Lenin *(letting out a derisive laugh)*: Sorry, Julius. I couldn't help it. Yes, comrade Ngombale recently told me how socialism became a single-person crusade for you, as you increasingly lost the support of your party people for your socialist project. BTW, ndugu, your longtime party ideologue Ngombale, a true Marxist I presume, recently joined me.

Nyerere: A Marxist 'man for all seasons'! He managed to survive all regimes, even those that veered away from my Ujamaa.

Lenin *(shrugging his shoulders)*: Ngombale is my nextdoor neighbour. Poor guy is roasting in hellish fire. He has refused aid from what he calls Chinese capitalist roaders!

To come back to the story. Ngombale told me how you lost your peasant base after your campaign of forced villagisation and also how you lost your proletarian base after putting down the workers' uprising. You abolished their elected bodies and imposed on them your statist trade union... You know what – Trotsky in his militarist moment wanted to abolish trade unions as well. I refused. "We have the intention to build a workers' state but the

Soviet state is not yet there. Workers need an organ to defend their interests against the state," I told him.

Nyerere *(interjecting)*: Comrades in glass houses shouldn't throw stones. You also dismantled your Soviets and your anointed successor, Stalin, enforced collectivisation, killing hundreds of peasants in the process, I am told.

Lenin *(calmly)*: I grant you that. You are right. During the civil war I had no option but to send some of our best working class cadres from the Soviets to the front. We lost many, leaving Stalin a freer hand to bureaucratise the party.

Stalin's forced collectivisation was a blunder of historical proportions. It broke the worker-peasant alliance that I had so painfully tried to put together. I know Stalin's intention was to procure food and surplus from the countryside to build industries, a kind of what we Marxists call 'socialist primitive accumulation.' I had tried to do that with the NEP (New Economic Policy), through the market. Stalin was too impatient. He was in a hurry to build industries, which he did. He couldn't wait for the market to do it. Had that not happened maybe the Soviet Union wouldn't have survived WWII. But industrialisation and success in the war came at a great cost. The destruction of the worker-peasant alliance accelerated further bureaucratisation of the party, creating a fertile ground for the subsequent triumph of the capitalist mafia under Gorbachev and Yeltsin.

Ngombale tells me something similar happened in your country. Your bureaucracy sabotaged your socialist project.

Nyerere: But what could I have done, Ilyich? I had inherited the colonial state, like you had inherited the Tsarist state. That was the only organised body I had at the time of independence. Once you accept the state you accept bureaucracy, you accept its security and repressive apparatus. The state comes with all its ugly features. And I am not, and I was not, an anarchist.

Lenin: Yes, you have a point there. I too don't agree with anarchism, but I think on bureaucracy anarchists have a point. Once Kropotkin, one of our brilliant anarchists, told me that the Soviet state had become very bureaucratic, "perhaps even people who yesterday were revolutionaries, changed as all authorities do, into bureaucrats, into officials, who want to twist their subordinates and who think that the whole population is subordinated to them." I responded thus: "We are always and everywhere against officialdom. We are against bureaucratisation, and we must pull up bureaucracy by its roots if it still nestles in our system. But you know perfectly well that it is extremely difficult to remake people and that, as Marx used to say, the most inaccessible fortress is the human skull."

(By now Nyerere was dozing off)

Lenin: I see you are falling asleep. Or are you praying again?

Nyerere: What time is it? I have lost all sense of time since coming here. No day, no night. No dry season, no wet season...

Lenin: Julius dear, you're taking your idealism too far. You see, man invented time just as he created god. But to make god different from himself man made god timeless...

Seeing Nyerere fast asleep, Lenin went back to writing his book, *How to bring the heavens down to earth: A foray into metaphysics*. He could hear Ngombale giggling from afar.

Issa Shivji is Professor Emeritus of Public Law & was First Julius Nyerere Professor of Pan-African Studies, University of Dar es Salaam, Tanzania.

49. Dictator Lenin vs. Democrat Churchill?

Jacques Pauwels

Democracy means the emancipation of what the Greeks called the *demos*, that is, the mass of ordinary people who have been exploited and oppressed for too long by a small minority. Today, this 'ninety-nine percent,' to use trendy terminology, includes not only the lower-class working people and the majority of women of the Western world but also the bulk of the denizens of the Global South; as for the 'one percent,' it consists of a demographically tiny elite of rich and powerful bankers, industrialists, oil and media barons, and large landowners, based mostly, though not exclusively, in the Global North. Democracy, then, is a system in which the *demos* not only provides input, e.g. via elections based on universal suffrage, but also receives a fair share of the output, mostly in the guise of social services such as free education and health care. In other words, democracy is a Janus with not only a political but also a social face. Keeping this definition of democracy in mind, let us compare the respective merits of two giants of the twentieth century, Churchill, lionised by most of our historians, politicians and journalists as a paragon of democracy, and Lenin, supposedly a vile dictator.

Lenin came to power in 1917, in the middle of the murderous 'Great War,' not via a coup d'etat, but because only his Bolshevik Party promised to achieve two things the Russian demos desperately needed and wanted, namely, an immediate end to the slaughter, as well as radical reforms not only of a political but also social-economic nature, including a redistribution of land in favour of the poor peasants. Once in power, Lenin kept this promise, in the first instance by concluding an armistice. Even though the conditions imposed by Germany were harsh, this decision was enthusiastically welcomed by the Russian people, who were tired of serving as cannon fodder for the glory of the czar. Churchill, on the other hand, like the other leaders of Britain, France and the US, abhorred losing Russia as an ally and wanted the Russian workers and peasants to keep on fighting and dying.[1] It is thus obvious that Lenin's position in this respect was democratic, while Churchill's was not.[2]

Then, under the auspices of Lenin's Bolshevik government, revolutionary Russia – soon to morph into the Soviet Union – introduced social-economic reforms that, like peace, were also badly needed and wanted by the country's *demos*. The democratic importance of these changes cannot possibly be denied: they included a redistribution of the land owned by

---

1 To keep Russia in the war and to save as much as possible of the country's extremely undemocratic czarist regime, which required preventing the radical reforms planned by the Bolsheviks, Britain's leaders, including Churchill, supported the reactionary 'Whites' who fought Lenin's revolutionary 'Reds.'

2 That Churchill was not a democrat at all is reflected in his attitude to war. When war broke out in 1914, the supposedly 'greatest Briton' was ecstatic, declaring that the conflict would be "glorious and delicious." Conversely, in 1917, he was disgruntled when the war ended as far as Russia was concerned.

aristocratic and ecclesiastical grandees, jobs and inexpensive housing, free education and health care, pensions, and, for women, the right to vote, equal pay for equal work, free childcare, and the legalisation of divorce and abortion. Such improvements in the lot of ordinary people were sorely needed in Britain too, where poverty was still widespread, but Churchill and the British elite in general opposed them as nefarious state interference with the supposedly natural and beneficial play of market forces.

After the war, when, inspired by the Russian Revolution, the British labour movement organised strikes to obtain higher wages and achieve other improvements, Churchill fiercely opposed such concessions; he was extremely upset with this plebeian seditiousness and proposed to have striking miners sprayed with machine gun fire. Mussolini, who had just established a fascist regime that rolled back significant gains made by the workers during Italy's quasi-revolutionary 'two red years' (1919-1920), was proclaimed by Churchill to be "the Roman genius" who "had rendered a service to the whole world" by showing how governments should treat recalcitrant workers. Later, as Prime Minister during World War II, Churchill was to find it necessary to promise to introduce major social reforms, of the kind pioneered by Lenin, at the end of the hostilities. But after the victory against Nazi Germany, made possible above all by the efforts and sacrifices of the Red Army, but to which Churchill had admittedly made a valuable contribution by providing his country with capable leadership, the British people knew that he was unlikely to keep his word and so he lost the general elections held in the summer of 1945. The winner was the candidate of the Labour Party, Clement Attlee, under whose auspices Britain witnessed the advent of the reforms collectively known as the 'welfare state.' With respect to the delivery of badly needed social services too, then, the conclusion is inescapable: Lenin was on the side of democracy, Churchill was not.

Let us now consider the two leaders' attitudes toward colonialism, unquestionably an extremely antidemocratic enterprise, since it involves one people expropriating, exploiting and oppressing another people. In his famous pamphlet *Imperialism, the Highest Stage of Capitalism*, written in 1916 and published the following year, Lenin carefully analysed and harshly condemned colonialism. Once in power, he proclaimed revolutionary Russia's solidarity with the oppressed colonial peoples of the world and proceeded to support their democratic struggle for independence in word and deed. As such, the Russian Revolution provided inspiration and guidance for the struggle for independence and democratic change in the colonies, making a profound impression on freedom fighters such as Ho Chi Minh. Lenin, in other words, promoted much-needed democratic change for the benefit of exploited and oppressed denizens worldwide, overwhelmingly people of colour, of the overseas possessions of European powers such as Britain.

Churchill, on the other hand, was a firm believer in the superiority of the white man, especially the 'Anglo-Saxon' white man, and in the latter's right to rule with an iron fist over millions of Africans, Indians and other colonial subjects. He was an unapologetic racist, who openly admitted to hating, inter alia, "people with slit eyes and pigtails," adding that he "did not like the look and smell of them." And he was a champion of imperialism, determined to preserve the British Empire and, if possible, to aggrandise it. The latter objective was achieved as a result of World War I, when Britain ended up pocketing virtually the entire oil-rich Middle East, which had actually been London's major war aim. According to the prevailing myth about the Great War, it was a war for democracy, but in the Middle East the decision-makers in London, including Churchill, did not allow democracy to blossom but established feudal, medieval-style kingdoms. And when the Arab population proved to be recalcitrant, as in Iraq, Churchill ordered their villages to be bombed from the air – with poison-gas bombs, no less – killing more women and children than resistance fighters.

As for the leaders in the colonies struggling for independence, Churchill had nothing but contempt for people like Gandhi, for example, whom he despised as "a half-naked fakir" and "a malignant subversive fanatic." Churchill found it immoral that Lenin and the Bolsheviks openly promoted the emancipation of people he considered inferior in Africa and Asia, including the jewel in Britain's own colonial crown, India, and he tarred the Russian revolutionaries with the same racist brush, denigrating them as "baboons."

In short, it is obviously an absurdity of Western mainstream historiography that Lenin is condemned as a nasty dictator, while Churchill is praised as one of the greatest democrats in recent history.

Jacques R. Pauwels, a Belgo-Canadian independent scholar with doctorates in history as well as political science, has taught at a number of universities in Ontario and is the author of books translated into many languages, including The Great Class War 1914-1918, *which also deals with the Russian Revolution.*

50. V.I. Lenin and Black Liberation

Joe Pateman

The revolutionary legacy of V.I. Lenin not only provides valuable insights into the oppression of black peoples. It also provides the key to black liberation. Lenin began exploring these matters early in his political development. Already in 1899, in *The Development of Capitalism in Russia*, Lenin linked the Tsarist policy of Russian settler colonialism, which colonised Russia's ethnic minorities, to European colonialism in Africa. Lenin recognised that both policies had a class root – the metropole's need for capitalist accumulation. His point was that racism and modern colonialism had a capitalist basis.

Lenin developed this insight in his 1913 article "Russians and Negroes," which compared African Americans to Russia's peasants. Noting that Russia abolished serfdom in 1861, and that America abolished slavery only two years later, during the Civil War, Lenin concluded that revolutionary struggle was the most effective route to emancipation. He demonstrated this point by showing that in 1913, Russian illiteracy dwarfed African American illiteracy. Lenin attributed this discrepancy to the fact that a "revolutionary war" abolished US slavery, whereas the Russians abolished serfdom through legal reform. That was why Russians still showed "more traces of slavery than the negroes." At the same time, Lenin pointed out that capitalism could fully liberate neither group.

Lenin also acknowledged that blacks were not the only victims of US slavery. The southern white working class suffered as well, as shown by the fact that their illiteracy rates remained double that of their northern counterparts long after slavery in the south had ended. Lenin's point was that racial capitalism oppressed all workers. White and black proletarians had a common enemy: the bourgeoise, and it was only by uniting against capitalism that they could achieve complete freedom.

From 1912 to 1916, Lenin studied the Black African situation in his "Notebooks on Imperialism." He made notes on dozens of books on colonialism in Africa, paying special attention to the European scramble for territory, the rampant exploitation, and the African struggles against it. Lenin acquired a mass of data on Africa's resource wealth, demonstrating its significance to global capitalism. Upon the basis of his Notebooks, Lenin placed black peoples at the centre of his analysis in his 1917 study, *Imperialism, the Highest Stage of Capitalism*. Lenin argued that Western imperialism depended for its survival on colonialism, most notably the exploitation of Africa. It was only after the colonisation of this continent that the imperialist epoch arose. Consequently, World War I was primarily a European conflict over the redivision of African territory. This meant that African liberation struggles would be crucial in overcoming imperialism and bringing socialism to victory.

The October Revolution was a landmark event in this regard. Lenin's Bolshevik party established the world's first socialist state. The Bolsheviks replaced the racist policy of Russian settler colonialism and what Lenin later called "Great Russian chauvinism" with a Leninist policy promoting the (ideally) harmonious development of all of Russia's nationalities, including the right to secession. Consequently, Blacks around the world saw the Soviet Union as a prototype of an (aspiring) anti-racist, anti-colonial society, and a beacon for black liberation. By way of example, the African American socialist W. E. B. Du Bois celebrated Leninist Russia as "the one modern state which outlawed racial discrimination. Even if this legislation did not always work perfectly, the Negro knew it worked better than...the caste laws of South Carolina."

Nonetheless, Soviet policies were sometimes divisive amongst black radicals. For instance, during the 1930s, the USSR promoted the Black Belt thesis, which presented African Americans in the deep south as an oppressed nation that, in line with Leninist principles, should seek national self-determination. Many black communists opposed this policy. They wanted a united socialist America, not an independent black state. Nevertheless, disagreements on specific policies did not deter blacks from upholding Leninism.

Lenin recognised that blacks had a unique revolutionary potential. Their super-exploitation brought them into conflict with imperialism, which arose upon a racist base. Blacks would realise that capitalism could not grant them freedom, and that only socialism could. This made the black working class a fitting vanguard for the proletarian movement. Lenin therefore refused to regard blacks as the mere objects of white paternalism. Rather, he recognised their ability to emancipate themselves, alongside the rest of the working class.

It was his belief in black self-emancipation that emboldened Lenin to raise the issue at the Second Congress of the Communist International in 1920, where it was agreed that black revolutionaries should participate in the organisation. In 1922, at Lenin's insistence, the Fourth Congress of the Comintern devoted a section to the black question, in which blacks played a leading role. Their discussion produced the "Theses on the Black Question," which consisted of four Comintern pledges. First, communists would support every black movement that undermined capitalism. Second, communists would fight for the full equality of blacks and whites. Third, communists would force trade unions to admit blacks and conduct special propaganda to do so; if they could not achieve this, communists would help blacks organise their own trade unions. Fourth, the International would plan the convening of a World Black Congress in Moscow. With these pledges, the Leninist International became a significant force for black liberation. Lenin's commitment to black emancipation earned him the respect of African American militants throughout the Soviet era. The Harlem renaissance poet Langston Hughes paid tribute in his 1933 poem "Ballads of Lenin":

> *I am Chico, the Negro,*
> *Cutting cane in the sun.*
> *I lived for you, Comrade Lenin.*
> *Now my work is done.*

Claude McKay – another poet who attended the Fourth Comintern Congress – recalled Lenin's voice and presence in his 1937 autobiography, *A Long Way from Home:*

> *And often now my nerves throb with the thrill*
> *When in that gilded place, I felt and saw*
> *The single voice and presence of Lenin*

Finally, in 1966, the Black Panther Party modelled their communist organisation on Lenin's Bolsheviks.

Lenin's Marxism also guided African socialism. Kwame Nkrumah, the leader of socialist Ghana, wrote his seminal 1965 work *Neo-colonialism: The Last Stage of Imperialism,* as a homage and sequel to Lenin's 1917 classic. It was as Leninists that many African revolutionaries overthrew imperialism and embarked on socialist construction. However, not all African socialists maintained a positive relationship with the official Leninism of the Soviet Union. Some, including the Guinean leader Sékou Toure, perceived the Soviets as infringing upon the sovereignty of their respective nations, while seeking to impose a socialist model unsuited to African conditions. Simultaneously, African socialists affirmed the general principles of Leninism. Thomas Sankara of Burkina Faso is representative: he argued that there could be no other path to liberation besides Leninism, for "as Lenin said, without revolutionary organisation, without revolutionary ideology, we will not achieve revolution."

To conclude, the collapse of Leninist governments across Europe and Africa weakened the global black liberation movement. Since then, black identity politics has obscured the class basis of racism, while African nationalism has facilitated exploitation. Both tendencies suit the capitalist oppression of black peoples. The only way forward is thus for blacks to re-arm themselves with Leninism. This means fighting for socialism, and not merely for equality under capitalism; it means opposing class exploitation, and not only anti-black racism; it means opposing neo-colonialism, and not just domestic oppression; and it means transcending incohesive movements, like BLM, for the vanguard organisation of a communist party. These Leninist principles are the key to black liberation.

Joe Pateman is an Assistant Professor in the Department of Politics at York University.

Artist: A.I. Kravchenko

51. Leninists[1]

John Holloway

No. ¡Ya basta! No, it doesn't have to be like that, it could be different. A refusal sustained by a scream, a dream and also a plan.
That has to be the starting point.
Let's talk of the Leninists, not Lenin. It's not so much the leaders but the people who follow them who are interesting. Lenin has become an easy target for criticism. The flow of struggle inseparable from a system of exploitation now moves in a different direction, with different forms of organisation and different ideas about how to change the world. A hundred years after his death, Lenin seems irrelevant. He plays little part in discussions of revolutionary change, other than as a warning: that's not the way we want to go, that led to disaster and great unhappiness.
If I take part in this collection of essays, it is not to rescue the image of Lenin, but because I think it is important to honour the Leninists. Not the bureaucrats, but the thousands and thousands and thousands of people who dedicated their lives and often their deaths to the struggle to build a different world. People who started from a ¡Ya basta!, a rejection of the brutality of capitalism, like we do, people who started from the dream that it would be possible to create a different world like we do, people who had a plan of change and worked to implement that plan, like we so often do not. We criticise that plan as misconceived, as authoritarian, as leading away from the self-determining society we want and need to create, and yet we have to respect, admire and regret the absence of the millions who shared that refusal-dream plan. Dying, often deliberately killed, they dropped their red banners on the ground. It is for us to pick them up. If we do not if we leave them lying there, we accept the capitalist dynamic of catastrophe and possibly extinction.
Perhaps too late to talk to them now, these revolutionaries of the last century. But what if we could, if we could interview them or just chat about their experiences in the early years of the Russian revolution, or the Chinese, or the revolutionary movements of Latin America or Africa? Not the leaders, but the ordinary participants. I would want to ask what was it that led them to devote their lives to the struggle to get rid of the oppression they experienced, how they understood that oppression, what was their experience of the revolutionary organisation, and what, if any, was their moment of disillusion, was it all a mistake, or would they still be revolutionaries today. What would they tell us? And how would we react, we who hate capitalism but have no clear plan for getting rid of it? Would the conversation be possible, or would it just get bogged down in the repetition of party dogmas and facile criticisms, or worse, go around and around in

---

1 I dedicate this note to the memory of the father/parents of two good friends, Sergio Tischler and Carlos Figueroa, who were killed for being communists.

sectarian accusations of betrayal? Would we be able to recognise our discontinuities and continuities? Would we be able to reach a point of laughing together, raising a glass and saying, "Whatever our differences, we are all communists"?

That is what the invitation to write something on Lenin makes me think about. Sitting comfortably at my desk, I think of all those who lived, were arrested, tortured, and killed because they wanted to create a different world. I can criticise their organisation and their authoritarian ways of thinking, but I can only think of them with enormous respect.

P.S. Ángela Navía (to whom many thanks), currently writing a doctoral thesis on the experience of members of the FARC in Colombia, sent me, after reading the note above, this extract from an interview with a long-term member of the FARC, which expresses perfectly what I had in mind:

> Ángela: Do you consider yourself a Leninist?
>
> O: Well, the truth, the truth is that I don't know how or with what you eat this Leninism thing. Even though I have gone through many schools on the matter. I always have done and do the best I can to change the world. I do consider myself to be a restless dreamer, utopian, romantic and whatever else you want to add ...

John Holloway is the author of the trilogy, Change the World without taking Power *(2002),* Crack Capitalism *(2010) and* Hope in Hopeless Times *(2022), and teaches in the Posgrado de Sociología of the Benemérita Universidad Autónoma de Puebla (Mexico).*

52. Dear Lenin

J. Moufawad-Paul

The first time I really thought about you was in denunciation. Before that I only thought about you as an abstract presence: a statue, a symbol of an empire that was crumbling before I was old enough to understand, a vague monument. In the early days of my political awakening, the communism you represented was understood to be a defeated enemy. Your meaning appeared to me as the ruins of the Berlin Wall came a month before I turned eleven. So, when I started to care about politics, when I began to think about your question of "what is to be done?", the kind of anarchist politics I gravitated to was less of a rejection of you and more an affirmation of what I felt could only matter in the shadow of these ruins.

There were of course signs of your supposed death throes. Like when I attended an activist meeting as an undergrad during International Women's Day to listen to my partner read something by Leila Khaled (who was also a Marxist-Leninist, but I didn't register that at the time), only to also listen to another woman read a passage you'd written, declaring you to be feminist. I was struck by this reading but not sold on its merits, largely because of its theatrical delivery. But it stuck in my mind, even if the identity of the performer has not. I wonder where she is now and whether she still thinks of you.

Eventually, as I started to care more about organising and activism, I also started to care about what these practices meant theoretically. As you said, though I'm pretty sure I did not know you said this at the time, "without revolutionary theory there can be no revolutionary movement." And as Mao would teach me later, without practice there would be no revolutionary theory. All of which is to say I craved more than the anarchism I had taken to be correct merely because, in 1990s Canada, communism was seen as passé.

It was during those moments, in which I was clawing my way out from this default anarchism, that I began to appreciate you, but only in reverse. Even though I was reading Marx and Engels I wasn't reading you, and it was only in the denunciation of your contributions that I found my way towards Marxism – through the negation of your thought. Because I didn't actually know, at that time, what you had written and theorised; I hadn't considered you as a thinker. Rather, my way into Marxism from anarchism was to think my thought as antiquated. I learned this first from Nick Dyer-Witheford's *Cyber-Marx* and then from Harry Cleaver, Antonio Negri, and the autonomist tradition. Learning an anti-Leninist Marxism taught me what your thought was supposed to mean. Without having read you, I was learning you in inverse; this tradition was telling me what your thought was meant to represent, why it was wrong (they opposed the notion of the party vanguard, of the revolutionary state), and of course, it dovetailed neatly with my default anarchism. I was permitted to make a smooth transition to Marxism by knowing you through this moment of denunciation. I thus became a Marxist by denouncing your theoretical contributions without having read them and being told how to think them through these autonomist avenues.

But thought does not remain autonomous. Eventually, I wanted to read your thoughts directly rather than presuming their meaning. International activist friends with experience in third-world struggles challenged me to think beyond this simplistic anti-Leninism; they were offended I hadn't read or thought you in a meaningful matter. So I read and thought you, encountered you in every moment. First the classic trilogy: *What Is To Be Done?*, *State and Revolution*, *Imperialism, the Highest Stage of Capitalism*. Then whatever piqued my interest, or what friends and mentors and eventually (years later) comrades in my organisational circles would suggest. "Have you read this?" one of my PhD supervisors, the late Amir Hassanpour, once asked when we were at an estate book sale of a communist professor who had passed, depositing a collection of your essays on colonialism and the national question upon the books I was already planning to buy.

I have learned from you and am still learning. The concrete analysis of the concrete conditions you always pursued. The clarity of your thought. My own work has been sharpened by studying yours; my organisational life has been transformed by engaging with your theory. When I read and re-read your work, I often recall that performance I witnessed in my undergrad days and can understand why someone would want to share you in such a way, no matter how weirdly performative it seemed at the time. I also feel the desire to share your theoretical contributions, though not in the same way – I'm not much of a performer. Like when I assign your work on various courses. I remember one course where I assigned part of *State and Revolution*, when a student who had never read you until then became enamoured with you: "He is so clear," she said in the class, "I'm not used to theory being so clear and complex at the same time." And so uncompromising: as a theorist of the general antagonism, you always approached everything with the understanding of class struggle and the necessity of making revolution. In short, you had ceased being a monument, a symbol of the ruins of the Soviet Union; you were no longer a theory to be read in reverse – to be denounced – but instead became symbolic, along with Mao, of a living Marxism.

There is such a terrible weight that lingers after every engagement with your thought. What is to be done here, in my concrete conditions, where a revolutionary movement requires a theory that can provide the concrete analysis? How would you apply your thoughts in my context, how would you think these circumstances? What would you say at this conjuncture? How do we think the universal aspects of your contributions beyond their particular applications? What do we do with the continuities and ruptures, this dialectical logic that you were so deft at comprehending? All of these questions you left for us to answer along with your legacy, which is indeed part of the weight upon the brain of living Marxism.

"Lenin walks around the world," wrote Langston Hughes, "Frontiers cannot bar him." This is true; he was correct about how your thought walks across innumerable boundaries. But sometimes I feel like the "sun sets like a scar" and there will be no dawn where "rises a red star." After all, we are living in capitalism's Armageddon, where plague and environmental devastation are the new normal. When I read your words, however, and the hopefulness behind them, I feel I can act according to the belief that, as Hughes also writes, "the world is our room." We can maybe inhabit this room; we can maybe bring a better world into being.

J. Moufawad-Paul works as a professor of philosophy at York University and is the author of several books, including Continuity and Rupture, Austerity Apparatus, *and* Politics in Command.

53. José Carlos Mariátegui and Lenin

Juan E. De Castro

One of the many unexpected aspects of *Seven Interpretive Essays on Peruvian Reality* (1928), José Carlos Mariátegui's masterwork, is the relative absence of references to Lenin. There are only three mentions of the leader of the Russian Revolution in a work often seen as the founding text of Latin American Marxism. However, this lack of engagement with the Russian leader should not lead one to believe that Lenin as a thinker and especially as a political example was of little import to the Peruvian Marxist.

Underlying the scarcity of references to Lenin is the fact that *Seven Interpretive Essays* was written, as Mariátegui notes, in part to "defend" himself against the "many who think that I am tied to European culture and alien to the facts and issues of my country."[1] However, even in *Seven Interpretive Essays* there is a brief passage that hints at the importance that Lenin actually had for Mariátegui. In it, Mariátegui quotes some verses from fellow Peruvian Alberto Hidalgo's poem *"Ubicación de Lenin"* ("Placing Lenin" or "Lenin in Context"), itself an important example of the presence of Lenin in 1920s Peruvian culture:

> In the hearts of the workers his name rises before the sun.
> The spools of thread bless him
> from the high spindles
> of all the sewing machines.
> Typewriters, pianos of the period, play sonatas in his honour.
> He is the automatic respite
> that eases the peddler's rounds.
> He is the General Cooperative of hopes.
> His message falls in the money box of the humble,
> helping them pay the instalments on their houses.
> He is the horizon toward which the poor open their windows.
> Hanging from the bellclapper of the sun
> he beats against the metals of the afternoon
> so that the workers may leave at five o'clock.[2]

In his discussion of the poem, Mariátegui counters Hildago's claim that for him Lenin and the revolution were a mere pretext, no different from "a mountain, a river or a machine," to write a poem. For Mariátegui, on the other hand, "Hidalgo deceives himself [...] in his belief that he is not affected by the emotion of historical events." His "poem to Lenin is a lyric creation."[3]

---

1 Mariátegui, José Carlos (1971), *Seven Interpretive Essays on Peruvian Reality*. Austin: University of Texas Press, 25.
2 Ibid: 207-208.
3 Ibid: 207.

In fact, here, as throughout his writing and action, Lenin is, for the Peruvian Marxist, the example, even the symbol, of true revolution.

Already in March 1924, in his eulogy to Lenin, Mariátegui rued that "the revolutionary proletariat has lost the greatest of its leaders," adding: "Communists, Socialists, and Anarchists, people belonging to all the revolutionary schools and parties, and even those belonging to none, all who desire social justice, are aware that the work and personality of Lenin do not belong to one sect or group, but to the totality of the proletariat, to the revolutionaries of the whole world."[4] It is hence not a stretch to suggest that implicit in this statement is the notion that admiration for Lenin is in fact a necessary condition for being a revolutionary. Those who don't mourn Lenin are therefore implicitly placed outside the "revolutionary school and sects," that is, outside the struggle for a different, more equal, and better world. In other words, Mariátegui clearly saw Lenin as an embodiment of what it meant to be a revolutionary.

Four years later, in his "Anniversary and Balance Sheet," as he declares his journal *Amauta* to be socialist – in response to the transformation of the APRA (*Alianza Popular Revolucionaria Americana*), led by his former political collaborator Víctor Raúl Haya de la Torre, into a political party – Mariátegui concludes: "Marx, Sorel, Lenin, these are the men who make history."[5] While Mariátegui's inclusion of Georges Sorel in his revolutionary trinity may surprise, Lenin is again present precisely as Mariátegui differentiates his socialist politics from those of the now-populist APRA.

Also, in several articles dealing with the history and development of the Russian Revolution, Mariátegui describes with admiration Lenin's actions. Yet, it is in his intellectual testament *Defensa del Marxismo*, using mostly material previously published in *Amauta* and published shortly before his early death in 1930, that he deals at greater length with Lenin not only as a historical figure but also as a revolutionary thinker who "philosophises both in theory and practice."[6]

Here one finds an acknowledgement of Lenin's importance as a Marxist thinker: "Lenin, leader of a great proletarian revolution [was] also the author of works on Marxist politics and economy as valuable as *Imperialism, the Highest Stage of Capitalism*." However, Mariátegui's emphasis in *Defensa del Marxismo* is on Lenin as a revolutionary "technician" and as a representative of true proletarian revolution.

Thus, as part of his criticism of Belgian politician Henri de Man's attempts at debunking Marxism, Mariátegui writes:

> And Lenin appears incontestably in our epoch as the most energetic and profound restorer of Marxist thought, whatever doubts plague

---

[4] See Mariátegui, José Carlos (1924), "Lenin." *Marxists Internet Archive*.
[5] Mariátegui, José Carlos (2011), "Anniversary and Balance Sheet," in Harry E. Vanden and Marc Becker (eds. & trans.), *José Carlos Mariátegui: An Anthology*, New York: Monthly Review Press, 130.
[6] See Mariátegui, José Carlos (1981), *Defensa del Marxismo*. Lima: Biblioteca Amauta.

the disillusioned author of *Beyond Marxism*. Whether the reformists accept it or not, the Russian Revolution constitutes the dominant accomplishment of contemporary socialism. It is to this accomplishment, of which the historical reach cannot yet be measured, that one must go in order to find the new stage of Marxism.[7]

In sum, for Mariátegui, Lenin's greatest achievement is the revolution. And it is through the revolution, both in terms of practice and analysis of this practice, that Marxism can be renewed.

Lenin for Mariátegui hence is not primarily a theorist or even a political tactician, even if the Peruvian Marxist admires the Russian revolutionary as both. Rather, for Mariátegui, Lenin fully represents both the idea and the practice of revolution. And it is this commitment to revolution that underlies even Mariátegui's most heterodox writings and actions.

Juan E. De Castro, professor of Literary Studies at Eugene Lang College, The New School, is the author of Bread and Beauty: The Cultural Politics of José Carlos Mariátegui *(Brill 2021; Haymarket 2022).*

---

7 Mariátegui, José Carlos (2011), "Defense of Marxism," in Harry E. Vanden and Marc Becker (eds. & trans.), *José Carlos Mariátegui: An Anthology*, New York: Monthly Review Press, 190.

54. Lenin Never Quoted Lenin

Juan Dal Maso

The above statement is obviously false, in a literal sense. Of course, Lenin did at one time or another refer to some of his own work in the course of a polemic or theoretical elaboration linked to previous debates. But from another point of view, metaphorical and related to Lenin's own attitude towards Marxism, it's true.

The fact is that, unlike the self-interested readings practised by both Stalinism and liberal historiography – which, for ideologically different reasons, present Lenin as a dogmatist whose ideas served as a precedent for the bureaucratic degeneration of the revolution – Lenin's thinking had as its outstanding characteristic the combination of doctrinal solidity, the capacity to analyse and incorporate the data of reality, and a strong openness to the emergence of the new. So, in that sense, it is true that Lenin never quoted Lenin.

By way of example, we have in Lenin an author capable of a research work like *The Development of Capitalism in Russia*, and at the same time of a theoretical-philosophical polemic like *Materialism and Empirio-criticism* (with ideas that were later corrected and reworked on the basis of his readings of Hegel during WWI).

We have in Lenin the organiser who laid the foundations of a highly centralised party organisation in 1903, and also the polemicist who in 1905, against the sectarianism expressed by the majority of the Bolsheviks towards the workers' councils or *soviets*, put forward the need to move away from the dichotomy 'soviet *or* party' and move towards the articulation of 'soviet *and* party' – both ideas guided by his conception that the hegemony of the proletariat was necessary for the revolution.

In fact, Lenin was even capable of going against his own formulas, as when in April 1917 he pointed out that it was necessary to fight for the power of the soviets, leaving aside the formula of the "democratic dictatorship of the proletariat and the peasantry" that he had coined in 1905 to define the character, tasks and class alliance of the Russian Revolution. And in the very course of 1917, in the heat of the development of the Revolution, he theorised on the centrality of the soviets as the basis of the proletarian state, deepening the reflections of Marx and Engels on the Paris Commune, the problem of the destruction of the bourgeois state and the transition to socialism.

However, his ability to contrast theory with reality also allowed him to take an early critical look at the workers' state itself, as when in the early 1920s, in the midst of the debate on the relationship between the trade unions and the state, he pointed out that this was a "workers' state with serious bureaucratic distortions" and that the working class organisations therefore had to defend the workers from their own state. In response to this, Lenin promoted cultural construction and education, within the framework of the New Economic Policy (NEP), and sought to counterbalance the tendencies towards the restoration of capitalism, the awakening of which he had no doubt about, by promoting "cooperation," seeking to create the conditions for the construction of socialism on the basis of everyday practice.

This last Lenin, the one who wrote on cooperation, the one who criticised the policy pursued by Stalin and Ordzhonikidze in Georgia, the one who unceremoniously stressed the disastrous functioning of the Workers' and Peasants' Inspectorate and recommended, in his "Testament," the removal of Stalin from the position of General Secretary of the party, is perhaps the most interesting of all. I say this because he is a Lenin who, combating the many challenges imposed by his state of health, grasps with extreme lucidity the dangers besetting the revolution and with his last strength fights an all-out battle against the rising soviet bureaucracy.

Then again, Lenin's entire revolutionary trajectory is ultimately marked by the same premises we pointed out at the beginning: attachment to theoretical foundations, analysis of concrete reality, openness to the emergent (even if it was bad news or even more so *because* it was bad news).

Because of this particular understanding of Marxist theory and practice, there are various testimonies to Lenin's disinterest in 'Leninism,' understood as a kind of cult of his exceptional gifts: from his speech during the official celebration of his 50th birthday, where he said something along the lines of "we should abolish these celebrations and stop imitating the bourgeoisie," to comments he made to Trotsky about tributes to him that he thought were "rubbish." Yet, if by 'Leninism' we mean Lenin's way of understanding Marxism, this idea of a 'Marxism of action,' theoretically rigorous and at the same time passionately committed to revolutionary practice, we are already a long way from and beyond the bureaucratic appropriations of his thought (reproduced historically and today by the bourgeois intelligentsia in order to bury his legacy along with that of the Revolution).

To finish, in his *Prison Notebooks*, Antonio Gramsci points out that Lenin lacked the time to deepen his reflections on the relationship between the tactics of the united front and the strategic problems of the revolution in Western Europe. This idea can be generalised: Lenin lacked the time, due to the accumulation of urgent tasks, to think about multiple problems on which he could have made major contributions. I am thinking in particular about the absence in the Third International of a theory of contemporary revolution, for lack of a systematisation of the conclusions of the Russian Revolution (which in certain respects Lenin himself left on standby by abandoning in fact, but not explicitly, his historic formula of the "democratic dictatorship of the proletariat and the peasantry"). Such a work of systematisation, overcoming the old formulas and thus disabling their use for the consolidation of the position of revolution by stages, would have provided a greater theoretical basis for fighting against the bureaucratisation of the communist movement, a task which Trotsky undertook later in the context of the rise of Stalinism.

This kind of incompleteness of his theoretical thought is also an expression of Lenin's power and, in a way, a lesson in method. Not to quote

Lenin, but to think with and through Lenin, in order to face the problems of this new historical situation. That's what we should do.

Juan dal Maso is a member of the weekly "Ideas de Izquierda" in Argentina.

55. Sasha and Volodya in Sri Lanka

Kanishka Goonewardena

Joseph Stalin was arrested in Sri Lanka on August 3, 2022.

This is not fake news, I must attest, having grown up in Sri Lanka. Even a non-Sri Lankan should, however, easily distinguish the one hailed as "a great man" by the legendary Black American writer W.E.B. Du Bois,[1] from the charismatic Secretary of the Sri Lanka Teachers' Union, who was indeed apprehended by police amidst the recent economic crisis and political turmoil, resulting from decades of odious debt and neo-colonial underdevelopment.

Sri Lankans of older generations, well acquainted with actually existing socialism in the heyday of the Non-Aligned Movement, were not unique in occasionally naming their kids after leaders of the Bolshevik Revolution. With ample optimism of the will, I myself suggested to the mother of my daughter and son that we name them *Lenin*.

Twice, to no avail.

But what is in a name? What does Lenin mean?

I've heard of a couple of Sri Lankan Lenins and know many Sri Lankan Leninists, whose Stalinist, Trotskyist or Maoist political parties would certainly have benefitted from a real dose of Leninism: first, to get their act together on the actuality of revolution in the three decades following the merely formal decolonisation of Ceylon in 1948; second, to resist imperialist globalisation and renegade nationalisms since the imposition of neoliberalism in Sri Lanka from 1977 onwards.

Lenin also springs to mind whenever I think of the perennial development of underdevelopment in Sri Lanka and elsewhere:

Communism = Soviet Power + Electrification!

I discovered Lenin in the early years of neoliberalism in Sri Lanka, as the once formidable Stalinist and Trotskyist parties were losing their touch with the masses, while an ultra-militant group of Narodnik nationalists masquerading as Maoists gambled on putschist tactics to overthrow a government taking its orders from Washington and Wall Street.

What moved me most in the Sinhala translation of *V.I. Lenin's Life Story,* published by Progress Publishers in Moscow, was however not Lenin, but his older brother Alexander Ilyich Ulyanov. His tragic involvement in an ill-conceived attempt to assassinate Tsar Alexander III gave me, while preparing for final high school examinations, food for thought. Reading about Lenin's childhood in this book yet again as an architecture student at the University of Moratuwa in the late 1980s, a time in Sri Lanka rife with political assassinations of the sort exemplified by Vera Zasulich and Maria

---

1 See Du Bois, W.E.B. (1953), "On Stalin," *Marxists Internet Archive.*

Spiridonova, I recognised Sasha, a hundred years after he was executed for attempting regicide, among some of my own left-wing communist friends.

I dwelled on the possible impact of Sasha's fateful political decision on his precocious younger brother, affectionately named Volodya, because what seemed like the mature Marxist discourse on this matter left something to be desired. We simply were told that Sasha made a terrible error of political judgement, but then Lenin learned from it how *not* to do the revolution. The moral of the story applied soundly to the Sri Lankan situation, which was unlikely to move any closer to socialism by way of a few T-56 shots fired at representatives of the ruling class. Yet, thanks to a stray copy of Isaac Deutscher's *Lenin's Childhood* that found its way to me, I had to reckon also with the fact that Sasha knew as well as anyone else the patent inadequacy of terrorism for revolution, but still joined the plot to kill the Tsar, and even took responsibility on the dock for much more than what he in fact did, to spare the worst for his partners in crime.

Upon Sasha's conviction, his recently widowed and anguished mother Maria Alexandrovna pleaded with him to beg for mercy from the Tsar, hoping to get the death sentence commuted. With sincere apologies for the grief he had caused, Sasha declined: "I cannot do that after all I have said in court." Even the Tsar's officials acknowledged the force of his conviction that life in Russia was not right and had to be made right.

Sasha's principled refusal to ask for forgiveness in that moment is all the more impressive in light of his profound reservations on the assassination plot, which he urgently communicated to 'the terrorist section' of *Norodnaya Volya*. As Deutscher notes, Alexander Ulyanov

> still argued against the plot, saying that it was absurd, and even suicidal, to engage in any political activity before one had clarified the principles on which it should be based. He felt the need for more theoretical work and for a more precise definition of aims and means... But [his co-conspirators] answered his scruples with a telling reproach: are we going to sit back, arms folded, while our colleagues and friends are victimized and while the nation at large is being oppressed and stultified? To engage now, they said, in the elaboration of theoretical principles would amount to surrender. Any philistine can theorise – the revolutionary has to fight.

The year before, practice – premised on a few dysfunctional bombs and revolvers – trumped theory tainted by philistines, Sasha had read the founding father of Russian Marxism, Georgi Plekhanov, who would later call Lenin "the alchemist of revolution" without intending it as a compliment. Plekhanov's Marxist analysis of Russia persuaded him that Narodnik political tactics were ineffective, that conceptions of socialism rooted in village communes were unrealistic and, above all, that terrorist attacks on the Tsar could not revolutionise an autocratic social order. Reading Marx's *Das Kapital* in the last summer of his life – while Volodya was absorbed in Ivan Turgenev – only strengthened these views in his mind. Yet Sasha could not help but also become convinced, in the prevailing circumstances of the

1880s, that the decisive task Marxists such as Plekhanov prescribed and practised on behalf of the revolution – raising the consciousness of the masses through propaganda (often from afar) – was well-nigh impossible in Russia amidst ramped up repression and censorship.

How did Volodya process all that? In the last paragraph of *Lenin's Childhood*, Deutscher observes:

> In all the fifty-five volumes of the latest and most complete Russian edition of [Lenin's] *Works*, Alexander is mentioned almost incidentally and only twice... So extraordinary a reticence could not be ascribed to frigidity of feeling: on the contrary, it covered an emotion too deep to be uttered and too painful ever to be recollected in tranquillity.

The question whether Lenin would have become a revolutionary if not for Alexander belongs to the realm of speculation. Yet the revolutionary Lenin did become is only intelligible with reference to the dilemma faced by his older brother – the apparent futility of all courses of action and inaction in a dire situation. In his autobiography, Louis Althusser memorably formulated this existential problem as a topological one: "the nub of all philosophical (as well as political and military) problems: how to escape the circle while remaining within it." Lenin's name matters because it bears the most exemplary solution to this riddle in *politics*, which transported masses from the impossibility to the actuality of revolution.

Today, it is not only Sri Lankans suffering from debt, underdevelopment and the dictatorship of the IMF who are wondering: what is to be done? Confronting the same question that killed Sasha, we all remain contemporaries also of Volodya, just as Vladimir Mayakovsky said when Lenin died:

> Lenin lived
> Lenin lives
> Lenin will live.

Kanishka Goonewardena was trained as an architect in Sri Lanka and now teaches a seminar called "Space, Time, Revolution" at the University of Toronto.

56. With Friends Like These…

Kaveh Boveiri

The recent accusations of one Vladimir against another Vladimir shattered the illusions of many self-acclaimed leftists, who had searched behind the former's visage some similarities with the latter. The first is Putin, the second Lenin.

But Lenin does not need the accusations made by Putin, or similar ones, to be hated even further by a large number of people on the left. The other day, a comrade sarcastically said that if someone asked her about the religion-like creed shared by the greatest number of people on the left in the contemporary world, the correct answer would be: "anti-Leninism."

Mind you, the left is not in principle opposed to remembering and celebrating revolutionary ancestors. Gramsci was the victim par excellence of Mussolini's Fascism; Rosa Luxemburg the martyr of the Freikorps; Trotsky one of countless victims of Stalinism. Today, there is an International Gramsci Society, a Rosa Luxemburg Foundation with offices worldwide, and several international Trotskyite organisations.

And Lenin? "No way, José!" I hear 'friends' scream. Just imagine an office of the Vladimir Ilych Lenin Foundation somewhere like Berlin. What percentage of the thousands of people who gather every January to commemorate the anniversary of the martyrdom of Rosa Luxemburg and Karl Liebknecht would show up for a similar event for Vladimir Ilyich?

But what is the source of all this aversion? Let us briefly review just some of the most oft-heard responses.

> You know, Lenin did not really follow Marx. He was not a faithful disciple to him, among others, because whereas Marx takes a mass movement of the working class as being the sine qua non constituent of any revolution, Lenin substituted this with his prescription of the vanguard party. In this way, he does nothing but confiscate the prestige and popularity of the soviets, and simply dissolves the Constituent Assembly of workers, to the benefit of the objectives of his so-called revolution in October. In so doing, he led in a Machiavellian way what may be better called a putsch, a coup d'état, or a military Bolshevik insurrection. And that neither a military insurrection nor a coup d'état does leave any room for democracy is a well-known fact. Hence, according to this reading, the democracy already prevalent in the soviets was lost thereafter. Furthermore, the reading goes on, what Lenin does also casts shadows on two other, 'authentic,' democratic revolutions, one preceding October and one following it: the Mexican revolution beginning in 1910 and the Spanish revolution in 1936. Thus, we learnt from him and the Bolsheviks how *not* to do revolutions and what is *not* to be done.

And the remedy? More reliance on the working class, more democracy, less centralism.

> You know, Lenin was too faithful to Marx and wanted to put into practice what the latter said as verbatim as possible. Hence, he failed to surmount the obstacles inherent in Marx's standpoint. Compare him with Trotsky for instance. In The History of the Russian Revolution, Trotsky dares to criticise Marx on several occasions – Lenin doesn't. He was simply too orthodox a follower.

And the remedy? Adopting a more courageous, 'critical' approach in reading Marx and the integration of the approaches of other, non-Marxist thinkers – Proudhon for one, Sismondi for another.

> You know, Lenin was not really a deep philosopher. One big philosophical problem in his thought is that he wrongly adheres to the theory of reflection. He forgets that there is no universe as a whole, and if there were a whole universe, this could only be observed by an observer outside this world. His *Philosophical Notebooks* are vague, and his *Materialism and Empirio-criticism* is sloppy, to say the least. That's why, like Napoleon, Lenin adopted the slogan: "First engage in a serious battle and then see what happens."

And the remedy? He should have been more circumspective and hence, once again, more critical of Marx. He should have changed Marx's famous thesis, "The philosophers have only interpreted the world in various ways, the point is to change it" into something like, "The philosophers have only interpreted the world in various ways, we should hence think deeply about it before attempting to change it." In a nutshell, Lenin should have been a better philosopher.

> You know, Lenin was not really a revolutionary character at all. Immensely influenced by Kautsky, and Engels instead of Marx, he was, as a matter of fact, a reformist, even a revisionist. That's why what he did was nothing but the recreation of state capitalism. His return to Russia – paid for by the German Kaiser – actually circumvented a possible genuine revolutionary path, which the course of events could and would have taken. His so-called New Economic Policy solidified his revisionism.

And the remedy? He should have stayed in Switzerland; or if he absolutely had to come and meddle with the revolution in course, he should have taken a more revolutionary and less authoritative standpoint in hearing his opponents. And so on and so forth. In short, Lenin should have been a different Lenin. A chapter, if not a whole book, could easily be written on each of these 'theses.' The shared logical conclusion of all this remains unequivocal and should not be forgotten: Lenin, and Leninism alike, must be avoided like the plague, and that at all costs!

Ironically, let us remind ourselves, one common feature among Gramsci, Rosa Luxemburg and Trotsky is that they were all ... victims, and that they all ... failed in realising their projects. (If you need an authority on this, read Lucien Goldmann's "*Pour une approche marxiste des etudes sur le marxisme.*")

Therefore, perhaps the current aversion lies in the fact that Lenin did have, albeit all too briefly, time to partly implement what he thought was right. This is not the case for the three persons lauded at different degrees by the contemporary left.

One thing is certain: parroting *any* leader or thinker of the past, in contradistinction with others, will get us nowhere – on the contrary, it demonstrates, once more, our current incompetence in having a rewarding impact on the status quo. A more fruitful approach to this problem might perhaps be to quest how each of these *comrades*, among others, saw what was missing in each case in the "concrete analysis of the concrete situation." Some sixty years ago, Lucien Goldmann invited us to take up such research. It is probably time to accept his invitation.

If not, with 'friends' like these on the left, Lenin does not need enemies, even one hundred years after his death.

Born and raised in Masjed Soleyman (with its exploitation of oil as a source of the current riches of the west, but the poverty of its own people), Kaveh Boveiri keeps dealing with the obsessions he developed since taken, as a kid, to the demonstrations of the Iranian Revolution – if not earlier.

57. Lenin and the Living Dialectic

Kevin B. Anderson

In 2023, as the 100th anniversary of Lukács' germinal text on dialectics, *History and Class Consciousness*, was being celebrated, one thing that came to the fore was his statement to the effect that the dialectical method, rather than any specific propositions or conclusions, was the most important and enduring legacy of Karl Marx. What was not mentioned, and has been little mentioned over the years, is that Lukács grounded – or at least saw an inspiration for – his far-reaching new perspective in Lenin's writings on the dialectic.

Here is what Lukács asserted in the preface to his work's first edition: "He [the author] believes that all good Marxists should form in Lenin's words, 'a kind of society of the materialist friends of the Hegelian dialectic.'"[1]

Lukács was quoting Lenin's 1922 programmatic article on the tasks of Marxist philosophers. But that article was just the tip of the iceberg. Within the decade, Lenin's 1914-15 notebooks on Hegel's *Science of Logic* began to be published, offering a more total view of what Lenin meant by "materialist friends of the Hegelian dialectic."

These "Hegel Notebooks" are one of the most extraordinary documents in the history of Marxism and political thought. An important leader of a large revolutionary socialist party is forced into exile by the shocking carnage and repression of the Left that marked the outbreak of World War I in August 1914. To be sure, he issues antiwar statements and tries to rally the party to take a principled antiwar stance that truly condemns all militarism and imperialism. Yet at the same time, he spends most of the initial months of the war on daily and painstaking studies of Hegel's *Logic*, as well as a few other works by the German philosopher. Evidently, he used the isolation of his Swiss exile to rethink his philosophical premises, by the deep study of the author whose writings Marx had called "the source of all dialectics."[2] While Marxists of Lenin's generation referred to the dialectic in general, the overwhelming majority saw any direct grappling with Hegel as unnecessary. This was because, Louis Althusser later intoned, since we have Marx on the dialectic, we can say that he absorbed what we need to know about Hegel and there is no need to read Hegel himself.

Be that as it may, many shocking and even liberating statements can be found in Lenin's Hegel Notebooks, ones that sweep away the cobwebs built up by decades of misinterpreting and misconstruing Hegel and the dialectic. The most famous statement in the Notebooks concerns Hegel and Marx's *Capital*: "It is impossible completely to understand Marx's *Capital*, and especially its first chapter, without having thoroughly studied and understood the whole of

---

1 Lukács, Georg (1971), *History and Class Consciousness: Studies in Marxist Dialectics*. Cambridge: MIT Press, xlv.
2 Marx, Karl (1976), *Capital Vol. I*. London: Penguin, 744.

Hegel's *Logic*."3 This is no mere generality, no mere crossing oneself by mentioning the dialectic and then going about one's business as a Marxist materialist. For Lenin adds in the next sentence a harsh critique of the generation that followed Marx, obviously including himself: "Consequently, none of the Marxists for the past half century have understood Marx!!"4

That is not all. To this writer, the most amazing statement in the Hegel Notebooks occurs where Lenin radically amends the materialist "reflection theory" of his youth and of his whole generation: "Man's consciousness not only reflects the world, but creates it."5 Of course, Lenin is not denying the material basis of social consciousness here, but he is arguing that consciousness, more specifically, revolutionary consciousness and revolutionary ideas, can "create" a new world.

This gives an entirely new basis for Marxist philosophy and for social action. To be sure, Lenin opposes a hyper-subjectivity that would seek to leap over the material circumstances facing us at a given juncture. At the same time, however, thoughtful revolutionary consciousness based upon deep digging into the dialectic can shape our world and therefore be a factor in changing it.

Lenin's Hegel Notebooks also widen our general approach to the Marxist analysis of society. He has escaped the prison of Engels' rigid dichotomy between materialism and idealism, taking us back to Marx's own critical appropriation of the best in the idealist tradition, above all in Hegel himself.

And unlike Lukács, Lenin connected his new dialectical insights to problems like the very structure of capitalism in his writings on imperialism and its dialectical opposite, national liberation, where he referred explicitly to the dialectics of history. He also used his new dialectic as a basis for his original work, *State and Revolution*.

On the one hand, Lenin did not, as did Lukács, explicitly attack Engels and his nearly positivist perspective, which coexisted uneasily with a great appreciation for Hegel and the dialectic. But on the other hand, Lenin never fell into Lukács' error of denying the dialectics of nature.

Nor, sadly, did Lenin live a long life, which might have allowed him to publish the results of his deep reflections on Hegel and the dialectic in 1914-15.

Nonetheless, the Notebooks remain as a rich legacy that helps us to keep the dialectical flame alive at a time when the world needs a living, revolutionary form of dialectics more than ever.

Rest in power, Vladimir Ilyich!

Kevin B. Anderson (he/him/his) is the author of Lenin, Hegel and Western Marxism, *and of* Marx at the Margins.

---

3 Lenin, V.I. (1976), "Conspectus of Hegel's Book The Science of Logic," in *Collected Works Vol. 38*, Moscow: Progress Publishers, 180.
4 Lenin 1976: 180.
5 Lenin 1976: 212.

Artist: V.I. Masik

58. Too Soon! Too Late? It's Time!

Lars T. Lih

Shortly after Lenin's death in 1924, the long-time Bolshevik activist Evgeny Preobrazhensky gave a brilliantly concise summary of his outlook in 1917: *Rano! Pozdno? Pora!* Here is my not-so-concise translation: Too soon! Too late? It's time!

Preobrazhensky's formula can only be understood by taking into account what I call the Bolshevik adjustment. When the Bolshevik leaders returned to Petrograd after the overthrow of the tsar – some from Siberia, some from Switzerland – they were all shocked and surprised to discover that the Bolsheviks were only a small minority. The soviet constituency of workers and peasant soldiers gave strong majority support to the tactic of what was called the agreement (*soglashenie*), according to which the Provisional Government would carry out essential revolutionary tasks (in particular, a democratic peace and land to the peasants) in return for essential political support. Consequently, the top Bolshevik leaders all made the same basic adjustment to this unpleasant reality: launch agitation campaigns to win majority support for installing a government based on the workers and peasants, one that excluded all 'bourgeois' representation. Here is how Bolshevik leader Lev Kamenev put it *prior* to Lenin's return to Russia:

> It is surprising that the Bolsheviks are not occupying a dominant position in the Petrograd Soviet of Worker and Soldier Deputies ... We are the representatives of the revolutionary element in Petrograd – but, in the meantime, it seems that the wide masses do not understand us. Evidently, since we are essentially correct, we are formulating our resolutions and decisions in a way that the masses do not understand [...] Have we developed to the point that we can create the dictatorship of the proletariat? No. What is important is not taking power – what is important is keeping it. This moment will come.

Too soon!

Let us now look at the course of the Bolshevik adjustment with the aid of Preobrazhensky's formula. Looking back in 1921, Lenin summed up the message of his famous April Theses of 1917 with these words: "On 7 April, I published my theses, in which I called for caution and patience." He further summarised the impact of the Theses by noting that "a left tendency [in 1917] demanded the immediate overthrow of the government," but that he, Lenin, "proceeded from the assumption that the masses had to be won over [first]." He then quoted his own words: "On 22 April, I wrote that the slogan 'Down with the Provisional Government!' was incorrect, since, if the majority of the people is not behind us, this slogan is either an empty phrase or adventurism."

Everybody (including, for a long time, myself) assumes that Lenin's April Theses were aimed at *speeding up* the revolution. And here we have Lenin claiming that the main objective of the Theses was to *slow things down*. And even more surprising, when we turn to the actual text of the Theses, we find that Lenin is right and all of us were wrong. The heart of the Theses is contained in these words: "As long as we are in the minority, we carry on the work of criticising and exposing errors and at the same time we preach the necessity of transferring the entire state power to the Soviets of Workers' Deputies." We must therefore use "patient, systematic, and persistent explanation."

In the weeks that followed, "patient explanation" became Lenin's mantra. It is indeed a useful phrase because it brings out the political thinking behind the Bolshevik adjustment. "Patient": the Bolsheviks committed themselves to refrain from overt attempts to overthrow the Provisional Government until such time as they had a solid majority in the soviet constituency. "Explanation": the Bolshevik message beamed day-in-day-out at the soviet constituency did not consist of learned explications of the difference between 'socialist revolution' and 'bourgeois-democratic revolution.' Rather, it was aimed at the most pressing and concrete issue of the day: the ineffectiveness of the revolutionary government. Here is a paraphrase of the Bolshevik message of March-October 1917: You workers and peasant soldiers have put your faith in an 'agreement' with elite society and its Provisional Government, in the expectation of painlessly achieving revolutionary goals. Well, friends, it won't work – this agreement is doomed to failure. Indeed, owing to infighting, sabotage, and profound policy differences, the Provisional Government is incapable of carrying out the essential duties of *any* government: external defence and internal order.

Too late?

Lenin was famously impatient in the autumn of 1917. His reasoning went something like this: We Bolsheviks confidently expected to receive majority support, and now everybody can finally see that the 'agreement' tactic is clearly leading the whole country over the cliff. We Bolsheviks have long claimed to have the key to carrying out commonly accepted revolutionary goals and averting the onrushing crisis – now is the time to put up or shut up! Any later may be too late!

Lenin argued that the Bolshevik message had finally obtained majority support, but this was a difficult judgment call, especially at a country-wide level. Arguments within the party were therefore unavoidable, but certainly *not* because of a profound split within the party over 'socialist revolution' or the desirability of soviet power. At least, Lenin thought so. In February 1918, Lenin wrote that "we not only thought, we knew with certainty, from the experience of the mass elections to the Soviets, that in September and in early October the overwhelming majority of the workers and soldiers had already come over to our side." Only this mass support "determined the correctness of the slogan 'for an insurrection' in October." The mistake of Zinoviev and Kamenev was that "they incorrectly evaluated the facts – they focused on details without seeing the main thing: that the Soviets had come over from agreementizing to us."

It's time!

Besides setting up an anti-agreement and therefore exclusively soviet government, the Second All-Russian Congress of Soviets in October used its brief two-day existence to pass two decrees that turned Russia upside down. The decree on peace jolted the peace process into motion, and the decree on land liquidated the gentry landowners as a class. These two decrees were the climax of the whole tactic of "patient explanation." The Bolshevik message throughout the year was that the agreement tactic prevented genuine movement toward the essential goals of the revolution. What better way to drive home this argument than to make dramatic moves the very moment that the agreement tactic was no more? The decrees were thus a brilliantly innovative bit of agitation.

Looking through his writings from autumn 1917, we see that these decrees were indeed a major motive for Lenin's insistence on an armed uprising. Lenin wanted to get an actual government in place because only a government could pass decrees with the force of law, and not just eloquent resolutions. The decrees were state acts and, as such, irrevocably transformed the political landscape. The meaning of 'counter-revolution' abruptly changed: it no longer meant 'restoring the autocracy,' but rather 'undoing peace diplomacy as well as the new order in the countryside.' Good luck with that! One could argue that the course of the subsequent civil war was determined during the few hours that the Second Congress was in session.

My short note, based on Lenin's own pronouncements, challenges some deep-rooted preconceptions. *Too soon!* The message of the April Theses was not 'speed up!' but 'slow down!' *Too late?* Divisions within the Bolshevik party in autumn 1917 were not over deep-seated principles but rather over tricky judgment calls. *It's time!* A central aim of the armed uprising was to show that only an anti-agreement government could pass truly revolutionary decrees, thus providing one last bout of "patient explanation."

Lars T. Lih is an independent scholar who lives in Montréal; his recent publications include What Was Bolshevism? *and* Lénine, une enquête historique: Le message des bolchéviks.

59. "All and Sundry"

Leo Zeilig

> *To imagine that social revolution is conceivable without [...] revolutionary outbursts by a section of the petty bourgeoisie with all its prejudices, without a movement of the politically non-conscious proletarian and semi-proletarian masses against oppression by the landowners, the church, and the monarchy, against national oppression, etc. to imagine all this is to repudiate social revolution [...] Whoever expects a 'pure' social revolution will never live to see it. Such a person pays lip-service to revolution without understanding what revolution is.*
> (Lenin)

Across the Global South, in Africa, throughout the Sahel, once the plaything of the imperialist armies – the French, British and Americans, their corporations – insurgent forces had taken power.

The movement was led by a diffuse popular army, neighbourhood groups, and worker cooperatives who had seized control of the entire extractive machinery, and, in coordination with a diverse range of radical groups and liberated zones, ran production for local consumption. No more exports to Europe, North America, or China, of oil, cocoa, gold, bauxite, or coffee. The textile industry – in years past broken up by decades of cheap imports from the north – was now producing affordable clothing for regional use.

Inspired by the popular events in Africa, Europe and North America had also – finally – woken from their game of sleeping beauty (workers' councils, people's courts and popular assemblies were beginning to lay siege to the rich in London, Paris, and Berlin).

Wasn't it Lenin who had once said, "The order of the links in the historical chain are not simple."

Everywhere the empires of capital, governments, and corporations, were trying to strike back, but with audacity and raw force the people were responding ... and winning. At last, the action left everything, everyone, everywhere transformed.

Lawrence Black

Where I stood in the queue at the port in the Albanian city of Vlorë I could see the other volunteers who were dressed like me, hoodies – mine now pulled off, and tied around my waist – jeans, trainers, and their faces open, wide, smiles to welcome conversation.

I held my book, bent back in my hands, and read: "this variegated and discordant, motley and outwardly fragmented, mass struggle, will be able to ... capture power, seize the banks, expropriate the trusts which all hate ... a mass struggle on the part of all and sundry of the oppressed and discontented elements."

And discontented I was, I had a belly full of fight.

The work I had done, in London's permanent gig-economy, left with me with little, except a taste for justice, and fury at the enduring privilege and poverty. My mother had spent her life scrubbing corporate office-blocks before the sun rose, then working as a cook in a restaurant when it set. "Always stand up, Larry, always fight," she taught me.

Now I was ready to follow her advice, though I realised that the fight for social change would mean that I was unlikely to see my home or family again – so be it, there was a home where I was traveling, and friends and comrades in the other volunteers around me.

I lifted the book again and continued to read.

Lenin had got me started years ago, the very book that I was now traveling with, thrust into my hands by an old militant I'd met on a picket-line. Annotated, and dog-eared, Vladimir Ilyich's words rattled in my ears still, "This struggle must be organised, according to the rules of art, by people ... engaged in revolutionary activity."

We were Lenin's 21st-century disciples!

Yet it wasn't Lenin's words which were written on banners or worn on tee-shirts in the parts of the world that were now free, but Walter Rodney's: *"The only great people among the unfree are those who struggle to destroy the oppressor."*

We were volunteers in the war against the mercenaries and armies of empire set on destroying our new world in the South. Yet, we were *also students* of the revolution, who might, if we returned, carry with us stories of liberation to spread the fires of revolt.

Bianca Ndour

I was privileged from childhood, there had always been money and private schools. But also ... a father who bullied me, and a mother who died when I was ten. My father was a Scottish engineer, who met my mother in a Dakar nightclub in 1965 where she was a singer.

I had lived in the UK as a radical academic festering in my scholarly void until I opened my eyes to what was happening in the world and realised that practice was the basis of all knowledge.

I had now found a new home in Ziguinchor, the southernmost city of Senegal – the home of my ancestors, and the HQ of our movement.

Comrade Lenin knew that we could only rely on our own power, and whatever weapons at our disposal: "They must arm themselves as best they can... [with] rifles, revolvers, bombs, knives, knuckle-dusters, sticks, rags soaked in kerosene for starting fires, ropes or rope ladders, shovels for building barricades, pyroxylin cartridges, barbed wire, nails... Under no circumstances should they wait for help from other sources, from above, from the outside; they must procure everything themselves."

And so we did, and I became one of the instigators of the global conflagration – *the* fighter of the first hour.

There has always been a single person who kneels low to the ground to ignite the touchpaper, to spark a wider revolt. Women are our stormbirds, in Paris in 1871, in Russia in February 1917, and in the revolutionary rehearsal in Tunisia in 2011 it wasn't Mohamed Bouazizi who triggered the great reckoning but HIS MOTHER. Always a woman!

At first it was modest. A few individuals, maybe a dozen fighters in total, until our numbers could no longer be counted, and we began to have supporters everywhere, gathering information about what Vladimir Ilyich had once called the weakest links – in this case, exposed bankers, corporate shindigs, political powwows.

We started in Senegal, which was an easy win considering the country's long history of revolt – workers had fought since independence, so we only needed to sustain the movement which had occupied workplaces, public spaces, and established agricultural collectives. The imperialists – white and black – who had controlled the country for 120 years had to be eliminated, and for this we set up people's tribunals and courts (and firing squads, of course).

Within two years the poor were in the saddle. We are now expanding further north into Europe, further south in Africa and spreading up from Mexico and across the border into the US. A frenzy of inspired struggle.

Next to the whitewashed former government building where I have set up my office the palm trees rustle noisily in the wind, and from the balcony I can see dolphins playing in the Casamance river.

I am close to the port where the volunteers from Europe and South America disembark, and occasionally I have time to marvel at our great, heterodox movement of revolt, open war, workers' control, and the systematic murder of the superrich wherever they are found.

Yet, there are still many we must convince, arguments that need to be won – heads to crack.

Nina Choto

In Zimbabwe I lived in a high-density area; in South Africa it's called a township. Before the 'crisis' threw us all to the ground once again, my mother had been a nurse in a state hospital, and my dad a mechanic.

My dad was a voracious reader when I was a kid, and between fixing his customers' cars, he had read acres of newsprint, and any political book he could lay his hands on. Lenin was his favourite, and he gave me a strange schooling; it was all carburettors and *What is to be done?*

In fact, Lenin's words often echoed in our home, after all wasn't Zimbabwe under Mugabe also a "country ruled by an autocracy, with a completely enslaved press, in a period of desperate political reaction in which even the tiniest outgrowth of political discontent and protest is persecuted"?

At 18, with thousands of others, I swam across the Limpopo, the river dividing Zimbabwe and South Africa, and found work as a live-in nanny, cook and cleaner to a wealthy Black family in Johannesburg – living in a lean-to in the garden, and eating scraps stolen from the kitchen.

Like all of us, I was surprised when the first killings took place in 2014 and everyone spoke of the 'Great Transformation.' Truth be told, I was full of questions about another 'struggle,' and another 'revolution.' As a child in Zimbabwe, we were reared on the 'heroes of the struggle' against colonialism and my father would say, "They might once have been heroes, but they are now our oppressors!"

Don't get me wrong – I wasn't jaded, I just doubted everything.

I began to attend meetings where the fighters, and workers, from the north of the continent addressed us. One of them spoke with such bombast, and force, "If we do not expand to the south, to Johannesburg, to the entire southern regions of the continent, then the caste of profiteers, and their militaries will eliminate us." His analysis of the concrete situation was flawless.

There was no time to waste.

So, later than many, still brimming with doubts but increasingly defiant, I joined the struggles beginning to rage across southern Africa, hell-bent on throwing in my five cents to make sure – unlike some of the previous great wars of liberation – ours became a genuine social revolution challenging global power.

The fight continues, and wins

Lawrence, Bianca, and Nina, each of them – in their own way – got pulled into the movement, the rippling contagion of popular democracy and civil war that spread across every corner of the globe.

Lenin's artisanal ragtag army of all and sundry, wielding guns, phones and computers, in the beautiful pollination of a new world.

The history of smooth, murderous men and women who had governed the world and controlled its wealth for centuries was coming to an end.

Leo Zeilig is a socialist, and Leninist. He writes on revolutionaries and modern African history, and political fiction.

60. Lenin and the Long Journey to the East: The Case of Qu Qiubai

Luka Golež

The full impact of the October Revolution in the historical development of the early 20th century was not only reflected in the geopolitical situation of the Russian Empire, nor in the changes that engulfed the whole of Europe in its revolutionary wave, but also had a global dimension. China was no exception to this process. During and after the 1919 May Fourth Movement, many Chinese intellectuals and students began to show an interest in Marxism, and the name of Lenin became widely recognised among progressives. This process heralds the beginning of the political activity of our protagonist – Qu Qiubai (1899-1935). While studying at the Russian Language Institute in Beijing, Qu Qiubai was an active member of various student organisations and developed a growing interest in communism. The Association for Marxist Theory Research at Beijing University, led by the famous Li Dazhao (in 1921 one of the founders of the Chinese Communist Party), introduced Qu Qiubai to the Marxist classics and encouraged him to write pioneering publications about the existing labour movement in China. In 1920, his growing fascination with the Bolshevik revolution, which he saw as a "materialisation of communist ideals," eventually led him to embark on a journey to Soviet Russia as a journalist for Beijing's newspaper *Zhenbao* (Morning Post), making him one of the first Chinese reporters to visit the newly formed socialist state.

During his two-year stay in Moscow, he wrote numerous reports, helped with translating into Chinese lectures on Marxism at the Communist University for the Toilers of the East, and attended two congresses of the newly established Communist International as well as the First Congress of Communist and Revolutionary Organisations of the Far East. In his famous travelogue "Impressions of the Red Capital," Qu Qiubai wrote that at the Third Congress of the Comintern, he felt for the first time all the political enthusiasm of the working masses from around the world. As a side note, he left us with an interesting detail. After the Congress, he met Lenin in the Kremlin corridors. A brief exchange ensued and Lenin, the "determined and sincere leader of the revolution,"[1] handed Qu Qiubai materials related to the 'Eastern question' in the quest for world revolution. Shortly after, in the spring of 1922, Qu Qiubai officially joined the CCP.

After returning to his homeland in 1923, Qu Qiubai quickly gained an increasingly important role in China's revolutionary movement. He translated and published Lenin's speech at the 4th Congress of the Comintern, lectured on Marxist philosophy and, thanks to his work as an

---

1 Qu Qiubai (1985), "Impressions of the Red Capital" in *Collected Works Vol. 1*, *Literature*, Beijing: People's Literature Publishing House, 161.

assistant and translator of Comintern representatives Henk Sneevliet ('Maring') and later Mikhail Borodin, became an important liaison between the Comintern and China's revolutionary political parties. His peak and decline in political participation was as part of the 'Great Revolution' that swept through China in the second half of the 1920s. During this period, he briefly assumed a leading role in the Politburo, but with the violent suppression of the progressive social forces and the betrayal of the revolution by the Nationalists, Qu Qiubai gradually became a target of criticism within the CCP for his alleged conciliationism towards both right- and 'ultraleft'-wing tendencies inside the party, ultimately leading to him losing power in the party. Consequently, he mainly dedicated himself to the problem of the literary artistic movement in China. As one of the leaders of Shanghai's League of Left-Wing Writers, he translated a series of articles on (Soviet) Marxist literary theory, including Lenin's writings on Tolstoy, and analysed historically and theoretically the question of 'Popular Revolutionary Art' in modern China. In 1934, he had the opportunity to put some of his ideas into practice when he became Commissar of Culture and Education in the Jiangxi Soviet (1931-1934), promoting experiments in revolutionary education, including the opening of countless 'Lenin Primary Schools.' On 18 June 1935, at age 36, Qu Qiubai, after having been arrested earlier in the year by Nationalist party guards, was executed for treason in Changting's Zhongshan Park. According to the local accounts, when Qiubai walked toward the execution place, he was singing the 'Internationale' (of which he had made one of the earliest translations into Chinese) and shouting "Down with the Nationalist Party" and "Long live the Chinese Communist Party."

Apart from being an active revolutionary, Qu Qiubai also made major contributions to the process of popularising and developing Marxist-Leninist thought in China. While teaching at Shanghai University in the mid-1920s, his lectures and articles on dialectical materialism received a broad response among the advanced strata of Chinese society. In this period, he made one of the most comprehensive interpretations of Lenin at that time in China. In a series of articles, which he published after Lenin's death in 1924, Qu Qiubai described Lenin as a "Historical tool of the world proletariat in the 20th century," whose revolutionary spirit and organisational form will live on and surpass biological death.[2] From a Leninist theoretical perspective, Qu Qiubai's role in explaining the historical conditions and content of the Chinese Revolution is even more important. To understand this problem, we must briefly explain the Comintern's historical meaning.

One of the turning points in the history of the communist movement that occurred with the establishment of the Comintern is the question of imperialism and its connection with the discovery of the revolutionary potential of national liberation struggles in the peripheries of the capitalist world. Lenin, in his interpretation of the imperialist era of capitalism, had

---

2 Qu Qiubai (2013), "Lenin: Tool of History" in *Collected Works Vol. 2, Political Theory*, Beijing, People's Literature Publishing House, 447-449.

discovered in colonial and semi-colonial nations a new subject of anti-capitalist struggle and thus expanded the spectrum of communist movements on the global level. This break with the Eurocentric Social Democratic tradition of the Second International is one of the central causes behind the rise of the Chinese communist movement. At the same time, the break posed a major challenge to Chinese Marxists with regards to reinterpreting social relations in China from the perspective of imperialism. Qu Qiubai was one of the first to address this challenge systematically and extensively. From China's subjective position, he provided a new interpretation of the economic and political causes of major social changes in China after the First Opium Wars period (1840-42), analysed the position of different social classes in the revolutionary movement, and investigated opportunities to unite and expand progressive forces in anti-imperialist struggles. In short, though contested, Qu Qiubai's translation of Lenin's works into the Chinese context had a major impact on the development of the Chinese revolutionary movement.

Given this brief description, readers may wonder why Qu Qiubai is still relevant today. When reading his works, we quickly notice that his 'translation' of Leninist-Marxist themes into the "concrete situation" of 1920s China is in no way reminiscent of more dogmatic recitations of Lenin's sayings, nor is it a mechanical interpretation of Chinese problems through the lens of dialectical materialism. On the contrary, his approach to Lenin's revolutionary thought is constantly intertwined with creative intellectual work, in which Lenin is understood as a historical "tool" for the interpretation of social problems and the organising of revolutionary movements, rather than as a final answer to the question of the specifics of China's national liberation struggle. In other words, Qu Qiubai strove constantly to re-invent and extend the concepts and methods of revolutionary praxis developed by Lenin.

The case of Qu Qiubai explains why the '-ism' repeatedly appears after Lenin's name: because Lenin's thought contains common qualities that can be applied differently in different historical spaces and times, albeit with the same revolutionary purpose. This reminds us of today's world, with its multiple interlocking crises, which differs in many ways from the economic and political picture of the 20th century, but where 'Leninism' is undoubtedly as relevant as ever. As the case of Qu Qiubai illustrates, returning to Lenin is necessarily a creative process that invites the invention of something new. Or as Lenin once wrote, "It is essential to grasp the incontestable truth that a Marxist must take cognisance of real life, of the true facts of reality, and not cling to a theory of yesterday."[3]

Luka Golež is a post-doctoral researcher at the Tsinghua Institute for Advanced Study in Humanities and Social Sciences, mostly working on Chinese revolutionary art and literature movements and the problem of Third Worldism in the 20th century.

---

[3] Lenin, V.I. (1974), "Letters on Tactics," in *Collected Works Vol. 24*, Moscow: Progress Publishers, 45.

61. Lenin's Way Out

Mahir Ali

In November 1922, five years after the October Revolution, Vladimir Ilyich Lenin was prepared to frankly acknowledge at the Fourth Congress of the Comintern: "Undoubtedly, we have done, and will still do, a host of foolish things. No one can see and judge this better than I."

It was an extraordinary confession to make, particularly in front of an international audience, in what turned out to be Lenin's last public speech. It would be more than 60 years before this level of glasnost would be encountered again in Moscow. And Lenin also had a spot of perestroika in mind.

He went on to attribute the Bolshevik-led government's follies and foibles to Russia's backwardness, the low level of education, the more or less universal international hostility to the infant revolutionary republic, and the largely inherited tsarist administrative machinery – "lightly anointed with Soviet oil," as he put it elsewhere.

This *mea culpa* was delivered by a visibly ailing leader who, after a series of strokes and bouts of semi-paralysis, was conscious that his days were numbered. There were occasional partial recoveries, but within a few months his debility robbed him of the power of speech.

"He was," as Isaac Deutscher puts it in his biography of Leon Trotsky, "in the mood of a man who, with one foot in the grave, uneasily looks back on his life's work and is seized by a poignant awareness of its flaws."

In a different country, the true story of a founding father's incredible intellectual endeavours to reset the nascent state's political and economic compass in his twilight years might have inspired some level of myth-making, but in the Soviet Union for decades even the bare facts could only be shared in hushed whispers.

In late December that year, Lenin, unable to write, managed to convince his irritating team of physicians about the therapeutic value of being permitted to dictate notes. In the roughly 70-day period between 22 December 1922 and 5 March 1923, he authored what became known as his political will or testament, even though it consists of a wide variety of documents, from letters to individuals and missives to the party to speech notes, as well as some thoughts that were intended to be locked away until his demise.

The three issues that particularly gripped his attention were state administration, party structure, and the question of autonomy and national rights within the incipient Soviet Union. More broadly, though, in this late period Lenin found himself aligning more closely with Trotsky, notwithstanding their past disagreements, while distancing himself from Josef Stalin, the recently elevated secretary general of the Communist Party.

Lenin had come around, for instance, to Trotsky's position on giving legislative powers to Gosplan, the state planning commission. In his last contribution to *Pravda*, published only after a debate within the Politburo, he proposed that the People's Commissariat of the Workers' and Peasants' Inspection effectively be merged with the party's Central Control Commission, because "no institutions are worse organised."

Stalin, who had been in charge of the commissariat, might have been even more alarmed when Lenin chose Trotsky to argue the case for a state monopoly on foreign trade, without retreating from the New Economic Policy (NEP) that sought to ameliorate the excesses of war communism, notwithstanding the resurgence of corrupting capitalist vices such as middlemen.

In the case of maintaining a state monopoly on international trade, he and Trotsky scored an easy win – "without firing a shot," as an elated Lenin put it in an appreciative note to Trotsky – which prompted Stalin to scream vile abuse at Krupskaya over the phone. Lenin was incensed when he eventually found out, recognising it as a personal attack. By then he had already dictated a note describing Stalin as too crude for the post of general secretary, and proposing his replacement. In an earlier comment, Lenin noted that Stalin had acquired too much power, and may not always use it wisely. On 5 March 1923, he wrote to Stalin threatening to break off relations unless the culprit unreservedly apologised.

That very day, he wrote a very different note to Trotsky, asking him to defend their mutual stance on "the Georgian affair." This involved Sergo Ordzhonikidze, in particular, riding roughshod over Georgian comrades in Tbilisi, and more broadly revolved around the shape of the enlarged Soviet republic. He had lost all enthusiasm for incorporating the Eurasian periphery into the Russian Federation, which remained Stalin's favoured solution.

Lenin was constantly – and consistently – on the lookout for instances of post-revolutionary imperialism. In an October 1922 message to the Politburo that reflects his residual sense of humour, he declared "war to the death on Great Russian chauvinism," adding: "I shall eat it with all my healthy teeth as soon as I get rid of this accursed bad tooth." Lenin also insisted that the proposed Union of Soviet European and Asian Republics must be a voluntary federation – with the imbalance corrected by the smaller republics having more rights than the potential Russian hegemon. Stalin relented, but only on paper.

By then, it was not uncommon for the secretary general to prompt his acolytes to condescendingly regard Lenin's missives as the incoherent ramblings of a dying man who was anyhow too much under the influence of women – his wife, sister, and the secretaries who jotted down his thoughts. What is remarkable, quite to the contrary, is the analytical clarity that Lenin demonstrated as long as he retained the power of speech. And parts of his brain continued to function to the very end. Nadezhda Krupskaya recalled his reactions as she read to him of an evening. "Sometimes, when listening to poetry, he would gaze thoughtfully out of the window at the setting sun." He would laugh when amused, or gesticulate to demonstrate his appreciation or dismay. In Lenin's last two days, he listened to stories by Jack London; one of them was titled "Love of Life."

In his final year or so, Lenin, to the best of his diminishing ability, raged against the dying of the light. Like everyone else, he failed to foresee where Stalin's "rudeness" would ultimately lead: to the burial of Bolshevism, followed by the defenestration, so to speak, of the finest Bolshevik minds. Perhaps inevitably, the triumph of tyrannical mediocrity also entailed the deification of a petrified Lenin and a selective calcification of what he stood for. To succeed, the cult of Stalinism required anointment by a few drops of Leninist oil.

That bred the myth of seamless continuity among both apologists for and trenchant critics of the evolving Soviet state. There can be little doubt, however, that had Lenin lived longer or been succeeded by a collective leadership, a substantially different future would have ensued.

It's not too late to rescue Lenin from the glass coffin on Red Square where his embalmed corpse was incarcerated a century ago, and to deploy his ideas as weapons – a far more fruitful response to the death throes of late capitalism amid the rising tide of fascism in Europe and beyond. Despite all the "foolish things," the Bolshevik experiment turned out to be globally transformative. It still has much to contribute to building bricks for the future.

Mahir Ali is a Pakistani-born journalist based in Australia.

62. Lenin in Bakhmut

Marc James Léger

The body of Vladimir Ilyich Lenin perished in January 1924. However, we all know that 2017 is the true centennial anniversary of the famed leader of the Bolshevik Revolution. The legacy and meaning of this first major test of communist politics after the Paris Commune is what defines for us the 'death' of Lenin today. In *Lenin 2017*, Slavoj Žižek called on us to remember, repeat and work through Lenin's legacy. Essentially, what Žižek means by this is repeating Lenin's questioning of teleological determinism, which for Lenin meant undertaking a communist revolution in a primarily peasant society. At this specific moment in time, navigating uncharted territories means responding as communists to the Russian invasion of Ukraine. In a 1922 memo, Lenin declared "war to the death" on "dominant-nation chauvinism." Those in Eastern Europe who prefer unification with the European Union and separation from their former Stalinist masters in Moscow can appreciate the stakes of what Žižek refers to elsewhere as the double blackmail. Without an internationalist perspective, all parties have ceded to the logic of a clash of civilisations. Instead of rejecting this double blackmail and building a socialist society, a Ukrainian regime that celebrates the fascist cult of Stepan Bandera, whose leader embezzled half a billion dollars from American taxpayers, has simply followed the diktat of NATO and the United States, leading to the deaths of half a million soldiers, the displacement of a third of the country's population, the decimation of political and labour rights, the sale of the country's resources to foreign investors, and the lurch of far-right tendencies, which is not altogether surprising since even before the 2014 Maidan Revolution, Ukraine was considered the most corrupt country in Europe. The counterpoint to this is not that the Russian regime is likewise riddled with right-wing, authoritarian tendencies, but that all sides are caught up in imperialist war games.

No one who repeats and works through Lenin can legitimately defend any side in this conflict since not one of these powers – as Leon Trotsky argued with regard to the imperialist actions of the Soviet Union before the Second World War – advances or defends the interests of the working masses. As Matthieu Renault has documented, Lenin was not always so conciliatory towards nationalities where there was no possibility that a workers' movement could take root. Quite the contrary. In the same respect, it is worth bearing in mind that Stalinism was not immanent to the revolution but that the revolution was betrayed, as Vadim Rogovin's work has demonstrated. In this case, one cannot but agree with the Class Wargames collective that the global left is not today called upon to act like amateur generals. Videos of Ukrainian press gangs forcing civilians into conscription indicate that many of the would-be soldiers understand the meaning of a suicide mission.

The death of Lenin is not unrelated to the renormalisation of fascism. However, before fascism re-became a thing, the postmodern end of history was widely accepted in academic, cultural and activist circles, with attention being shifted from class issues to language, identity, the body, affect, new materialisms, and so on. Slavoj Žižek and Alain Badiou are arguably the two intellectuals who have done the most to divert the attention of young comrades away from the postmodern abyss that new social movements had sunk into. The prescription to this malady is some version of dialectical materialism, the method that from the outset has saved Marxism from vulgar economism, nihilism, subjectivism, objectivism, historicism and the various offshoots of structuralism. Lenin was himself exemplary of those followers of Marx who understood Marxist materialism as a living form of knowledge and who, on this basis, appreciated the contributions of bourgeois thought to materialist praxis.

The person who did the most to make the dialectical Lenin known and understood to Europeans is the French Marxist philosopher Henri Lefebvre. Lefebvre began his life's work among those who opposed Bergsonism and championed the nascent avant-garde artists and intellectuals among Constructivists, Dadaists, Surrealists and CoBrA. Through the struggle against fascism and the Situationist explosion of May 68, Lefebvre was the first of the Marxists, well before Žižek and Badiou, to clue his compatriots in on what was problematic about Foucault, Barthes, Kristeva, Baudrillard, Derrida, Deleuze and Guattari. Unlike the latter, Lefebvre had fought within and against the French Communist Party. He understood not only the problems but the necessity of organisation. For Marxists like him, Lenin represented a revolutionary form of non-state socialism. And it was mostly cultural figures and thinkers like Lefebvre who in the prewar era challenged the call for the stabilisation of international communism. The questions they confronted at that time and that still concern us are how and why it is that the international proletariat did not accomplish its historical mission and create a world beyond capitalism. How is it that consciousness could be lured by what appears to be a conflict between peoples, that is, rather than consciousness organised in a struggle against the exploiting class? The contradictory passage of alienation, from the realm of ideas or subjectivity, through production relations and everyday life, is ultimately received as history. And humanity, for good and bad, makes history. While many see in such Hegelianism a form of bourgeois mystification, Marxist-Leninists see in it the necessary and eventual overcoming – *dépassement* – of Marxism-Leninism. Lenin was meant to die, but not at the hands of bourgeois nationalists and fascists.

After the Stalinisation of communist parties, countless strategies have been attempted to go beyond stilted forms of orthodoxy: phenomenology, existentialism, linguistics, cultural revolution, third-worldism, informalism, sexuality, deconstruction, difference, etc. None of these has realised the impossible that they set out to conquer, and the humanism that most of them opposed is in a rather miserable state. Opposite this, the bureaucratically organised society of spectacular disintegration rages on. Think of the themes raised by businessman Vivek Ramaswamy in his August 2023 Republican Party presidential primary speech: God is real; there are only two genders; fossil fuels are a requirement for human prosperity; reverse racism is racism; an open border is not a border; parents determine the education of their children; the nuclear family is the greatest form of governance known to man; capitalism lifts us up from poverty; the Constitution of the United States is the greatest guarantor of freedom in human history. Clearly none of these are passable as criteria of truth and each would need to be unpacked rather than sold as ersatz political products. What is true, however, is that the globalisation of relations of production is at the centre of the American state's obsession with war and the shift towards authoritarian and fascist politics.

One place where global capital flows come to an abrupt end, among many others, is in the Eastern Ukrainian 'meat grinder,' a 600-mile battle line near Bakhmut. If this fault line is not to grow deeper, intellectuals and artists must persist in relating to the international working class the means of its prospective annihilation. This insufferable reality is why we return to Marx and Lenin and why it is that only action can reveal reality in all its truth. So why Lenin? Not because Lenin was the leader of a well-organised workers' movement, but the contrary, because he cunningly confronted the movement's idealist, populist, moralistic and ontologistic disorientation in the midst of imperialist war.

Marc James Léger is a Marxist cultural theorist living in Montreal.

63. The Need to Dream and the Importance of (Re)Believing in Lenin

Marcela Magalhães

There is something inherently human about the ability to dream. The ability to envision a better *futuro*, to transcend present circumstances and aspire to something greater, is what distinguishes us as conscious beings.

Throughout history, dreams (*sonhos*) have acted as beacons that guide humanity towards extraordinary achievements and social transformations. However, as time progresses, it has become increasingly evident that we have lost faith in 'utopia,' in the possibility of a more just and equitable world. The collapse of the Soviet Union in 1991 apparently marked the end of a systemic alternative to capitalism, which in a way consolidated the false idea that capitalism is the only viable economic model on a global scale. In this sense, we are increasingly seeing the influence of what has been called "capitalist realism" and of the pessimistic idea that "it's easier to imagine the end of the world than the end of capitalism," the latter of which has not only spread, but seems to have become a constituent part of the (Western) imagination itself. It is within this context that I turn my gaze to the teachings of Vladimir Lenin, the centenary of whose death invites us to reconsider the *importância* of dreaming and the need to (re)believe in ideals capable of moulding a more just future.

By turning to Lenin, I recognise the importance of the necessity to transform dreams into concrete actions, and it is this connection between ideal(ised) vision and effective practice that led me to join the *Partido Comunista Português* (PCP) in 2021. Just as the poet João Cabral de Melo Neto reminds us that *"um galo sozinho não faz a manhã"* (a rooster alone does not make the morning), it is clear that there is no communist without a party. It is in organised unity that we find our real chances of bringing about significant change.

Unfortunately, the influence of "capitalist realism" has profoundly shaped the way many of us regard the possibility of social transformation. The idea that it is easier to conceive of the collapse of the world than the end of capitalism expresses resignation in the face of established, entrenched social structures. Lenin, however, reminds us that resignation is never the answer. On the contrary, we must always recover and nourish our capacity to dream as a means of imagining and, in turn, creating a more just world.

Over the years, I have witnessed the decline of faith in the ideas that once inspired remarkable revolutions in the world. The 20th century brought with it different ideologies that promised equality, social justice and prosperity for all, but most of these aspirations were eventually overshadowed by oppression, corruption and conflict. In the midst of these vicissitudes, Lenin's ideas – paradoxically – resurface as a voice that challenges resignation and stimulates reflection on what can be achieved when we dare to dream. As such, dreaming is not an escape from reality, but a way of creating a vision that guides our actions. Lenin, in his quest for a more just society, believed in the possibility of radical transformation. His ideas were hence not mere theoretical abstractions: they were calls to action, to build a society that would transcend the inequalities and violence intrinsic to the capitalist-colonial system. If, on the one hand, the practical interpretations of these ideas have not always corresponded to the original intentions, it is nonetheless crucial to recover the essence, truth and strength of the dreams that once fuelled the revolutions of the past.

Lenin's (his)story is full of challenges and adversity, but he remained steadfast in his conviction that humanity could achieve a higher state of equality and justice. It is this Leninist resilience, this intrepid faith in the transformative power of collective vision and action, that deserves to be re-examined on the occasion of this centenary. In a world marked by ever-growing inequalities and multiple intersecting global crises, the need to dream-fight (*sonhar-lutar*) must not be underestimated.

Yet, (re)believing in Lenin is not about blindly accepting all his proposals or ignoring the historical flaws in their implementation. Instead, it is about recapturing the spirit of questioning, of challenging the status quo, that Lenin embodied. It is about looking at the fundamental ideas that permeate his writings and asking ourselves how we can apply these principles in a relevant way in today's context. At a time when many of us feel increasingly disillusioned with the dominant political and economic order, it is crucial to revive the notion that it is possible to conceive and build a better future. The act of dreaming is thus not a sign of naivety, but a means of overcoming our intellectual pessimism about the possibility of genuine systemic alternatives. It is an expression of hope and the assertion that complacency is not an option. It is an affirmation that, despite all the challenges, we can and must shape our collective destiny.

Our reverence for Lenin today does not demand an unquestioning surrender to the socialism of Lenin's times, but rather symbolises the urgency of dismantling and reinventing current social structures in order to (finally) overcome inequality. This conviction resonates with the vision of the 'new wo/man' intrinsic to 20th century socialist and communist thought, which aimed at a profound metamorphosis of human essence in post-revolutionary society. Both perspectives converge in the search for more just and equitable societies, encouraging the bold exploration of new forms of governance, economic organisation and social interaction. The message is clear: it is imperative not just to change, but to seek genuine alternatives that transcend the constraints of pre-existing models.

By (re)believing in Lenin, we are invited to re-examine our own conceptions of justice, equality and progress, as well as our doubts, fears and hesitations. We are challenged to ask ourselves how we can contribute to building a radically more just world, where the ideals of freedom and solidarity are not mere words, but tangible realities in our daily lives.

In *What is to be done?*, Vladimir Ilyich reminds us of the essential need to dream, emphasising that it is through audacious imagination and action towards a more humane future that change becomes possible. This lasting legacy transcends the historical figure of Lenin as a leader, echoing as a timeless call to persist in the search for a better world, even in the face of adversity. It is in dreams that the eternal flame of transformation resides, where what some call utopia becomes the path we follow, daring to mould a more just and equal today-tomorrow. After all, as the great Brazilian *comunista* architect Oscar Niemeyer reminds us: "*É preciso sonhar, senão as coisas não acontecem*" – it is necessary to dream, otherwise things won't happen.

Marcela Magalhães has a PhD in Iberian Studies/Postcolonial Literature and writes on politics for various media in Italy and Brazil.

Translated from the Brazilian Portuguese by hjje.

64. Lenin and the Deep History of Inner Eurasia

Marcus Bajema

On 18 April 1919 Lenin signed a decree establishing the Russian Academy of the History of Material Culture (RAIMK), giving birth to Soviet archaeology[1] – with two main consequences. First, there was an enormous expansion of archaeological research as both the young and the mature Soviet state invested heavily in science. Tsarist Russia had previously seen high-quality research, but on such a limited scale that Soviet archaeologists were able to revolutionise the understanding of Inner Eurasia by discovering hitherto unknown ancient cultures and civilisations, such as the 'Bactria-Margiana Archaeological Complex' uncovered by Sarianidi.[2] Second, and just as important, was that Soviet archaeologists needed to rethink how the long-term history of Inner Eurasia, roughly coterminous with the territory of Tsarist Russia and the USSR, had to be understood. Early Russian archaeologists had adopted the cultural historical approach initially developed in Scandinavia and widely applied in Europe, which recognised distinct cultures that were increasingly identified with ethnicity.[3] The key then was to find enough archaeological remains to establish such cultures, and to relate them to other cases that could be securely dated such as ancient Egypt.

In the 1920s and early 1930s, however, Soviet archaeologists proposed novel approaches to apply Marxism to their discipline. One group developed the 'ascending method,' which started from the archaeological remains themselves to work up to productive forces, the relations of production, and to the political and ideological superstructures.[4] This method lost out to a rival scheme of the endogenous unfolding of universal stages of social development, later codified in the Stalinist *Short Course* with the 'five set' or *pyatichlenka*, from the primitive-communal stage to the slaveholding, feudal, capitalist and socialist modes of production.[5]

Some positive developments came from this approach, such as the interpretation of social relations from settlement and burial evidence that would not be applied in Western archaeology until the 1960s.[6] In the main, however, the *pyatichlenka* was more of an ideological concept applied to scientific evidence, rather than being open to criticism and revision.

---

1 Klejn, Leo (2012), *Soviet Archaeology: Trends, Schools, and History*. Oxford: Oxford University Press, 15.
2 Kohl, Philip (2007), *The Making of Bronze Age Eurasia*. Cambridge: University of Cambridge Press, 241-242.
3 Trigger, Bruce G. (2006), *A History of Archaeological Thought: Second Edition*. Cambridge: University of Cambridge Press, 230-232.
4 Klejn 2012: 240-243.
5 Persisting long after Stalin's death, see Markwick, Roger (2001), *Rewriting history in Soviet Russia: The politics of revisionist historiography, 1956-1974*. New York: Palgrave Macmillan, 45-46.
6 Trigger 2006: 334-336.

Archaeological cultures and even languages previously seen as unique were now subsumed under universal stages. In this way, the traditional interpretive frameworks of archaeology and linguistics were turned upside down, while the Japhetic theory of Nikolai Marr was applied in a way that was often questionable in terms of objective scientific practice.[7]

In 1950, Stalin criticised Marr in his *Marxism and Problems of Linguistics*.[8] Partially this was due to a change in official Soviet ideology and policy as a result of which a new emphasis was placed on the origins and history of Slavic peoples.[9] Thus, traditional cultural-historical and linguistic methods again came to the fore, coexisting with the new Marxist approaches. This in turn led to Soviet archaeology becoming a patchwork of sequences of development in distinct geographical or cultural areas.[10] Consequently, even the best of scholars were at a loss to make sense of the interactions between these regions, much less of the overall long-term history of what preceded the USSR and Tsarist Russia.[11]

In the end, it was not so much ideas and theories, but the actual study of the material remains that provided the solution. Evgeny Chernykh used the results of the analysis of many thousands of metallurgical samples to provide a new interpretation of what he called the "Early Metal Age" of Eurasia. He argued that it was possible to recognise strong similarities in the forms and manufacturing techniques in areas stretching for thousands of kilometres and persisting for centuries. He named such patterns "metallurgical provinces," consisting of different metal-producing and metal-working zones, often occupied by distinct cultures. According to Chernykh, the use of metals combined with the domestication of plants and animals of the earlier Neolithic revolution engendered a "complex productive economy."[12] How this worked can be seen in the first metallurgical province recognised by him, the 'Carpatho-Balkan Metallurgical Province' (CBMP). After the initial domestication of cereals, sheep and goats, among others, spread from the Fertile Crescent, other areas took the lead. It was in the Balkans that metallurgy proper first developed in the fifth millennium BCE,[13] with copper mines like Ai Bunar supplying ores for the production of as much as 1,000 tonnes of smelted copper.[14]

---

7 Klejn 2012: 202-203.
8 See Stalin, J.V. (1950), "Marxism and Problems of Linguistics," *Marxists Internet Archives*.
9 Klejn 2012: 32-35.
10 As can be seen in the overview of Soviet archaeology in Mongait, Alexander (1959), *Archaeology in the U.S.S.R.* Moscow: Foreign Languages Publishing House.
11 The famous Australian Marxist archaeologist Vere Gordon Childe in the 1950s provided a devastating critique of the state of Soviet archaeology. Among his criticisms was the lack of a reliable chronology, which did not allow him to make any sense of Russian prehistory (Klejn 2012: 172). On the other hand, it might also be that the substance of Inner Eurasian prehistory was simply too different from Childe's experience with its European counterpart.
12 Chernykh, Evgeny (1992), Ancient Metallurgy in the USSR: The Early Metal Age. Cambridge: Cambridge University Press, 4-5.
13 See Radivojevic, Miljana, Benjamin Roberts, Miroslav Radic, Julka Kuzmanovic Cvetkovic and Thilo Rehren (eds.) (2021), The Rise of Metallurgy in Eurasia: Evolution, Organisation, and Consumption of Early Metal in the Balkans. Oxford: Archaeopress.
14 Chernykh, Evgeny (2017), *Nomadic Cultures in the Mega-structure of the Eurasian World*. Brighton: Academic Studies Press, 122.

Analysing the chemical composition of metal samples, it was determined that this copper was used not just in the Balkans but exported to the steppes of modern day Ukraine and Russia – a metallurgical province covering an area of 1.4 million square kilometres in the later fifth millennium BCE.[15] As such, the CBMP encompassed different modes of production and social formations, from the class differentiation evident at Varna and Durankulak on the Bulgarian Black Sea coast to the more egalitarian Cucuteni-Tripolye sites of the Ukrainian steppe, to the lesser-known pastoralists of southern Russia. Unfortunately, the precise means of exchange of metals within the CBMP zone is not yet well understood, but some form of a 'prestige exchange system' can be credibly inferred.[16]

A succession of new metallurgical provinces followed the eventual demise of the CBMP, marked by important shifts in technology, as well as the scale and spatial extent of metal production. In the first millennium BC the shift from bronze to iron, more plentiful and evenly distributed, led to the obsolescence of the metallurgical province as a unit of historical analysis. Instead different systems of long-distance interaction emerged, such as the Greek and Phoenician worlds of commerce and city-states, the great empires of the Middle East and later the Mediterranean, but also the vast Scythian world on the steppe.

There is never, then, one single unit of history, neither the archaeological cultures modelled on the nation states of 19th-century Europe nor the autochthonous unfolding of stages of development in this or that region. None of these cultures and regions were ever independent to begin with, but were always part of larger, interacting wholes such as Chernykh's metallurgical provinces. History is bewildering. And as it is for us today, so it was for Lenin when he grappled with the analysis of Russia's capitalist path and the transition to socialism. Tsarist and early revolutionary Russia presented him with a variety of socio-economic formations (*uklady*).[17]

Lenin showed how these different formations were in the end connected to the birth and development of Russian capitalism, for instance, through the phenomenon of "buyer-up."[18] Here we see not fixed ethnic particularities or evolutionary stages, but rather a 'world' of interwoven socio-economic phenomena that shared a common fate (of developing towards industrial capitalism) but at the same time retained some independence. Soviet historians of the 1960s and 1970s re-engaged with these ideas of Lenin under the banner of 'multistructuredness' (*mnogoukladnost*), emphasising also

---

15 Ibid: 116-117.
16 Kohl 2007: 38.
17 See Lenin, V.I. (1974), "Left-Wing Childishness and the Petty-Bourgeois Mentality," in *Collected Works Vol. 27*, Moscow: Progress Publishers, 335-336.
18 See especially section VI of chapter VI of Lenin's *The Development of Capitalism in Russia* as well as the discussion in Milios, John (1999), "Preindustrial Capitalist Forms: Lenin's Contribution to a Marxist Theory of Development," *Rethinking Marxism*, 11(4), 38-56.

their potentiality for drafting a non-capitalist path for a decolonised Africa and Asia.[19]

Despite all the crucial and undeniable differences between late Tsarist Russia and the CBMP, both contained a variety of distinct socio-economic formations that were linked, in highly distinct ways to be sure, by strong connecting threads. The 'multistructuredness' of Russia's recent past in fact stretches back for many millennia of Inner Eurasian history, and can be compared to similar but not identical processes in other world regions. By thinking about a plurality of historical worlds, both scientifically and in a Leninist, political way, we can thus both deny a singular path from prehistory to an 'end of history' and think again about how a non-capitalist path might take hold in our own globalised present.

Marcus Bajema, PhD (2015), Leiden University, is an independent scholar living in the Netherlands who has recently published Throwing the Dice of History with Marx *(Brill, 2023).*

---

19 Markwick 2001: 89-103, see also Monogarova, L.F. & B.V. Andrianov (1976), "Lenin's Doctrine of Concurrent Socioeconomic Systems and its Significance for Ethnography," *Soviet Anthropology and Archaeology*, 14(4), 3-26.

65. Ecological Leninism and Proletarian Agency

Matt Huber

It is often said we live in an age of crisis. So did Lenin. Crisis in Lenin's era meant inter-imperial rivalry and the catastrophe of World War I. While the prospect of a similar crisis always lurks in the background today, many socialists and Leninists agree the primary crisis of the 21st century is cascading ecological breakdown. Thus, it should be no surprise that leading Marxist thinkers are proposing new versions of ecological or climate Leninism to map out the expected revolutionary upsurges to come.

Andreas Malm's "Ecological Leninism" argues we must look carefully in the socialist tradition for models today. In an interview for *Jacobin*, he says, "The obvious choice [...] of using state power in a situation of chronic emergency is the anti-Stalinist Leninist tradition." Specifically, and elaborated in his book *Corona, Climate, Chronic Emergency*, Malm invokes the example of 'War Communism' when the Bolsheviks, after they had seized state power, in the context of civil war, expropriated land and property and attempted to implement an immediate transition to a communist economy.

In an essay for the socialist journal *Spectre*, "Climate Leninism and Revolutionary Transition," Kai Heron and Jodi Dean similarly explain how impending ecological emergency will thrust the question of *revolutionary transition* back into the fore, "There will be insurrections. Revolution is on the table." Rather than invoking the already-in-power Bolsheviks as their model, however, they acknowledge rightly our current problem is a lack of organised power. Thus, they insist "Climate Leninism" must be rooted in the formation of a revolutionary party organisation that lays the groundwork for the seizure of state power in the crisis conjunctures ahead: "We thus use Climate Leninism as the name for the politics needed at this conjuncture of imperialism and climate emergency. The revolutionary party is its basic premise." Their wager is that history does not move linearly or incrementally, but famously, as Lenin claimed, "in leaps." The revolutionary party of the future must be ready for the leaps to come.

What both these perspectives lack, and what we too often forget, is the foundation of Leninism and Marxism alike: what Mike Davis called Marx's theory of "proletarian agency," or the idea that only the working class has the strategic capacity to deliver the revolutionary transition that Malm, Heron, Dean and others so desperately seek. For Malm, state power is already assumed to implement 'war communism,' but how revolutionary socialists might find themselves in this position is not specified. Given his other writing in *How to Blow Up a Pipeline*, he definitely acknowledges the need for a "mass movement" but focuses most of his attention on a proscribed "radical flank" of militants engaging in sabotage and property destruction. Malm writes mostly as if the current youth-based climate movement will somehow scale up to "mass" status, but does not indicate much role for the traditional working class party, union or other such organisations. For Heron and Dean, the working class is simply absent – only mentioned partially and derisively: "Climate Leninism reminds us that we cannot – as many Marxists do – fetishize the industrialized, unionized, worker of the Global North." Rather than the proletarianized masses, Heron and Dean seem keen on fetishizing – as many self-styled academic revolutionaries do – land-based peasant and "indigenous and pastoralist leaders" as key actors in a "coalition of the oppressed."

In order to succeed politically, an Ecological Leninism for the 21st century must reassess the revolutionary agency of the proletariat – that is, the class separated from the means of production, most notably the land and the ecological means of subsistence itself. While the class composition of the proletariat has surely changed, we have witnessed a period of its enormous expansion with the proletarianization of China, the collapse of the Soviet Union and the depeasantization of much of the planet. A mere three decades ago, according to World Bank figures, 45% of the earth's labour force worked in agriculture. Today, the figure is around 25%. Lenin confronted a revolutionary situation in a predominantly peasant country; much of the world looks nothing like this today.

A proletarian Ecological Leninism might find more insight by revisiting an earlier Lenin of the "What is to be Done?" era. As Lars Lih's argues in his incisive contextualisation, *Lenin Rediscovered*, Lenin at the time was first and foremost "a Russian Social Democrat." He was a follower of Karl Kautsky, and the Social Democratic Party of Germany, whose entire orientation as expressed in the "Erfurt Program" emphasised the *democratic power of the emerging proletarian majority*. As Lih explains, in autocratic Russia, Lenin placed special importance on the struggle for *political freedom* and democratic rights. More specifically, Lenin subscribed, along with his social democratic Erfurtian comrades, to the 'merger formula,' which insisted revolutionary socialism could only emerge via a 'merger' between committed revolutionary leaders and the mass, working class movement.

Above all, Lenin believed revolutionary change only comes via *mass politics*. Late in his life, in *"Left-Wing" Communism: An Infantile Disorder*, he famously declared that revolutionary change requires that "…one must not count in thousands […] in these circumstances one must count in millions and tens of millions." It is precisely this mass orientation rooted in the 'merger formula' that is so lacking among the middle class left and socialist revolutionaries today. Lenin's description of socialists detached from the workers' movement, as quoted by Lih, applies to many self-styled 'ecosocialists' today: "…the socialists kept their distance from the worker movement and created teachings that criticized the contemporary capitalist bourgeois social system and demanded the replacement of that system with a higher, socialist system." Isolated on college campuses or within undemocratic NGOs, these radical ecosocialists often diagnose rightly the need for 'system change not climate change' but seem more concerned with the moral purity of their advocacy for the 'Global South' (a quite wide abstraction) or 'marginalised frontline communities' than with directly engaging the proletarianized majority that possesses the social power to confront the cause of ecological crisis (capital).

In conclusion, an Ecological Leninism that vaguely calls for a 'coalition of the oppressed' or assumes we can conjure in the next decade revolutionary war communism from above, ultimately sidesteps how we must build a broad-based and popular working class ecological politics. In 2023, fossil capital posts record profits while the world burns, and political leaders act as if this is completely out of our collective control. What other force besides the global proletariat has the potential social power to reverse this situation? Such a politics must necessarily begin with the primary ecological threat to proletarian life: the insecurity of market-based survival itself. Thus, a green agenda rooted in universal public goods like energy, housing and transport could speak to what the 'Yellow Vest' movement called 'end of the month' struggles (as opposed to the elites concerned with the 'end of the world'). The public provision of working-class necessities around a broader decarbonisation program could also enrol the democratic participation of workers themselves in the collective definition of needs. But no such program will come about without the agency of workers to engage in strike action, create political crises, and organise around a set of core political demands that resonate with and mobilise the broad masses. This is an Ecological Leninism worthy of his name.

Matthew T. Huber is a Professor in the Department of Geography and the Environment at Syracuse University and the author of Climate Change as Class War *(2022, Verso).*

66. Lenin Against Stalin: The National Question

Michael Löwy

In this strange 21st century, in this world given over to 'ethnic cleansing,' tribal wars, and to the fierce rivalry of financial sharks for control of the world market, it is not without interest to revisit Lenin's dream and that of his comrades: a free socialist federation of autonomous republics. In numerous texts before 1917, Vladimir Ilyich had always fought for the right to self-determination of the different nations that made up the Tsarist Empire. Consequently, barely a week after taking power, the October revolutionaries published a declaration which solemnly affirmed the equality of all the peoples of Russia and their right to self-determination up to the point of secession. The new Soviet power would fairly quickly recognise – in part, as a fait accompli, but also due to an authentic desire to break with imperial practices and recognise national rights – the independence of Finland, Poland and the Baltic countries (Lithuania, Latvia, Estonia). The fate of Ukraine, the nations of the Caucasus and other 'peripheral' regions, on the other hand, would be decided over the course of the civil war, with, in most cases, a victory for the 'local' Bolsheviks, aided to differing extents by the new Red Army in the process of becoming.

Concerning Ukraine, here is what Putin, this worthy heir of the Romanovs, declared in a speech on February 22, 2022, justifying the invasion that would take place a few weeks later:

> So let me start with the fact that modern Ukraine was created entirely by Russia, or more precisely, by Bolshevik and Communist Russia. The process began almost immediately after the 1917 revolution, and Lenin and his comrades-in-arms did it in a very crude way to Russia itself – through secession, tearing away parts of its own historical territories. (...) From the point of view of the historical destiny of Russia and its people, the Leninist principles of state building were not only a mistake, they were, as we say, even worse than a mistake.

In this speech Putin demonstrates his preference for Stalin, who aimed to build "a unified state," and against Lenin, who proposed "odious and utopian fantasies inspired by the revolution." Continuing his virulent polemic against Vladimir Ilyich, Putin added:

> Bolshevik policy resulted in the emergence of Soviet Ukraine, which even today can rightly be called 'Vladimir Lenin's Ukraine.' He is its author and architect. (...) It was Lenin's ideas on an essentially confederative state structure and on the right of nations to self-determination up to the point of secession that formed the foundation of the Soviet state: first in 1922, they were enshrined in the Declaration of the Creation of the Union of Soviet

Socialist Republics, then, after the death of Lenin, in the 1924 Constitution of the USSR.

In fact, Ukraine did not 'secede' but, following the victory of the 'reds' in the civil war in this region of the former Empire, joined the USSR as an autonomous nation. The Bolsheviks simply recognised Ukraine as a nation separate from Russia – as they did with many other nations-cum-republics of the Soviet Union. Putin's reactionary speech is thus an unintentional homage to Lenin's progressive nationalities policy.

It was particularly over the national question that the confrontation between Lenin, already seriously ill, and Stalin took place in 1922-23: "Lenin's last struggle," according to the title of Moshe Lewin's famous book. While Lenin insisted on the need for a tolerant attitude towards peripheral nationalisms, and denounced "Great-Russian chauvinism," Stalin saw centrifugal national movements as the main adversary and strove to build a unified and centralised state apparatus.

Conflict also arose over the degree of autonomy to be allowed to the Soviet Republic of Georgia in the emerging Soviet Union. Beyond specific local questions, the issue at stake was quite simply the future of the USSR. In a late and desperate struggle against the Great Russian chauvinism of the growing bureaucratic apparatus, Lenin devoted his last moments of lucidity to confronting its main leader and representative: Joseph Stalin. In notes dictated to his secretary in December 1922, Lenin denounced the Great Russian chauvinistic spirit of this "rascal and tyrant, such as the typical Russian bureaucrat is," and the attitude of a certain "Georgian [...] who carelessly flings about accusations of 'nationalist-socialism' (whereas he himself is a real and true 'nationalist-socialist,' and even a vulgar Great-Russian bully)." In fact, he did not hesitate to openly name the People's Commissar for Nationalities: "I think that Stalin's haste and his infatuation with pure administration, together with his spite against the notorious 'nationalist-socialism,' played a fatal role." Returning to the Georgian affair, Lenin insisted: "The political responsibility for all this truly Great-Russian nationalist campaign must, of course, be laid on Stalin and Dzerzhinsky."

While Stalin's approach was fundamentally statist and bureaucratic – strengthening of the apparatus, centralisation of the State, administrative unification – Lenin was above all concerned with the international scope of Soviet policy: "the harm that can result to our state from a lack of unification between the national apparatuses and the Russian apparatus is infinitely less than that which will be done not only to us, but to the whole International, and to the hundreds of millions of the peoples of Asia, which is destined to follow us on to the stage of history in the near future." For him, nothing would be as dangerous for the world revolution as "when we ourselves lapse, even if only in trifles, into imperialist attitudes towards oppressed nationalities, thus undermining all our principled sincerity, all our principled defence of the struggle against imperialism." The conclusion of what came to be known as "Lenin's testament" was, as we know, the proposal to replace

Stalin as the head of the General Secretariat of the Party. Alas, it was too late... Lenin's immobilisation by another stroke at the beginning of 1923 removed the main obstacle to Stalin's control of the party apparatus.

The struggle of Ukraine against Putin's "Great-Russian chauvinist" war of conquest illustrates the relevance of Lenin's democratic views on the right of nations to self-determination in our times.

Michael Löwy, born in Brazil in 1938, has lived in Paris since 1969, and is presently emeritus research director at the CNRS (National Centre for Scientific Research); his books and articles have been translated into thirty languages.

Translated from the French by hjje.

67. Lenin and the Invention of Politics

Michael Neocosmos

The fact that Lenin's thought still elicits interest 100 years after his death is surely indicative of its central importance in world history. That he was the core thinker and guide of the first successful socialist revolutionary transformation in the world is, of course, the main reason for this. This does not mean that Lenin was always right, but rather that such study allows us to understand the core features of this first successful development of a revolutionary politics. What is arguably the case is that Lenin was indeed the first to develop a conception of emancipatory politics as a distinct thought-practice with its own rationality which was informed by, but irreducible to, political economy. It is in this sense that Lenin can be said to have been the inventor of politics.

So what is revolutionary (emancipatory) politics? How can such a politics be thought? Lenin's answer consists in demarcating the proletariat politically, i.e., he develops a way of thinking the slogans and actions which will constitute the proletariat as a political subject. His core orientation is structured around three broad principles: first to build a political party that will represent the working class in the political arena; second to outline and fight for a uniquely dialectical proletarian politics, the horizon of which was to be a communist future; and third to insist on the party showing confidence in the independent action of the broad masses and not just that of the working-class.

I will not discuss the first principle as it is well known and has been debated at length other than to recall that, after much reflection, Lenin in 1902 proposed a solution to the disastrous defeat of the Paris Commune in the form of a vanguard party of professional revolutionaries, which was meant to address a universalistic political outlook of opposition to the entire socio-political capitalist order that is distinct from the particularism of trade unions.

Much less well known is Lenin's consistent development of an original political subjectivity which can be said to have been uniquely proletarian in orientation. This is the second principle underlying Lenin's thought of politics, and it consists first of all in his insistence on thinking a political theory and practice that would demarcate the proletariat politically from all other classes and their parties, including others on the 'left.' In this way, the proletariat was to acquire a clear *political* physiognomy unique to it so that it may become a political subject via its party. That is to say, not only must the party be able to address all important political issues of the day, but it had to do so in a manner that secured the greatest advantage for all the oppressed. Second, what was unique to proletarian politics was thus not so much the party form of organisation, but rather the devising of a political thought-practice which was uniquely political; in other words, the devising of a politics which was not reducible to economic trends however progressive they may be, for it was such reduction that led to bourgeois politics. This thought-practice prioritised what was of importance for the benefit of the broadest sections of working people (including the peasantry) and thus had to fight for the deepest and most extensive forms of democracy, because "Marxists know that democracy ... makes the class struggle more direct, wider, more open and pronounced, and this is what we need."[1] It is in this context that Lenin develops a political critique of what he terms "economism." For Lenin, politics is not derivative, it must be developed on the understanding of what the proletariat was striving for in the future.

Two important examples from his writings serve to illustrate this: what was known as the debates on the "agrarian question" (1907-8) and much later what came to be known as the "national question" (1916-22) both internationally and within the Russian Empire itself. In the former case, despite the economically progressive capitalist expansion of landlord property, and contrary to the Mensheviks, land had to be expropriated and redistributed to peasants as it was democratically necessary to do so, for this would sweep aside all remnants of feudal relations and enable modern peasant accumulation on a democratic basis. In the second case, the right of nations to self-determination had to be strictly adhered to by Marxists because it was the only progressive democratic position to take into account the oppressive conditions of imperialist domination of colonised nations. The economic tendency towards monopolies and larger imperial entities may have been economically advanced but it was politically reactionary, and oppressive of the democratic yearnings of the masses.

Crucially "one should know how to *combine* the struggle for democracy and the struggle for the socialist revolution, *subordinating* the first to the second. In this lies the whole difficulty; in this is the whole essence."[2] The politics of the present should be subordinated to the future goal one aimed for, thus: "victorious socialism cannot consolidate its victory and bring humanity to the withering away of the state without implementing full democracy."[3] In other words, democracy is not advocated for itself but for what it will enable.

Emancipatory politics for Lenin then consist in addressing current struggles in such a way that they are subordinated in thought and practice to a communist vision of the future. Democratic demands are conceptualised and pursued in relation to the attainment of socialism; struggles within socialism (the dictatorship of the proletariat over the bourgeoisie along with the broadest forms of democracy for the masses) are pursued in relation to facilitating the withering away of the state (communism). Thus, Lenin's political thought is oriented towards a future to which the present can only lead if politics are correctly handled; or again more abstractly, his conception

---

1 Lenin, V.I. (1974), "A Caricature of Marxism and Imperialist Economism," in *Collected Works Vol. 23*, Moscow: Progress Publishers, 73.
2 Lenin, V.I. (1973), "To Inessa Armand," in *Collected Works Vol. 35*, Moscow: Progress Publishers, 267, emphasis in original.
3 Lenin 1974: 74.

can be said to be dialectical because it enables a process of the becoming of the proletariat as a political subject with a view to universalising popular egalitarian conceptions throughout a society in constant change. It is this openness to egalitarianism (and this is the third principle underlying his politics) which pushes Lenin to advise "don't be afraid of the people's initiative and independence. Put your faith in their revolutionary organisations"[4] – hence also his 1917 slogan "All Power to the Soviets" – and to remind his comrades that "every ... workers' gain, can only be secure when it is based on the independent action of the working people themselves, on their own organisation, on their endurance and revolutionary determination."[5]

Finally, it is the inherent dialectic character of Lenin's politics which disables any form of dogmatism, for any political position taken by the party must be founded on a detailed understanding of all the aspects of a given problem: "dialectics requires an all-round consideration of relationships in their concrete development."[6] Unsurprisingly, when "the Party is sick"[7] Lenin turns to the broad masses for a solution. For Lenin, it is imperative to understand the future in the present, not to think in terms of self-contained stages, but rather to insist that "politics ... take precedence over economics. To argue otherwise is to forget the ABC of Marxism."[8]

To sum up, given the weakness today of emancipatory political thought, it is thus crucially important to return to Lenin, to elucidate how he went about developing his politics, to learn from it, to retain what is relevant and to discard what is obsolete for the benefit of current popular struggles for freedom.

Michael Neocosmos is Emeritus Professor in Humanities at Rhodes University, South Africa and a lifelong militant in emancipatory struggles. He is currently writing a book entitled Transcending our Colonial Place: Africa and the dialectics of emancipation.

---

[4] Lenin, V.I. (1974), "One of the Fundamental Questions of the Revolution," in *Collected Works Vol. 25*, Moscow: Progress Publishers, 374.
[5] Lenin, V.I. (1974), "Speech at a meeting of Delegates from the Poor Peasants' Committees of Central Gubernias," in *Collected Works Vol. 28*, Moscow: Progress Publishers, 172.
[6] Lenin, V.I. (1973), "Once again on the Trade Unions, the current situation and the mistakes of Trotsky and Bukharin," in *Collected Works Vol. 32*, Moscow: Progress Publishers, 91.
[7] "The Party Crisis," Ibid: 43.
[8] "Once again...," Ibid: 83.

68. President Putin is somewhat right[1]

Michał Kozłowski

> *Yesterday Lenin came, and up to today he has been here four times already. I enjoy talking with him, he's clever and well educated, and has such an ugly mug, the kind I like to look at.*
> (Rosa Luxemburg to Kostya Zetkin)[2]

On February 21, 2022, on the eve of his attack on Ukraine, President Putin floated historiosophical musings on the origin of nations: "Soviet Ukraine is the result of the Bolshevik's policy and can rightfully be called 'Vladimir Lenin's Ukraine.' He was its creator and architect." This was not praise of Vladimir Ilyich, on the contrary Lenin's actions were supposed to be "extremely harsh on Russia – by separating, severing what is historically Russian land." Lenin created Ukraine like God created woman – from a Russian rib. Mr Putin must be well aware of Ulyanov's demiurgical powers. After all, his office is seated on top of Lenin's dead body, miraculously preserved in nearly immaculate form. "They have been concerned with maintaining not the body's biological flesh, but its physical form. This form includes the body's look, shape, weight, and colour, as well as its dynamic characteristics – its overall suppleness, elasticity of skin, flexibility of joints, internal pressure in muscle tissues" – notes scrupulously an anthropologist. Sceptics claimed that what is left is only 10% of his body, but were rebutted by an independent investigation that showed the mummy contained as much as much as 23% of the corpse.[3]

Regardless of which number is correct Ukrainians seemed unimpressed. They coined the term Ленінопад (*Leninopad*, 'Leninfall') to describe the process of destruction of Lenin's monuments once profusely scattered throughout the land, which began in earnest after the Russian annexation of Crimea in 2014. Thus, in 2022, the invading Russian army engaged in the highly confusing practice of reinstating monuments of Mother Russia's great tormentor. President Putin may be solemnly overstating Lenin's role in creating modern Ukrainian identity, but he is not wrong when he claimed Lenin was harsh on Russia.

Ulyanov emphatically quotes Chernyshevsky's description of Russia as "a wretched nation, a nation of slaves, from top to bottom – all slaves." And he spices it up: "Nobody is to be blamed for being born a slave; but a slave who not only eschews a striving for freedom but justifies and eulogises his slavery (e.g., calls the throttling of Poland and Ukraine, etc., a 'defence of the

---

1 Ironic disclaimer: the views on the nature of Russian imperialism expressed in this memo are not those of President Putin or the author. Nor should they be associated with the views of the contemporary radical left. They are solely the opinions of V.I. Lenin.
2 Luxemburg, Rosa (2011), *The Letters of Rosa Luxemburg*. New York: Verso, 298.
3 See Yurchak Alexei (2015), "Bodies of Lenin: The Hidden Science of Communist Sovereignty," *Representations*, 129, 116-157.

fatherland' of the Great Russians) – such a slave is a lickspittle and a boor, who arouses a legitimate feeling of indignation, contempt, and loathing."[4] Ulyanov believed that the socialist task was to combat nationalism of every kind, but above all, Great-Russian nationalism. This unequal treatment of nationalisms was not accidental. According to Lenin Russia was not the world's only imperialist power but she definitely "set a world record for the oppression of nations with an imperialism that is much more crude, medieval, economically backward and militarily bureaucratic."

Lenin was in fact obsessed with the idea of decolonising the Russian empire at any cost. Not everyone agreed. Rosa Luxemburg, the leader of the Polish social democrats vigorously opposed separatism as a vehicle for Polish nationalism. The brawl between the two promising revolutionaries attracted much attention among European socialists. Trotsky recalls: "As a pupil of Rosa Luxemburg, Dzerzhinsky spoke against the right of nations to self-determination, accusing Lenin of protecting separatist tendencies which weakened the Russian proletariat. To Lenin's answering accusation of giving support to Great-Russian chauvinism, Dzerzhinsky answered: 'I can reproach him (Lenin) with standing at the point of view of the Polish, Ukrainian and other chauvinists.' This dialogue is not without a political piquancy: the Great-Russian Lenin accuses the Pole, Dzerzhinsky, of Great-Russian chauvinism directed at the Poles, and is accused by the latter of Polish chauvinism."[5] Despite the "piquancy" involved Lenin had no dilemmas: "in her fear of the nationalism of the bourgeoisie of oppressed nations, Rosa Luxemburg is actually playing into the hands of the Black-Hundred nationalism of the Great Russians." That is, for Lenin, Russian nationalism is always the greater evil. Sometimes even greater than the bourgeoisie itself: "The bourgeois nationalism of any oppressed nation has a general democratic content that is directed against oppression, and it is this content that we unconditionally support,"[6] wrote Lenin in 1914.

Vladimir Illich was not in the habit of weighing his words. In 1922 during the conflict on nationality policies he called his dear comrades Dzerzhinsky and Stalin "Great-Russian chauvinists." In October of the same year, in one of the last memos sent to the Politburo, he solemnly pledged: "I declare war to the death on Great Russian chauvinism. I shall eat it with all my healthy teeth as soon as I get rid of this accursed bad tooth." The tooth, however, never healed and the war never took place. Lenin was declining in health, which the comrades took advantage of to remove him from state affairs. He died soon thereafter and was mummified.

Some say Lenin's extravagant Russophobia came from an early grievance. After his brother was executed for rebellion against the Tsar, Russian 'educated society' in his hometown Simbirsk turned its back on the

---

4 Lenin, V.I. (1974), "On the National Pride of the Great Russians," in *Collected Works Vol. 21*, Moscow: Progress Publishers, 104 (translation altered).
5 See Trotsky, Leon (2017), *History of the Russian Revolution*. London: Penguin, 329.
6 All quotes are taken from Lenin, V.I. (1977), "The Right of Nations to Self-Determination," in *Collected Works Vol. 20*, Moscow: Progress Publishers, 393-454.

whole family; they crossed to the other side of the street. Consequently, Lenin's family allegedly socialised with Chuvashs, Tatars, Polish exiles and even some Jews. This imperial rainbow-crowd allegedly infected him with a phobia of all things Great-Russian. But this may just be wicked tongues.

Michał Kozłowski is a philosopher, historian and sociologist. He works at the University of Warsaw.

69. Hiding

Minna Henriksson

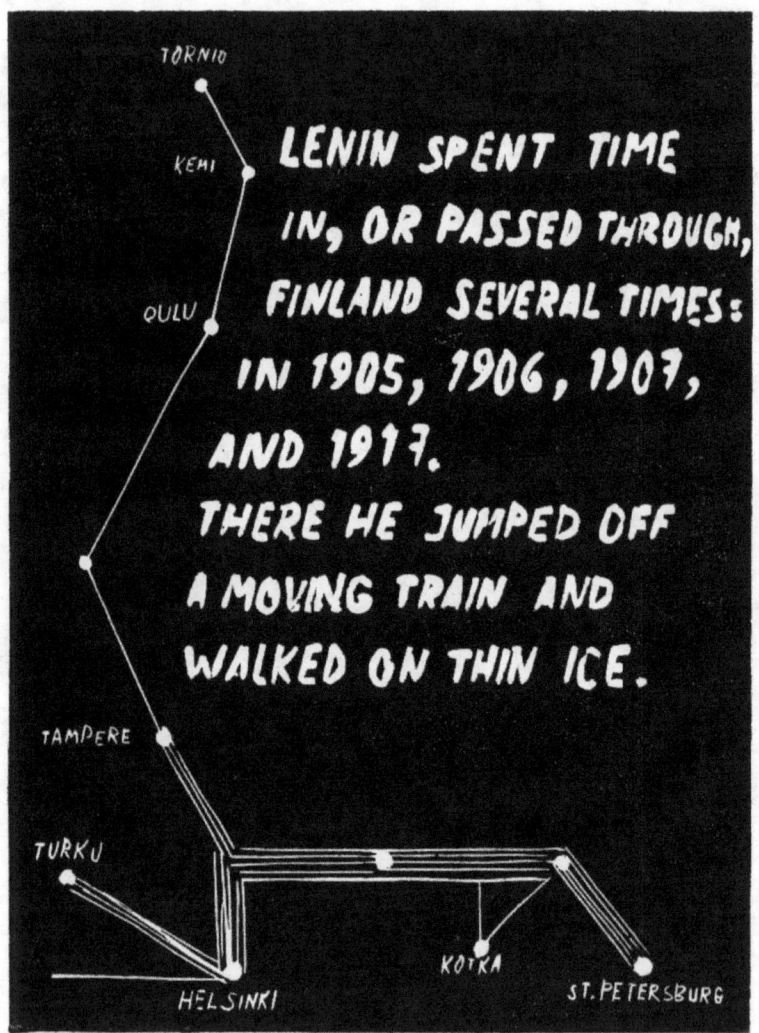

IN 1946, A LENIN MUSEUM OPENED IN TAMPERE. BETWEEN 1957 AND 1979 TWO OUTDOOR STATUES, ELEVEN MEMORIAL PLAQUES, AND A PARK WERE ESTABLISHED TO COMMEMORATE HIM.

Over the past decade artist Minna Henriksson (b. 1976, lives in Helsinki) has made several installations in Finland, Estonia and Latvia, including in the Tampere Lenin Museum, based on her observations of disappearance of commemorations to Lenin.

70. Thinking (In) the Conjuncture

Natalia Romé

I.

What could Lenin offer us today? Is there a way in which his thought, like a living anachronism, can usher in a fresh breeze?

If yes, then likely in the form of his persistent concern, expressed in various ways, to think together that which does not allow itself to be easily linked. The difficult encounter between the heterogeneous and incommensurable forces of theoretical practice – the methodical, Lenin might say – and the political, is one of the pillars of his thought, as expressed in classic texts such as *Materialism and Empirio-criticism*, on the risks of leftist declarations based on right-wing theoretical positions such as those of the Machian Otzovists, as well as more marginal texts, such as the 1920 "The Tasks of the Youth Leagues," where he explores the inherent tensions in the encounter between tradition and practical experimentation, a problem of particular importance in the training of future generations, on whom the construction of the communist society would fall.

There is thus no doubting Lenin's emphasis on the importance of theory as a "guide to action." Yet the complexity of this idea was generally evaded under the countless images that attributed to Lenin's thinking a rigid subordination of political practice to theory, which translated into top-down or vanguard strategies. Double confusion: equating the leader with the practice of thinking and the collective with the 'body' of action rests on an epistemological reduction of thought to theory and of politics to bare action. The price paid for this idealist treatment, against which Lenin wrote, expresses itself today in the multiple forms of profound disconnection between theoretical elaboration and concrete political experiences.

From this insistence on the impossible conjunction between theoretical thought and political-strategic thought, emerged one of Lenin's greatest legacies. Therefore, perhaps it is indeed time to step back into some of our 'old traditions,' because sometimes the future takes the form of a legacy that we must decipher in response to the questions of our current conjuncture.

II.

In the 1960s and 70s, in the context of the so-called 'crisis of Marxism,' Louis Althusser returned to Lenin as the architect of an exercise in attentive reading of the productive silences of the Marxist text, which Lenin unfolded, like creases in the fabric of history, thereby opening up heuristic potential for new elaborations.

The 'theoreticist' Althusser knew how to read in the 'theoreticist' Lenin the force of politics as the limit of theory. Excess upon excess, the Althusserian gesture allows the previously unseen to appear in Lenin's text, just as Lenin's reading revealed the unseen in Marx's text. An opening of theory before the Real of history, which points, in turn, to the unfinished condition of the latter. In *Materialism and Empirio-criticism*, Lenin does not fail to draw attention to the absolutely fundamental requirement that constitutes the specific function of Marxist philosophy, i.e. that of pointing out – in the words of Althusser and Balibar – that "a science only progresses, i.e., *lives*, by the extreme attention it pays to the points where it is theoretically fragile."[1] This fragility coincides precisely with the gaps in the theoretical inheritance in its *current* becoming.

Now, this place is the opening to political practice in the present. Lenin reads Marx as a *political* reader, that is, as a reader of the political force *in(side)* theory. A reader who reads politically and in that singular exercise, which is the action itself, recognises on the surface of theoretical discourse that which exceeds it. Only in this way does the "philosophy at work" in Marx's writing encounter the Real of history and makes of this Real the immanent and constitutive dislocation (*décalage*) of the materialist position in theory. That is what it means to produce theory, to persevere in theory in order to see what it can do and to verify in its *limits* that which no longer corresponds to it, because it is what unfolds from history itself in the moment of its practical imagination, of practice capable of transforming social matter.

It is the political reading, informed by the challenges of action in the concrete situation, which allows the theory to expose its "points of fragility." These points act as indications of its conjuncture. Lenin deliberately avoids all abstract generalities that blur the singularity of the conjuncture, considered as a mere field of the "practical application" of theory to a "case." Rather, in his consideration of the conjuncture, history enters into theory, whips it up, breaks it down and produces in its immanence the previously unseen of its explanatory and mobilising power.

III.

Political practice maintains its specificity when acting upon the concrete of the situation, as Lenin vehemently reiterates in his writings of April 1917. The "present moment" defines political practice as such and affects Marxist theory, thereby opening its spatio-temporal boundaries, because it concerns the disjunct unity between heritage and current task(s). Lenin asserts:

> "Our theory is not a dogma, but a guide to action," Marx and Engels always said, rightly ridiculing the mere memorising and repetition of "formulas," that at best are capable only of marking out *general* tasks, which are necessarily modifiable by the *concrete* economic and political conditions of each particular *period* of the historical process.[2]

Here lies, for Althusser that which

---

1 Althusser, Louis & Balibar, Etienne (2009), *Reading Capital*. London and New York: Verso, 31.
2 Lenin, V.I. (1964), "Letter on Tactics," in *Collected Works Vol. 24*, Moscow: Progress Publishers, 43.

is irreplaceable in Lenin's texts: the analysis of the structure of a conjuncture, the displacements and condensations of its contradictions and their paradoxical unity, all of which are the very existence of that 'current situation' which political action was to transform, in the strongest sense of the word, between February and October, 1917.[3]

In other words, political practice does not engage history in the same way as the *theoretical practice* of the historian, "who analyses the past." Politics in action makes of the present not the seat of the concept, but the space of its vacillation, not the connection with an expressive causality in which Truth presents itself as an essence finally recovered, but the space emptied of metaphysical guarantees, the paradoxical condition of a unity expressed in the displacements and condensations of a determination whose last hour never comes.

Exercising the *political* reading in the situation of its conjuncture, which is that of the political question about the task(s) to be done, Lenin expounds the profound epistemology of the materialist dialectic. In so doing, he induces inescapable effects in the philosophical field, effects that philosophy as such is not capable of absorbing because it is blind to its inherent politicity.

In sum, Lenin makes of politics an exercise of practical, agonal, unfinished, partisan reading, required by the singularity of his conjuncture. He reads in Marx the unfinished limit of his theory and the paradoxical assumption of politics as the practice and thought of the limit. And it is from this limit that Lenin turns to us, where theory assumes the form of an interplay between *norm and exception*, at the exact point where the theory of history cannot account for the singularity of the current moment if it does not understand itself as knowledge that tends to *intervene in the conjuncture*.

That is one of Lenin's greatest legacies. A *political* love for what is true. A love that we can and must recover as a heritage of the future.

Natalia Romé, PhD in Social Sciences, is a professor and researcher at the Gino Germani Institute, Faculty of Social Sciences, Universidad de Buenos Aires.

Translated from the Argentine Spanish by hjje.

---

[3] Althusser, Louis (2005), *For Marx*. London and New York: Verso, 79.

71. Eulogy of Lenine by a Cuban Marxist

Natasha Gómez Velázquez

"*Lenine ha muerto.*" Lenin is dead. The news circulated in the Cuban press and its most influential national and local newspapers for approximately 30 days.[1] Using the most common name by which the Bolshevik leader was known in Cuba at the time, various journalistic pieces described the days of mourning in Russia, the construction of the mausoleum and even possible struggles for power. There were also comments on the Bolshevik transition from utopia to reality, i.e. Lenin's adaptation of the originally envisioned socialist project to "backward" Russian conditions. Yet other texts spoke of Soviet socialism as a unique social experiment. Finally, the press reported the important decision of Mr. Antonio Bosch y Martínez, the socialist mayor of the town of Regla in Havana, to build a monument to Lenin, in recognition of his "immense social work" and for being a "citizen of the world." The historical site, known as *Colina Lenin* (Lenin Hill), remains to this day.

In fact, Russian issues had already had a certain presence in the media: The 1904/05 Russo-Japanese War; the Revolutions of 1905 and 1917; the nascent socialism. Magazines such as *Social* frequently wrote about events in Soviet Russia, for example, the Bolshevik celebrations of Tolstoy's centenary and the plan to publish all of his literary work.

It is in this context that one of the most prominent Cuban revolutionaries of the time, Julio Antonio Mella (1903-1929), decided to write about the death of *Lenine*. Today, Mella is considered, along with the Peruvian José Carlos Mariátegui, one of the most creative Latin American Marxists. Mella began his political activities as a student leader at the University of Havana, though his activism quickly went beyond the university environment. In 1925, he was one of the founders of the original Communist Party of Cuba (PCC), from which he was soon expelled due to his heterodox theoretical and practical interpretations of Marxism, which did not conform to party "discipline and statutes," as established by the Communist International. Mella, on the other hand, aimed to develop tactics and strategies of struggle informed by and appropriate to the Cuban context.

Shortly after, however, a Comintern official who discussed the 'Mella case' with PCC leaders in Havana stated that the expulsion was a mistake. Consequently, the party itself confirmed that: "We have received the resolution of the International..., in which the 'Mella case' was resolved. We are ordered to reconsider our ruling regarding the sentence imposed by the

---

[1] For a Spanish-language overview of some of the publications about the death of Lenin and other Soviet-related themes, see Gómez Velázquez, Natasha (2017), *Palabras de Lenin, conclusiones de hoy*. La Habana: Editorial Félix Varela.

Party's judgment." Subsequently, the organisation "resolves" to "readmit" Mella, reinstating all of his party duties and rights. ²

Returning to the year of Lenin's death, in February 1924, Mella wrote, "*Lenine coronado*" (Lenin crowned), a somewhat strange title that alluded to the post-mortem glorification by the bourgeois press of the Bolshevik leader. In particular, Mella referred to an article by "Yankee journalist" Arthur Brisbane, which had been widely circulated, and in which, now that Lenin's death was a fact, the author allowed himself to be condescending towards him.

In Mella's short text, one of his recurring theses is present: the possible revolution in Cuba has to be creative. Admiration of the Bolsheviks' work and achievements offered inspiration and experience, but socialism, Marxism, and revolutions had to be theorised and carried out according to historical contexts: "we do not intend to implant in our environment servile copies of revolutions made by other people in other climates. In some points we do not understand certain alien transformations, in others, our thinking is more advanced. In any case, we would be blind if we denied the step forward taken by humanity in the path of its liberation." He concludes by expressing that what is needed are "people who act based on their own thinking and by virtue of their own reasoning, not by the thinking and reasoning of others."³ It is this conviction, converted into political action, that later led to his ideological conflicts with the PCC. Yet, Mella was not only a man of thought, but his practical work as part of the student, workers', intellectual and communist movement was immense (especially if one bears in mind that he was murdered in exile in Mexico at the age of 26). Like Lenin, Mella understood very well that it was political subjects who organised and made revolutions. Perhaps for this reason, in his eulogy he highlighted that: "There were two phases in Lenin. A first phase: [marked by] the idea, followed by a second: [the idea put into] action, which characterises every great man. A first period of romantic dreams, and a second of the realisation of those dreams somewhat modified by contact with reality."

Apart from the eulogy, in many of Mella's other writings the works of "Nikolai" Lenin, "the most accurate and practical of the interpreters of Karl Marx," constitute an important reference point. This is evident in texts such as "*Por la creación de revolucionarios profesionales*" (Towards the creation of professional revolutionaries) and "*Nuestras enfermedades infantiles*" (Our infantile disorders). The titles chosen already indicate the Leninist genesis that inspired the young Cuban communist: "the professional revolutionary, if s/he is a [true] Marxist..., knows how to apply Marxism to all problems." As examples of "infantile disorders," Mella mentions the division between workers and intellectuals inside the Communist parties, and the introduction

---

2 For the "Mella case", see, e.g., Jeifets, Víctor L. & Schelchkov, Andrei A. (eds.) (2018), La Internacional Comunista en América Latina. En documentos del archivo de Moscú. Moscú-Santiago de Chile: Ariadna Ediciones.
3 For all Mella quotes, see Mella, Julio Antonio (2017), *Mella. Textos escogidos. Tomo I & II*. La Habana: Ediciones La Memoria, Centro Cultural Pablo de la Torriente Brau.

of "reformist" and "opportunist" ideology into these organisations. Echoing Lenin, what was needed was "to create workers of the revolution!" For him, as long as they were all Communists, there could not be any division between workers and intellectuals, because: "what is a communist? The sincere revolutionary who accepts the party program and contributes daily with their work to carry it out."

The following year, on August 6, 1925, in an act inspired by his admiration for the revolution in Russia, Mella visited the Soviet sailors of the *Vorovsky*, anchored in the port of Cárdenas (it had not been authorised to enter the port of Havana), waiting to be loaded with sugar produced by the "proletarians of the lands of Cuba." He identified himself with his membership card from the "*Agrupación Comunista de La Habana*," and was immediately received with the joy typical of comrades. Next, he was taken to the "Lenin Corner" with its "red-clothed table, its bookshelf, its portraits of Lenin, Marx and Vorovsky, the Martyr of Lausanne, and the red flags made of silk and gold given by the Uruguayan proletariat." And so, "*una tarde bajo la bandera roja* (one fine afternoon under the red flag)," Mella and the Soviet sailors talked about politics, the world revolution, Gorky, and ... the institution of marriage in the USSR, the latter now no longer "an eternal yoke born out of economic interest, but of love."

Perhaps it is in this sense that Mella, in his eulogy, refers to *Lenine* as someone who "in his time and circumstances was an advanced man, a superman, who with the power of his genius, knew how to give a powerful impulse to the transformation of a civilisation."

Natasha Gómez Velázquez is professor of the Theory and History of Marxism at the University of La Habana (Cuba).

Translated from the Cuban Spanish by hjje.

72. Lenin Will Rise Again Like a Phoenix

Naweed

As a young child, I witnessed the Soviet Union's occupation of Afghanistan. My father, a Maoist, recognising the growing danger to people like him, decided to flee with our family – by bus, truck and on foot – across the border into Pakistan. It was during this journey that I first experienced the bitter taste of migration, finding myself in remote areas lacking the most basic of life's necessities. In those tumultuous times, the Islamist Mujahideen groups were engaged in extensive propaganda in the many refugee camps against the 'Red Soviets.' Although I cannot pinpoint the exact moment, I first heard the name Lenin from the Mujahideen's constant use of it in this anti-Soviet propaganda; to most Afghans, "Lenin's descendants" had occupied Afghanistan and were responsible for massacring innocent people.

How did it come to this? In 1978, the People's Democratic Party of Afghanistan (PDPA), calling themselves Marxist-Leninist, seized power through a military coup and called on the population to defend the impending socialist revolution based on Lenin's theories. Afghanistan's populace, long oppressed and impoverished, was yearning for transformative change and the PDPA had initially lured people with the promise of *"Kor, Kali, Dodai"* ("Shelter, Clothes, Food" in Pashto), during the oppressive presidency of Dawood Khan (1973-1978), but once in power it ultimately delivered only "graves, shrouds, and bullets" to the vast majority of the people. Thousands of intellectuals, both left-wing and religious, as well as ordinary citizens, were imprisoned without trial, tortured and murdered, disappearing forever in secret mass graves. These atrocities forced countless Afghans to abandon their homes and seek refuge in neighbouring countries, with some of them joining the nascent Mujahideen groups determined to resist the 'red infidels,' with generous support from the West.

The USSR's occupation of Afghanistan in 1979, nominally to defend its 'communist' ally in the context of the Cold War, combined with the crimes committed by the PDPA and Soviet soldiers, deepened the people's general aversion to communist ideology, and in particular Leninism, because the PDPA leaders mentioned Lenin or Leninism in every single slogan. In addition, Western media waged an aggressive propaganda campaign against communism, equating it with murder, robbery, rape, torture and destruction, thereby distorting Marxism and Lenin's legacy in the minds of many Afghans.

However, despite this propaganda onslaught, several anti-Soviet Maoist groups held fast to their belief in Marxism-Leninism. The Great October Revolution led by Lenin and the subsequent Chinese Revolution led by Chairman Mao had played pivotal roles in first introducing and promoting socialist ideals in Afghanistan. Beginning in the 1950s and 60s, various groups, inspired by Lenin's ideas, engaged in political activism, even at the cost of imprisonment and torture. Their goal was to introduce Lenin's principles to workers, peasants and intellectuals, especially in urban centres, in a simple and understandable manner. One of these organisations, *Shola-e-Jawid* (Eternal Flame), soon became the most powerful Maoist movement, whose approximately fifty thousand members started demonstrations against the government but also clashed with the PDPA (founded in the 60s) and radical Islamist groups. In one of these confrontations, the most well-known Maoist poet at the time, Saidal Sokhandan, was shot dead in 1972 at Kabul University by Islamist radicals. Then, when the PDPA took power, most Maoist leaders such as Akram Yari and hundreds of rank-and-file Maoists were imprisoned and/or killed by successive PDPA governments. The remaining Maoists were thus forced to wage an underground struggle against the PDPA and, in fact, all subsequent Afghan regimes, continuing to this day.

It was during the late 1980s, when my family was part of a newly formed organisation that embraced Mao Zedong Thought, that I, along with my peers from the refugee camp – all of us not yet teenagers – began to receive a socialist education by reading short stories written by socialist writers for youth.

Many of these Marxist works in the Persian language entered Afghanistan from Iran, and I vividly recall the short story "When Will You Come Back, Big Brother?" by Ali Ashraf Darvishian, an Iranian left-wing writer, in which Lenin was mentioned. I questioned my teachers about this Lenin and his role as a leader of the Soviet Union and we learned about Lenin's role in launching the socialist revolution and disseminating Marxist ideas across the world. These classes were held in clandestine houses that had to be abandoned at the slightest suspicion that a neighbour might have found out and denounce our activities.

My first deep dive into Lenin's ideas, however, came through his text, "Three Sources and Three Components of Marxism," which, like a beacon, illuminated the path of Marxist thought for me and my comrades. We learned that to be a Marxist, one must be a materialist first. From that point on, Lenin was a constant presence in our discussions and daily life. We matured with Lenin's teachings, understanding that the only way to eliminate class society was through the socialist revolution and the dictatorship of the proletariat. This literally led to hundreds of young Marxists in Afghanistan sacrificing themselves for their convictions. The Afghanistan Liberation Organisation (ALO), the Maoist organisation to which I belonged after the demise of *Shola-e-Jawid*, had several secret military bases inside Afghanistan from which to launch the fight against the puppet government of the soon to be last 'communist' president, Dr. Najibullah. Hundreds of our cadres went to war and were killed.

After the fall of Najibullah's government in 1992 (the Soviet troops had withdrawn in 1989), and the subsequent eruption of civil war involving various Islamic factions in Kabul and across Afghanistan, my family and I moved to one of our organisation's own camps in Pakistan, with families coming from different parts of Afghanistan. This camp was unique in Pakistan, being the sole clandestine operation run by a Marxist-Leninist organisation. Within the camp, a series of classes focused on Marxism were conducted, catering to both beginners and those at advanced levels of understanding. My role was first as a student, but later I taught younger kids as well.

The curriculum centred on the foundations of Marxism, Leninism and Mao Zedong Thought. But it was not just about theory; it was about embodying the principles of a Marxist-Leninist way of life. The lives of the great leaders of the proletariat served as guiding examples. We imbibed their teachings, living simple lives, and showing kindness and sincerity when interacting with the less educated masses. Our commitment was to assist them in becoming literate and gradually raising their level of class consciousness while never placing ourselves above them. Consequently, in order to earn the camp population's trust, we actively engaged in building and repairing people's (mud) homes and provided medical care. When people saw the simple, proletarian lifestyle of our organisation's members, they recognised that we genuinely cared for the masses and did not consider ourselves separate from them.

These activities continued in various forms until the United States invaded Afghanistan on October 7, 2001, toppling the Taliban government. Following the fall of the Taliban, most Maoists returned to Afghanistan with their families. For the next 20 years, we seized the opportunity to re-engage (still clandestinely) in political activities, and began publishing newspapers and magazines with leftist ideas – using pen names – to expose the hypocrisy of American democracy and human rights claims, and to highlight the atrocities committed by NATO and US forces against the Afghan people. Simultaneously, the different Afghan Maoist groups, not always in agreement with each other, sought to integrate themselves into society, sharing Marxist ideas through the re-establishment of underground educational programs.

However, with the Taliban's return to power in August 2021, many of these groups were forced to curtail their activities. Some members went into hiding or were compelled to leave Afghanistan due to the imminent threat of arrest or harm by the Taliban. My family and I once again faced the painful experience of emigration, leaving our country behind to seek refuge in a foreign country, far from the people alongside whom we had worked for so long. Yet, I maintain contact with my comrades and continue my efforts to coordinate and collaborate with other leftist groups and organisations inside Afghanistan. Given the adverse context, our current, more modest goal is to create a unified nationwide organisation consisting of Marxist-Leninist revolutionaries, enabling us to actively contribute to the evolving political landscape of Afghanistan. Our final goal, however, has not changed: proletarian revolution.

In short, colossal anti-Leninist propaganda and decades-long catastrophic wars have not been successful in erasing Lenin's name from the minds of (not only) the Afghan masses. Lenin's legacy endures, and the world's proletariat will once again stand as a united front against imperialism and its servants. *Zendabad Lenin!* Long live Lenin!

Naweed is a member of the Afghanistan Revolutionary Organisation.

73. Lenin on the Moon

Nicholas Bujalski

Within the vast, neglected archives of Soviet visual culture – tucked away in Eurasian bookstores, piled on the stalls of provincial *barakholki*, lurking like digital ghosts in the remote corners of the internet – it is still possible, at times, to encounter peculiar pieces of space-age ephemera.

One of the most obscure and powerful works of this type is the 1960 painting *Lenin on the Moon* by Soviet-Ukrainian artist Vyacheslav Aleksandrovich Khovaev (1911-1977).

Artist: V.A. Khovaev

In the centenary year of V.I. Lenin's death, as we join our thoughts upon a century of 'Ilyich without Ilyich,' this strange image of a lost Soviet future might prove a fertile site for reflection.

Lenin's stern jaw emerging out of the lunar night, with industrious cosmonauts hard at work in the foreground and the 'pale blue dot' rising beyond... To begin: for those of us who grew up in lands on the opposite side of the 'Iron Curtain,' there's something that might feel visually familiar in Khovaev's piece.

This is a work from the heady years between the launching of Sputnik in 1957 and Yuri Gagarin's 1961 spaceflight, when American political cultures, too, set their sights on a future promising bold, interstellar feats. Indeed, the aesthetics here – the sharp lines and saturated colours of a slightly estranged realism – evoke the pulpy cover illustrations of U.S. science-fiction paperbacks from the same period. Not to mention the resonances this image holds with the presidential heads of Mount Rushmore: that peculiar artifact from the twilight of the 'heroic age' of the American bourgeoisie.

Furthermore, there's something to this piece that might appear *conceptually* familiar to viewers today. An initial interpretative glance at *Lenin on the Moon* seems to evoke many of the 'black legends' of bourgeois historiography. For – the petty demons of liberalism might whisper – isn't it obvious that this painting is simply another artifact of a socialist 'cult of personality'? A graven idol of Lenin, as sterile as the lunar soil from which it emerges; a Lenin entombed as a piece of dead heritage on the surface of a dead planet; a phantasmagoric corollary to Lenin's embalmed, lifeless body on Red Square? There is much grist for the mill here for the eternal Cold Warrior who would smugly paint Lenin as somehow both 'too volitional' (a Blanquist, a coup-mongerer, a power-hungry centraliser) and 'too mechanistic' (deterministic, cold, the worst son of the Second International). Isn't it both tyrannical and banal to envision the surface of the moon as simply another site for the rote reduplication of the body of 'the leader' – a spiritless, thankless labour, emerging from and itself witnessing the impoverished imaginary of the Soviet experiment as a whole?

But let us ward away these initial thoughts. Perhaps this liberal reading should be seen, instead, as symptomatic of the impoverished imaginary of our own twenty-first century.

In the United States, in the year 2024, the moon has never felt farther away. Today, even the flawed feats of the Apollo space missions – helmed as they were by the sons of officer families, private schools, and oil wealth; vibrating as they did with the inner strains of a white Christian nationalism – seem to have held a futurity far beyond anything within the reach of our present moment. Space travel in the year 2024 (when it is discussed at all) is now accepted to be little more than the preserve of 'public-private partnerships,' nationalist point-scoring, and the obscene leisure of Silicon Valley billionaires – with, as a faint promise, hopes of this 'final frontier' one day being opened up for resource extraction, speculative investment, and the privatisation of the cosmic commons.[1]

It can be difficult to grasp that, for Khovaev and his generation, things were quite different. These were people who inhabited a site of experience

---

[1] Cf. The popular internet meme "Born too late to explore the earth, born too early to explore the stars." Could we say that this phrase is not just another expression of the petty-bourgeois ennui of the imperial core, but also a worthy epitaph for our current regime of accumulation? One which, in the absence of new frontier zones and 'spatial fixes' of the type that outer space might offer, has embraced neoliberal cannibalization to ward off the tendency of the rate of profit to fall? Trapped upon an exhausted firmament, 'Accumulation by Dispossession' is engraved on the walls where Ugolino devours his children.

and a horizon of expectation truly alien to our own. The lunar surface, the sea of stars, the raw stuff of the future itself – all of this possessed a far more concrete, revolutionary, even tactile existence.

Khovaev was born in Eastern Ukraine in 1911, and over the course of his life he would have experienced 'the future' time and time again as an agitating energy and a living presence. Khovaev was from an age that had the cracked open the prison house of semi-feudal Romanov rule and had leapt into the actuality of building socialism; an age that had repelled the assaults of white guardists, foreign interventionists, and fascism's reactionary hypermodernism; an age that had just launched the first artificial satellite into the earth's orbit and which would soon lift a former foundryman (Y.A. Gagarin) and a textile worker (V.V. Tereshkova) into the cosmos. This was a generation that understood, and had lived, a natural through-line from 1917 to 1957: from proletarian revolution to the exploration of outer space, from the cruiser *Aurora* to the satellite *Sputnik*.

Khovaev's lunar fantasy is thus the product of a time when the future really existed, when it was a physical thing to be wrested with calloused hands from the dead grip of the past and shaped in startling new ways through collective labour and proletarian struggle. To adapt the words of the late David Graeber: *Lenin on the Moon* is a speculative vision produced in a time when the working-class imagination was a material force in human history.[2]

And in this sense, perhaps we should see our lunar Lenin's tremendous visage not as a sterile idol, nor a dead weight upon this 'line of flight,' but rather a guardian of the future's very conditions of possibility and a sigil of its eternal renewal.

The Lenin that Khovaev speculatively carves into the surface of the moon is the Lenin of the concrete analysis of the concrete situation; the Lenin who embraced the entire earth in its terrestrial totality with an eye for the weakest link in the imperialist chain; the Lenin who turned theory into a weapon in the hands of the dispossessed; the Lenin who strove to arm a counter-*Katechon* against a counter-revolution that, in our twenty-first century, reigns preemptively ascendant; the Lenin who affirmed the Dictatorship of the Proletariat as the only true vehicle through which human agency could begin to flourish against the millennial march of social domination.

This is Khovaev's *Lenin on the Moon* – this is the Ilyich envisioned as a watchful sentinel in the night sky, in permanent revolution around the earth.

***

But – of course – Khovaev's vision didn't come true. It gazes at us as an artifact from a past future, a future that passed, foreign and obscure. And as

---

2 Graeber, David (2012), "Of Flying Cars and the Declining Rate of Profit," *The Baffler*, 19.

this brief reflection has attempted to show, it can be extremely difficult to access the living energies that once coalesced into visions like this.

In the reigning imaginary in our year 2024 towards the cosmos – deferred, alienated, privatised – there is no room for Lenin on the moon. If Lenin does look down on us from anywhere through the dark night of space, it is perhaps only from Saturn – that most melancholy and dialectical of all the old celestial bodies, cast out and dethroned, lost amidst its long, weary wanderings.

But let us remember that, in Walter Benjamin's telling, the sorrow of Saturn holds a secret compact with the principle of hope: a traveller whose lonely course "embraces dead objects in its contemplation, in order to redeem them."[3] And just as Lenin lived, lives, and will live, so too might the now-foreign futurities of the Leninist project once more emerge from seemingly-infertile soils – even if working-class cosmonauts have not, as of today, carved Lenin's face into Selenian hills.

For although we dispossessed have yet to inherit the earth (or the moon), Althusser once took pains to remind us that "to change the world is not to explore the moon. It is to make the revolution and build socialism without regressing back to capitalism. The rest, including the moon, will be given to us in addition."[4]

Nicholas Bujalski is a Visiting Assistant Professor in the Department of History at Oberlin College, where he teaches courses on the Russian, Soviet and European revolutionary past.

---

3 Benjamin, Walter (1998), *The Origin of German Tragic Drama*. London: Verso, 157.
4 Althusser, Louis (1972), *Politics and History: Montesquieu, Rousseau, Hegel and Marx*. London: NLB, 186.

74. Lenin and Great Russian Chauvinism

Nigel C. Gibson

The past keeps fast hold of us, grasps us with a thousand tentacles,
and does not allow us to take a single forward step,
or compels us to take these steps badly.
(Lenin, 1919)

One of Lenin's last fights was against "Great Russian chauvinism" in his own party, the party of the revolution, the party which had not, like most of Europe's social democratic parties in 1914, betrayed the working class and international socialism by voting for the imperialist war. But now Great Russian chauvinism was threatening the Communist Party and the revolution.

Earlier in the debate on trade unions in 1920, Lenin had expressed a deep concern about the party's bureaucratisation and its "passion for bossing,"[1] arguing that the workers needed to be defended against their own state (which he called a "workers' state with bureaucratic distortions"). Both this and emphasis on the self-activity of revolutionary subjects connected with his philosophic concepts of national self-determination and revolution. Lenin insisted that socialism could not be introduced by party diktats but "only by tens of millions when they have learned to do it themselves."[2] In other words, "tens of millions" of workers and peasants had to become involved in participating in, deciding on, and determining the administration on a daily basis and thereby in the process of their own self-rule and self-determination. It was a difficult task, a task set by the revolution which was "not the product of a Party decision but [...] a revolution that the masses themselves create."[3]

Lenin was never under the illusion that somehow the great betrayal of social democracy in Europe and particularly the most powerful Marxist party, the German, did not also permeate the Bolsheviks. Indeed, great power chauvinism had an objective basis in the latest stage of capitalism, that is monopoly imperialism. The Marxist parties themselves were not immune since an aristocracy of labour was being produced in the imperialist countries, which became one of the bulwarks of the Second International. While Marx had written about the English workers' chauvinistic attitude towards the Irish as the source of the former's impotency, Lenin conceptualised the dialectics of history as the objectivity of a new subjectivity of self-determination. Rather than just a principle, the possibility of new anti-imperialist revolutionary forces became almost immediately concrete. The

---

1 Quoted in Dunayevskaya, Raya (2017), *Russia: From Proletarian Revolution to State-Capitalist Counter-Revolution*. Leiden: Brill, 75.
2 Lenin, V.I. (1974), "Seventh Congress of the R.C.P.(B)," in *Collected Works Vol. 27*, Moscow: Progress Publishers, 135.
3 Ibid.

1916 Easter Rising in Ireland realised Lenin's revolutionary anti-war slogan, by turning the imperialist war into civil war. The Irish, despite their military inferiority, struck an enormous blow at the heart of the empire which, Lenin hoped, would encourage others.

Lenin was adamant, arguing with some of the best of Europe's anti-war revolutionary left as well as his Bolshevik colleagues: "The dialectics of history is such that small nations, powerless as an independent factor in the struggle against imperialism, play a part as one of the ferments, one of the bacilli, which help the real power against imperialism to come on the scene, namely, the socialist proletariat." To conceive of revolution without this ferment, Lenin added, was to conceive of revolution as a battle where one side says, '"We are for socialism,' and another [...] says, 'We are for imperialism' [...] Such a person pays lip-service to revolution without understanding what revolution is."[4]

The importance of Lenin's position, the centrality of self-determination, would deepen after the success of the Russian Revolution as the Bolsheviks came to power, especially as the motion of the masses was stalled by famine and civil war, and the promise of revolution in Europe violently stilled after the Spartacist uprising and the murder of Luxemburg and Liebknecht in Germany. Lenin's hope for international revolution shifted with the 1920 "Theses on the National and Colonial Question" becoming an important focus for international communism, importantly including "American Negroes" among "the dependent and underprivileged nations."[5] The theses were not disconnected from his argument that the capitalist stage was not inevitable and countries where capitalism hadn't developed could "go over to the Soviet system and [...] to communism, without having to pass through the capitalist stage."[6]

Earlier, in March 1919, Lenin's comment "scratch some Communists and you will find a Great Russian chauvinist" summed up his concern as the party took over more functions of the state. In his "Speech Closing the Debate on the Party Program," Lenin immediately mentioned the importance of the Bashkirs' distrust of the Great Russians who "have utilised their culture to rob the Bashkirs." For the Bashkirs, "the term Great Russian is synonymous with the terms 'oppressor,' 'rogue'."[7]

Aware of how revolutionary socialists would easily support movements for self-determination in principle, far from home, Lenin responded to Nikolai Bukharin's willingness to support self-determination "in some cases," mentioning "the Hottentots, the Bushmen and the Indians." Again referencing the Bashkirs, Lenin asked, "how is it that Comrade Bukharin has

---

4 Lenin, V.I. (1974), "The Discussion on Self-Determination Summed Up," in *Collected Works Vol. 22*, Moscow: Progress Publishers, 356.
5 Lenin, V.I. (1974), "Draft Theses on National and Colonial Questions," in *Collected Works Vol. 31*, Moscow: Progress Publishers, 148.
6 Lenin, V.I. (1974), "The Second Congress of the Communist International," in *Collected Works Vol. 31*, Moscow: Progress Publishers, 244.
7 Lenin, V.I. (1974), "Eight Congress of the R.C.P. (B.)," in *Collected Works Vol. 29*, Moscow: Progress Publishers, 195.

forgotten this small tribe?" "There are no Bushmen in Russia, nor have I heard that the Hottentots have laid claim to an autonomous republic, but we have Bashkirs, Kirghiz and a number of other peoples, and to these we cannot deny recognition."[8]

In Lenin's view Bukharin, one of the party's leading intellectuals, was a consistent "imperialist economist."[9] Similarly, the revolutionary internationalist Rosa Luxemburg, who was one of the first to note the brutality of German militarism, never considered the Irish struggle against imperialism revolutionary, calling the rebellion a putsch. Like Bukharin, she did not recognise the new revolutionary subjectivity of the revolts, in the same text also denying that Ukraine had ever been a nation and calling an independent Ukraine "Lenin's hobby."[10]

In fact, Lenin's last written statement on the "national and colonial question" directly concerned Ukraine as he outlined basic principles for socialists and anti-imperialists: "A distinction must necessarily be made between the nationalism of an oppressor nation and that of an oppressed nation, the nationalism of a big nation and that of a small nation. In respect of the second kind of nationalism we, nationals of a big nation, have nearly always been guilty, in historic practice, of an infinite number of cases of violence; furthermore, we commit violence and insult an infinite number of times without noticing it. [...] That is why internationalism on the part of oppressors or great nations, as they are called (though they are great only in their violence, only great as bullies), must consist not only in the observance of the formal equality of nations but even in an inequality of the oppressor nation, the great nation, that must make up for the inequality which obtains in actual practice. Anybody who does not understand this has not grasped *the real proletarian attitude* to the national question."[11]

It is always remarkable how ideas that seemed to be buried in their context become newly alive as a new crisis reveals the fault lines on which the possibility of a new revolutionary consciousness emerges. One hundred years after Lenin's 1922 statement, Vladimir Putin ordered the invasion of Ukraine. He did it in the name of Great Russia, criticising Lenin and the Communists for breaking up the Czarist empire by wishing for the defeat of Russia. Perhaps more remarkable is the support Putin's Great Russia war has among today's anti-war left, and among the anticolonialist left who often couch this support in geopolitical and decolonial terms. How would Lenin respond? What would be "a real proletarian attitude"? An example can be found in a post by the Russian *Militant Anarchist*. A Russian victory, they say, would "give the regime what it currently lacks...*carte blanche* for any action." As the

---

8 Lenin, V.I. (1974), "Draft Program of the R.C.P.(B.)," in *Collected Works Vol. 29*, Moscow: Progress Publishers, 171-172.
9 On "Imperialist Economism" see Lenin, V.I. (1974), "The Nascent Trend of Imperialist Economism," in *Collected Works Vol. 23*, Moscow: Progress Publishers, 13-21.
10 Luxemburg, Rosa (1961), *The Russian Revolution: Leninism or Marxism*. Ann Arbor: University of Michigan Press, 52-54.
11 Lenin, V.I. (1977), "The Question of Nationalities or 'Autonomisation'," in *Collected Works Vol. 36*, Moscow: Progress Publishers, 608 (my emphasis).

war drags on and opposition to it is silenced, talking to Russian soldiers over the heads of their leaders and organising underground resistance to conscription becomes imperative. *Militant Anarchist* concludes, "The defeat of Russia, in the current situation, will increase the likelihood of people waking up, the same way that occurred in 1905, or in 1917 – opening their eyes to what is happening in the country."[12]

Nigel C. Gibson's latest books are Fanon Today: Reason and Revolt of the Wretched of the Earth *(Daraja Press: 2021) and* Frantz Fanon: Combat Breathing *(Polity Press: 2024).*

---

12 See "Russian Anarchists on the Invasion of Ukraine (2022)", *Crimethink*.

75. The Star of Lenin Still Shines

Olya Murphy

From left to right, critics of Vladimir Ilyich Lenin associate him with the authoritarian features of the Soviet experiment and the failure of socialism during and after the revolution. Conversely, as Vijay Prashad has eloquently argued with a focus on the Global South, for many others Lenin remains a symbol of worker (and peasant) power and liberation, a model of strategic thinking and revolutionary organisation, and a beacon of hope for a socialist future.[1] I count myself in the latter group.

My personal road to appreciating Lenin had many twists and turns, including ideological traps set by the Western anti-communist propaganda war inside the USSR that had a tremendous influence on the Moscow intelligentsia and professional elites. In the rich capitalist countries – I now live in Canada – Lenin's legacy has been forever demonised. Growing up in Moscow during the 1970s and 80s, I knew that Lenin was the central historical figure, our primary national hero. No Soviet citizen could avoid knowing something about Lenin's life and historic role in establishing the first workers' state. Nevertheless, in the long run, Soviet education and propaganda were not as effective as that of its Western adversaries – the educated, cultural elites, with considerable power and influence, especially in Moscow, to a large extent came to embrace anti-communist ideology and developed rather negative views of Lenin. (This was not the only factor contributing to the downfall of the Soviet bloc, but it was an important one.) Many internalised the messaging of the CIA-funded Radio Liberty and Voice of America, while selectively reading 'samizdat,' some even lamenting the Bolsheviks' historic expropriation of the ruling elites. 70 years of the Soviet regime were insufficient to overcome such tendencies, and the relentless hostility and machinations of the Western capitalist states, led by the US, helped put the final nail in the coffin.

Yet this is not reason enough to cease the struggle for socialism and discard Lenin's contribution to this history. The Soviet Union provides valuable lessons, and it was not without significant achievements – for example, the great reduction in economic inequality, the lifting of millions out of dire poverty, the defeat of Nazi Germany, the support for anti-colonial movements, among other things.

In the final years of the USSR, Gorbachev's reforms created an impressive level of press freedom. An unintended result, however, was that the anti-communist intelligentsia became the dominant voice in the cultural and ideological production of the late 1980s, paving the way for the overthrow of the regime, the destruction and theft of national wealth, and the establishment of a particularly brutal form of capitalism. This counter-revolutionary process was supported by a minority but was met with little

---

1 Prashad, Vijay (2017), *Red Star Over the Third World*. New Delhi: Leftword Books.

resistance. Among those who supported it, many believed that capitalism and liberal democracy would bring a better world, while those who opposed it either felt disempowered or hoped (as Gorbachev did) that some more democratic form of socialism would win the day – a major miscalculation, as Gorbachev's reforms removed necessary protections of the system in the context of the Cold War, in effect delivering victory to the enemy without a fight. During the process, with the transformation of the state, the economy, and of the social safety net, workers' voices vanished together with state protections and industrial jobs. The trauma of this *anti-Leninist* experiment, crystallised in the reign of Boris Yeltsin, should never be forgotten.

In the countries formed by the breakup of the Soviet Union, Lenin's legacy as well as knowledge about him and the revolution has waned considerably. The Russian state sought legitimacy in the imperial past and religion. Nevertheless, according to recent polls many Russians retain positive views of Lenin's historical role. The Communist Party remains the main opposition party and though it is strongly nationalist, it strives to keep the memory of Lenin, and of socialism, alive. In the international arena, though Russia is capitalist and socialism is no longer the prevailing ideology, Western capitalist imperialism has never left Russia alone and the current US-led proxy war with Russia in Ukraine has led to an historic turn of Russia eastward toward China as well as to the Global South. What does this mean for world socialism?

Lenin believed that socialism in Russia would not be fully achieved without revolutions in the capitalist centres. But what happened with the workers' revolutionary movements in those countries and the possibilities for world socialism? Since Lenin's death, several processes have proved decisive. One is the co-opting of workers' movements by the reformist welfare state and the adoption of 'welfare capitalism' by large corporations in the post-World War Two era. This brief period was followed by the turn to 'neoliberalism,' financialisaton, the politically disabling debt peonage imposed on workers and the reversal of workers' economic and political gains. Concurrently, deindustrialisation decimated large sections of the working class in the Global North and transnational capital has spawned a larger but also more dispersed and divided working class in the Global South in a fit of imperialism that was glossed as 'globalisation.'

Today, the ground under the global status quo is rapidly shifting. As Lenin purportedly said, "There are decades where nothing happens; and there are weeks where decades happen." A strange and *perhaps* promising alliance has formed between Russia and China; an alliance, including many other non-Western countries, inching toward de-dollarisation of global trade and a multipolar world in opposition to the US-dominated capitalist global order. The battle lines are being drawn, so to speak.

In this context, I can't help but think of Lenin's steadfast anti-imperialism, his solidarity with colonised peoples, and his capacity to think strategically in non-ideal circumstances. Of course, as socialists we want workers' democracy, but the road will not be as straightforward or 'pure' as we wish. Revolutionaries need to be pragmatic realists as well. Socialists should, I would suggest, side with a bloc of countries developing alternative institutions for trade and cooperation, without imposing capitalist austerity or relinquishing control over all the crucial productive resources in the Global South or submitting to the financial oligarchy of the North. Socialists should be able to see the qualitative difference between, on the one hand, the predatory nature of the imperial capitalist state and private corporate 'credit' (essentially plunder) advanced to the Global South by the Global North, and, on the other, the Chinese financial system controlled by the Communist party, with clear differences in the contractual and practical conditions attached to loans and developmental projects. How else, in the given conditions, could the Global South gain access to urgently needed capital and technology? Even if the multipolar vision is not socialist at present, it is surely more open and conducive to socialist developments than a US hegemonic order. For example, isn't trade with Russia and China better for Cuba and Venezuela to develop socialism than complete isolation and capitalist subversion?

In conclusion, however flawed the Soviet Union was, the world was a better place with it than without – the history of the Global South and of the unhinged imperialism of the 21st century is naked proof of that. The same applies to China's global initiatives. China, whatever its shortcomings, mistakes and failures, has not abandoned its goal of building socialism. In fact, after the brief experiment with neoliberalism, it seems to have returned to the path toward that goal.[2]

As a young Muscovite during the demise of the Communist regime, I did not see what was really in store and I even naively supported Yeltsin. Forgive me Lenin, for I knew not what I was doing. Over thirty years later, inside the belly of Western capitalism, teaching about global economic and working-class history, I have come to see more clearly what was lost – including advances made by women in the USSR. All around, the workers' world is as precarious as ever, while it is becoming ever clearer that socialism – a socialism that learns from past experiments – is the only way out, and the best alternative to the rising tide of fascism in many parts of the world. For that reason, the star of Lenin still shines. He fought for a kind of world that has yet to be fully realised. It seems to me the only hope for us.

Olya Murphy (she), received her PhD at York University in history, specializing in global economic history, and currently lectures in the fields of 'business and society' and labour studies in the department of social science at York University, Toronto, Canada.

---

2 Martinez, Carlos (2023), *The East is Still Red: Chinese Socialism in the 21st Century*. Glasgow: Praxis Press.

76. Lenin on the Buses

Owen Hatherley

In 1902, Lenin, and various members of the Russian Social Democratic Labour Party, visited London. Some, like Lenin himself, settled in the city for a short time. You can find commemorations of this, still – there has been no *Leninopad* in London, though the monuments are inconspicuous. The office where he edited *Iskra*, at the back of what is now the Marx Memorial Library, is a miniature museum; he appears with Marx, Engels and an idealised burly worker in a mural in the same building. Another mural on a construction hoarding opposite has Lenin's goateed silhouette on it. The house in Percy Circus, in what was then the slum district of Finsbury, where Lenin lived, has a blue plaque; in the public space in the middle of the circus there was for a time a memorial, designed by fellow socialist and émigré Berthold Lubetkin, before it was removed at the start of the Cold War. Finally, a nearby council housing block to Lubetkin's design was slated to be named Lenin Court, but this was changed to Bevin Court, after the decidedly anti-communist Labour foreign secretary. Today, radical history tours will guide you to where Lenin may or may not have liked to go to the pub. This is perhaps still possible because of the historic lack of fearsomeness of Britain's Communist movement or perhaps because there is less need to purge the record in a country which has never been remotely Leninist. But it may also be owed to something else: that Lenin was a good Londoner.

In *My Life*, published in 1930, Trotsky writes of spending time in the English capital with Lenin on arrival in 1902. Trotsky liked to walk the streets of London, but he was easily lost in this vast and apparently interminable metropolis: "with my usual penchant for systematic thinking, (I) called this defect 'a topographic cretinism.'" Lenin was not lost. When Trotsky describes going through London on foot with Lenin, you immediately sense that the walking partner was someone with a sharp eye, keen to understand and take in what was then the world's largest and richest city.

> From a bridge, Lenin pointed out Westminster and some other famous buildings. I don't remember the exact words he used, but what he conveyed was: "This is their famous Westminster," and "their" referred of course not to the English but to the ruling classes. This implication, which was not in the least emphasised, but coming as it did from the very innermost depths of the man, and expressed more by the tone of his voice than by anything else, was always present, whether Lenin was speaking of the treasures of culture, of new achievements, of the wealth of books in the British Museum, of the information of the larger European newspapers, or, years later, of German artillery or French aviation. They know this or they have that, they have made this or achieved that – but what enemies they are! To his eyes, the invisible shadow of the ruling classes always overlay the whole of human culture – a shadow that was as real to him as daylight.

There, a sense of deep exile, not just from the Russian Empire, but from the capitalist world in general. An apartness, a distance, an ability to see capitalist civilisation from *outside*, to alienate it.

In her own book of reminiscences, *Memories of Lenin*, published in the same year, Nadezhda Krupskaya remembers her and Vladimir Ilyich's battles with English. They *thought* they knew the language – "I had studied English in prison from a self-instructor" – and she and Lenin had even translated Sidney and Beatrice Webb, but "when we arrived in London we found we could not understand a thing, nor could anybody understand us." Like so many visitors, Krupskaya and Lenin were struck by London's scale – "the immensity of London staggered us" – and by the "filthy" weather. But together, they discovered the best way to see, and to understand London – the top deck of a bus. On these,

> Ilyich studied living London. He liked taking long rides through the town on top of the bus. He liked the busy traffic of that vast commercial city, the quiet squares with their elegant houses wreathed in greenery, where only smart broughams drew up. There were other places too – mean little streets tenanted by London's work people, with clothes lines stretched across the road and anaemic children playing on the doorsteps. To these places we used to go on foot. Observing these startling contrasts between wealth and poverty, Ilyich would mutter in English through clenched teeth: "Two nations!"

Over time, these top-deck bus journeys became a fixture for the exiled revolutionaries. Krupskaya writes about them with great affection and vividness, and an eye for the city's grotesque inequalities – a feature of the city that endures 120 years later. From the bus, they saw "ill-clad lumpen-proletarians with pasty faces (hanging) around the pubs, and often one would see among them a drunken woman with a bruised eye wearing a trailing velvet dress from which a sleeve had been ripped off." She continues:

> Once, from the top of a bus, we saw a huge 'bobby' in his typical helmet and chin strap hustling before him with an iron hand a puny little urchin, who had evidently been caught stealing, while a crowd followed behind them whooping and whistling. Some of the people on the bus jumped up and began hooting at the little thief too. "Well, well!" Vladimir Ilyich would mutter sadly. Once or twice we took a ride on top of the bus to some working-class district on pay-day evening. An endless row of stalls, each lit up by a flare, stretched along the pavement of a wide road; the pavements were packed with a noisy crowd of working men and women, who were buying all kinds of things and satisfying their hunger right there on the spot.

Krupskaya and Lenin would take comrades with them to see these contrasts – among them an English socialist named Raymond, with whom they were unimpressed. He had "been nearly all over Europe, lived in Australia and other places, and spent most of his life in London, [but] had not seen half of what Vladimir Ilyich had managed to see in London during his one year's stay there. One day Ilyich dragged him off to a meeting in Whitechapel. Like most Englishmen, Mr. Raymond had never been in that part of London, inhabited mostly by Russian Jews who lived a life of their own there unlike that of the rest of the city. He was astonished at what he saw." The couple also availed themselves of the more pleasant conveniences of the London bus network.

> More often than not we went to Primrose Hill. It was the cheapest trip – the fare only costing sixpence. The hill commanded a view of almost the whole of London – a vast smoke-wreathed wilderness of houses. From here we took long walks into the parks and country lanes. Another reason we liked going to Primrose Hill was because it was near the cemetery where Karl Marx was buried.

Both in Primrose Hill and on the top deck of the bus, Lenin saw London not as a set of 'villages,' discrete and incomprehensible, as generations of neoliberal urban theory would have it, but as a totality – a place that could be understood, and once understood, transformed. This is what made him a good Londoner. Lenin's curious, alienated eye helped him to see what sort of a city London is – a place at once deeply international and deeply insular, a place with vast extremes of rich and poor, a place where people know nothing about the people who live next door to them, a place where capitalism appears unquestioned, until you look beneath the surface – and a place of surprising refuge to revolutionaries. It is that city still today.

Owen Hatherley is a writer and editor living in south-east London. He favours the 176 bus route from Penge to Tottenham Court Road.

Artist: V.A. Serov

77. Lenin: Responding to Catastrophe, Forging Revolution

Paul Le Blanc

The free-spirited revolutionary Rosa Luxemburg once said of Lenin: "I enjoy talking with him, he's clever and well educated, and has such an ugly mug, the kind I like to look at." Angelica Balabanoff, who had worked closely with Lenin, was able to specify: "From his youth on, Lenin was convinced that most of human suffering and of moral, legal, and social deficiencies were caused by class distinctions." She explained, "he was also convinced that class struggle alone ... could put an end to exploiters and exploited and create a society of the free and equal. He gave himself entirely to this end and he used every means in his power to achieve it."

From the right end of the political spectrum, Winston Churchill sought a balanced measure of his mortal enemy. He hated what Lenin represented and even hailed Mussolini's fascist dictatorship in Italy for its "triumphant struggle against the bestial appetites and passions of Leninism." Yet he wrote of Lenin: "His mind was a remarkable instrument. When its light shone it revealed the whole world, its history, its sorrows, its stupidities, its shams, and above all its wrongs ... It was capable of universal comprehension in a degree rarely reached among men." It is worth adding an insight from erstwhile supporter Max Eastman, who suggested that one of Lenin's contributions in "the theory and practice of Marxism" was a rejection of "people who talk revolution, and like to think about it, but do not 'mean business' ... the people who talked revolution but did not intend to produce it."

Today, some would-be revolutionary organisations still seem to feel it is sufficient to develop and express revolutionary thoughts, and revolutionary 'positions.' Defining and expressing 'politically correct' positions remains primary for some groups. This may take the form of arguing against the capitalist ruling class, or against non-revolutionary groups, or against other would-be revolutionary groups. Of course, Lenin was fully prepared to engage in polemics and arguments, but what was primary for him was helping to mobilise *practical struggles* capable of materially defending and advancing the urgent needs of workers and the oppressed. He favoured struggles that can make sense to people in the here and now but also tilt toward mass revolutionary consciousness and, if fought effectively, insurgency and power shift – ultimately, revolution.

In addition, Lenin held that without the accumulation of experience, cadres, relationships, and authority within the working class, a would-be revolutionary organisation cannot *actually become* a revolutionary organisation. This can only be achieved through practical activism. This approach was simply expressed in the explanation of Vincent Raymond Dunne, leader of the militant and victorious Minneapolis teamster strikes of

1934: "Our policy was to organise and build strong unions so workers could have something to say about their own lives and assist in changing the present order into a socialist society."

But what other ways does Lenin's orientation offer us in our own time? In working towards an answer, we first must dispense with six historiographical myths: 1) Lenin favoured dictatorship over democracy; 2) his so-called 'Marxism' was a cover for his own totalitarian views; 3) he favoured a super-centralised political party of 'a new type' – with power concentrated at the top, himself as party dictator; 4) he favoured rigid political controls over culture, art and literature (to instil 'politically correct' thoughts and feelings); 5) he believed that through such authoritarian methods a socialist 'utopia' could be imposed on backward Russia; and 6) flowing naturally from all this, he became one of history's foremost mass murderers. Humanistic revolutionaries can find no 'helpful hints' from such stuff as this.

Faced with the complex swirl of Lenin's life and times and ideas, one can select elements adding up to a 'Leninism' from which decent people must turn away. In her critique of the Russian Revolution which Lenin led, however, Rosa Luxemburg emphasised her determination to "distinguish the essential from the non-essential." Her critique of the non-essential was designed to help advance the triumph of the *essentials* in Lenin's revolutionary approach. She was particularly concerned to separate problematical 'emergency measures' of the Russian civil war (1918-21) from the profound workers' democracy animating the 1917 Bolshevik revolution. Based on the proven effectiveness of this revolutionary-democratic quality in 1917, Luxemburg concluded that "the future everywhere belongs to [Lenin's] Bolshevism."

So, what are the essentials in Lenin's approach for revolutionaries of today? Here are six:

1. One essential revolutionary principle for Lenin involves the political independence of the working class – the refusal to subordinate the struggles of the working class to the leadership of pro-capitalist parties. "No democracy in the world puts aside the class struggle and the ubiquitous power of money," Lenin noted, adding that while in a country such as the United States capitalists and workers had equal political rights, in fact "they are not equal in class status: one class, capitalists, own the means of production and live on the unearned product of the labour of the workers; the other, the class of wage-workers, ... own no means of production and live by selling their labour-power in the market." He warned that the "so-called bipartisan system" of the pro-capitalist parties, Democrats and Republicans, "has been one of the most powerful means of preventing the rise of an independent working class, i.e., genuinely socialist party."

2. Another essential involves opposition to all forms of racism, ethnic bigotry, or oppression based on gender or sexuality. Disagreeing with the 'economist' tendency that argued for the workplace's primacy, Lenin argued our "ideal should not be the trade union secretary, but *the tribune of the people*, who is able to react to every manifestation of tyranny and oppression, no matter where it appears, no matter what stratum or class of the people it affects."

3. A third essential involves opposition to imperialism and war.

4. A fourth principle is a commitment to genuine democracy (rule by the people) as essential both to our future world and within the movement to create that better future.

5. A fifth principle involves an internationalist orientation – solidarity across borders, a commitment to global collaboration among the workers and oppressed of all countries.

6. Finally, today, we must add another essential. A voracious market economy designed to enrich already immensely wealthy elites is intimately connected with the environmental destruction engulfing our world. Such catastrophe is the framework for efforts of today and tomorrow.

The Leninism of Lenin, however, cannot be encompassed in a checklist of 'essentials.' It is a dynamic method, fuelled by the commitments, the critical intelligence and the creative energies of many comrades. Also, the process of testing perspectives and learning from actual struggles – accompanied by debates and sometimes even splits, but also united efforts and sometimes fusions – will be necessary on the way to creating a revolutionary party worthy of the name: "people who will devote the whole of their lives," as Lenin put it, building a multi-faceted, cohesive revolutionary collective of the working-class majority.

Flowing from this, Lenin insisted "we must at all costs set out, first, to learn, secondly, to learn, and thirdly, to learn, and then see to it that ... learning shall really become part of our very being, that it shall actually and fully become a constituent element of our social life." But he also insisted we must learn through doing – through actual struggles against oppression and exploitation, collectively evaluating that experience, and thinking through what to do next for a future of the free and the equal.

Paul Le Blanc (he/him), a long-time scholar and activist who has lived most of his life in Pittsburgh, is one of the editors of the Complete Works of Rosa Luxemburg *(Verso) and the author of* Lenin: Responding to Catastrophe, Forging Revolution *(Pluto).*

78. The Three Tragedies of Vladimir Ilyich Lenin

Peter Hudis

Is Lenin best understood as a tragic hero? There was surely much that was heroic about Lenin: his determination to build a viable revolutionary Marxist party from the late 1890s onward, his pathbreaking study of Hegel's dialectic in 1914-15 in response to the Second International's capitulation to imperialism, and most of all, his audacious decision to seize power from the provisional government in 1917 in order to initiate a transition to socialism. Yet as Aristotle noted long ago, the deepest tragedies afflict the most heroic figures. And the following three unmistakable tragedies mark Lenin's life and legacy.

1. Lenin is often associated with forging an original concept of revolutionary organisation, but that is to accord him too much honour as well as too much discredit. Lenin did not invent the concept of a vanguard party, let alone "democratic centralism" (the term was first used by a Menshevik). These were all staples of the Second International, in which he spent two-thirds of his political life. As an unstinting follower of Karl Kautsky before 1914, Lenin largely applied the organisational principles of German Social Democracy to Russian conditions – an admirable task, given the vast difference between the quasi-republican states of West Europe and autocratic Russia. Despite claims to the contrary, the 1903 split between Mensheviks and Bolsheviks was not over principled organisational differences; it was a *tactical* debate over what defined membership in the RSDLP. The real divide came in 1907, when the Mensheviks moved to the Right in holding that the defeat of the 1905 Revolution meant the working class was too weak to lead the Russian Revolution.
    So, what about organisation? Lenin upheld the need for a centralised, disciplined party in the face of tsarist repression, but that was hardly unique: it was just as true of the Bund, the SRs, and most Mensheviks. In fact, he pined for the day when a bourgeois-democratic revolution in Russia would enable his party to operate along the same lines as the SPD in Germany. He was not an original on the question of organisation. The tragedy is that his autocratic approach to opponents in the RSDLP between 1908 and 1914, and even more importantly, his imposition of a single-party state in 1918 and his banning of factions in 1921, created the impression that his increasing reliance on hierarchical and centralist organisational practices was a model for all to follow. This had disastrous consequences – in the developing world, where 'Leninism' became for many associated with the suppression of revolutionary democracy, and in the developed world, where efforts to build 'vanguard parties' in countries having little or nothing in common with the Russia

of the early 20th century led to little more than the formation of innumerable marginalised sects.

2. But Lenin *was* an original – if not on organisation, then surely on other matters. He developed a profound critique of the new stage of imperialism, dialectically linking it to its opposite – the struggle for self-determination by subjugated national minorities. He added three little words to Marx's declaration "Workers of the World Unite" – *and colonised peoples*. This is what made Lenin's ideas come alive to masses of people in the non-Western world, especially when they saw his words put into action from 1917 to 1923 in providing aid and assistance to anti-colonial movements in Central Asia, the Middle East, China, Indonesia and Latin America.

What is often overlooked, however, is the new conceptual point of departure that impacted his analysis of imperialism and view of struggles for national self-determination as a "bacillus" for proletarian revolution – his six-month engagement with Hegel's *Science of Logic* in 1914-15, following the shock of the Great Betrayal of 1914. Lenin became enthralled with Hegel's notion of "transformation into opposite" for illuminating the transformation of competitive into monopoly capitalism and the transformation of part of the organised workers' movement into an aristocracy of labour defending imperialism. In the face of both, he held, it was necessary to go "lower and deeper" into the *non-organised* masses – especially the colonised masses.

In delving into Hegel with new eyes, Lenin went far beyond the vulgar materialism that defined the orthodox Marxists of the time (such as Plekhanov) – which included himself, who earlier (in 1908/09) upheld the naïve realism of the photocopy theory of reality in Materialism and Empirio-Criticism. In 1914-15 he broke from the notion that thought is "nothing but" the reflection of material conditions, proclaiming, "cognition not only reflects but creates the objective world." And he writes, the "whole chapter on the 'Absolute Idea' [in the Science of Logic] ... contains almost nothing that is specifically idealism ... in this most idealistic of Hegel's work there is the least idealism and the most materialism."

The tragedy, however, is that Lenin never published his "Hegel Notebooks," keeping the break from his philosophic past to himself. As a result, it became harder for many to discern the *process* that led to the political conclusions embodied in his break from the Second International. The interconnection between philosophy and revolutionary politics became obscured, both on the part of activists and academics.

3. Lenin's greatest accomplishment was to call for the seizure of power in October 1917 – in direct contradiction to his insistence, voiced for decades, that the most that could be achieved in "backward" Russia for

the foreseeable future was a bourgeois-democratic revolution. In proclaiming "All Power to the Soviets," he placed the transition to socialism on the agenda – albeit with the understanding that it could not be achieved without proletarian revolutions in the West. It was a gamble – and he knew it. The odds of success were slim, and became slimmer still in the face of counter-revolution, civil war, and the failure of the West European revolutions.

Lenin knew socialism could not exist in one country; but in the face of external and internal threats, he severely curtailed free expression, independent political activity, and whatever power still remained in the soviets – as if relying on the "thin stratum of Bolsheviks" would allow the regime to weather the storm. But it didn't. In his last days he could feel the revolution reeling backwards, but it never occurred to him to loosen the party's tight grip on the monopolisation of power. 1921 was the turning point: instead of accommodating demands for greater political democracy now that the civil war was over, he cracked down on opponents (especially leftist ones) ever harder. This made Stalin's rise to power possible, if not inevitable. With that, one of the greatest tragedies in human history occurred – the transformation of a putatively proletarian revolution into a state-capitalist totalitarian dictatorship.

Marxism had always insisted on combatting the claim that capitalism defines the horizon of human possibility. It is therefore one of the greatest ironies of history that nothing has done more to give capitalism a new lease on life than revolutions led by self-proclaimed Marxists that ended up creating statist variants of capitalism. Once 'socialism' and 'communism' became associated with single party states and the annulment of political and economic democracy, it was inevitable that the effort to envision the end of capitalism would become harder than ever. That is why today it is easier to envision the end of the world than the end of capitalism.

The struggles for freedom never stop, but today the absence of a viable conception of an alternative to capitalism provides the ruling class with the most powerful weapon it could ever hope for. That is not Lenin's tragedy but ours. But given the depth of this tragedy, and the responsibility he partly bears for it, the time is long past to shed tears for Lenin.

Peter Hudis is Distinguished Professor of Philosophy and Humanities at Oakton College (USA) and author of Marx's Concept of the Alternative to Capitalism *(Brill, 2012) and* Frantz Fanon: Philosopher of the Barricades *(Pluto Press, 2015), and has edited or coedited six volumes of writings of Rosa Luxemburg.*

79. Lenin in Thailand[1]

Puangchon Unchanam

At first glance, Lenin and his ideas are not the first thing that come to mind in a discussion of Thailand. Lenin was a Marxist revolutionary. Under his leadership in the Russian Revolution, the Bolshevik Party ended Tsarism, abolished the monarchy, and founded the Soviet Union. Thailand has long been a kingdom. In fact, for the last few decades it has been a highly conservative, ultra-royalist, and anti-socialist kingdom. Although the Communist Party of Thailand (CPT) once played a crucial role in mobilising peasants and workers against American imperialism during the Cold War, the party has long become inactive and disappeared from the political scene. And even when the CPT was in its prime, the person whose ideas the party looked to most was not Lenin, but Mao. It was his ideas and tactics in guerrilla warfare that the CPT studied and accepted. Beyond this, thanks to the royalist ideology that has dominated the kingdom since the middle of the last century, Lenin, the October Revolution, Bolshevism, and Marxist-Leninist theory remain alien to most Thais. Instead, as students at school and in university, Thais are still bombarded by textbooks and historical writings with nostalgic stories of the long and close relationship between Russian tsars and Thai kings and even a famous romance between a Thai prince and a Ukrainian noblewoman from the Russian Empire. In this way, rather than a familiar face, Lenin has been a total stranger to most Thais.

However, if we examine Thai history closely, Lenin has not always been a foreign unknown. In fact, from time to time his name and legacy appeared in the public space. For instance, in the early 20th century the formation of the Soviet Union made Thai elites, especially the royals, concerned about their fates. Facing demands for political rights by his subjects, the last absolutist monarch of Siam, King Prajadhipok, tried to maintain his grip on power by portraying any democratic reform in his kingdom as a road to serfdom which, according to him, had been paved by and was on display in the Soviet Union.[2] Then, during the Cold War, the Thai state banned hundreds of leftist books and pamphlets because they were deemed an ideological threat to the kingdom's conservative order. Alongside the writings of Marx, Engels, and Mao, Lenin's classic works such as *The State and Revolution, Imperialism, the Highest Stage of Capitalism*, and *"Left-Wing" Communism* were prominent on the list.[3] Most importantly, in recent years Lenin's name has often (re-)appeared in newspapers, newly released books, activist training courses, and social media. How could the Russian revolutionary who passed away a century ago become relevant again to the

---

[1] Editors' note: All cited works are Thai-language publications with titles translated into English.
[2] King Prajadhipok (1999), "His Majesty's Review of the Economic Plan," in *The Economic Plan*. Bangkok: Pridi Banomyong Institute, 61-100.
[3] The Ministry of Interior, "Announcement of prohibited Documents and Publications," March 3, 1977.

kingdom in which he never set foot? There are several reasons for this development.

In 2020-2021 the most recent protest movement swept across Thailand. Led by university students, the movement demanded major reforms in the kingdom which for too long had been dominated by the monarchy and the military. While most of the activists and participants in the movement were liberals, some were attracted to the ideas of social democracy and Marxism. Thus, what distinguished this movement from its predecessors was the leftward drift of its demands and rhetoric. In addition to concepts such as liberty, civil rights, and democracy, catchwords included *capitalism, exploitation, class struggle, the working class* and *social inequality*. With its demands for significant reform of the monarchy, the military and the bureaucracy, the movement soon faced a strong reaction from the state, including criminal charges, arbitrary detention and police intimidation. Before the movement began to peter out, however, some of its factions shocked state authorities by launching a new movement, Restart Thailand (RT). Using the hammer and sickle as its symbols and "Workers, not any great monarch, built the nation" as its main slogan, the RT movement invoked images of the October Revolution and Marxist-Leninist ideology.[4] Although the protest movement finally disbanded by the end of 2021, the emergence of the RT and its rhetoric were remarkable. They reminded the elites that the newest generation of activists were no longer simply liberals. Standing among them were radical dissidents whom the elites fear the most: republicans and socialists.

Thanks to the leftist ideas and rhetoric that were used during the protests, many young people have since been eager to explore socialist literature. Publishers have responded to this demand by releasing new translations and editions of writings related to Lenin and the October Revolution. These include *Ten Days That Shook the World* and *Revolution at the Gates*. In addition, Marxist study groups and activist training courses have discreetly formed in major universities, focusing on reading Marx, Lenin, and Thai socialists.[5] But the legacy of the protest movement goes beyond bookshops and study groups. It has penetrated into and influences parliamentary politics. Once presenting itself as a liberal party, the Move Forward Party (MFP) heard the protesters' angry voices and rebranded itself as a social democratic party. With a campaign that promoted universal welfare, social equality, support for worker unions, and monarchy reform, the party won the 2023 general elections. Although the MFP was not able to form a government because its reformist policies were deemed too radical for other major parties, its election victory sent a signal to the establishment that millions of Thais want significant change. Notably, the two politicians who

---

[4] "Workers, not any great monarch, built the nation," *Prachatai*, August 12, 2020.
[5] A representative of this trend is Thammasat University Marxism Studies.

played a key role in the party's success, Thanathorn Juangroongruangkit and Piyabutr Saengkanokkul, are avid readers and admirers of Marx and Lenin.[6]

Undoubtedly, the massive protests of young dissidents and the rise of a social democratic party does not sit well with those on the political right. The latter perceive all reformist demands, whether raised on the streets or in the parliament, as a threat to the political order, with the monarchy at its apex. To fight against this threat, right-wing writers in newspapers and social media needed to find whipping boys, and they landed upon Thanathorn and Piyabutr. Consequently, the pair have been accused of manipulating the MFP and the protest movement for their own sinister purposes, conspiring to abolish the monarchy, and planning to found a socialist republic. Where did their masterplans come from? For the right, the conspiracy to overthrow the throne is certainly inspired by Lenin, the hero of Thanathorn, Piyabutr and many young activists.[7]

In sum, Lenin has been locally perceived in Thailand in distinctive ways. While those with a leftist orientation recognise the importance of Lenin's major ideas such as imperialism, the vanguard party, and the proletarian revolution, those on the right see, portray and despise him as anti-monarchist, republican and regicidal. It remains uncertain which side will prevail in this debate between those inspired by Lenin's legacy and those who reject all it represents. What is certain, however, is that a hundred years after his death, Lenin is once again relevant in Thailand. Like an unvanquished spectre, he haunts the kingdom where being a communist is considered a crime.

Puangchon Unchanam is an Assistant Professor in Political Science at Naresuan University, Thailand, and the author of Royal Capitalism: Wealth, Class, and Monarchy in Thailand *(University of Wisconsin Press, 2020).*

---

6 Wanchai Tantiwitthayaphithak and Wirapha Angkunthatniyarat, "Interview with Thanathorn Juangroongruangkit," *Sarakadee Magazine*, January 14, 2007; Piyabutr Saengkanokkul (2022), *Great Teachers in Politics*. Bangkok: Shine Publishing House; Piyabutr Saengkanokkul, "The Ideas of Marx and Lenin," February 14, 2021. Available online.

7 "Eddy unmasks Thanathorn!," *Thai Post*, March 14, 2023; "Eddy Teaches Piyabutr," *Thai Post*, July 13, 2022; "Exactly like Lenin: A Hundred Years Later, Thai Youngsters Do Not Dare to Lead A Revolution," *Thai Post*, July 12, 2022; Phak Kat Hom, "From Lenin to Piyabutr," *Thai Post*, July 12, 2022; "A Former 'Friend' of Thanathorn Criticises Piyabutr," *Manager*, September 29, 2021.

80. Six Links of Leninism

Redrock

In the history of the international communist movement, there have been several relatively complete theoretical analyses of revolutionary experience, namely Marx's analysis of European Revolution and the Paris Commune, Lenin's analysis of the Russian Revolutions in 1905 and 1917, and Mao Zedong's exploration and summary of New Democratic Revolution, Socialist Revolution and Cultural Revolution. In the concrete case of Lenin, he established a revolutionary party by founding a nation-wide political newspaper, helped grow the advanced proletarian class and led the democratic revolution towards socialism in a formerly autocratic imperialist country with no political freedoms. This task and the conditions for its eventual completion are very similar to the situation faced by contemporary China. For us, therefore, Lenin's works are of outstanding value. In our view, his revolutionary theory contains the following six links.

The first link is to ideologically establish Marxism and only Marxism as the theoretical basis for revolution. Lenin fought against populism and legal Marxism for precisely this reason. Today, revolutionary Marxist-Leninists have reached a certain ideological consensus that China has become an autocratic imperialist country and that its contradictions can only be fundamentally resolved through a new proletarian revolution.

Since we advocate revolution, we must first find the power of revolution. The second link in Lenin's revolutionary theory is hence to instil a principled socialist consciousness into workers and create an advanced stratum of the working class to consciously lead the socialist revolution. To this end, in his own time, Lenin carried out a fierce struggle against the Economists and the Socialist Revolutionary Party. The Economists worshiped the spontaneity of workers and catered to the purely economic requirements of the backward strata of the working class, consequently moving towards trade unionism. The Socialist Revolutionary Party, on the other hand, became ultra-left and believed that the masses could be moved into action through the creation of political events (= assassinations), rather than by inspiring them through engaging with their everyday life problems. Both tendencies have their representatives in contemporary China and are thus in need of study. It is necessary to systematically understand how and against whom Lenin organized the Bolshevik Party and its growing mass basis through the all-Russian political newspaper, propaganda, agitation and other means.

Instilling a principled socialist consciousness into the working class requires a democratic centralist organisation. The third link is thus to establish a strong proletarian party with a secret party central committee, and secret local organisations, publish a national political newspaper, educate and organise the proletariat. Ideological influence can only be consolidated through organisational forms, and only an organisationally unified party can ensure that an ideologically victorious Marxism can be transformed into the concrete practical actions of the masses to defeat capitalism.

Once we have created a solid party ideologically, politically, and organisationally, and with the conscious support of hundreds of thousands of advanced workers, we must dare to win strategically. The fourth link advocates establishing the leadership of the proletariat over the democratic revolution and leading the democratic revolution towards socialism. Lenin fought against the Mensheviks' views on strategy. The revolutionary storm of 1905 caused the latter to abandon their organisational views. They worried that the bourgeoisie would withdraw from the revolution, so they supported the liberal leadership of the democratic revolution. Lenin, on the other hand, knew that the bourgeoisie would withdraw from the revolution as demands radicalised. The proletariat should therefore compete with the bourgeoisie for leadership over the petty bourgeoisie and prepare for socialism through the democratic dictatorship of workers and peasants. Neither the state bureaucracy nor the bourgeoisie in current China are progressive in any way. Only when the alliance with the petty bourgeoisie led by the proletariat overthrows the alliance of the autocratic government with the monopoly bourgeoisie can more political freedoms be leveraged to prepare for the next step of the proletarian revolution.

The fifth link is the defence of the secret party and its legal struggle at the low ebb of the revolution, for which Lenin fought against both the Otzovists and the liquidators. The 1905 revolution failed, but the impact of the revolution made it impossible for the tsar to rule as he had before, that is, to rule mainly by violence, as is the case in contemporary autocratic imperialist China. This gave rise to two tasks: on the one hand, the preservation of the secret party and secret newspapers in order to continue to educate the masses politically, and prepare forces for the next revolution; on the other hand, the parliament established by the tsar had to be used to carry out legal work, thereby turning the tsarist institutions used to deceive the masses into spaces for attacking the tsar. Most of the Mensheviks became liquidators and wanted to turn the secret party into an exclusively legally operating parliamentary party. A section of the Bolsheviks became Otzovists, refusing any type of legal work or the use of legal channels of propaganda. Currently, China does not have its own 1905 revolution, nor does it have a secret party, but this does not rule out the possibility that China's autocratic imperialism will make concessions in the future after being impacted by mass revolution.

The sixth and final link in Lenin's revolutionary theory is to uphold internationalism and oppose chauvinist defencism in imperialist countries. The main means by which imperialism divides workers and the masses is nationalism, especially the defence of the motherland in imperialist competition. Kautsky distorted Marxist internationalism into the right of the working class of all countries to defend their homeland, kill each other in wartime, and forgive each other after the war. In response, Lenin demonstrated the relationship between monopoly capitalism, imperialism, war and revolution, and put forward the correct slogan: turning imperialist war into civil war. China's autocratic imperialism also uses nationalism to corrupt and divide workers. For example, the state describes the ongoing Sino-US trade war as national oppression rather than an imperialist struggle for hegemony, and attributes responsibility for the Russian imperialist war of aggression against Ukraine exclusively to the intervention of US imperialism and the expansion of NATO. Some workers and leftists are also influenced by chauvinism and believe that opposing US imperialism takes precedence over the task of domestic proletarian revolution. If we do not take a clear-cut stand against all forms of nationalist propaganda and agitation, we will not be able to truly inspire workers to understand that it is the reactionary government which makes workers love their country, that is, love the very same autocratic imperialism that directly oppresses them.

In sum, these six links constitute, for us, the organic structure of Lenin's revolutionary theory: Only when the uniqueness of the theoretical basis of Marxism is ideologically established can we have the political task of instilling socialist consciousness into the masses and the necessity of organisationally consolidating the results of political education. Although a series of revolutionary movements after the October Revolution ultimately failed, we should be prepared before each new major revolutionary movement. Today's China has very sharp class contradictions, which can in time become a weak link in the imperialist system. Since China wants to compete with the more powerful US imperialism for global hegemony, it must intensify the exploitation, suppression and deception of the proletariat and working people domestically. In response, the Chinese proletariat will have to fight resolutely and win. This, in turn, will provide a solid foundation for the world proletarian revolution.

'Redrock' is the name chosen by an anonymous contributor.

81. Building Strength in the Weakest Link: Lenin and the Philippines' Internationalist Solidarity

Regletto Aldrich Imbong

Regarded as the Marxist theoretician who successfully led a proletarian revolution towards its victory and established the first socialist state in history, Vladimir Lenin advanced Marxism to a new and unprecedented level of development. Lenin tempered himself and Marxism through the life and death struggles he led against both class enemies and the opportunists of the Second International. Thus, he not only succeeded in building a socialist state but in creating a Third International based on a renewed affirmation of the revolutionary internationalist principles of Marxism and informed by its adaption to unique Russian circumstances.

Lenin's creative application of Marxism to the specific conditions of Soviet Russia enabled the development of concepts that, while retaining and sustaining a certain fidelity towards the Marxist project, reinvented it to respond to the unfamiliar constellation which Lenin and the Bolsheviks confronted, ruptured and reorganised. Among these concepts is imperialism, which Lenin also described as the highest stage of capitalism. Lenin made sense of the specific stage of capitalism at that time and repositioned Marxism against the opportunistic currents of Kautskyism. He saw how the capitalism of the time "ha[d] grown into a world system of colonial oppression and of the financial strangulation of the overwhelming majority of the population of the world by a handful of 'advanced' countries."[1] Anti-colonialism is thus an important component of Lenin's concept of imperialism – and, therefore, also of Leninism. Indeed, if Leninism has to be reinvented today, as Slavoj Žižek has contended, it must take into account the present worldwide conditions of imperialism and (neo)colonialism. This makes living Leninism relevant not only to the experiences of industrialised centres but even more so to the struggles taking place in the peripheral (neo)colonial regions.

One important theory that developed from Lenin's concept of imperialism is that of the weakest link. Here, Lenin conceived of a socialist revolution to commence not in capitalist strongholds or in the 'advanced' industrial countries, but in the relatively 'backward' agrarian and (neo)colonial regions, i.e., the weakest link of the imperialist chain. Against charges hurled about the supposed dogmatism of Marxism being impotent and thus incapable of making sense of the situation of (neo)colonial and non-

---

[1] Lenin, V.I. (1974), "Imperialism, the Highest Stage of Capitalism," in *Collected Works Vol. 22.* Moscow: Progress Publishers, 191.

industrial regions,[2] Lenin's theory of the weakest link and the more general concept of imperialism are among the many "theoretical ingenuities that would define Marxism in the colonial world of the 20th century,"[3] and one might add, the 21st century.

Today, the notion of Leninist anti-imperialism is once again gaining relevance and is still championed by militant organisations in the Philippines that continue to build internationalist and democratic solidarities, amidst and despite the heightening repression at the home and international fronts. For example, this anti-imperialism is embraced by the *Bagong Alyansang Makabayan* or *BAYAN* (New Patriotic Alliance), an alliance of national democratic organisations. Founded in 1985 at the height of the dictatorial regime of Ferdinand Marcos Sr., *BAYAN* brings together multisectoral formations of workers, peasants, professionals, church people, indigenous people, and other marginalised sectors in the struggle for "national liberation against imperialism, feudalism, and bureaucrat capitalism." It acknowledges how until today, the Philippines "remains a nominal republic under the hegemony of US Imperialism and the world capitalist system."[4] Concretely, it has waged various campaigns that oppose the continued subjugation of the country under imperialist designs and has likewise offered alternatives built on the principles of national sovereignty, people's empowerment, and social justice.

The revolutionary armed communist movement centred in the Philippine countryside is another force that champions this anti-imperialism. It has waged a war of national liberation and democracy for over five decades,[5] outliving dictatorships and fascist regimes then and now.

Finally, beyond the confines of the nation, anti-imperialism has also been expressed in the International League of Peoples' Struggle (ILPS). Founded in 2001 by 218 mass organisations from 40 countries, the Philippines included, the league seeks to promote, support and develop the "anti-imperialist and democratic struggles of the people of the world against imperialism and all reaction."[6] This inspiration was taken from what Lenin[7] himself described as genuine internationalism: "There is one, and only one, kind of real internationalism, and that is – working whole-heartedly for the development of the revolutionary movement and the revolutionary struggle in *one's own* country, and supporting (by propaganda, sympathy, and material aid) *this struggle*, this, and *only this*, line, in *every* country without exception." Despite the global backlash against leftist politics after the demise

---

2 See e.g., Mpofu, William (2022), "The Philosophy of Liberation: Troubling the Marxism of the 21st Century in Africa," in Sabelo J. Ndlovu-Gatsheni and Morgan Ndlovu (eds.), *Marxism and Decolonization in the 21st Century*. London and New York: Routledge, 31-48.
3 See Smith, Michael N. (2022), "The Limits of Postcolonial Critique of Marxism: A Defence of Radical Universalism," in Sabelo J. Ndlovu-Gatsheni and Morgan Ndlovu (eds.), *Marxism and Decolonization in the 21st Century*. London and New York: Routledge, 49-67.
4 See BAYAN website.
5 See Guerrero, Amado (1970/71), *Philippine Society and Revolution*. Marxists Internet Archive.
6 See ILPS website.
7 Lenin, V.I. (1974), "The Task of the Proletariat in our Revolution," in *Collected Works Vol. 24*. Moscow: Progress Publishers, 75.

of the USSR, the league has endured in answering the challenge of creating an "international rallying force in the struggle for national independence, democracy, and social liberation," and attempting to create the conditions for the advance of the revolutionary movement throughout the world.

As a matter of fact, *BAYAN* is among the founding member organisations of the ILPS. It has repeatedly recognised the importance of forging internationalist solidarities especially given the waves of forced migrations of Filipinos to developed countries. Many of these Filipinos, paradoxically honoured today by successive Philippine governments as modern-day heroes, suffer the most exploitative working conditions abroad. Lenin himself saw a "decline in emigration from imperialist countries and the increase in immigration into these countries from the more backward countries where lower wages are paid."[8] With an export-oriented import-dependent economy, the Philippine government is structurally inclined to export its own labour rather than to emancipate it from a depressed economic condition instigated by ongoing imperialism.

In the face of a worsening imperialist crisis, working people the world over today bear the brunt of having to produce super-profits, which ironically alienate them from a wealth they themselves created. In the spirit of Lenin's anti-imperialism and internationalism, the local as well as international anti-imperialist forces must hence strengthen themselves to confront and resist imperialism. The anti-imperialist forces in the Philippines, amidst many years of brutal repression, could strengthen themselves only by forging internationalist solidarities. In this way, they also embody the legacy of the late, great Filipino revolutionary, internationalist and ILPS chairperson emeritus Jose Maria Sison. Commenting on how Lenin expanded and further informed the development of an internationalist Marxism as "a guide to revolutionary action," Sison explained that, following Marx, "Lenin [called] on all oppressed nations and peoples to unite against monopoly capitalism in the era of modern imperialism and proletarian revolution."[9] In other words, Lenin saw in the weakest link not only objective conditions but also a subjective force whose strength – when combined with the comradely relations it will forge with other anti-imperialist formations – could finally break imperialism's chain of oppression.

Regletto Aldrich Imbong is Associate Professor of Philosophy at the University of the Philippines Cebu.

---

8 Lenin 1974: 282.
9 See Sison, Jose Maria (2021), "On Internationalism." Available online.

82. Against the Capitalist Scaremongers from 1917 to 2024, 2025, etc.

Richard Gilman-Opalsky

V.I. Lenin was serious about revolution, about the active processes of abolishing the capitalist form of life and creating something new. He was a serious scholar, a deep reader of philosophy and history, a comrade invested in the hopeful becoming of a different world.

I also have many criticisms of Lenin at my own far remove from his life and times, and even share some of those articulated while he was living. In the web of disagreements between Rosa Luxemburg and Lenin, for example, I always found myself closer to Rosa; and today, only the most ideological and reactionary (i.e., only the worst) Marxists would flippantly discount anarchist insights like those in Emma Goldman's *My Disillusionment in Russia*. I may even identify as one of the left-wing communists who suffer from what Lenin called an "infantile disorder," an identity I might defend today as utterly necessary for the future of Marxism.

Left-wing communists have always worried about the practical permutations of Marx's philosophy that might ultimately undermine anti-capitalist struggles and aims. We know that Marx himself did not take kindly to editorial modifications of his thinking. Communists today must therefore go back to basic principles like the left-wing communists of old. On the other hand, it is crucial to understand that Lenin lived in a context of active revolutionary change, and that he could thus not remain fixed on theoretical questions while the question of "what is to be done" was being raised anew every day and demanded fast answers and action. One has to respect the difference between thinking about revolution when it is far away as opposed to when the abolition of the *status quo* is actively underway.

Whatever else happened around Lenin, whatever obstacles he faced and navigated, whatever debates he took up against his critics, whatever mistakes... he has to be honoured and appreciated for his unrelenting defence of Marx and Engels' revolutionary work, and for his conviction that revolutionary ideas could indeed be practised so long as they were not falsified or distorted by opportunists, liberals, and other ideological axe-grinders.

In 1917 (after February but before the October Revolution), Lenin wrote a short piece; "How the Capitalists Are Trying to Scare the People."[1] Some facts of 1917 remain facts of the present. One of the greatest of all obstacles facing revolutionaries then and now is the fear that what is bad may get worse, that what little we have may be lost. Certainly, liberals and conservatives fear any overturning of the *status quo*, but revolutionaries too

---

1 Lenin, V.I. (1974), "How the Capitalists Are Trying to Scare the People," in *Collected Works Vol. 24*, Moscow: Progress Publishers, 439-440.

must take serious risks in the face of few certainties. The rationale of liberals and conservatives favours even a miserable *status quo* over the possibility of a more miserable *status quo* with fewer of the perks. One iteration of the fear: imagine the same nightmare as this, but without our phones!

Lenin read an editorial of capitalist scaremongering published in the *Finansovaya Gazeta* (Financial Newspaper), which provoked him to write his rebuttal. The editorial worried about destabilising upheaval, class war that would lead to financial crash, and millions of people losing their property. It warned that all "non-socialists" would be rounded up and arrested. In warning readers about financial and social instability and property-less millions, the author of the editorial may as well have been describing the terrors of their own capitalist reality, or even the terrors of a future capitalism, the one we now call the present.

In any case, Lenin had to fight against a capitalist politics of fear. We must do that still. Revolutionary politics, and a caricatured Marxian left, are still targeted in political discourses around the world. You may find this in the United States as recently as in the summer and fall of 2023 in the speeches and interviews of former president and clown-hero of racial-capitalism, Donald Trump. If you have the stomach for such bile, search the transcripts of Trump's speeches where he constantly and explicitly invokes the threats of Marxism, socialism, communism, and anarchism, to the rapt attention of millions. No doubt, a spectre still haunts. Perhaps that is good news and bad news.

To offer just one example, in March 2023, at the meeting of the Conservative Political Action Committee, Trump said, "We're now in a Marxism state of mind, a communism state of mind." In the same speech, he said that "sinister forces trying to kill America have done everything they can to stop me, to silence you, and to turn this nation into a socialist dumping ground for criminals, junkies, Marxists, thugs, radicals, and dangerous refugees that no other country wants... If those opposing us succeed, our once beautiful USA will be a failed country that no one will even recognise. A lawless, open borders, crime-ridden, filthy, communist nightmare."[2]

Lenin rebutted in 1917 that "the capitalists are deceiving themselves and the people." Deception about communism, and a spectacular mythology about capitalism, predate and outlive the defining discourses of the Cold War. They are as constant as capital itself.

It is tempting to make light of Trump's idiotic remarks. Lenin, however, knew to take idiotic remarks about Marxism, socialism, and communism seriously, to combat them. Thankfully, we need not read Trump's transcripts or address him by name. However, following Lenin, we must continue to find ways to counteract the scaremongering of our enemies. That old challenge remains.

---

2 See "Trump speaks at CPAC 2023 Transcript." Available online.

Capitalism is a nonstop engine of extraction, exploitation, and ecological destruction, which is also responsible for a psycho-social crisis that may prove more catastrophic more quickly than financial or ecological catastrophe. Naturally, the ruling class never opposes capitalism because capitalism reliably consolidates that class's wealth and power. Further, capitalist scaremongers always insist – from 1917 to 2024, 2025, etc. – that capitalism gives everything to everyone and that its opponents would take everything you love and desire away. Scaremongers say you will have to abdicate everything from your property to each individual joy, no matter how intermittent those joys may be.

Lenin responds: "Socialists are out to make only the landowners and capitalists 'abdicate.'... it is sufficient to make a few hundred, at the most one or two thousand, millionaires, bank and industrial and commercial bosses, 'abdicate' their property... This would be quite enough to break the resistance of capital. Even this tiny group of wealthy people need not have all their property rights taken away from them... The question at issue is merely that of breaking down the resistance of a few hundred millionaires."

Today, over a century later, we would speak of billionaires, although perhaps no more than the few hundred to one or two thousand of the same class. That is to say, we communists seek the abolition of the wealth and power of a tiny subset of the world population. But that tiny cabal will not give up anything by law, certainly not by laws that are written and upheld by and for the ruling class. And the ruling class will not voluntarily abdicate their wealth and power simply because they've heard a strong argument. For that abdication, we need revolution, as necessary in 2024, 2025, etc. as in 1917.

Richard Gilman-Opalsky (he/him) is Professor of Political Theory and Philosophy in the School of Politics and International Affairs at the University of Illinois, Springfield. He is the author of many books, including The Communism of Love, Communist Ontologies, *and* Imaginary Power, Real Horizons.

83. Lenin and Me

Ronald Grigor Suny

I was in the Soviet Union in 1970, the one hundredth anniversary of Lenin's birth, and while ceremonies of commemoration were ubiquitous, so were jokes about the founding father of the USSR. One I remember was about a young boy who sees an old man fishing on the bank of a river. The curious kid asks, "Any luck?" The old man snarls, "Get out of here. Don't bother me. Can't you see I'm fishing?" A few years later the boy passes by the river again, and there is the old man. He shyly asks: "Have you caught anything?" Again, the man, irritated, shouts, "Get the hell out of here. I'm fishing." Many years later, when the boy himself is an old man, he publishes his memoirs: *Moi vstrechi s Leninym* (My Meetings with Lenin).

I never met Lenin (I am not that old), but I feel like I have lived with him for much of my 83 years. At home there is a Lenin in almost every room, and guests are encouraged to try to find them. I can say I am an admirer of Lenin as well as a reluctant critic. While I am a biographer of the young Stalin rather than of his mentor, Lenin is a powerful presence in most of my published work. In *The Soviet Experiment*, a survey textbook of the history of the USSR from Vladimir Il'ich Lenin to Vladimir Vladimirovich Putin, the dominant emotion is regret: regret that Lenin's project did ultimately not succeed in creating a democratic socialist Russia. This makes me remember another anecdote from half a century ago. Lenin returns to the Soviet Union on that hallowed anniversary and looks around. Saddened by what happened to his dream, he comments: "*My khoteli stroit' Sovetskuiu vlast', no nepolochilos*" – "We wanted to build Soviet Power, but it didn't work out."

Speaking of which, when I first went to the Soviet Union as an exchange student in the mid-1960s, it was a moment when what was known as the 'Thaw' was just beginning to freeze. It was the year that the dissident writers, Andrei Sinyavskii and Yuri Daniel, were arrested, the first sign of retreat from greater liberty in the post-Stalin years. Yet, there was still faith in the socialist project among the people I met. Party officials spoke of a return to Leninism, though it was not clear what that meant. There was optimism about the future, combined with the living memory of the great catastrophe that the Soviet people had gone through only twenty years earlier, the Great Fatherland War. A sober sadness coexisted with stoic commitment to building something better than what they imagined was the West, at least among the gifted and privileged students with whom I lived in the Moscow State University dormitory in the Lenin Hills.

I would eventually conclude that Soviet history was about change and the expectation of change, change for the better. The whole enterprise was about creating a new and better society, something called socialism, and then communism. Marxism, a dedicatedly secular humanism, held firmly to the promise of progress presented in the Enlightenment. This was fundamental to the Soviet's rhetoric of legitimation, and I was convinced that if greater democracy were finally introduced, the experiment would flourish. Instead, the Brezhnev regime attempted to conserve what had already been built. With the crushing of the Prague Spring in 1968, it was clear to me that a turning point had failed to turn. The disillusion with the Soviet project began from the top, with intellectuals, and through the next decades, as I observed in my trips to the USSR in the 1970s and 1980s, it inexorably spread downward to the broader public. A brief eruption of hope in the Gorbachev years sputtered into despair as the economy tanked.

Yesterday and today, conservative historians argue that the apex of Soviet history was Stalinism. In their deductive model, which they glean from their superficial readings of Marx and Lenin, they see the failure of the Soviet experience inscribed in the DNA of the revolution. My own work, on the other hand, argues that Soviet history is better understood as a series of improvisations with little a priori guidance from the classics. Lenin and the Bolsheviks attempted to build their elusive socialist society under extraordinarily difficult and perilous conditions. Lenin and Trotsky knew that one had to work with what one had. Thus, in the first years after the revolution, their original hopes and ambitions were repeatedly compromised as Soviet society moved back to reinstating old hierarchies. Commands from above substituted for initiatives from below. Their growing suspicions of the capacity of ordinary people to fulfil the promise of 1917 led to dominance by party and state officials, centralisation of decision-making within the party elite, and the atrophy of soviet democracy. But even with the fatal outlawing of organised factions within the RCP(b) in March 1921, throughout the early 1920s raucous and divisive debates continued. After Lenin's death, however, his practice of treating politics as a form of war helped steadily to erode debate and dissent. By 1928 criticism became dangerous, and Stalin and his closest followers reduced disputes to savage, often fabricated, accusations against their opponents and imagined enemies. The descent into despotism accelerated.

Lenin and Stalin stand on opposite sides of the great divide that make up understandings of the Soviet experiment. Lenin remains a figure of possibilities, of lost opportunities, but also of the original inspiration that suffused Russian Social Democracy, that is, to create a popular democratic revolution that could found a socialist society. As Trotsky put it so vividly at the time of the Great Purges, between Bolshevism and Stalinism there exists "not simply a bloody line but a whole river of blood." The revolution had been betrayed, and Stalin stood on the opposing bank. And yet, Marxists must face squarely the fact that Stalinism did not grow out of Buddhism but from Leninism.

To admire Lenin critically is thus to preserve the promise of 1917 when ordinary women and men, in that order, went out on the streets to overthrow a tyrannical regime. They were joined by soldiers and sailors, and tsarism fell. A euphoria of freedom was briefly experienced. As violent as the February, July, and October days were, followed by civil war, people had taken power and political initiative into their own hands. Their sacrifices belie the Western stereotype that Russians and the other peoples of that defunct empire desire autocracy and/or the rule by strong, despotic men.

But the promise of 1917 (as well as 1989-1991) was not fulfilled, and neither were those of other democratic uprisings of ordinary people in the non-Western world, like the 1979 Iranian Revolution, the Arab Spring or many anti-colonial revolts. Rather than resorting to essentialist views of Russians or Slavs, Muslims or Africans, I believe the cause of political degeneration lies not with the *demos* but with elites, who in the chaos of revolution use the opportunity of institutional destruction along with, when necessary, the most brutal force, to seize and hold onto power.

In sum, it is the Lenin of the decades before and immediately after the revolution that continues to inspire, the revolutionary who risked all to fight autocracy. It was that Lenin whose image, as a naïve, untenured assistant professor of history attempting to understand as neutrally and objectively as possible what was transpiring in the designated enemy of the country in which I was born and lived, I dared to hang on my office door at Oberlin College. That six-foot long poster read: *Lenin zhil, Lenin zhiv, Lenin budet zhit'* (Lenin Lived, Lenin Lives, Lenin Will Live). Nowadays, my Lenin posters, old banners and busts as well as other relics of Soviet times are at home with me, reminders of what had been attempted, achieved, and lost.

Ronald Grigor Suny is Professor Emeritus of History and Political Science at the University of Michigan and the University of Chicago.

84. Whatever Would Lenin Have Said? – We Owe Him an Answer!

Ronald Matthijssen

In these *organic* times the advice for the revolutionary at heart is to let a movement aimed at leading to a takeover of power grow *organically*. In the days of my coming of age, that would have been a daunting idea. Any leftist movement of acceptable size was steered by a party. And so, at 17, I joined the Dutch Radical Policy Party (PPR), because of their environmental policies and their opposition to the boycott of the Moscow Olympics. And then, personally and politically (which feminism declared synonymous), things began to accelerate. 1979 saw the rise of the Squatter Movement in the Netherlands, as part of an international movement directed at solving the housing crisis by occupying and appropriating capitalist investment objects. There was no party, no theory, not even a formal organisation (at least not in the early years). It looked more like a spontaneous revolution, challenging the power of the state at the local level.

In 1980, I left the PPR, because the party was too keen on getting back into government (i.e. too opportunistic) and disregarded the grassroots movements popping up everywhere. Suspecting a revolutionary potential, I joined the Communist Party of the Netherlands (CPN), whilst joining the squatter movement at the same time. This proved to be quite a stretch. Besides being a district board member and responsible for the distribution of the Dutch *Pravda* in that district, I was reading and discussing Marxist-Leninist theory on the one hand and participating in direct action on the other. Simultaneously I was also involved in the anti-racist movement, centring on the abominable housing conditions of immigrants from the former (Suriname) and continuing (Dutch Antilles) colonies. Unsurprisingly, this movement was also split between an 'organic' (i.e., 'anarchist') and a theory-led faction. Debate was everywhere.

In short, a perfect backdrop for studying V.I. Lenin's *What Is to Be Done?* Reading it felt like being let in on a secret regarding the next level of revolutionary consciousness, something I like to call the 'Gaze Beyond.' "Without revolutionary theory, there can be no revolutionary movement."[1] This issue was usually the start of every debate within the different movements at the time. Many of my comrades-in-arms rejected all theory as a form of limitation of their freedom to act spontaneously. They simply wanted to be in permanent opposition to the powers that be, or to put it plainly: they wanted the freedom to riot randomly. The idea that at one point a new order must set in to claim victory and change the system for ever seemed to scare them. This new order might curtail their newly acquired

---

[1] Lenin, V.I. (1977), "What Is To Be Done?," in *Collected Works Vol. 5*, Moscow: Progress Publishers, 369.

freedoms, including the freedom to 'not belong' or, worse, to be incorporated into a broader movement. I thus began to understand the importance of what Lenin wrote: "Only those who are not sure of themselves can fear to enter into temporary alliances even with unreliable people; not a single political party could exist without alliances."[2] In the context of the time, the idea of an alliance as *temporary* and directed at a single purpose dawned on me as the only logical and viable path, as opposed to what was happening in Italy (the so-called '*Compromesso Storico*' between the PCI and the DC) but also in other European countries, i.e., the beginning of the *continuous* alliance between a growing number of parties of the so-called Left and the representatives of capitalism. But there was a 'but': what did it mean "to be sure of ourselves"? Sure in terms of being *convinced*, politically, philosophically, intellectually and even morally or rather, sure as in "being in a position of power"?

I decided that Lenin had meant the latter, because being merely convinced about anything was tantamount to self-righteousness. I was pretty sure that conviction alone did not win battles. Most people around me, however, were satisfied with their convictions without wanting to reflect on seizing power as the ultimate and necessary consequence of their activism, something I see being repeated today. In short, in the early 1980s neither the squatter movement, nor any segment of the real Left in general, regarded or even imagined itself as being in a position of power as meant by Lenin. On the contrary, it was the Reagan/Thatcher/Pinochet era, the Backlash Years. No reason for alliances of any sort, opposition was the only acceptable word.

But was this an accurate analysis or an historic failure? By abandoning the playing field, and perhaps at the most aspiring to sabotage the system, didn't we simply end up accepting defeat without genuine struggle? In fact, weren't we in reality already in a position of power, both in numbers (the working class) as well as in means (the mass demonstrations of the early 1980s opposing the deployment of nuclear missiles were the largest in history)? The term '99%' wouldn't be coined until 30 years later, but why weren't we conscious of our historical role and opportunities (or as Lenin put it, "widest perspectives") at the time?

Today we see that in most countries there is once again a total lack of theory when it comes to acting on the "the widest perspectives"[3] regarding the projected image of what is to be done when a position of power is achieved. In fact, it appears to have become increasingly difficult to even conceive of these widest perspectives with regards to a) the path to revolution (because of major doubts about who's in on it), b) what follows a successful revolution (the dictatorship of the proletariat?), and c) who is the real enemy to be defeated (external or internal). Moreover, as mentioned at the beginning, the obsession is on keeping movements 'organic,' that is, relying on spontaneism, which in itself is tantamount to "unbound opportunism."[4]

---

2 Ibid: 362.
3 Ibid: 392.
4 Ibid.

By way of example, look at today's Climate Change movement: millions are raising hell, challenging the exploiters of the planet, but I see no strategy to change the course of history. Instead, some people have joined reformist Green parties, while the majority seem to be eagerly anticipating a spontaneous revolution, and when that turns out be a pipe dream, this frustrated revolutionary energy will eventually lead to premature civil war in their own ranks, as opposed to "marching in a compact group along a precipitous and difficult path, firmly holding each other by the hand. [...] for the purpose of fighting the enemy."[5]

To conclude, the contemporary Left owes it to Lenin to work out the theory behind the future "position of power," in which alliances can be forged, and the civil war can preferably be waged against the enemies of the working class. Acknowledging that we are no longer living in early 20th-century Russia or even mid-20th-century Cuba, we must develop our own equivalent of the Dictatorship of the Proletariat. We must fight and win and know how to proceed thereafter. The question is still burning.

Ronald Matthijssen (*The Hague 61): social worker, teacher, translator and Theatre of the Oppressed practitioner, fell in love with Lenin as a young man and has enjoyed his company ever since.

---

[5] Ibid: 355.

Artist: Y.N. Tulin

85. Lenin on Women and Social Reproduction ... in Vietnam

Ly Hoang Minh Uyen
(Sally Mju)

Karl Marx laid the foundations for a Marxist theory of 'social reproduction' long ago, asserting that capital does not recognise the value of women's reproduction work, despite its vital importance to the maintenance of the capitalist system. Without women, who would cook for the industrial workers? Who would look after them when they are sick? Who would take care of the children, the home? Who would produce the next generation of toilers? Similarly, at the beginning of the 20th century, Rosa Luxemburg placed a strong emphasis on the value of 'unpaid' women, as shown in her 1912 "Women's Suffrage and Class Struggle," in which she highlights working women's "immense expenditure of energy and self-sacrifice in a thousand little tasks." Nevertheless, capitalism has thoroughly exploited this work while seemingly excluding it from the process of surplus production; as a result, social reproduction work has been marginalised in society, including in my own country, the Socialist Republic of Vietnam. In the words of Lenin, "it does not immediately strike the eye."

In recent decades, however, several waves of feminist movements have increasingly recognised the value of housework. Demanding wages for housework has become widespread in the US and Europe, as analyses of social reproduction have been expanded by Marxist-Feminists like Federici, Brown, Fortunati, Bhattacharya, and others. Interestingly, most studies on reproduction today do not mention Lenin's writings about women. Yet, as a man who prioritised people's liberation from all types of oppression, Lenin's major concern with women and children is important to keep in mind. I, therefore, aim to make a short argument that Lenin indeed made several contributions to women's liberation as well as the theory of social reproduction. Moreover, I would like to relate his work to the current situation of women in Vietnam.

In the first place, Lenin conducted extensive studies on the working conditions of women in the agricultural and public service sector, and even at home, for his early writings on capitalism. For example, Lenin addressed the unfairness of forcing women and children "of the tenderest age" to work long hours for very little pay in *The Development of Capitalism in Russia*:

> The working day in the woman's industries in general is as much as 18 hours [...] the wages of those who obtain their livelihood exclusively by factory labour [are] below their minimum needs.

Lenin also saw early on that although the capitalist class had repeatedly modified its method of exploitation, the covert exploitation of women workers in the shape of household work remained, thereby concealing its fundamental importance in the reproduction of capitalist social relations. Hence, Lenin referred to exploited housewives as "household slaves" and "unpaid labour" because they had to perform their unpaid reproduction work first for their husbands, second for capitalist society.

> No matter how much democracy there is under capitalism, the woman remains a 'domestic slave,' a slave locked in the bedroom, nursery, kitchen.

Likewise, after the revolution, at the 1918 First All Russia Congress of Working Women, Lenin voiced his concern about the treatment of women in the capitalist countries and the prospects of their liberation under socialism:

> In all civilised countries, even the most advanced, women are actually no more than domestic slaves. Women do not enjoy full equality in any capitalist state, not even in the freest of republics.

Finally, social reproduction also includes birth-giving and the right to abortion. In this regard, it is important to mention that already in 1913, Lenin affirmed that under conditions of Tsarist capitalism:

> [i]t goes without saying that this does not by any means prevent us from demanding the unconditional annulment of all laws against abortions [...] Such laws are nothing but the hypocrisy of the ruling classes.

Consequently, in the aftermath of October 1917, Soviet Russia became the first country in the world to legalise abortion, on "medical and social grounds," though the right to abortion was revoked under Stalin in 1936 and only decriminalised again in 1956 under Minister of Health Maria Kovrigina. As the latter put it in her unpublished autobiography: "The ban on abortion humiliated the personality of the woman herself, it controlled the intimate side of her life, not to mention the fact that many women paid for it by their health and even life itself."[1]

In my country, the majority of recent strikes and rights campaigns have been led by Vietnamese industrial workers, both men and women, in response to salary issues; however, despite some emerging debate on whether housework, known also as 'no-name work,' should be recognised and compensated,[2] there have been no explicit campaigns, movements or more systematic research to address the social reproduction issue. In general, in Vietnam there is still limited acceptance and understanding of the concept of social reproduction, as women continue to be expected to undertake unpaid reproductive work as a holy responsibility and a labour of love.

Concerning abortion, as a woman, what I want for myself and for other women is first and foremost to take care of my own health and basic personal needs such as access to birth control, medicine for menstrual pain and sanitary napkins, all of which should be considered fundamental human rights.

---

1 See Talaver, Sasha (2020), "When Soviet Women Won the Right to Abortion (for the Second Time)," *Jacobin*.
2 See Viet Nam News (2016), "Women's housework should be part of GDP: researchers."

Moreover, as currently seen across the world, we women want to have the right to control our own body. Or in the words of Silvia Federici, "Control over our bodies has two aspects: we want to be free to decide not to have children, but we also want the right to have children."[3] In Vietnam, although women have the choice to get an abortion legally, they often cannot decide freely but are dependent on the state and the economic policies of the government.

To give an historic example, after the end of the Vietnam War in 1975, a two-child family policy was introduced by the new

Socialist government to achieve a reduction in poverty and food shortages. The government promoted phrases like "a family with two children is happy" and forced women to have abortions if they became pregnant with a third child, which was obviously a highly distressing experience for women. The two-child policy is still in place today, albeit less strictly applied as part of an effort by the current government to boost the working population. However, it is still a serious regulation for women who work in the public sector. In general terms, abortion has been legal throughout the country since 1975, but because it is not covered by the government-sponsored health insurance, women incur high charges at both public and private facilities. Also, Vietnamese society generally considers abortions to be 'sinful.' Hence, a woman who has an abortion will often be called a murderer, regardless of whether she is a single mother or a party member who does not want to violate official population policies. In addition, in the case of teenagers and religious women, it would be 'shameful' if their family knew, so they frequently 'choose' to have the procedure in secret clinics, which do not ensure their health, so as to avoid having to face isolation by society.

To conclude, this article provided a brief summary of some of Lenin's views on the issues of women's exploitation, through the lens of today's situation in Vietnam. These views, together with those of Luxemburg and many contemporary scholar-activists, are still valuable for the worldwide woman's movement, in order to obtain fundamental rights and emancipation, such as the right to be recognised for our labour at home and the right to abortion. Lenin concluded that movements to liberate women from oppression must necessarily embrace the theory and practice of socialism:

> The status of women up to now has been compared to that of a slave; women have been tied to the home, and only socialism can save them from this.

I concur with Lenin that only socialism can bring all of humanity freedom. In this sense, given that Vietnam is officially a socialist country, women's issues should (finally) be given top priority.

Ly Hoang Minh Uyen (Sally Mju) is a translator and educator in Ho Chi Minh City, Vietnam.

---

[3] See Ashton, Catrin and Federici, Silvia (2022), "Not a Labor of Love. The Radicalization of Motherhood," *PS*.

86. Lenin on Imperialism: Wrong, But Also Right

Sam Gindin

Though emerging out of economic dynamics, Lenin understood capitalist imperialism as ultimately a political phenomenon based on the politicisation of competition. Analysed in his Imperialism, the Highest Stage of Capitalism, this modern imperialism came into being as competitive capitalism gave way to monopoly capital.

With the surge in the economic power of industrial and financial capital, monopoly capital acquired, in Lenin's argument, direct control over its respective states and these states came to win, on behalf of domestic capital, privileged access to foreign resources and markets. The resultant inter-imperial rivalry for dominance would bring the breakdown of international capitalism and signal "the eve of the social revolution of the proletariat."

Lenin was writing in the midst of WWI and given that war, the Great Depression that came soon after and another world war that followed, Lenin's prognosis seemed ratified. Yet capitalism proved stubbornly resilient. Capitalism persisted, the capitalist states that were at their "highest stages" did not suffer successful revolutions, and a distinctly new phase of capitalism, overseen by the hegemony of the American state, emerged towards the end of WWII. In spite of various mutations, this phase remains in place some eight decades later.

It would seem a hard sell to argue for hanging on to a theory tied to a conjuncture of a 100-plus years ago and proven wrong even for its own times. Yet many on the left insist that *specific* claims made by Lenin retain their relevance for grasping the dynamics and contradictions of capitalism today. The irony is that attempts to resuscitate Lenin's mistaken details get in the way of appreciating Lenin's more general insights. A good many Marxists have as a result appropriated much of what he got wrong and missed what he got right.

The devil is in the details: where Lenin fell short

There are a good many assertions in *Imperialism* that could be challenged: capitalism's tendency to underconsumption, the casual references to a "labour aristocracy," the over- generalisations about finance from the experiences of specific countries. But three analytical points are especially significant.

i) Monopoly capital

The development of capitalism did indeed concentrate capital into fewer but larger units. But greater concentration is not synonymous with less competition; in fact, the trajectory runs in the opposite direction. Capitalism's development actually *intensifies* competition.

Aside from pressures to offset the higher capital costs through aggressively trying to increase market share and the acceleration of capital mobility that came with transformations in finance, there are competitive capacities linked to greater size. Institutionalised market research, technical know-how, administrative organisation and access to financial resources enabled the scope of competition to be extended from local/regional spaces to national/international ones and to crossing sectoral boundaries.

Against the expectations implied in Lenin's emphasis on the rise of monopolies, of the twenty largest US corporations when Lenin was writing, only two are still on that list today (Ford and Exxon). Notable too is that Amazon, the second largest US corporation by sales and a common example of monopolistic power, is battling the largest corporation, Walmart, in the retail sector while competing with search engines and social media platforms for the advertising dollar, with Google and Microsoft over the Cloud, and with all of high tech and a host of start-ups over AI.

ii) State theory

Lenin's description of monopoly capital's capture of the state is far too instrumental. Private corporations and factions of capital have different, often inconsistent, interests and in any case are not always sure about the best answers to capitalist crises and future directions. It is states that, over time, developed the capacities to unite capital, address crises, look beyond issues of current profitability, disorganise and contain labour, and address the international context.

These capacities, fundamental to reproducing capitalism as a whole, provide the state a degree of autonomy from particular capitalist interests, thereby imbuing it with an aura of democratic legitimacy (succinctly captured by Angela Markel's marvellously honest expression "market-conforming democracy").

iii) Inter-imperial rivalry

Kautsky had suggested the possibility of capitalist states coming together in an agreement that served their collective interests ("ultra-imperialism"). Lenin scoffed at this; the uneven development of capitalism and the consequent jockeying for leadership would undermine any such agreement. He did not foresee – it is hard to imagine anyone foreseeing – the possibility that the material conditions might be created for effecting such a period of relatively peaceful economic competition.

The American state pulled this off through materially integrating capital into an empire that it itself oversaw. It would be guided by the 'rule of law' whereby the distribution of benefits would be determined not by force but through competition in free markets for goods, services and capital flows. And each state would take responsibility for establishing – with appropriate repression as needed – the conditions, within its own territories, for global accumulation (with foreign capital having the same rights as domestic capital).

Did Lenin get anything right about imperialism?

Definitely! Three aspects of Lenin's formulation of the imperialist moment are especially valuable. First, he starts with what is specific about capitalism as a mode of production – its political economy – and analyses where that is heading.

Second, he distinguishes between capitalist exploitation and imperialism. Investment abroad and international trade may exploit workers in other countries, but like exploitation domestically, that is just capitalism doing its thing. It is when strong states step in and limit the political sovereignty of weaker states that Lenin sees imperialism at work. This allows imperialism to be understood in broader terms than invasion and direct control over a territory or state: countries may have formal sovereignty but in reality that sovereignty is compromised through economic and legal mechanisms.

Third, the emphasis on the export of capital as a prime attribute of imperialism can lead to baffling conclusions. Would we say that the massive capital investments of China and Japan in the US, or Germany building expensive auto plants in the US, makes them imperialist actors? Lenin's theorisation allows us to escape such confusions by emphasising the general tendency of *all* capital, at a particular stage of capitalist development, to look to capital exports. That is, he moves beyond the acts of individual corporations or states and analyses imperialism as a totality, as a *system*. This offers a clearer and richer characterisation through which to approach modern imperialism.

From imperialism to the American Empire

Looking back from the end of the 1970s, Giovanni Arrighi commented that by the end of the 1960s, the theory of imperialism had become "a 'Tower of Babel,' in which not even Marxists knew any longer how to find their way." What was the relevance of the theory of imperialism when the clear hegemony of the United States of America pushed aside inter-imperial rivalry? Or when formally sovereign states were internationalised in the sense of taking on the responsibility within their own territory for the accumulation of global capitalism? Or when manufacturing was moving to the global south and though very uneven, the global south was often growing faster than 'the west'?

The question clearly wasn't whether uneven relations between states had disappeared. In overseeing this new world order, only the American state could essentially decide whether any particular state qualified for 'sovereignty.' The rhetorical criterion was 'democracy;' the substantive criteria were, however, not popular freedoms but the economic freedoms of property rights, free markets and American hegemony. Alongside this, as the 'indispensable nation' the American state retained the 'flexibility' to adjust rules to guarantee its special status. Though the states dependent on this order sometimes complained, they generally accepted this 'reality.' And as hegemonic powers often do, any autonomy expressed to its absolute power – e.g. as with China or Russia – was and is identified as a 'threat.'

Conclusion

There is a seduction in predictions that promise that "objective contradictions" – like inter-imperial rivalry – will do much of the heavy lifting for us. This is not just bad analysis, but bad politics. In the context of our (i.e. the left's) weakness, if capitalism does go into a deep crisis, the beneficiaries are as likely to be the right as our side; international rivalry may strengthen nationalism and marginalise rather than stimulate a class response; and workers may, given their limited options, put their faith in fixing the system so they can return to a past now looking far better than it did before the crisis.

Therefore, the most important crisis to discuss isn't the one confronting capitalism but the one confronting the left. In this regard, we might set Lenin's pamphlet on imperialism aside and turn to Lenin's explicitly political challenges. How much longer can we avoid the obvious necessity of a socialist party to serve as a space for making socialists and spreading socialist ideas, strategizing, and deliberating soberly over lessons learned? How to build a working class with the vision and capacities to put socialism on the map again? And how do we find/make the time to do this in the face of economic pressures – including those brought about/facilitated by 'imperialism' – and do so with the joy that sustains our humanity along the way?

Sam Gindin spent his working life as Research Director of the Canadian Auto Workers and is co-author with Leo Panitch of The Making of Global Capitalism: The Political Economy of American Empire.

87. Lenin as Method

Sandro Mezzadra

Remember the lines written by Vladimir Mayakovsky soon after Lenin's death: "I'm anxious lest rituals,/mausoleums/and processions,/the honeyed incense/of homage and publicity/should obscure/Lenin's essential/simplicity." It happened, we know, and not only in the USSR. In many versions of Marxism-Leninism, Lenin became an icon at the cost of turning his words into eternal truths, seemingly solid like rock but in fact doomed to be shattered by the stormy winds of history.

It is even too easy to contrast such a frozen image of Lenin with his understanding of dialectics. Take his struggle with Hegel in 1915-16, his reading of *Science of Logic* while Europe was in flames and he was in search of theoretical tools that would soon become political weapons. In his *Philosophical Notebooks*, Lenin writes about "the idea of universal movement and change," he takes due note of "self-movement," "change," "movement and vitality," "impulse," "activity," as key elements of being and history – against any "*dead Being.*"

But there is more to be said here. What really matters is the way in which Lenin's political thought and practice have been 'received' and understood, more often than not by friends and enemies alike. Lenin's style, the inflexibility and even violence with which he led political struggles in and outside the party, may have contributed to the idea that he was obsessed by orthodoxy. Or take his famous words, written in 1913: "the Marxist doctrine is omnipotent because it is true. It is comprehensive and harmonious, and provides men with an integral world outlook." It would be difficult to write such words again today, and even reading them causes a sense of unease.

Nonetheless, Lenin's style was, in essence, politically motivated, and aimed at keeping united a party that he considered – at least since he had published *What is to Be Done?* in 1902 – the only adequate tool for revolutionary politics in Russia in an age of turmoil, repression and war. Too often, the peremptory tone of his writings and his emphasis on the 'correct line' in theory and practice have obscured what seems to me the main characteristic of Lenin's method – a method that is focused on the elements of *rupture* and *discontinuity*. Needless to say, these are elements that exist in tension with any 'frozen' orthodoxy, and rather require a constant adaptation to shifting circumstances.

This is something that Lenin himself writes regarding the tactics of the Bolsheviks in the Russian revolutionary process of 1917. "It is important to realise," we read in *Letters from Afar*, "that in revolutionary times the objective situation changes with the same swiftness and abruptness as the current of life in general. And we must *be able to adapt* our tactics and immediate tasks to the *specific features* of every given situation." The awareness of the novelty of the political conjuncture opened by the February

Revolution leads Lenin to struggle within his own party, denouncing what he calls arguments of "routinism," "inertia" and "stagnation."

Sure, 1917 was an exceptional year in Russia, and Lenin is talking about tactics here. But in what I called a method based on rupture and discontinuity, there is much more at stake. One can get a sense of that method by reading, for instance, *The Development of Capitalism in Russia* (1899), his first major work written in the Siberian exile. The polemic with the populists in that book is passionate, accurate and well known, what is less explored is the notion of capitalism that Lenin extrapolates from his analysis. With a conceptual clarity that was completely new in Russia, Lenin emphasises the disruptive effects of capitalist development, what he calls its "spasmodic character," and takes this tendency towards permanent change as the background against which revolutionary politics is to be rethought. One can even say that such an analysis foreshadows the break with any gradualist understanding of socialism that later became a hallmark of Lenin's politics, a politics that was always strictly intertwined with theory.

"Without revolutionary theory," Lenin famously writes in *What is to Be Done?*, "there can be no revolutionary movement." It would not take much work to show that each contribution he made to revolutionary theory – on such issues as the party and the state, to mention just two – and to revolutionary politics – in 1905 no less than during the Great War and in 1917 – is predicated on a method that emphasises and is informed by rupture and discontinuity. And this is a method that retains its power and effectiveness today, while we face a set of new "spasmodic" ruptures and discontinuities at the global level that tend to take the catastrophic form of proliferating wars and conflicting imperialisms.

Let me conclude with some words on this topic. It would be easy, but wrong, to hark back to Lenin's work on imperialism and to adapt it literally to the current global predicament. Capitalism has changed too rapidly over the last century, as has the relation between capital and state, which was a key point in Lenin's theory. However, his *Imperialism* (1917) builds a perfect instantiation of the method I have been outlining thus far. What is at stake in the book is a radical transition within capitalism, a profound transformation of the mode of production. "The old capitalism," Lenin writes here, "the capitalism of free competition with its indispensable regulator, the Stock Exchange, is passing away." While the original analysis outlined in *Imperialism* later nurtured theories of "state monopoly capitalism" (or stamocap) often deemed to represent the last configuration of capitalism, there is a lot to learn from Lenin's struggle to grasp and respond to the new contours of the mode of production in his times in the context of its momentous transformations today. To put it with Leninist "simplicity": a new capitalism requires a new revolutionary theory and politics.

Of course, Lenin was writing about imperialism in a conjuncture of unprecedented war in Europe, when the basic elements of the world order (British hegemony, according to Giovanni Arrighi) were in ruins. There is no shortage of analogies with the time we are currently living through. Once we follow Lenin's politics in the years of the war, *he can become a method for us* – first and foremost in his fight to include "geopolitical" factors within his understanding of class struggle and communist politics in Russia and on the world scale. It is precisely this articulation between world politics and social struggles that becomes crucial again today.

And Lenin has more than one lesson to teach in this respect. His writings in the years of the war (for instance on the national question) are so striking also because they signal his steady awareness of the relevance of anticolonial struggles, of a new world ("India, China, Persia, Egypt," he writes in 1915) that leads him to break with any Eurocentrism and to understand communist politics as world politics. This is a powerful shift in the history of Marxism, one from which we can draw inspiration today to once again analyse, understand and name the tremendous shifts of power – the multiple crises and transformation of the current world order – that we are witnessing from the angle of the revolutionary potentialities hidden behind them. I repeat, Lenin as method: this is for me the best way to celebrate the centenary of his death and his fully terrestrial afterlife. Under the sign of his "simplicity," to echo the words of Mayakovsky.

Sandro Mezzadra teaches political theory at the University of Bologna and has been participating for many years in autonomist movements in Italy and elsewhere in the world.

88. 'Lenin' is the Name of a Man

Sara Katona

'Lenin' is the name of a man
created for a revolution.
He is a character built for his duties.
Someone created to suffer for his cause
with no function but revolution,
no work but revolutionary work,
no passion but for revolution.

Vladimir Ulyanov is the name of a man
who chose revolution.
His character built out of middle-class money.
A man who chose to suffer for his cause
with no function demanded of him,
no work, but duties he selected,
no passion but for revolution.

I am not a communist because of Karl Marx or Vladimir Ulyanov.
In them, I find kinship and cause.
They have grounded my ideals in theory and logic,
but they never professed to have instruction manuals,
or prophesied their application to this era.
How amused and ashamed would they be,
to see their works idolised, worshiped, divisive?

Those theorists we deify would argue
their role was mandatory,
but their person ephemeral.

But today,
"In unity,"
"In solidarity,"
We, us, our "comrades"
pin "The Movement"
stagnant between our tomes.

Why do we hold to them so tightly,
as if ideas are nonrenewable resources,
and with their finiteness,
we reject anything else in fear
that a loosened hold
will wither not our idolatry, but our idols?

In solitude and desperation,
we join leftist communities,
only to become part of the problem.

Organisations claim "multi-tendency,"
but we know better.
Leftist infighting:
Tankies and brocialists,
reds and the dirtbag left.
"Are you demsoc or an actual communist?"

Is accessibility our goal today?
Coded language,
unclear delineation.

In America, we ask:
IMT, PSL, DSA, SPUSA…?
Choose your acronym,
"I'll tell you why you're wrong."

New here?
Don't be.
There will be no elaboration.

It is the job of those privileged with time and ability
"To enlighten and organise
forces for the struggle."[1]
While chairing an anti-war anti-imperialist group
For a socialist party,
I was kicked out of a communist book club,
for asking questions.

We are not Plekhanov and Lenin,
with whom divides came to head
at a time of great change.
Praxis makes perfect.
"It is, of course,
much easier to shout, abuse, and howl
than to attempt to relate, to explain."[2]

---

1 See Lenin, "The Three Sources and Three Component Parts of Marxism."
2 See Lenin, "April Theses."

Communism is the name of an ideology
created for equity.
It is a philosophy built for compassion.
An idea created from suffering to give cause,
with no function but what we give it,
no work but what we put into it,
no passion but our passion.

Sara Elizabeth Katona (they/them) is an off-brand academic who enjoys researching and deconstructing traditional colonial institutional discourse by listening to how people construct, perceive and situate their own identities.

Artist: Ernst Jazdzweski

89. On the Eve of Revolution When Ilyich Visits Rosa...

Sevgi Doğan

February 1916. Berlin. Barnimstrasse Womens' Prison. Outside it is snowing, "a soft breeze is blowing from above through [her] dormer window into the cell causing [her] green lampshade to stir slightly, gently blowing the pages of"[1] open books and letters on the tiny table.

Rosa Luxemburg is either reading or writing as a scent of loneliness permeates the damp, mouldy cell. The table is full of her favourite books, among them Vladimir Korolenko's *A History of My Contemporary*, which she is currently translating into German, and Goethe's *Faust*, open at the page of what she knows to be **Ilyich**'s favourite line, where Mephistopheles says: "Theory, my friend, is grey, but green is the eternal tree of life." There are open letters in Russian, German and Polish, and another one that she has just begun to write that begins, "My dearest Klara!"

Luxemburg appears to be deep in thought as she looks at the letter she holds in her freezing fingers. When the cell door is opened, she startles and turns around.

Luxemburg: Did he arrive?

Wardress: Yes, he is waiting in the courtyard.

Rosa takes her shawl and wraps it around her shoulders. She tidies her messy grey hair in the tiny mirror on the wall and makes a sign to the guard that they can go. She walks, staggering left and right, through the cold, damp and gloomy corridor towards the courtyard. Outside, with his ever-balding head and well-groomed beard, Lenin stands deep in thought, caressing his beard. In earlier years, Luxemburg had once described him as clever and well educated with "such an ugly mug, the kind [she] liked to look at,"[2] not forgetting to add how much – all differences aside – she enjoyed talking with him.[3] Their common friend and comrade Clara Zetkin had informed her that **Lenin** wanted to see her. Now, finally, he was here.

Luxemburg: My dearest **Vladimir**, I was waiting for you, what a pleasure to see you again. I remember the first time we met in May 1901 in Munich where I saw you with Parvus. I guess you were there anonymously for the

---

1 Luxemburg, Rosa (2011), *The Letters of Rosa Luxemburg*. London: Verso, 175.
2 Ibid: 298.
3 Ibid: 298.

publication of your wretched *What is to be done?*[4] But when was the last time we saw each other, I do not remember, help me please?

Lenin: Rosa, the pleasure is all mine! Actually, according to your future biographer Elzbieta Ettinger,[5] we first met in Berlin in 1901. But it does not really matter, does it, the important thing is that we met, although sometimes we may have preferred to be far away from each other!

They both laugh.

Lenin: By the way, I fondly recall your beloved cat, Mimi. I remember how "she impressed [me] tremendously, [...] she was a *barskii kot* – a majestic cat." I think she might have even "flirted with [me], roll[ing] on her back and behav[ing] enticingly toward [me], but when [I] tried to approach her, she whacked [me] with a paw and snarled like a tiger."[6] The two of you are quite alike.

Luxemburg: Ohh! **Vladimir**, believe me, "I can grieve or feel bad if Mimi is sick or if [my dear friends] are not well."[7] The other day, "I was so tired and had such a hangover mood of depression, that thoughts of suicide came to me."[8]

Lenin: My dearest eagle, "We realise all the difficulties. We see all the maladies, and are taking measures to cure them methodically, with perseverance [...]. My advice is: do not give way to despair and panic." Trust me, "We, and those who sympathise with us, the workers and peasants, still have an immense reservoir of strength. We still have plenty of health and vigour."[9] We are on the eve of the revolution, I can feel it.

Luxemburg: Oh, *caro mio*! Are you sure something will change? Just look at the world. Imperialist war everywhere. In Europe, in Palestine, in Russia and Ukraine, in what will one day be known as Kurdistan. Millions of workers slaughtered. We have to stop producing weapons and funding research on it, otherwise nothing will fucking change, *tovarish*. "I know that life will go on, that one must continue and remain firm and courageous and even cheerful, I know all that [...],"[10] but frankly what "makes me happy [these days are] music and painting and clouds and doing botany in the spring and good books and Mimi and [good friends] and much more."[11]

---

4 Laschitza, Annelies (2010), *Her şeye rağmen tutkuyla yaşamak (Rosa Luxemburg – Im Lebensrausch, trotz alledem)*, Istanbul: Yordam kitap, 149.
5 See Ettinger, Elzbieta (1986), *Rosa Luxemburg: A Life*. Boston: Beacon Press, 121.
6 Luxemburg 2011: 298.
7 Ibid: 366.
8 Ibid: 243.
9 Lenin, V.I. (1973), "A Letter to G. Myasnikov," in *Collected Works Vol. 32*, Moscow: Progress Publishers, 508.
10 Luxemburg 2011: 443.
11 Ibid: 366.

Lenin: I hear you, my dear *Genossin*, and I know what will make you happy right this moment. Right hand or left?

Luxemburg: Despite everything, left, always left.

Lenin (handing her a book): My favourite author, whom I met before Marx and who radicalised me in some way, Nikolay Chernyshevsky.

Luxemburg: Such a nice surprise! What can make a person happier than a good book? Especially when it comes from a true comrade. I will read it with pleasure and write you what I think of it, but don't be upset again if I do not agree with you.

While she takes a brief look at the book, Lenin lifts what he is holding in his left hand up to **Rosa**.

Lenin: And is that all? Of course not! I know we both like Beethoven. In fact, "I know of nothing better than the *Appassionata* and could listen to it every day. What astonishing, superhuman music! It always makes me proud, perhaps with a childish naiveté, to think that people can work such miracles! … But I can't listen to music very often, it affects my nerves. I want to say sweet, silly things, and pat the little heads of people who, living in a filthy hell, can create such beauty."

Luxemburg: Don't be too harsh on yourself. You cannot imagine "how much joy you have given me with"[12] this special surprise! I know what you want to say. "Ah, music! How painful it is to be deprived of it and how I yearn for it!"[13] in here. Thank you so much, my dear **Vladimir Ilyich**.

Lenin: You are very welcome, but you know why I am really here. I want to talk to you about two things: first, the Russian revolution we've been waiting for, the revolution that you will in 1918 describe as "a deed of world-historical significance and a genuine milestone;"[14] and second, a very much related question, that is, the right to self-determination.

Luxemburg (rolls her eyes): Oh dear! From the topics of suicide, nature and art to the revolution and your never-ending, false obsession with self-determination… honestly, if I had the chance to choose, I would prefer to continue chatting about the former.

Both laugh raucously.

---

12 Ibid: 460.
13 Ibid: 337.
14 Ibid: 447.

Luxemburg (continues): Having said that, you know more or less what I think about revolution, it should come from below, from the masses, and as I underlined many times: after the revolution, we have to be very careful about democratic centralism, and especially about the party amassing too much power. We must not stifle "the initiative of the workers" and we must not allow "bureaucratic distortions"[15] to rise and destroy the spirit of the revolution.

Lenin (yawns): Yes, yes, the eternal question of centralisation, but say (laughing), did you just steal my expression "bureaucratic distortions"? Regarding "the question of the political self-determination of nations and their independence as states in bourgeois society," **Rosa**, you have wrongly "substituted the question of their economic independence." Why won't you understand that "the national state is the rule and the 'norm' of capitalism,"[16] without which soci...

Luxemburg (interrupts): Oh, you stubborn man! How you love to point out my so-called mistakes, even when I am long dead...

Lenin takes **Rosa**'s arm as they continue arguing in the courtyard, under the falling snow. Today, in 2024, they are still feverishly discussing these issues.

Sevgi Doğan (she/her) is a precarious post-doc researcher at the Scuola Normale Superiore, Italy. She is the author of Marx and Hegel: On the Dialectics of the Individual and the Social *(Lexington Books, 2018).*

---

15 See Mishra, Vinod (1988), "Vladimir Ilich Vs. Rosa Luxemburg: A Study Based on Lenin's Writings," *Marxists Internet Archive.*
16 Lenin, V.I. (1977), "The Rights of Nations to Self-Determination," in *Collected Works Vol. 20,* Moscow: Progress Publishers, 400.

90. Publishing as Scaffolding

Sezgin Boynik

Publishing as a collective organiser was Lenin's idea. In "Where to Begin," written in 1901, he compared publishing to "scaffolding round a building under construction, which marks the contours of the structure and facilitates communication between the builders, enabling them to distribute the work and to view the common results achieved by their organised labour."[1] Scaffolding would also create the possibility of "unit[ing] the activists not by a congress, which under those conditions would be too costly, but around a newspaper published abroad and out of reach of the police."[2]

Collective, democratic, common and inexpensive[3] – the role of publishing as scaffolding was also to catalyse and unite the fragmented energy of impoverished and disorganised masses into a revolutionary political party. It should perform this not merely by reporting on the "economism" of workers' struggles, but by expanding the scope of publishing from the narrow understanding of daily injustices to a larger political force affecting *"all the people."*

Those who were frequent targets of Lenin's critique, especially those who denied the political primacy of workers' struggles, a group Lenin called opportunists and "economists," criticised as abstract the idea that publishing could be a collective organiser of the working class. For them, this was the fantasy of a political mastermind. They called Lenin an "armchair" revolutionary editor.

What is to Be Done? was Lenin's answer to them. "The scaffolding is not required at all for the dwelling; it is made of cheaper material, is put up only temporarily, and is scrapped for firewood as soon as the shell of the structure is completed."[4] In other words, publishing was introduced as a provisional activity in permanent movement. After the breakup with the Mensheviks and *Iskra*, the Bolsheviks' publishing adventure was in constant flux; between 1905 and 1912 they published *Vperyod, Proletary, Novaya Zhizn, Volna,*

---

1 Saifulin, M. (ed.) (1972), *Lenin About the Press*. Prague: International Organisation of Journalists, 71.
2 See "Vladimir Ilyich Lenin," in Georges Haupt and Jean-Jacques Marie (eds.) (1974), *Makers of the Russian Revolution: Biographies of Bolshevik Leaders*, London: George Allen and Unwin, 55.
3 The Bolsheviks' publications were 'inexpensive' compared to the bourgeois press, but every kopek was to be counted in order to print them. Lenin paid special attention to "the collection of funds for a workers' daily newspaper." In his remarkable statistical study on the funding of three legal Bolshevik papers published in St. Petersburg between January 1 and June 30 1912, *Zvezda, Nevskaya Zvezda* and *Pravda*, Lenin insisted on the autonomy of the workers' press existing on "their own." His conclusion was that "a newspaper founded on the basis of five-kopek pieces collected by small factory circles of workers is a far more solid and serious undertaking (both financially and, most important of all, from the standpoint of the development of the workers' democratic movement) than a newspaper founded with tens and hundreds of rubles contributed by sympathising intellectuals" (Saifulin 1972: 36-7).
4 Ibid: 96.

Ekho, *Sotsial-Demokrat*, *Zvezda*, *Pravda*, *Mysl*, and *Prosveshcheniye* in different cities under very unfavourable conditions.[5]

Proletary was published in Helsinki (1906-07), Geneva (1908) and in Paris (1909). In all these cities, the printing workshops had to be established from scratch, as makeshift printworks. The Paris story is particularly interesting.

Based on the recent research by Antoine Perriol, we now have a better picture of the early years of the workshop printing *Proletary* and *Sotsial-Demokrat*.[6] Lenin arrived in Paris with two Latvian typographers with whom he had worked in Geneva, Dimitry Snegaroff and Volf Chalit. They were immediately instructed to establish the press, which according to correspondence Lenin had with Zinoviev at the time, was not an easy task. Alexei Aline, who was coordinating the Bolshevik press, gave first-hand testimony about the importance of printing to Lenin and the special relationship he had with his typographers.[7]

During this time, and still with the support of Lenin, Snegaroff and Chalit established '*Kooperativna tipografiya soyuz*' (Cooperative Printing House Union), which they renamed '*L'Imprimerie Union*' (Union Printing House) in 1910.

Both printing houses published left periodicals by Russian emigres in Paris, as well as some art magazines. With the printing of Guillaume Apollinaire's *Les Soirées de Paris* in 1913, '*L'Imprimerie Union*' gradually shifted its activities into contemporary art. It was only Snegaroff and Chalit, Lenin's typographers, who could typeset Apollinaire's calligrammes (visual poems), which made them sought-after printers among avant-gardists.

After *Les Soirées de Paris*, '*L'Imprimerie Union*' continued to publish some of the most experimental artists' books – the surrealist magazines, Dadaist posters, pataphysical treatises, and Zaum poems. Then, at the end of 1921, Ilya Zdanevich-Iliazd, a Georgian Futurist, arrived in Paris, joined '*L'Imprimerie Union*' and helped turn it into a leading symbol of avant-garde art publishing.

The fact that from the shell of a Russian, Eastern, temporary, makeshift, militant, semi-illegal and revolutionary printing press, emerged one of the most refined, Parisian, advanced, beautiful, and experimental contemporary art printing houses of the West reveals much about the obscure histories of the Leninist underground.

The typographers and printers, and their 'technique,' were an important aspect of this subterranean revolutionary world. They formed the cosmos of socialism. As Régis Debray, in one of his more recent texts on the "typographic soul of socialism," claimed: "The professional typographer occupies a special niche within the ecosystem of socialism, the key link

---

5 Ibid: 19-20.
6 Antoine Perriol edited a dossier "Iliazd & L'Imprimerie Union," *Les Carnets de L'Iliazd Club*, No. 7, Paris, 2010, 11-86. See also the excellent website on L'Imprimerie Union: https://imprimerie-union.org/.
7 Aline, Alexei (1929), *Lénine à Paris: souvenirs inédits*. Paris: Les Revues, 16-23.

between proletarian theory and the working-class condition; herein lay the best technical means of intellectualizing the proletariat and proletarianizing the intellectual, the double movement that constituted the workers' parties."[8] This 'technique' also required a knowledge of smuggling, evading censorship, hiding from the police, and constant improvising, especially under conditions of Tsarist repression, even when printed in exile.

There is thus no better metaphor against the Eurocentrist contemporary art culture than the Russian Bolsheviks' "scaffolding," which became a beacon of the Parisian avant-garde with the help of two Latvian and a Georgian typographer. History should be written from this point of view, not from delusions based on a missed encounter of Lenin and Tristan Tzara at Cabaret Voltaire.

Scaffolding was not only a reference to transitory, improvised and collective aspects of revolutionary print. It was also a philosophy refusing to accept the standing permanency of indissoluble legal capitalist reality. As Lenin wrote: "We know the fragile nature of 'legality,' we shall not forget the historic lessons of the importance of an illegal press."[9]

Sezgin Boynik runs Rab-Rab Press in Helsinki. He edited Coiled Verbal Spring: Devices of Lenin's Language *in 2018 and published an artist's book* On Lenin: Atlases, Herbariums, and Rituals *in 2017.*

---

8 Debray, Regis (2007), "Socialism: A Life-Cycle," *New Left Review*, 46, 5-28.
9 Saifulin 1972: 12.

91. Words: 26 October 1917[1]

Sheila Delany

"We shall now proceed
to construct the socialist order."
Lenin said it,
Trotsky tells it –
decades compressed
(supernova, red star)
everything in it
the most amazing words of our time
at last, at first,
or any time so far.
Imagine: having to speak those words!
Incantatory, bringing into being,
only prose, more moving than any spell
or even Matthew Arnold at Chartreuse
lamenting his two worlds,
"one dead, the other
powerless to be born" –
but here, in October, born.

For now, the prosaic takes over:
my sons arrive from other cities
a neighbour brings plums from her tree
a comrade, depressed about Cuba,
sends bad news online. We
aren't likely to hear those words.
I hope that others will.

Sheila Delany is a lifelong activist and literary scholar, now emerita from Simon Fraser University in Vancouver.

---

1 Trotsky, ever meticulous, writes that the minutes of the Second Congress of Soviets did not survive. This was the congress at which the Bolsheviks were able to assume governance and at which Lenin – appearing undisguised in public for the first time in weeks – spoke these words. For this moment, Trotsky relies on his own memory and on the account by John Reed. See Leon Trotsky, *History of the Russian Revolution Vol. 3*, pp. 300 ff. in the Sphere Books (London, 1967) paperback edition, and John Reed, *Ten Days That Shook the World*, International Publishers (New York, 1967), p. 126. Reed uses the Russian calendar, so his date is November 7.

92. Lenin at His Worst... Or at His Best?

Slavoj Žižek

Lenin observed (from a balcony overlooking the hall) the last session of the Russian Constituent Assembly, on 6 January 1918. Afterwards, the Assembly was *de facto* disbanded, never convoked again – democracy (in the usual sense of the word, at least) was over in Russia, since this Assembly was the last multiparty elected body. Here is Lenin's reaction, which merits a longer quote:

> 'Friends, I have lost a day,' says an old Latin tag. One cannot help but recall it when one remembers how the fifth of January was lost.
> After real, lively, Soviet work among workers and peasants engaged on *real tasks*, clearing the forest and uprooting the stumps of landowner and capitalist exploitation, we were suddenly transported to 'another world,' to arrivals from another world, from the camp of the bourgeoisie with its willing or unwilling, conscious or unconscious champions, with its hangers-on, servants and advocates. Out of the world in which the working people and their Soviet organisation were conducting the struggle against the exploiters we were transported to the world of saccharine phrases, of slick, empty declamations, of promises and more promises based, as before, on conciliation with the capitalists.
> It is as though history had accidentally, or by mistake, turned its clock back, and January 1918 for a single day became May or June 1917!
> It was terrible! To be transported from the world of living people into the company of corpses, to breathe the odour of the dead, to hear those mummies with their empty 'social' Louis Blanc phrases, was simply intolerable...
> It was a hard, boring and irksome day in the elegant rooms of the Taurida Palace, whose very aspect differs from that of Smolny approximately in the same way as elegant, but moribund bourgeois parliamentarism differs from the plain, proletarian Soviet apparatus that is in many ways still disorderly and imperfect but is living and vital. There, in that old world of bourgeois parliamentarism, the leaders of hostile classes and hostile groups of the bourgeoisie did their *fencing*. Here, in the new world of the proletarian and peasant, socialist state, the oppressed classes are making clumsy, inefficient ... [manuscript breaks off at this point].[1]

It is, of course, easy to mock the quoted passage, seeing in it just the first step towards the Stalinist dictatorship, and to strike back: what about the meetings and debates within the Bolshevik party itself? Did they not in a couple of years also turn into "the world of saccharine phrases, of slick, empty declamations," a world of empty rituals in which members acted like zombies, and in which one could also "breathe the odour of the dead"? But,

---

1 Lenin, V.I. (1977), "People From Another World," in *Collected Works Vol. 26*, Moscow: Progress Publishers, 431-433.

on the other hand, is Lenin's brutally icy description not perfectly applicable to today's large-scale international meetings about global warming, like the Glasgow 2021 Climate Change conference, which also transport us "to the world of saccharine phrases ... of promises and more promises based, as before, on conciliation with the capitalists"? Is it not that, if we are to confront seriously our challenges, from ecological crises to immigration, we will have to change our entire political system along the lines suggested by Lenin?

Slavoj Žižek, Hegelian philosopher and Communist based in Ljubljana, Slovenia.

93. What to Do with *Chto Delat?*

Soma Marik

As Lenin was becoming increasingly ill, with fewer activities and writings, Stalin and Zinoviev contributed heavily to building a Lenin cult, focused on an 'infallible' Lenin and his true 'disciples.' The immediate target was Leon Trotsky, who had been a non-Bolshevik before 1917 and had clashed with Lenin. In this cult-building, *What Is To Be Done?* represented a key element of official 'Leninism.' This had longer term consequences, as a Stalinist image of *What Is To Be Done?* as a model for party building emerged.

Looking at *What is to Be Done?* through Stalin's Lens

When the *History of the CPSU(B) – Short Course* was written (published in 1938), under Stalin's guidance, in relation to *What is To Be Done?* it was said:

"The historic significance of this celebrated book lies in the fact that in it Lenin:

> 1) For the first time in the history of Marxist thought, laid bare the ideological roots of opportunism, showing that they principally consisted in worshipping the spontaneous working-class movement and belittling the role of Socialist consciousness in the working-class movement;
> 2) Brought out the great importance of theory, of consciousness, and of the Party as a revolutionising and guiding force of the spontaneous working-class movement;
> 3) Brilliantly substantiated the fundamental Marxist thesis that a Marxist party is a union of the working-class movement with Socialism;
> 4) Gave a brilliant exposition of the ideological foundations of a Marxist party."

As Stalin elaborates: "The theoretical theses expounded in *What is To Be Done?* later became the *foundation* [emphasis mine] of the ideology of the Bolshevik Party," not just a phase of Marxist practice. This became the dominant way of reading the book by those calling themselves communists internationally. In fact, since the mid-1930s any type of Party-building practices and theoretical considerations had to fit into this *recognised interpretation of the book.*

Lenin's Evolving Views

Yet this was far from how Lenin saw it, and far from its only relevance. Lenin did not see the book as conclusively showing the ideological roots of opportunism. During WWI, for example, Lenin and Zinoviev would trace opportunism in different ways, connecting it to imperialism and to a theory of "labour aristocracy." Nor did Lenin see himself as unique in showing the relationship between the working class and Socialism. As for the ideology of the Bolshevik party, Lenin's own remarks on *WITBD?* suggest he saw it as a practical and polemical work related to one particular phase of party building, and not at all as a foundation of Bolshevik ideology. It could not be, since *WITBD?* was written from the common standpoint of all the *Iskra*-ists against *Rabocheye Dyelo* and *Rabochaya Mysl.*

Lenin's positive statement of aims in *WITBD?*

Revolutionary theory did not develop just because one was a member of a class, but because of scientific reflection upon reality.

The unity of theory and class movement called for a revolutionary party.

Class consciousness could not come to workers only from inside the factory and the struggle between labour and capital, but from outside, that is, by looking at the relations between all the classes.

In Russia the mass movement was forging ahead, while the revolutionaries still operated on a cottage industry *(kustarnichestvo)* level. By this, Lenin was making a comparison between the handicraft industry versus modern industry, and crude, amateurish revolutionary work versus systematic, modern revolutionary work. When the inevitable popular *stikhiinyi* (spontaneous) explosion came, the party had to be prepared. This actually indicates Lenin saw spontaneous explosions as likely.

When a few years later *WITBD?* was included in a collection of his writings, entitled *Twelve Years*, Lenin reminded readers in the preface that it should be read keeping in mind its polemical character. In his words:

> The basic mistake made by those who now criticise *What Is To Be Done?* is to treat the pamphlet apart from its connection with the concrete historical situation of a definite, and now long past, period in the development of our Party.

Finally, when party-building issues arose in later times, he did not refer back to *WITBD?* In other words, he did not see *WITBD?* as a *global and timeless party building theoretical statement.*

Reading the text today?

My reading is different from the Stalinist one, and also partially from the new orthodoxy sponsored by Lars T. Lih, who in my view makes Lenin a permanent Kautskyian.[1] Indeed, *WITBD?* saw the German SPD as a model party. But it stressed the social, economic, cultural and political specificities of Russian conditions. Building a revolutionary mass working-class movement called for building a layer of organised cadres committed to

---

1 See Lih, Lars T. (2008), *Lenin Rediscovered: What Is to Be Done? in Context*. Chicago: Haymarket Books.

revolution as a profession and committed to *konspiratsiia* (underground work, not conspiracy) of necessity as the Tsarist police carried out constant repression. The political task of the party was to develop political agitation.

Achin Vanaik, Kunal Chattopadhyay, and the present author, have argued at different times that in addition to the above, based on Lih, there is a need to look at Lenin's "inside-outside" metaphor more carefully.[2] His principal aim of that period was the political centralisation of the fragmented experiences of various struggles in the Tsarist autocracy where underground work becomes a necessity.

This could not be done only by trade union struggles within the factory or a group of factories. Rather, it required the bringing of theory, which was the accumulation and processing of past practice and experience, into the working class by a revolutionary disciplined unified party. And theory could not be a spontaneous product. No single worker could have that total experience. Only the party, as the collective brain of the class, could draw in all the best fighters into its ranks and ensure development of theory on the basis of class struggle. Having the worker as a professional revolutionary was vital to building a revolutionary working-class party.

Sectoral oppressions within the class

In that context, I have argued[3] that as long as the specific problems faced by women workers were not addressed, the concept of the professional revolutionary tended to marginalise women and peripheralize their role in the revolutionary party. I have suggested that sexism was inadequately theorised in *WITBD?* and subsequently, whereas left-wing women activists like Clara Zetkin had made efforts to develop a vanguard layer of women more seriously.

Because Lenin was engaged in one specific debate, his use of terms like advanced workers, vanguard, etc., did not look at specificities of socially situated workers, their gender or ethnicity. If a professional revolutionary is a full-time worker-leader, then where is the space for women vanguards here, who are not given respite from family work? Consequently, the pre-existing sexism was not addressed. The party that would be built would have a much less resolute orientation to organising women workers as a distinct category. It would only be through the transformation of the working class during the war years, so that by 1917 women made up some 43% of the labour force in Petrograd, that de facto changes would be forced on the Bolsheviks.

In sum, the problem that remains with us is, if *WITBD?* with its emphasis on organising the vanguard layer is read without examining our own built-in gender, caste and community-linked images, then the

---

2 See, e.g., Vanaik, Achin (2019), "The Question of Organisation: Beyond Marx, the Enduring Legacy of Lenin," *Economic and Political Weekly*, 54(28).
3 See e.g. Marik, Soma (2004), "Gendering the Revolutionary Party," in Biswajit Chatterjee and Kunal Chattopadhyay (eds.), *Perspectives on Socialism*. Calcutta: Progressive Publishers, and Marik, Soma (2017), "Bolsheviks and Feminists," *Economic and Political Weekly*, 52(44), 81-89.

marginalised and doubly or trebly oppressed will be made secondary even in the party building project. Class unity means inclusivity of all the sectoral oppression within the class. All in the name of Lenin, even though he did not mean it, unless we ascribe to *WITBD?* the world-shaking foundational role that Stalinism gives it.

Soma Marik, Associate Professor in History, RKSM Vivekananda Vidyabhavan, India, is a Marxist-feminist engaged in political movements and research on Marxist theory, women's history and oral history.

Source: Ády

94. The Finest Statue of Lenin Ever Made

Stefan Gužvica

Mohács is a small town in Southern Hungary, rich in history even for the standards of Central European places of similar size, which have often seen their fair share of momentous events. It is perhaps most famous for the battle between Hungarians and the Ottomans in 1526, resulting in the Ottoman conquest of Hungary, which lasted for over a century and a half. To ethnographers, it is known for the UNESCO-listed *Busójárás* carnival, a local variant of the many pagan end-of-winter festivals throughout the world. For those interested in the history of the labour movement, however, there isn't much to speak of, which is quite unusual for a country that saw a communist revolution in 1919, was a workers' state for forty years, and had another upheaval in 1956 inspired by the anti-Stalinist communist reformers. Having said that, Mohács ought to be notable for something else, which is both politically and artistically significant: its (former) statue of Lenin.

The sculpture was made by Imre Varga, probably the finest modernist sculptor in Hungary. Passing away at the age of 96 in 2019, Varga lived long enough to see what the Hungarians usually euphemistically refer to as 'regime change,' and to adjust his artistic output accordingly, spending the final decades of his life making stylistically rather postmodern (and still quite good) statues of Hungarian national heroes that displaced those from the communist pantheon. The many well-deserved commendatory obituaries only referred in passing, if at all, to the Lenin statue in Mohács, merely listing it as one of the many works of the prolific artist. This is no surprise. Virtually all the statues by Varga which explicitly reference the now-undesirable period(s) of Hungarian history had been removed. The statue of Béla Kun, the leader of the Hungarian Soviet Republic of 1919, was among the lucky ones, exiled to the "Memento Park" outside of Budapest (despite the Orbán regime's serious efforts to completely vilify what is easily the most glorious moment in the country's long and illustrious history). Even Mihály Károlyi, the President of the liberal republic which preceded Kun's Commune, was forcibly removed from its place next to the Hungarian Parliament and relocated to the sculptor's hometown of Siófok on lake Balaton. The destruction of the monarchy is also considered politically unacceptable in the reactionary Hungary of today, and Lenin in Mohács was no exception to this iconoclastic trend: the statue was removed on November 22, 1990.

What makes this Lenin statue so special that I deem it worth salvaging, at least in words and images, for I could certainly not in any way achieve its restoration?

The statue, unveiled in 1974, portrays a massive (presumably red) banner with a larger-than-life face of Lenin. It is a well-known image from Soviet propaganda, dating back to at least half a century before. It is not an homage, it is a cliché, and a very intentional one. Its true meaning lies in the contrast that is provided by the second part of the sculptural narrative. The

Lenin banner was, appropriately and predictably, set on a pedestal which one could climb: a pedestal which was, not by accident, envisioned to also serve as a staircase on which people could sit. Not too far from the banner, a climbing spectator would encounter the second figure in the composition, a regular man descending the stairs: short, indistinguishable, disinterested. He is pensively looking down at the ground, hands in pockets, not even noticing the huge banner overhead. The man has some distinguishing features, however: a newsboy cap and a goatee. This is another, human Lenin. The *real* Lenin.

Suddenly, the human's disregard transforms from ignorant to intentional. Lenin has a very good reason for ignoring the man on the banner: it is not him. The cult is not him; the symbolism is not him; and the particularly daring observer must certainly have come to this conclusion: the workers' state in which this monument is located is *not him*. The reality is as far from the grandiose propaganda as from the designs of the historical Lenin. Certainly, this most radical of possible conclusions did not go over the heads of the staff working in the Soviet Embassy in Budapest. Someone, either intuitive but ignorant or a master of *doublethink*, lodged a formal complaint. They were not the only ones. It allegedly took years of administrative back-and-forth between various party committees, in Budapest and in Mohács, before the monument's erection was finally approved.

In other words, the real Lenin of Varga condemns the system which took up the banner of 'Leninism.' Most evidently, it also condemns the 'personality cult.' Certainly, the phrase was a bit of a buzzword at the time, since in the communist jargon it presented a convenient scapegoating of Stalin by Khrushchev. Khrushchev conjured the phrase to partially rehabilitate Stalin's victims without ever bothering to rehabilitate the original Marxist science which had been battered with equal brutality as the heads that had studied it.

Nevertheless, the condemnation of the personality cult is important. Lenin famously loathed it, and those who knew him best, starting from Krupskaya, were against any exuberant displays of Lenin's corpse. Later they would find out that this was among the lesser wilful misinterpretations of Lenin's legacy by self-proclaimed 'Leninists.' Varga helps Lenin and his comrades to rectify this historical injustice, as much as art can rectify any injustice. If nothing else, he does so by inspiring the thought that the bizarre embalming of Lenin within a pyramid was not exactly what he would have had in mind. The image of the imposing banner rendered powerless by the existence of the real Lenin is so powerful that it almost rights the wrong of posthumously treating him as if he were an Egyptian pharaoh.

The Mohács Lenin was certainly one of Varga's finest and most underappreciated works. It is also easily the finest statue of Lenin ever made. The winds of change which supposedly represented newfound freedoms failed to recognise and appreciate such an evident expression of artistic freedom. As they mocked the Stalinist censorship for its inability to recognise valuable art, the 'liberators' of 1989 acted the same way. As they repeated the liberal cynical cliché that "inside every revolutionary is a policeman," their 'revolution' immediately embarked on a policing of the past of which they still stubbornly refuse to let go. This policing continues to indoctrinate us all throughout Eastern Europe in the name of 'freedom' as we navigate our lives through a region devastated by the harshest economic depression in human history.

As it happened, the police officers posing as freedom fighters sentenced the Lenin banner to death, and the real Lenin to exile. About a decade ago, a Hungarian blogger discovered the real Lenin in an outdoor storage facility, resting against the wall, looking as casual as ever, as unbothered by the events of the past thirty years as he was unbothered by the formidable banner. The real Lenin knows that defeat is never final, and that the 20th century was more than just a tragedy. The staircase-pedestal, which could hold him again, is also gone. In 2004, a Youth Centre was built in its stead. But that is okay. I dare say that this is the outcome that the human Lenin would have found most fitting anyway.

> *When people discover the secret of greatness*
> *The squares will become devoid of monuments*
> (Branko Miljković)

Stefan Gužvica is a Yugoslav historian and communist.

95. Lenin's *"Left-Wing" Communism* and ISO-Zimbabwe in Late 1990s Working-Class Struggles

Antonater Tafadzwa Choto

For the International Socialist Organisation (ISO)-Zimbabwe, 2024 marks not only the 100th anniversary of Lenin's death but also 25 years since we attempted 'entryism' into the Movement for Democratic Change (MDC), guided by Lenin's 1920 pamphlet *"Left-Wing" Communism: An Infantile Disorder*. In September 1999, the pamphlet became useful to ISO comrades of my generation when we were confronted with the question of how to relate to the newly formed, trade union-backed opposition to President Mugabe and his ZANU-PF, the Movement for Democratic Change (MDC). The MDC, created in response to the massive working-class struggles against the neoliberal policies of the IMF and World Bank-backed Economic Structural Adjustment Programme (ESAP) introduced in 1991, in fact supported the same neoliberal policies the workers had so vehemently rejected. Its main emphasis was on electoral reforms for an improved democracy, largely the result of civil society and middle-class intellectuals taking over the leadership, in the process marginalising the very workers who had started the struggles. The ideologically immature working class not only supported the new opposition MDC but were at the forefront of setting up party structures, believing that, through it, they could get rid of both Mugabe's government and the neoliberal policies.

As ISO, at the height of the struggles in the 1990s, we had supported and intervened directly in the strikes by workers against the adverse effects of ESAP, radicalising their demands against capitalism, as epitomised by the slogan *"Shinga Mushandi Shinga! Qina Msebenzi Qina!"* (Worker, be resolute! Fight on!). Thus, when workers called for the trade unions' parent body, the ZCTU, to initiate the formation of a workers' party, we welcomed the move. Unfortunately, what materialised was a mildly social democratic party, the MDC, throwing us into disarray on how to relate with a party that sought merely to reform neoliberal policies instead of overthrowing them. We therefore debated whether we should attempt some type of entryism into the MDC. On the one hand, if we did not try to influence the MDC from the inside, there was a danger of becoming politically irrelevant; on the other, entryism risked what Lenin called "right liquidationism," that is, "lean[ing] towards liberalism." What was to be done? In discussions with members of our International Socialist Tendency (IST) in other countries who had had similar experiences, it was recommended that we read Lenin's *"Left-Wing" Communism: An Infantile Disorder*. So, we did.

At that time ISO had close to a hundred members nationally with the majority having joined at the height of working-class struggles in 1996/97. In Harare, about ten of us who had recently been introduced to Marxist revolutionary politics formed a study circle. We met daily at the ISO office after work for about two hours to read together and discuss the pamphlet. Unfortunately, due to the double burden placed on women, we were only two females, as the other women comrades had to go home after work to cook for and attend to their children. We also took the risk of travelling at night. The study group discussions were exciting and allowed comrades with a working-class background such as myself to gain a better understanding of Marxism. Nonetheless, when we started our reading sessions, it did not make sense for us to join the MDC, as the latter was evidently going to betray the working class, with its reform-based program.

We therefore sought to understand Lenin's argument on why some compromises are necessary, as we prepared ourselves for discussing with ideologically advanced comrades, often with a university background, who included those who had led the formation of ISO-Zimbabwe in 1992. Our study circle also read a section of *What is to be Done?* – "The Spontaneity of the Masses and the Consciousness of the Social-Democrats." In it, Lenin argues that "the history of all countries shows that the working class, exclusively by its own effort, is able to develop only trade union consciousness, i.e., the conviction that it is necessary to combine in unions, fight the employers, and strive to compel the government to pass necessary labour legislation, etc." Consequently, socialist class consciousness must be introduced into the working class from the outside, which is precisely the role that ISO would play through entryism into the MDC, radicalising the working class.

We thus gradually became convinced of the need to enter the MDC, seizing what seemed to be an historic opportunity to develop further the workers' class consciousness, while helping to raise their self-confidence to eventually take over the leadership of the party they themselves had created. In November 1999 we had a two-day members' meeting to come up with a position on the relationship with the MDC. After intense discussions and debates, a consensus was reached to do entryism armed with Lenin's underlying argument, which called on revolutionary socialists to "maintain the closest contact [...] with the broadest masses of the working people" and never fall into the trap of "doctrinairism." We agreed to join the MDC as an organisation based first and foremost on the non-negotiable principle of absolute freedom of expression. This enabled us to criticise MDC's neoliberal manifesto and advocate for an anti-neoliberal programme through our *Socialist Worker*. We also resolved to use the MDC platform to relate to and recruit the radicalising rank-and-file workers, and we soon successfully ran for a parliamentary seat in Highfield, a township in Harare, which in turn led to the building of rank-and-file industrial committees in the areas surrounding the constituency.

In short, for a time our entryism was a success, but we soon came under attack from the MDC leadership, with the scales tilted firmly against us, as we sought to radicalise the working class by proposing radical social democratic demands. The MDC leadership, on the other hand, pursued class collaboration and managed to hold back mass struggles in the hope that US and British imperialism would intervene with a regime change agenda. The UK, as Zimbabwe's former colonial power, had continued to play an intimate role in Zimbabwean affairs, publicly blaming Mugabe and ZANU-PF for the country's political and economic crisis, and had poured in funding to NGOs involved in advocating for democracy. The ISO's situation was worsened by the lack of a sizeable number of revolutionary intellectuals to counter the theoretical arguments of middle-class intellectuals within the MDC, who began branding us as ZANU-PF apologists, as we supported some of the anti-imperialist positions taken by Mugabe's government including back-tracking on the neoliberal ESAP. Also, in 2001 the ISO supported ZANU-PF's land distribution program, arguing for the opposition to do the same. As a result of this support, our MP was recalled and the ISO fired from the MDC towards the end of 2001. After our expulsion, ISO continued to work within the working class while attempting to radicalise rank-and-file members of union, student and community organisations.

In conclusion, guided by Lenin's *"Left-Wing"* pamphlet, our organisation, the ISO, survived and was not swept aside by the workers' movement, with which it continued to relate after the formation of the MDC. Though it did not grow as anticipated, our entryism offered valuable lessons for our contemporary period and struggles, whether in Zimbabwe or elsewhere. The need to build a solid revolutionary working-class organisation remains. We continue the struggle.

Antonater Tafadzwa Choto, a member of the International Socialist Organisation (Zimbabwe) since 1995, is currently a PhD candidate at the University of Johannesburg, Sociology Department.

96. Lenin's Legacy – An Alternative to Capitalism

Tamás Krausz

Lenin is the voice of the political and social awakening of the subordinated classes and the historical embodiment of their revolutionary will on a global scale.

The more aspersions the capitalist media casts at Lenin, the clearer the gigantic significance of his legacy becomes. Namely, the capitalist propaganda knows that for both small and large nations the practical-political alternative to capitalism – next to Marx and Engels – starts with Lenin. Lenin left to the workers of the world the revolutionary objectives and practical experiences with which they can defend themselves even today against the world of capital. For the peoples of the world the destruction of the Soviet Union places the most important political and theoretical message of the founder of the Soviet state – socialism – into a new perspective. In light of the Hungarian and Eastern European socialist experiences, many people in Hungary today see that the social and cultural emancipation of the working class is inseparable from Lenin's original socialist project, the tradition of the Russian revolution of 1917, the soviets, the Hungarian Soviet Republic and the workers' councils (which appeared in many other countries, were defeated and re-established).

In the literature inspired by the totalitarian paradigm, Lenin is often represented as a 'predecessor' to the Stalinist dictatorship. Lenin, of course, envisaged a totally different society, even though he was very much conscious of the historical realities and constraints imposed by the relative economic backwardness of Russia. His speech at the 11th Party Congress of the RCP(B) in the spring of 1922 stressed in particular that during the New Economic Policy (NEP) period – a 'reformist,' gradual and cautious approach to the solution of the fundamental problems of economic development – Soviet Russia would develop within the framework of a transitional multisectoral mixed economy, in which the various forms of economy compete and mobilise different social forces: "When I spoke about communist competition, what I had in mind were not communist sympathies but the development of economic forms and social systems."[1] This in practice meant that the direct realisation of socialism was transferred to the distant future, and concessions were made to the system of market economy. However, capitalism was only partially restored because firstly, the Soviet state limited the existence of private property and secondly, because the state guaranteed the existence of socialist self-governing structures. Thus, various economic forms – small proprietors, the state capitalist, state socialist, and self-

---

[1] Lenin, V.I. (1973), "Eleventh Congress of the R.C.P. (B.)," in *Collected Works Vol. 33*, Moscow: Progress Publishers, 287.

governing cooperative sectors – coexisted in a system, which in the literature is known as a socialist mixed economy. In Lenin's view, this form would constitute a transitional period to socialism in the context of a post-revolutionary Soviet Russia ravaged by WWI and civil war.

During the 1920s NEP, direct communal ownership and production was realised either in the form of voluntary associations or through state mediation, though only in a small fraction of agricultural and industrial units or fields. Towards the end of his life Lenin focused much of his attention on 'self-governing' and 'cooperative socialism' – the historical possibilities of an economic system built on direct democracy – which he called "islands of socialism."

The significance of the experiments with cooperatives was of immense importance to Lenin, because in the Soviet state the working class "owns all the means of production" and thus "the only task [...] that remains for us is to organise the population in cooperative societies [...] Socialism [...] will achieve its aim automatically."[2] In other words, in the developed form of socialism, cooperatives and other voluntary economic associations will exist without the tutelage of the state and capital, on the basis of workers' democracy.

Lenin often underlined that socialism cannot be "introduced;" rather, after the socialist revolution, a whole historical period is needed to "learn" the practice of the "commune state" and economic self-governance, which is the main function of the above-mentioned mixed economy of the transitional period: "Now we are entitled to say that for us the mere growth of cooperation [...] is identical with the growth of socialism, and at the same time we have to admit that there has been a radical modification in our whole outlook on socialism. The radical modification is this: formerly we placed, and had to place, the main emphasis on the political struggle, on revolution, on winning political power, etc. Now the emphasis is changing and shifting to peaceful, organisational, 'cultural' work. I should say that emphasis is shifting to educational work, were it not for our international relations, were it not for the fact that we have to fight for our position on a world scale."[3] That is, cultural revolution goes hand in hand with economic revolution.

But Lenin's successor did not learn. On the contrary, the years 1928-33 marked a turning point in the history of the NEP and the history of socialism. The multisectoral economic system was abolished with Stalin's 'revolution from above,' and the Stalinist dictatorship swept away – next to the institution of private property – also the "islands of socialism." At the level of political propaganda, nevertheless, the realisation of socialism was officially declared as accomplished in the 1936 Constitution. In reality, however, a new social and economic system was established, which markedly differed from the society that Lenin envisaged. We call this system state socialism, indicating our recognition that the regime was not capitalist because it

---

2 Lenin, V.I. (1973), "On Cooperation," in *Collected Works Vol. 33*, Moscow: Progress Publishers, 467.
3 Ibid: 474.

eliminated private ownership and the capitalist mode of production; but instead of the voluntary economic associations, cooperatives and a society based on self-organising democracy of the working class, the state controlled the means of production, which in fact eliminated the opportunity for the development of a different socialism, in which Lenin continued to believe until his death.[4]

In the Soviet Union and Eastern Europe, in the final years of state socialism before its demise, the power elites reformed the system not towards the direction of socialist self-governance but towards the re-establishment of a capitalist market economy. After the regime changes (1989-91), this elite, aligned with global capital, accomplished mass-scale privatisation and the restoration of capitalism. That is, counter-revolution.

But as the permanent crises precipitated by this shift towards capitalism clearly demonstrate, Lenin's life work remains of great significance to the peoples of the world until the realisation of socialism, since there has been no other relevant alternative to capitalism during the last centuries. However complicated the history of state socialism is, its experience shows us that even in this form there have been important social and cultural achievements for the subordinated classes in Eastern Europe and the Soviet Union. The main lesson is still that these socialist achievements can only be durable if the workers take the state property under their control through their own organisations.

In short, the socialism-communism that Lenin fought for remains a historical opportunity against the genocidal world order of capitalism. Its realisation, however, depends on the collective action of the subordinated classes.

Tamás Krausz (1948), a historian and leftist intellectual, is professor emeritus at the University of ELTE in Budapest. He wrote his main works on the history of the USSR.

---

[4] See also Bartha, Eszter; Krausz, Tamás & Bálint Mezei (eds.) (2023), *State Socialism in Eastern Europe: History, Theory, Anti-Capitalist Alternatives*. London: Palgrave Macmillan.

97. Lenin, Theorist of the Integration of the National, Colonial and Social Questions

Thierno Diop

Showing that capitalism was destined to give way to another system was the main objective of Marx, for whom the national question was secondary in countries that had become nations thanks to the birth and development of capitalism. Yet, as revolutionary activists privileging class struggle as the driving force of history, Marx and Engels followed closely political events in Europe and the rest of the world to identify factors favourable and unfavourable to revolution. This soon led them to pay closer attention to the national and colonial question in Ireland, Russia, India, China and among "the slave peoples."

In the late 19th century and early 20th century, it was especially in Eastern and Central Europe that this question was on the agenda. In 1887, Karl Kautsky wrote "*Die moderne Nationalität*," followed by his 1907/08 "Nationality and Internationality," whose theses were debated by Marxists until 1914. In 1908/09, Rosa Luxemburg wrote "The National Question and Autonomy," a work in which she placed the class struggle above all else. However, it was in the Austro-Hungarian Empire, bringing together several nationalities fighting for the recognition of their specificities, where the national question arguably arose most acutely and provoked a great deal of reflection. In his 1899 *State and Nation*, Karl Renner argued in favour of a "personality principle" through which "the nations should be constituted not as territorial entities but as personal associations, not as states but as peoples," while Otto Bauer, in dialogue with Renner, defended so-called "national-cultural autonomy" in his 1907 *The Question of Nationalities and Social Democracy*. Finally, in 1912, Anton Pannekoek wrote "Class Struggle and Nation," published by Josef Strasser, who in turn authored *The Worker and the Nation*, in which he criticised Bauer's conception.

Also at the beginning of the 20th century, the colonial question was added to the national and social question. Lenin, critical heir of his predecessors and confronted with the national question in the era of imperialism, analyses the relationship between class struggles in capitalist countries and national liberation struggles in oppressed and colonised countries. In their *Les Marxistes et la Question Nationale, 1848-1914*, Georges Haupt, Claudie Weill and Michael Löwy take stock of Lenin's treatment of the national question, emphasising his punctual interventions on the issue from the end of the 19th century (especially in relation to the Jewish Bund), and the fact that the right to self-determination of the nations of the Russian Empire was first proclaimed in article 9 of the party program adopted in 1903 by the Third Congress of the Russian Social Democratic Labour Party (RSDLP). This article 9 would become the constant point of reference for Lenin's writings on the national question.

It was, however, not until the 1912 Sixth (Prague) All-Russia Conference of the RSDLP, which consummates the 1903 split between the Bolsheviks and the Mensheviks, that the national question found itself at the heart of Lenin's theory and politics: "the tsarist autocracy in alliance with the reactionary nobility and the growing industrial bourgeoisie, is now endeavouring to satisfy its predatory interests by means of crude 'nationalist' politics, directed against the more cultured regions (Finland, Poland, North-Western Area), and, through colonial conquest, against the peoples of Asia (Persia and Mongolia) who are waging a revolutionary struggle for freedom."[1] In the years after, Lenin devoted a series of articles to the issue, in particular "Critical Remarks on the National Question" (1913), and the 1914 "The Right of Nations to Self-Determination." In the first text Lenin states, "It is obvious that the national question has now become prominent among the problems of Russian public life", and refutes the positions of the Jewish Bund and its bourgeois conception of "national culture" as well as Bauer's and Renner's related notion of "national-cultural autonomy." In the second, he sharply criticises Rosa Luxemburg and her attack on article 9. Then, after the outbreak of the World War in 1914, according to Haupt, Weill and Löwy, the issue "was elevated to the category of an essential means, an instrument for the seizure of power, without altering the project of international revolution." Grégoire Madjarian, in his *La question colonial et la politique du Parti communiste français 1944-1947*, writes, "Two conditions of Russian reality favoured a broader and deeper understanding of the national and colonial question: firstly, in the tsarist empire, where non-native peoples were found both in the centre and the periphery, the national question and the problems of nationalities appear less distinct than in the Western colonial empires; secondly, Russia's economic and social development blended features of capitalist Europe and semi-feudal Asia, with a powerful, concentrated proletariat a minority within a vast peasantry."

Thus, in his *Imperialism, the Highest stage of Capitalism*, written in 1916 and published in 1917, Lenin manages to combine the national and colonial question in a single theory. "The theory of imperialism," writes Madjarian, "at once a culmination and a break with the past, provides the framework for systematising and uniting the theses on the right of nations to self-determination developed from the problems raised in the tsarist state, the positions taken with regard to the revolutionary movements of colonial countries, the analysis of the modern phase of capitalism and the experience, finally, of the integration of the social-democratic workers' movement. The revolutionary function of this theory is that it establishes a necessary link between the system of capitalist exploitation and national oppression, that it links the anti-feudal and national struggle of the colonial peoples to the struggle against capitalism, that it rejects against the liberals and social democrats (Hobson, Kautsky, Schumpeter) the possibility of a non-

---

1 Lenin, V.I. (1977), "Sixth (Prague) All-Russia Conference of R.S.D.L.P.," in *Collected Works Vol. 17*, Moscow: Progress Publishers, 455-456.

imperialist capitalism, and that it refuses to reduce imperialism to political domination alone, that is to say, to its colonial form. This was the foundation of an anti-capitalist strategy uniting the proletarians of the metropolises and the colonial peoples, a strategy that became truly global for the first time."

Consequently, the Second Congress of the Communist International held in July-August 1920 adopted Lenin's anti-capitalist strategy for democratic revolution. Next, the First Congress of the Peoples of the East held in Baku from September 1 to 8, 1920, marked by the confrontation between Lenin and the Indian delegate M.N. Roy, endorsed and disseminated the conclusions of the Second Congress of the Communist International for the use of the peoples of the Orient. Despite some hesitations and errors in implementing the conclusions of this congress, Lenin shows the importance of linking class struggles in Europe with national liberation struggles outside the continent, in order to defeat imperialism: "World imperialism shall fall when the revolutionary onslaught of the exploited and oppressed workers in each country, overcoming resistance from petty-bourgeois elements and the influence of the small upper crust of labour aristocrats, merges with the revolutionary onslaught of hundreds of millions of people who have hitherto stood beyond the pale of history, and have been regarded merely as the object of history."[2]

To conclude, the theory of imperialism developed by Lenin enabled him to demonstrate the relationship between class struggle and national questions and to integrate national, colonial and social questions. This theory greatly influenced leaders of national liberation struggles in Africa, in particular, Kwame Nkrumah, first President of Ghana, author of the book, *Neocolonialism, the Last Stage of Imperialism*, and Amical Cabral, leader of the liberation struggle in Guinea-Bissau and Cape Verde, author of *The Weapon of Theory*.

Today in Africa, where we are witnessing the resurgence of the national question, as manifested by the recent partition of Sudan into two states and by inter-ethnic struggles in other countries, Lenin's updated approach could once again be an important starting point for analysis.

Thierno Diop, Doctor of Philosophy, taught at Cheikh Anta Diop de Dakar (Senegal).

Translated from the French by hjje.

---

[2] Lenin, V.I. (1974), "The Second Congress of the Communist International," in *Collected Works Vol. 31*, Moscow: Progress Publishers, 232.

98. The Vanguard Question

Will Cameron

"What is to be done? *Chto delat'?*"

The most famous question Lenin ever asked, one that would change the course of history.

It is often taught that Lenin posed this question in a spirit of desperation: "Why aren't the wheels of history moving forward?" he seemed to be asking, "Why is capitalism not producing its own gravediggers?"

It is also often taught that Lenin offered a straightforward answer to this question: organise a vanguard party. Like a "spirit hovering over the formless void," bring "consciousness from without" to the "spontaneous trade unionism" of the workers' movement. Accept that the proletariat needs a disciplined officer corps to issue its marching orders, lest it stray into the historical cul-de-sac of conciliatory reformism with its class enemy.

And thus endeth the lesson: Lenin, as Kautsky and Martov would have wished, a grave object lesson in the dangers of political impatience and revolutionary hubris. Generations of similarly melancholic leftists – despite their frustration at the non-formation of the revolutionary class in and for itself – have agreed, for all their differences, on one thing: we must not ask *Lenin's question*, for democratic ends require democratic means. To ask "what is to be done?" betrays a brutish instrumentalism, a belief that politics is a technical problem that the enlightened vanguard can solve on behalf of the benighted masses. Leninism – *vanguardism* – is simply a betrayal of the self-emancipation of the oppressed.

But how else might Lenin's question speak to us – what lessons might it teach – beyond these all-too-familiar Cold War nostrums, so inadequate for grappling with the "burning questions" looming here at the shores of the end of history's other side?

Chto Delat'? was already a well-worn question in 1902, when Lenin chose it as the title for his pamphlet advocating higher professional standards in the Russian Social-Democratic Labour Party. It was, most famously, the title of the 1863 literary blockbuster by the intelligentsia icon N.G. Chernyshevsky. In the guise of a trashy *Bildungsroman*, Chernyshevsky presented the Russian reading public with his "tales of the new people," the growing ranks of those going underground to prepare the way for social revolution. Following its young heroine Vera's emancipation from patriarchal bourgeois society, the novel traces her gradually expanding political consciousness. In an underground world of free love and cooperative labour, Vera sheds her alienated and individualistic scepticism (a scepticism that Chernyshevsky's narrator never tires of detecting in the novel's "perspicacious reader"), and is granted with visions of a post-revolutionary future where the efforts of the "new people" have culminated in an egalitarian and abundant utopia. Despite its notorious didacticism (its utilitarian "rational egoism" was most famously lampooned in Dostoevsky's *Notes from Underground*), the novel nonetheless succeeded in preaching its social gospel: all over Russia, imitators of Chernyshevsky's "new people" experimented with the alternative lifestyles portrayed in the text.

If (as its English translators Michael Katz and Robert Wagner assert) Chernyshevsky's *What is to be Done?* "supplied the emotional dynamic that went to make the Russian Revolution," Lenin's *What is to be Done?* is usually read as picking up on one partial strand of this emotional dynamic. The novel's superhuman folk hero, Rakhmetov – a seven-foot-tall advanced-theory-devourer, working behind the scenes at every global revolutionary uprising – is said to have furnished the Bolshevik leader, like the great terrorists during the heyday of Russian populism before him, with the highest ideal of conspiratorial asceticism. When his older brother Alexander was executed over a plot to assassinate the tsar, a young Vladimir Ilyich inherited his copy of *What is to be Done?* and pored over it. The disciplined cadres of the professional vanguard party would succeed in living up to the Rakhmetovian ideal where the older generation had failed.

But this common interpretation – trotted out by everyone from liberal historian Orlando Figes to left-wing luminary Tariq Ali – relies on very shallow readings of both *What is to be Dones?* It ignores the role Rakhmetov plays in Chernyshevsky's novel, and the avowed opposition to conspiratorial terror in Lenin's pamphlet. In the novel, Rakhmetov appears very briefly; the narrator carefully introduces him, explicitly stating that he serves no purpose in advancing either plot or characterisation. He is only there, we are told, to illustrate an unattainable ideal of revolutionary discipline, so absurdly hard to instantiate that the good works of the main characters seem modest and achievable by comparison. Lenin's pamphlet, meanwhile, does not lionise Rakhmetovian heroism but the daily struggles of organisers to distribute propaganda and maintain regular contact with workers under conditions of extreme repression. For Lenin, these efforts are bringing the Russian party as close as possible to the exemplary professional party machine – the German Social Democrats – and represent a clear break with the ineffective (if inspirational) tactics of the pre-/non-Marxist underground. As scholars like Lars Lih have shown, Lenin was not "worried about the workers" when he wrote *What is to be Done?*, but rather felt convinced that their growing militancy was being stifled by a socialist intelligentsia incapable of developing the organisational infrastructure to build solidarity at the national level.

If not in plaintive worry about the workers, then, in what spirit did Lenin ask his eponymous question? Let's dig even deeper to find out. Chernyshevsky – an erstwhile seminarian – had the gospel of Luke in mind when he hit upon the title of his novel. "What is to be done?" was the question asked of John the Baptist when the word of God came upon him in the wilderness of Judea, and he announced the coming of the messiah. How to "prepare the way of the Lord," and "make his paths straight"? If the messianic axe is coming to hew down "every tree which bringeth not forth good fruit," how to avoid the "unquenchable fire" that awaits the unchosen? John has a modest answer: "Anyone who has two shirts should share with the one who has none, and anyone who has food should do the same." Of course, Chernyshevsky (and Lenin after him) were no mere advocates of charitable works. They were (obviously) revolutionary opponents of liberal or Marxist-revisionist faith in the providential amelioration of social conditions under capitalism. But there is something about this way of figuring the *anticipation* of messianic revolutionary rupture – the connection of modest acts of everyday social change to a coming horizon of total transformation – that I think finds the most compelling traces in Lenin's famous question.

Luckily, Lenin's pamphlet actually rephrases its initial question in a way that might make these traces clearer. "What must we dream of?" he asks. Against the party's 'economistic' advocates of keeping party propaganda to workplace issues directly affecting the working class – who "ask whether a Marxist has the right to dream at all" – Lenin lets Pisarev (another 1860s luminary) answer on his behalf: "If a person were completely devoid of all capability of dreaming ..., if he were not able to hasten ahead now and again to view in his imagination as a unified and completed picture the work which is only now beginning to take shape in his hands, then I find it absolutely impossible to imagine what would motivate the person to tackle and to complete extensive and strenuous pieces of work in the fields of art, science, and practical life."

What if asking "what is to be done?", then, was another way of asking "what must we dream of" – of opening up space for such "hasten[ing] ahead now and again," of positing that "a unified and complete picture" does, indeed, await us on the other side of whatever smaller efforts we are undertaking right now? Or, as the gloss on this passage that introduces Ernst Bloch's study of utopian thinking puts it, what if we treat the question as a "forward signal which enables us to overtake, not to trot behind"?

This is the lesson of Lenin's vanguard question: not a monolithic idol stultifying our modest good works, but the opening of the space to dream that revolutionary action requires.

Will Cameron wrote a doctoral dissertation on the concept of the 'revolutionary vanguard.' He currently teaches political theory and organises graduate workers in Ithaca, NY.

99. What Lenin did not say

Wladislaw Hedeler

Some of what Lenin actually said and wrote fell victim to the red pen of the censors in the Soviet Union and did not find its way into the five editions of his *Collected Works* (the planned sixth edition was never published), nor into the *Selected Works* (*Leninskie Sborniki*, discontinued in 1985 after the publication of the 40th volume) that accompanied these editions. To fill this gap, in 1999 employees of the Central Party Archive, renamed the 'Russian Centre for the Preservation and Study of Documents of Recent History' (and known today as RGASPI – Russian State Archive of Social-Political History), compiled a selection of these 'unknown documents.' From 600 secreted documents they selected 422 for publication.[1] When Andrei Sorokin presented the second, unchanged edition in 2017, among the editors who had been responsible for the original selection only Vladlen Loginov, born in 1929, was still living. The final volume of the Lenin biography he compiled, which marks the temporary end of 'Leniniana' in Russia, is eagerly anticipated.[2]

The only finding aids available in the RGASPI for its Lenin holdings are item lists corresponding to the fifth edition of the *Collected Works* and to the *Selected Works*; in other words, there is no separate finding aid for the entire Lenin inventory. To facilitate searches, the signatures of the relevant documents have been printed in each publication. In addition to the volumes that can be viewed in the reading room of the RGASPI, there is also a card index created during the development of the 'Biographical Chronicle' completed in 1982 (the register for the 12 volumes was available from 1985) and a catalogue of Lenin's library in the Kremlin. It took some time and effort to obtain permission to see this card index and the original manuscripts, but as my work on the new German-language editions of Lenin's *Imperialism*,[3] *Marxism and the State* and *The State and Revolution*[4] demonstrated, it was well worth comparing the published texts with the original sources. In the postscripts of the new editions, the history of the origin and publication of the texts in the Soviet Union and Germany is dealt with in some detail. In the process, an aspect that had been inadequately investigated in the historical academic treatment of the works emerged, to which the legal historian Hermann Klenner made reference in his commentary on the revised editions:

---

1 Lenin, V.I. (1999/2017), *Neizvestnye dokumenty 1891-1922*. Moscow: Rosspên.
2 Editors' note: A short English-language version of Loginov's multiple volume biography was published in 2019 under the title: *Vladimir Lenin – How to become a leader* (London: Glagoslav).
3 Lenin, V.I. (2016/2018), *Imperialismus als höchstes Stadium des Kapitalismus*. Critical new edition with essays by Dietmar Dath and Christoph Türcke. Edited and annotated by Wladislaw Hedeler and Volker Külow. Berlin: Verlag 8. Mai.
4 Lenin, V.I. (2019), *Der Marxismus über den Staat/Staat und Revolution*. Critical new edition with essays by Hermann Klenner and Wolfgang Küttler. Edited and annotated by Wladislaw Hedeler, Volker Külow and Manfred Neuhaus. Berlin: Verlag 8. Mai.

In Lenin's *The State and Revolution*, the rights of the individual play little or no role. Lenin was a lawyer, so he knew exactly what he was doing when he chose not to talk about something. To begin with, his definition of dictatorship as "authority untrammelled by *any laws* [my emphasis], absolutely unrestricted by any rules whatever, and based directly on force"[5] is not particularly congruent with an understanding of state and constitutional law as *vinculum juris*, as a relationship between state organs and citizens predicated on mutual rights and obligations. His conception of legality, *'Dual' Subordination and Legality*,[6] contains only the demand that the laws for all of Russia must be *uniform*; however, it avoids the recognition that the very concept of legality means first (or at least also!) that all state interventions in the lives of citizens are bound by laws. If, by contrast, the law is seen and used one-sidedly or even exclusively as a *means of power*, it is easy to forget that it loses its essential legal quality when it is denied the ability to act equally as a *measure of power*. Where there are no subjective rights, there is actually no objective right either. Where legality is only understood as the strict observance by the people of orders issued by the authorities, instead of also as a claim by the citizens who constitute the power of the state that any intervention by the authorities into the sphere of freedom of these citizens must be legally regulated, the power of the state is in any case not socialised.

The contempt for the law, which went as far as the dissolution of the legal framework, was also evident during the Russian Revolution in the various attempts to determine its *differentia specifica*. The preamble to the 'Guiding Principles of Criminal Law', enacted in December 1919 by the People's Commissariat of Justice stated that, in its struggle with its class enemies, the armed proletariat had used various forceful measures without any particular rules or system, on a case-by-case basis and in an unorganised manner.

A socialist-appropriate law is, however, not an interchangeable set of arbitrary behavioural instructions. The people's right to self-determination is simply not possible without a corresponding right of self-determination for individual citizens. Insofar as citizens are not granted any subjective rights vis-à-vis the state, the people are also merely an object of the law, and the state is an authoritarian state [*Obrigkeitsstaat*], whatever its other objectives may be.[7]

This touches on an important point that highlights both Stalin's subsequent interpretation and abuse of the law, and clarifies the nature of the knout (a Russian whip) that Lenin placed in the hands of his successor.

Dr. Wladislaw Hedeler (born 1953), a historian, publicist and translator based in Berlin, specialises in the history of the CPSU and the Comintern.

Translated from the German by Patrick Anderson.

---

5 Lenin, V.I. (1978), "The Victory of the Cadets and the Tasks of the Workers' Party," in *Collected Works Vol. 10*, Moscow: Progress Publishers, 246.
6 See Lenin, V.I. (1973), "'Dual' Subordination and Legality," in *Collected Works Vol. 33*, Moscow: Progress Publishers, 363-367.
7 Klenner, Hermann (2019), "The 'Classical' Lenin. Justice and Injustice of and in 'The State and Revolution,'" in V. I. Lenin *Der Marxismus über den Staat/Staat und Revolution*, 13.

100. Lenin's Death in China

Yuan Xianxin

On January 21, 1924, Lenin died. The news quickly spread across the world, including to China.

China at the beginning of 1924 was in chaos. Since the founding of the Republic in 1912 the country had been in a state of almost constant civil war and people had gradually become extremely discontented with the rule of the so-called Beiyang warlords. In 1919, the Chinese government's poor showing at the Versailles Conference, particular concerning the future status of Shandong province, sparked what is arguably the most famous cultural and political protest movement in recent Chinese history, the May Fourth Movement and with it an increased general interest in radical modernising ideas, including communism. Hence, when two months later Soviet Russia stated that it would relinquish all territorial and economic privileges accrued during the Tsarist era, many Chinese became even more curious about everything Soviet. Historian Zhou Yuefeng went as far as calling it the "Leninist Moment" in China.

In this atmosphere, the Chinese Communist Party (CCP) was born in 1921. At the same time, Sun Yat-sen, the sidelined founder of the Republic and leader of the Kuomintang Nationalist Party (KMT), who had endeavoured for years to end the corrupt rule of the Beiyang warlords, began to meet more frequently with Soviet and Comintern envoys. As a result, Sun gradually moved to the left and planned to work with the CCP to launch a new national revolution – this time in a Leninist sense. Yet, the onset of the Mongolian Incident in 1921 complicated matters. When Soviet Russia sent troops into Outer Mongolia and backed it up with the discourse of national self-determination, the Beiyang government and a large number of Chinese citizens expressed severe anger. This directly affected the diplomatic relations between Moscow and Beijing.

Concretely, at the time of Lenin's death, the Beiyang government still had not officially recognised the USSR. Thus, when young students in Beijing and Nanjing tried to organise rallies in memory of Lenin, the authorities banned them. Nevertheless, for most Chinese, both the new-born Soviet regime and Lenin as its leader were still wrapped in Janus-liked mystery. The Russian Revolution had created great achievements and promised the world a bright future, but it had also been accompanied by appalling horrors and bloodshed. Five days after Lenin's death, a prominent Chinese government official, Zhang Shizhao, wrote what was perhaps the first commentary on Lenin's death in the Chinese press. Although Zhang did generally not approve of Lenin's political ideas, he recognised Lenin's outstanding personality: "The existence of Lenin was a significant event in and for our human society at the beginning of the 20th century. It would hence be no surprise if the life and death of the human mind would change as a result of it."

Zhang's comments, which approve of Lenin's character while disapproving of his deeds, were shared by many Chinese intellectuals. Thus it was undoubtedly the Communists who were most enthusiastic about introducing more about Lenin to the Chinese public. Two weeks after Lenin's death, *China Youth*, the organ of the Chinese Communist Youth League published a special issue devoted to Lenin. In it, Liu Renjing summarised some of the main points of Lenin's thought: the relation between state and revolution, imperialism as the highest stage of capitalism, social revolution in the West and national revolution in the East, the revolutionary party, the peasant question, the NEP, among others. This was perhaps the first time that Lenin's ideas were comprehensively presented to Chinese readers. Liu, had travelled to Moscow to attend the Fourth Congress of the Comintern two years earlier, and was one of the rare CCP members to ever have met Lenin in person. Nonetheless, apart from the summary of Lenin's thinking, the question of how to actually relate Lenin's legacy to China's ongoing revolution was not explicitly concluded, possibly because many Chinese remained sceptical of Communism. Even Yun Daiying, the chief editor of *China Youth*, sounded very similar to Zhang Shizhao on this question. He merely urged Chinese youth to learn from Lenin's character so as to better serve the revolution yet to come.

Another significant event at the time was the First National Congress of the Kuomintang in late January 1924. This congress signalled that the KMT was beginning to embrace the ideas and organisation of a Leninist party. In addition, under the instruction of the Comintern envoys, all CCP members joined the KMT as individuals. The two political parties decided to join hands to fulfil the revolutionary path that the Soviet Union had indicated for China: to carry out the national revolution first and complete the transition to a bourgeois society. After that, one would see.

In fact, Lenin's death significantly interrupted the rhythm of the congress. Upon hearing the news, Sun Yat-sen immediately decided to adjourn the proceedings and to hold a grand memorial meeting, at which a teary Sun said to his followers: "My heart is connected with Lenin's although we are separated by thousands of miles." After the Congress resumed, the KMT and CCP agreed to officially cooperate, thereby setting the direction for a stronger emphasis on dealing with Lenin's legacy, in particular in relation to the colonial and national revolutions. In mid-February, as the leaders of the CCP and KMT returned to Shanghai, they began preparations for a Lenin memorial conference in early March. According to press reports, a 'German doctor' made a major speech at the conference. He suggested that Lenin's two greatest works were the liberation of all peoples in Russia from tsarist oppression and the establishment of the Comintern, which commanded the national liberation of colonial and semi-colonial peoples. Such a summary was, of course, meant to serve as preparation for the forthcoming national revolution. Therefore, it was no surprise that he ended his speech by calling Sun Yat-sen "the Lenin of China" and advocating the youth to follow Sun's leadership.

From this point on, in Chinese public opinion, Lenin and his ideas were deeply bound up with the colonial question and the national revolution. In June 1924 another young Chinese communist, Zhao Shiyan, published a long essay called "On Lenin," in which he talked specifically about Lenin's various hitherto unknown comments on China after the 1911 Revolution. Zhao was pleased to find Lenin highly praising the revolution and its leader Sun Yat-sen. He even quoted the last sentence of "Backward Europe and Advanced Asia" as his concluding paragraph: "But all young Asia, that is, the hundreds of millions of Asian working people, has a reliable ally in the proletariat of all civilised countries. No force on earth can prevent its victory, which will liberate both the peoples of Europe and the peoples of Asia."

The texts 'discovered' by Zhao Shiyan were later repeatedly cited by the CCP. In fact, at the end of 1924, *New Youth*, an organ of the CCP, published a special issue devoted to the national revolution, including translations of the Lenin pieces mentioned by Zhao. In another special issue commemorating the first anniversary of Lenin's passing, the national question continued to be the focus of the CCP's interpretation of Lenin. Chen Duxiu, General Secretary of the CCP, said in his essay "Leninism and China's National Movement" that the reason why Leninism made Marxism more complete was because of his two theories, "the dictatorship of proletariat as the phase between capitalism and communism, and the global national movement of anti-imperialism."

Then, in March 1925, Sun Yat-sen also died. For Dai Jitao, Sun's former secretary, Soviet Russia could not be trusted, and the Soviet attitude on Outer Mongolia showed that the principle of national self-determination did not lead to world revolution and liberation, but only to competitions and wars among nations. Consequently, the different understandings of nation and national liberation constituted a central theme in the subsequent (violent) split between the KMT and the CCP.

Finally, immediately after Lenin's death, Guo Moruo, a young romantic poet, composed a poem titled *The Sun is Gone*. In one of the stanzas Guo wrote: "His inflamed light wave would expel Lucifer/ His torrential heat-flow would destroy icy walls/ The poor with no clothes and jobs/ accepted his sacred fire stolen from the heaven/." For the Chinese revolution, the suns of Sun Yat-sen and Lenin set one after another in 1924-25. The subsequent tensions, complexities and twists of the Chinese revolution resulted to a large extent in the different understandings of how the national revolution, inspired by Lenin's ideas, should be conducted. The sun was gone, but the people on the ground continued to explore the way of revolution, painstakingly and urgently. In the PRC Lenin's birth and death anniversaries have been commemorated ever since. Lenin's image as well as the interpretation of his legacy is still in constant flux. As long as this is the case, Lenin's power will not easily perish.

Yuan Xianxin is Associate Professor at the Department of Chinese Language and Literature, Tsinghua University.

101. Eleven Theses on the Contemporaneity of Tovarish Lenin

Yağmur Ali Coşkun

1. All Marxism leading up to Lenin did not know what the physiognomy of the proletarian revolutionary organisation should look like for the "expropriation of the expropriators" to happen. Marx fought hard to preserve the unique place of *politics* in proletarian struggle; but he could not have specified the tools to be used with the limited experience the early socialist sects and artisanal, guild-like structures that dominated the First International provided. The Paris Commune swept away the conspiratorial and corporatist aspirations of these early organisations and posed the question of a mass organisation with discipline. But posing the question is not answering it. As a result, second generation Marxists were bifurcated between contemplative materialism (Kautsky, Bernstein) and heroic mythologism (Sorel). The avatars of this bifurcation still haunt us today. Neither camp understands that the "sensuous, practical activity" (Marx) of the proletariat is *part and parcel* of the objective struggle and must assume a specific shape to be successful. The Leninist Party is the physiognomy of the proletariat tarrying with the negative in socialism's becoming.

2. Standpoint of the proletariat or the objective Truth? Both, please! The objective structures of imperialist capitalism can be explicated only from the standpoint of the proletariat. Without revolutionary theory, no revolutionary practice, sure; but the ultimate test of the theory (which is necessarily based on a standpoint) is mass politics.

3. Who educates the proletariat's educator, i.e., the Party? The proletariat itself. The Party and its individual militants bring to the working class "the ABCs of communism; to the ignorant, instruction about their condition; to the oppressed, class consciousness" (Brecht); but what makes a militant? *Working* in the Party Committees, working in the Soviets, working in the unions. This is the essence of the Bolshevik-Menshevik division. It is *revolutionary activity* itself amidst the actual proletarian and oppressed masses – that is the ultimate education for the militant. If the militant hails from the proletariat, the making of the militant coincides with the proletariat's self-transformation, i.e., *praxis*, as the militant is theorising about the class he or she has come from and is bringing the theory back to its origin. If the militant happens to come from bourgeois, petty-bourgeois etc. origins, this practical education allows him or her to drop all pseudo-intellectual pretensions, class prejudices, and parliamentary cretinism. All this massive work is embodied in the collective that is the Party, which, to ensure the

continuity of this (self-)transformative activity, must operate with an iron discipline. And where does the Party learn this discipline from? From the factory, the workplace – that is, once again, the daily life of the proletarian masses themselves. Further, if the Party is going to represent the proletariat as a whole and not just some 'corporate' interests, it also must make alliances with other oppressed strata without abandoning class politics. The figure of the militant is thus intimately linked to the theory of hegemony.

4. How to deal with nationalist or religious bigotry within the proletariat? The Enlightenment-liberal preaches to the workers their own dumbness. The mysticist poses socialism as a new religion. Lenin explicitly rejects these two harmful attitudes, because he understands that these forms of identification constitute the "heart of a heartless world" (Marx), especially in the case of oppressed religious or national groups. Do not fight the shadows, fight the material basis that gives rise to those shadows.

5. There are no 'two cultures' in Marxism. Marxism is the science of history and therefore the guide to revolutionary proletarian action. It is not science but positivist metaphysics that clogs the way of both Marxism and other creative activity (including science), exposed by Engels and Lenin alike. The distance between Mach and Berkeley is no greater than that between Mach and post-structuralists. The cure? Materialist dialectics. In the capitalist era, the self-movement of knowledge = proletarian politics.

6. The "concrete analysis of the concrete situation" is always intimately linked to the universal, because "the concrete is concrete because it is the concentration of many determinations" (Marx). Never dispense with abstractions, but never be satisfied with them either. The highest point of this in Lenin is the theory of imperialism.

7. The chief theoretical defect of all Reformism and its negative mirror-image, Ultra-Leftism, old and new alike, is not understanding dialectics. The road from the Philosophy section at Berne Library to the Finland Station can be short – if you know the "science of interconnections" (Engels).

8. All dichotomies that political life throws up in consciousness are resolved in practice. The Soviet and the Party, party-building and mass work, vanguardism and hegemony are all moments of one another. Even 'victory' and 'defeat' are meaningful only in the context of socialist construction (something that apparatchiks can never understand).

9. And what happens when you rip one side of the dichotomy from the other? You always end up by necessity in individualism or corporatism, which is aggregate individualism.

10. None of this makes sense without Communism as the final goal; but this final goal is made possible by capitalism itself. If there is teleology in Marxism, it is suggested by history itself. The blasts of the capitalist historical continuum generate the Subject whose telos it is to "blast the continuum of history" (Benjamin).

11. How, then, do we change the world? The answer is poetic:

With Lenin

To plunge into life
like plunging into the summer sunlight,
to find the key to that
'Why was I born,
why am I alive' plight,
to remain bright like the coming days,
to remain bright with the coming days,
to remain bright,
an earth green,
a flag red,
a dove white,
to be with Lenin
from the same song,
same trench, same river,
    same construction site...

Nâzım Hikmet, 1960
(trans. Yağmur Ali Coşkun)

Yağmur Ali Coşkun is a revolutionary Marxist organiser, internationalist, proud union member, translator, sociologist-in-training at UC Berkeley PhD program, who tries his hand at music and creative writing.

Artist: Yevgeniy Fiks

102. Lenin of February 24th

Yevgeniy Fiks

After February 24, 2022, Lenin's legacy in relation to the issues of imperialism, international class solidarity, decolonisation, self-determination and national identity is largely being ignored, and yet seems as urgent as ever. But what were Lenin's actual views on all these pressing questions, developed at the beginning of the 20th century, yet still important in our times? For instance, while Lenin's positions were always dynamic, dialectical and tactical, he consistently remained a staunch supporter of a nation's right to self-determination, including secession:

> What Ireland was for England, Ukraine has become for Russia: exploited in the extreme, and getting nothing in return. Thus the interests of the world proletariat in general and the Russian proletariat in particular require that Ukraine regains its state independence, since only this will permit the development of the cultural level that the proletariat needs.

The project *Lenin of February 24th* focuses on the dialectical re-reading of Lenin in the face of the present-day moment. We applaud *Leninopad*. It is right that Lenin monuments fall. When they fall, they reveal Lenin's writing to us. Lenin the monument is being replaced with Lenin the thinker.

For generations, Lenin monuments concealed from us Lenin's texts. Lenin of 24th February uncovers Lenin.

Yevgeniy Fiks is a Moscow-born, New York-based artist, author and organiser of art exhibitions.

103. "Truth [is] Not in 'Systems'": *Our* Politics of the Event

Yutaka Nagahara

Natura non facit saltum...[1]

War is an act of social intercourse.[2]

The qualification of the regime of the One leaves a remainder which I call an event, and, thus, the event is the dysfunction of this regime. The event is not given, for the law of all donation is the regime of the One. The event is thus the product of an interpretation.[3]

On January 30, 1946, Colonel Razin sent a letter to Stalin and "respectfully ask[ed]" two questions: "Have Lenin's theses in his appraisal of Clausewitz grown obsolete?" and "What should be our attitude with regard to the military and theoretical heritage of Clausewitz?"[4] On February 23, Stalin answered these questions with political and rhetorical cunning, as was his habit.[5]

He solemnly declared, from the outset, that Razin's "question is wrongly put": this first blow, as a discursive manoeuvre designed to undermine Razin's starting point, allows Stalin himself to *carefully blemish* the revolutionary *symbolon* called Lenin in advance, by way of a theoretical circumlocution: "there are no such 'Theses' of Lenin on Clausewitz's teachings on *the art of war*." Stalin's answer is 'correct' in a sense that I will discuss later; it is, however, also a form of *tone policing*. In other words, Stalin concluded at the very commencement, armed with the commandment[6] that Lenin *is* obsolete and outmoded in so far as his reading of Clausewitz's *military theory* is concerned; indeed, so much so that it *was already* redundant in terms of his *political theory as such*.[7]

It would be interesting to unearth the details of Stalin's art of coaxing and crafty reasoning, as well as the metaphors he mobilises to thwart his

---

1 Hegel, G.W.F. (1989), *Science of Logic*. Atlantic Highlands: Humanities Press International, 170.
2 Quoted in Davis, Donald E. & Kohn, Walter S.G. (1977), "Lenin's Notebook on Clausewitz," *Soviet Armed Forces Review Annual*, 1, Gulf Breeze: Academic International Press, 198.
3 Badiou, Alain (2018), *Can Politics Be Thought?* Durham: Duke University Press, 78. Hereafter emphases are mine unless otherwise indicated.
4 Society for Military History (1949), "Colonel Rasin's Letter," *Military Affairs*, 13(2), 75-77.
5 Stalin, J.V. (1946), "Answer to a letter of 30 January, from Col.-Professor Rasin." *Marxists Internet Archive*.
6 Derrida, Jacques (1996), *Archive Fever: A Freudian Impression*. Chicago: University of Chicago Press, 1.
7 Editors' note: In his letter to Razin, Stalin confirms Lenin's "interest" and "acknowledgement" of Clausewitz and his "need[ing]" him in order to disprove both the social chauvinists and the left Communists. However, given that Lenin was not a "military expert," and that "there are no restrictions on us [the successors of Lenin] in the criticism of the Military doctrine of Clausewitz, as there are no remarks of Lenin that could hinder us in our free criticism," he affirms that "we have" reasons to criticise the military doctrine of Clausewitz, thereby implicitly condemning Lenin's own engagement to be obsolete.

political enemies by stigmatising them as an "enemy of the people," from Trotsky to everyone else around him. However, in this essay, I will not pursue that task, but rather focus on the Lenin who – far from the Lenin counterfeited by Stalin – grappled with Clausewitz's famous dictum that "war is nothing but the continuation of state-politics by other means"[8] in relation to his readings of Hegel.

As is well known, Lenin's notes on Clausewitz are omitted from the official edition of the Philosophical Notebooks. Balibar calls it "a dissociation" and "an astonishing lacuna [...] even though in his writings of the following period explicit references and allusions to both Hegel and Clausewitz almost always go together."[9] Leaving the secrets of Soviet party politics at that moment to Balibar's superb chronological lectures on Lenin and the work of other specialists, I would instead like to pay attention to a comment Lenin made in the margin on the following excerpt from Clausewitz's On War:

> While there may be no system, and no *apparatuses for discerning the truth*, yet truth does exist. To discern it one generally needs *seasoned judgment* and the *rhythm of long experience*. Thus history here presents no formulas, but here as everywhere it does present the *exercise for judgement*.[10]

By paying particular attention to this excerpt, is Lenin upholding the so-called professional or artisanal revolutionaries even without "popular and workerist singularities"?[11] This question remains crucial even for the Lenin I am talking about here, but the point on which I would like to focus is none other than the coup-like jottings or a sort of Badiouan 'intervention,' Lenin noted in the margin: That is, "truth [is] not in [the] 'systems'."[12]

This brusque or dictum-like epitaph, or rather exergue, that truth does *not* dwell in "system*s*," should be grasped, with an emphatic alteration, as the (historical) fact that truth *never* dwells in circular "system*s*" as something that is ostensibly neither too much nor too little and therefore statically and stably closed and completed[13] – and is the one thing that never divides into two.[14] To paraphrase this "intervention" through which the "interpretation" of the truth can "realise itself" as the actual "truth (event)" to come, Lenin's inserted jotting acts as "the supernumerary [or say, incommensurable] statements and facts" or, from a different angle, as the supplementary "remainder" of the "systems" without which they cannot be what they are

---

8 Clausewitz, Carl von (1976), *On War*. Princeton: Princeton University Press, 69. Lenin and his 'comrades' quote this dictum by inserting "i.e., violent" into the space between "other" and "means."
9 Balibar, Etienne (2007), "The Philosophical Moment in Politics Determined by War: Lenin 1914-1916," *in* Sebastian Budgen, Stathis Kouvelakis & Slavoj Žižek (eds.), *Lenin Reloaded: Toward a Politics of Truth*, Durham: Duke University Press, 213.
10 Clausewitz 1976: 517.
11 Badiou 2018: 78.
12 Davis & Kohn 1977: 205.
13 On Hegelian "circularity," see Rockmore, Tom (1986), *Hegel's Circular Epistemology*, Bloomington: Indiana University Press.
14 E.g., Badiou, Alain (2007), *The Century*. Cambridge: Polity Press.

supposed to be, since "systems," *by definition*, are to be "dysfunctional" or half-open with inevitable "remainders" in order for them to be repeatedly *re-closable*.[15]

To be sure, as A. S. Bubnov, whose name we can find in the list of the victims of the *Great Purge*, pointed out in the introduction to Lenin's Notes on Clausewitz, Engels wrote to Marx on January 7 1858, referring to Clausewitz's "weird way of philosophising, but *per se* very good,"[16] with an emphasis not only on the fact that "Clausewitz's thinking [...] was fertilised by Hegel"[17] but also on his "adaptation" of "ideas [dialectics]" to "the relationship of war to politics".[18] For the Lenin who scrupulously read Hegel's *Logic* like a young student, despite already having written *Materialism and Empirico-criticism* (1909), the truth is something not simply different from but definitely other than or outside "systems," and in this sense only, is the event – the *tangential* "leap" – that contravenes the inside-outside dichotomy on which systems are established, and that in turn post-eventally re-establishes the system as "the regime of the One." The truth is therefore also the "apparatus," to use Clausewitz's neologism "*Wahrheitsapparat,* or say the Foucaultian "dispositive," by which to discern what the truth is and how it can be politically narrativized as an *ongoing* process: Only through these processes does the new subjectivity arise from the "*entre-deux*" as such, to which Badiou will give a name, "the empty set."[19] If so, then, the characteristics of the Lenin who co-opted Clausewitz's "weird way of philosophising" should be explored in more detail.

Lenin, making a long excerpt from Hegel's *Logic,*[20] might have had in mind Hegel's insistence that "the new quality in its merely quantitative relationship is, relatively to the vanishing quality, an indifferent, indeterminate other, and *the transition is therefore a leap*, both are posited as completely external to each other"[21] when he notes in the margins, "gradualness explains nothing without leaps." He declares this under the heading "Breaks in gradualness." In this sense, Lenin emphatically *repeats*, in the margin, the word "Leaps" *three times in a row,*[22] as if they were carved seals engraved on the copper plate of the capitalist *campo santo*.

We cannot ignore that this is the initial "*mot d'ordre* [slogan]"[23] or the "intervention" that started October.

For Lenin, truth *does not* dwell in systems; that is, truth can be and/or be-come the truth for the first time only in the course of the tangential *leaps* from the circular orbits of the systems in which the truth abides statically as

---

15 Badiou 2018: 78.
16 Bubnov in Davis & Kohn 1977: 192. (Translation altered)
17 Ibid.
18 Ibid: 192-194.
19 Badiou 2018: 78.
20 Lenin, V.I. (1976), "Philosophical Notebooks," in *Collected Works Vol. 38*, Moscow: Progress Publishers, 85-315.
21 Hegel 1989: 368.
22 Lenin 1976: 123.
23 As to the mots d'ordre, see Deleuze, Gilles and Guattari, Félix (1987), *A Thousand Plateaus: Capitalism and Schizophrenia*. Minneapolis: University of Minnesota Press, 79.

~~non~~-truth, to use a Derridian "erasure." This, then, is exactly the truth called event; however, at the same time, as Badiou says, "event[s] are not given" and therefore do not exist *yet* without something other than systems (givenness). Thus, no one can know when it will come with an "exact calculation."[24] For Lenin, the creation of the "leaps," "breaks," and catching the "rhythm" of the *move* or *wave* required by the political *agogics* – or "Truth procedure" as Politics[25] – is, consequently, nothing other than the truth discovered through a *"weird way* of philosophising." If the leap as the truth is nothing but the event which can never be stably dwelt in and as a part of systems, the event deserves to be called the Revolution-as-Truth: in other words, the revolution takes *place* inside and outside at once – "entre-deux." This is exactly the seminal point of Lenin's readings of Hegel and Clausewitz "fertilised by Hegel" together, especially that of the Lenin who confronted WWI as the moment [*Kairòs*] or *"Augenblick"* of the "revolution at the gates"[26] and who awaits the revolutionary Bolshevik-qua-"Universal-singular" to create themselves *neither* spontaneously *nor* by way of any so-called "external injection," *but* as the minoritarian lever of "the unrepresentable, [...] an empty set."[27]

Although Lenin did not make notes on it in the *Notebooks*, Clausewitz wrote the below, which is just next to the sentence which Lenin quoted; it is impossible to imagine that he overlooked it:

> We admit, in short, that [...] we cannot formulate any principles, rules, or methods: history does not provide a basis for them. On the contrary, at almost every turn one *comes across* peculiar features that are often incomprehensible, and sometimes astonishingly odd.[28]

Toporkov, in his "Explanatory Notes" to Lenin's notes on Clausewitz, comments that "Clausewitz denies the possibility of any dogma, of any everlasting and unchanging principles of military science. [...] The excerpts taken by Lenin from this section develop the argument of why it is impossible to construct a theory of war in an abstract form. Clausewitz points to the presence of *moral* elements which defy exact calculation."[29] Regardless of whether it is appropriate to use the word "moral" or not, in this sense, the point Stalin introduced at the outset of this essay, i.e. there are no "Theses" of Lenin on Clausewitz, is *counter-revolutionally* 'correct' and at the same time absolutely wrong.

Lenin here attempts to grasp the *"Kairòs"* of the Politics of the Event, the Althusserian "aleatory encounter" or the Deleuzian *clinamen,* which is and must "often [be] incomprehensible, and sometimes astonishingly odd"

---

24 Toporkov in Davis & Kohn 1977: 217.
25 Badiou, Alain (2005), *Metapolitics*. London: Verso, 141ff.
26 See Žižek, Slavoj (2011), *Revolution at the Gates: Selected Writings of Lenin from 1917*. London: Verso.
27 Badiou 2018: 78.
28 Clausewitz 1976: 516-517.
29 Toporkov in Davis & Kohn 1977: 217.

when seen from the viewpoint of the stable orbit where there fictitiously resides the static truth glaring like a 'gatekeeper' at the closed gates of the systems, and which is destined to be dismantled by the "breaks in gradualness" with "exercise for judgement," only through which can we not merely "discern" but realise "*a failure of the regime of the One.*"[30] In this sense, Lenin here is *himself* the event as such, *ontically* speaking, by which the pre-evental and the post-evental can encounter one another as the leap called Revolution-qua-Truth, where the rupture of history is sutured momentarily for the next "breaks in gradualness" that will inevitably come.

Yutaka Nagahara, Professor Emeritus at Hosei University and Researcher at the Ohara Institute for Social Research, is the author of numerous books and articles, including the forthcoming The Apparatus of Capture: Capital and Governance.

---

30 Badiou 2018: 78.

104. Lenin's Time

Jodi Dean

My goal for when shops reopened after the initial COVID-19 lockdown was getting a quote from Lenin tattooed on my arm: "There are decades where nothing happens; and there are weeks when decades happen." It was perfect for the moment, for the strange experience of time where March 2020 lasted five months and protests went on all summer. The problem was that Lenin never said it. I did some research, checked with Russian friends, posed the question on social media. He didn't say it. He could have said it; we can imagine him saying it, feel him saying it, but there is no record of Lenin actually saying it.

Maybe I was being too literal. That Lenin said, "There are decades where nothing happens; and there are weeks when decades happen" is asserted in multiple places. It's easy to find statements to this effect online. It's like we want him to have said it. Some amorphous 'we' needs to attach his name to this idea, to speak through him and in speaking through him have him speak for us. This need suggests that Lenin's words are more than the words that came out of his mouth. He speaks with many mouths. Or the name for the speech of many mouths is Lenin.

Everybody knows that there are decades where nothing happens. That's our sense of day-to-day drudgery – of struggling for years on end to make even the smallest difference – of our encounter with futility. But Lenin, Lenin is the one who knows that there are moments when everything changes. Lenin's time is a time of leaps and rupture, when old patterns fall away and the impossible becomes the inevitable. In the lines that Lenin didn't say, but we wish he did, we mark our revolutionary break with the sad repetition of the uneventful. Anyone could have said it, but because it's attributed to Lenin, we know the weeks when decades happen hold the promise of a new society, new ways of being.

Lenin's time isn't linear. Lenin isn't bound by the regular rotations of the earth and the moon, the expected sequence of day by day, week by week, year by year. Building power takes discipline, organisation, and persistence, the decades where nothing happens. But Lenin knows, and we know through Lenin, that we are preparing for the moment when the time is right. The hundreds will become millions. Change will come rapidly, the revolution teaching us skills and capacities we can barely imagine.

When our collective Lenin mouth says, "There are weeks when decades happen," the imperialists tremble. It's a threat! The July days of 1917 were a time of counterrevolution. The popularity of the Bolsheviks declined. Lenin went into hiding. In but a few short months, the provisional government was overthrown, and the Bolsheviks came to power. Is that when we imagine he said it? Preparation, defeat, victory.

The lines from Lenin ultimately tattooed on my arm are from *"Left-wing" Communism: An Infantile Disorder*. It is only when the "lower classes do not want to live in the old way and the 'upper classes' cannot carry on in the old way that the revolution can triumph." Lenin's guidance isn't a clock or a calendar. It focuses on the class struggle: when workers are no longer willing to live as they've been living and the bosses can no longer force us to, that's the time of revolution. As we approach that time, it will feel like nothing is happening. Then everything will.

Jodi Dean teaches and organises in Geneva, NY.

Artist: S.D. Merkurov

"I will return and I will be millions."
Tupac Katari

About KickAss Books

KickAss Books is a 3-person collective – Hjalmar Jorge Joffre-Eichorn, Patrick Anderson and Johann Salazar – with roots in Bolivia, India, Australia, Germany, Portugal and Canada. Inspired by the current spate of anniversaries of comrade-ancestors, we are attempting to create a new style of left-activist publications: edited volumes dictated by the actually lived struggles, questions and convictions of our contributors, expressed in a variety of forms that speak to their own personal-political reality. Our motivations for doing this are many, including a desire to amplify lesser-heard voices, to combat revisionist histories, and to reclaim the dignity of past victories and defeats, thereby illuminating their ongoing potential to overcome present-day oppressions. Above all, our hope has been to provide a platform for a truly broad range of authors and artists to express their thought, vision, pain – in prose, poetry, song, image… – people for many of whom this struggle against oppression is an awful necessity.

Since 2020, we have collaborated with 200+ contributors from 75+ countries across all five continents. While forging left relationships on this scale has certainly had its challenges – cooperation, especially digital, can be messy and exhausting at times – our experience so far has primarily been of solidarity. And of generosity: none of our contributors has received payment for any of these projects. The three of us, all self-employed, have also invested literally countless hours (days, weeks, months!) of our unpaid time and energy.

Thanks to this intense communisting, we have, to date, managed to publish four books (listed below). While, as is the case for so many of us, our energy and mental/physical health is often precarious, we continue to believe (perhaps foolishly) that there may be more that still needs to be said.

La lucha continúa.

Publications:
- *Lenin150 (Samizdat)* (2020; 2nd edition 2021, Daraja Press)
- *Post Rosa: Letters Against Barbarism* (2022, Rosa Luxemburg Stiftung, NYC)
- *Left Alone: On Solitude and Loneliness amid Collective Struggle* (2023, Daraja Press)
- *Lenin: The Heritage We (Don't) Renounce* (2024, Daraja Press)

 The production of the visuals in this book was supported by a grant to KickAss books from the Rosa Luxemburg Stiftung.

About Daraja Press

Daraja Press publishes to reclaim the past, contest the present and invent the future.

Daraja Press is a non-profit publisher, based in Quebec, Canada, that seeks to reclaim the past, contest the present and invent the future. Daraja is the KiSwahili word for 'bridge'. As its name suggests, Daraja Press seeks to build bridges, especially bridges of solidarity between and amongst movements, intellectuals and those engaged in struggles for a just world. We seek to build upon, develop and support interconnections between emancipatory struggles of the oppressed and exploited across the world. In a phrase, our aim is to:

Nurture Reflection, Shelter Hope and Inspire Audacity.

Daraja Press publishes print books, e-books, pamphlets, campaign materials, and video and audio content. We actively encourage cooperation with other publishers and have co-published with some 20 other publishers. Many of our titles are published in Kenya by Zand Press for distribution at local prices in East Africa.

Awards

- *Love after Babel* and other poems by Chandramohan S won the Nicolás Cristóbal Guillén Batista Outstanding Book Award from the Caribbean Philosophical Association.
- *Decolonization and Afro-Feminism* by Sylvia Tamale won the 2022 FTGS Book Prize.
- In addition, the poetry book *29 leads to love* by Salimah Valiani, published by Inanna Publications, won the 2022 International Book Awards Winner for Contemporary Poetry. Salimah is the author of *Cradles* and *Love Pandemic* published by Daraja Press.
- Daraja Press's publisher, Firoze Manji, was the recipient of the 2021 Nicolás Cristóbal Guillén Batista Lifetime Achievement Award from the Caribbean Philosophical Association.

Our full catalogue is available at https://darajapress.com

Bibliography

1. Works by V.I. Lenin
All references to the Progress Publishers (Moscow) edition of the *Collected Works*.

1972
"Explanation of the Law on Fines Imposed on Factory Workers," *Vol. 2*, 29-72.

1973
"The Party Crisis," *Vol. 32*, 43-53.
"Once again on the Trade Unions, the current situation and the mistakes of Trotsky and Bukharin," *Vol. 32*, 70-107.
"A Letter to G. Myasnikov," *Vol. 32*, 504-509.
"Eleventh Congress of the R.C.P. (B.)," *Vol. 33*, 259-326.
"'Dual' Subordination and Legality," *Vol. 33*, 363-7.
"Fourth Congress of the Communist International," *Vol. 33*, 415-432.
"On Cooperation," *Vol. 33*, 467-475.
"To Inessa Armand," *Vol. 35*, 266-269.

1974
"On the National Pride of the Great Russians," *Vol. 21*, 102-106.
"Imperialism, the Highest Stage of Capitalism," *Vol. 22*, 185-304.
"The Discussion on Self-Determination Summed Up," *Vol. 22*, 320-360.
"The Nascent Trend of Imperialist Economism," *Vol. 23*, 13-21.
"A Caricature of Marxism and Imperialist Economism," in *Collected Works Vol. 23*, Moscow: Progress Publishers, 28-76.
"The Tasks of the Proletariat in the Present Revolution," *Vol. 24*, 19-26.
"Letters on Tactics," *Vol. 24*, 42-54.
"The Task of the Proletariat in our Revolution," *Vol. 24*, 55-92.
"How the Capitalists Are Trying to Scare the People," *Vol. 24*, 439-440.
"One of the Fundamental Questions of the Revolution," *Vol. 25*, 370-377.
"The State and Revolution," *Vol. 25*, 385-498.
"Extraordinary Seventh Congress of the R.C.P.(B)," *Vol. 27*, 85-158.
"The Immediate Tasks of the Soviet Government," *Vol. 27*, 235-278.
"Left-Wing Childishness and the Petty-Bourgeois Mentality," *Vol. 27*, 323-354.
"Speech at a meeting of Delegates from the Poor Peasants' Committees of Central Gubernias," *Vol. 28*, 171-178.
"Draft Program of the R.C.P.(B.)," *Vol. 29*, 97-140.
"To the Working Women," *Vol. 30*, 371-372.
"Draft Theses on National and Colonial Questions," *Vol. 31*, 144-151.
"The Second Congress of the Communist International," *Vol. 31*, 213-263.
"The Eight All-Russia Congress of Soviets," *Vol. 31*, 461-534.

1976
"Conspectus of Hegel's Book The Science of Logic," *Vol. 38*, 85-237.

1977
"What the 'Friends of the People' Are and How They Fight the Social-Democrats," *Vol. 1*, 129-332.
"The Economic Content of Narodism and the Criticism of it in Mr. Struve's Book," *Vol. 1*, 333-508.
"The Development of Capitalism in Russia," *Vol. 3*, 25-658.
"Casual Notes, I. Beat – But Not to Death!" *Vol. 4*, 387-402.
"What is to be done?" *Vol. 5*, 347-530.

"The Three Sources and Three Component Parts of Marxism," *Vol. 19*, 23-28.
"The Right of Nations to Self-Determination," *Vol. 20*, 393-454.
"Marxism and Insurrection," *Vol. 26*, 22-27.
"For Bread and Peace," *Vol. 26*, 386-387.
"People From Another World," *Vol. 26*, 431-433.
"The Question of Nationalities or 'Autonomisation'," *Vol. 36*, 605-612.

1978
"The Socialist Party and Non-Party Revolutionism," in *Vol. 10*, 75-82.
"The Victory of the Cadets and the Tasks of the Workers' Party," *Vol. 10*, 199-276.

Lenin in other languages
Lenin, V.I. (1999/2017), *Neizvestnye dokumenty 1891-1922*. Moscow: Rosspėn. In Russian.
Lenin, V.I. (2016/2018), *Imperialismus als höchstes Stadium des Kapitalismus*. Critical new edition with essays by Dietmar Dath and Christoph Türcke. Edited and annotated by Wladislaw Hedeler and Volker Külow. Berlin: Verlag 8. Mai. In German.
Lenin, V.I. (2019), *Der Marxismus über den Staat/Staat und Revolution*. Critical new edition with essays by Hermann Klenner and Wolfgang Küttler. Edited and annotated by Wladislaw Hedeler, Volker Külow and Manfred Neuhaus. Berlin: Verlag 8. Mai. In German.

2. Other works
Aline, Alexei (1929), *Lénine à Paris: souvenirs inédits*. Paris: Les Revues.
Althusser, Louis (1972), *Politics and History: Montesquieu, Rousseau, Hegel and Marx*. London: NLB.
Althusser, Louis (2005), *For Marx*. London and New York: Verso.
Althusser, Louis & Balibar, Etienne (2009), *Reading Capital*. London and New York: Verso.
Amado, Abel Djassi (2021), "The União Nacional in Cabo Verde, 1937-1945: Local Politics in an Imperial Political Party," *Portuguese Literary & Cultural Studies*, 36/37, 129-155.
Ashton, Catrin & Federici, Silvia (2022), "Not a Labor of Love. The Radicalization of Motherhood," *PS*. Available online.
Badiou, Alain (2005), *Metapolitics*. London: Verso.
Badiou, Alain (2007), *The Century*. Cambridge: Polity Press.
Badiou, Alain (2018), *Can Politics Be Thought?* Durham: Duke University Press.
Balibar, Etienne (2007), "The Philosophical Moment in Politics Determined by War: Lenin 1914-1916," in Sebastian Budgen, Stathis Kouvelakis & Slavoj Žižek (eds.), *Lenin Reloaded: Toward a Politics of Truth*. Durham: Duke University Press, 207-221.
Bartha, Eszter; Krausz, Tamás & Bálint Mezei (eds.) (2023), *State Socialism in Eastern Europe: History, Theory, Anti-Capitalist Alternatives*. London: Palgrave Macmillan.
Benjamin, Walter (1998), *The Origin of German Tragic Drama*. London: Verso.
Bergin, Cathy (ed.) (2016), *African American Anti-Colonial Thought, 1917-1937*. Edinburgh: Edinburgh University Press.
Brecht, Bertolt (1967), *Gesammelte Werke 19*. Frankfurt: Suhrkamp.
Broussard, Nicholas (1995), "Napoleon, Hegelian Hero," *Napoleon.org*. Available online.
Budgen, Sebastian (2020), "The Phallic Road to Socialism," *Salvage*. Available online.
Burbank, Jane (1995), "Lenin and the Law in Revolutionary Russia," *Slavic Review*, 54(1), 23-44.

Burliuk, David; Kruchenykh, Alexander; Mayakovsky, Vladimir and Victor Khlebnikov (1917), "A slap in the face of public taste," *Marxists Internet Archive*. Available online.
Cabral, Amílcar (1969), *Revolution in Guinea: Selected Texts*. New York: Monthly Review Press.
Cabral, Amílcar (1970), "Une Lumière Féconde Éclaire Le Chemin de La Lutte," *Arquivo Amílcar Cabral*. Available online.
Cabral, Amílcar (1973), *Our People Are Our Mountains: Amílcar Cabral on the Guinean Revolution*. London: Committee for Freedom in Mozambique, Angola and Guinea.
Cabral, Amílcar (2008), *Unity & Struggle: Selected Speeches and Writings*. Pretoria: Unisa Press.
Chabal, Patrick (2003), *Amílcar Cabral: Revolutionary Leadership and People's War*. Trenton: Africa World Press.
Chernykh, Evgeny (1992), *Ancient Metallurgy in the USSR: The Early Metal Age*. Cambridge: Cambridge University Press.
Chernykh, Evgeny (2017), *Nomadic Cultures in the Mega-structure of the Eurasian World*. Brighton: Academic Studies Press.
Clausewitz, Carl von (1976), *On War*. Princeton: Princeton University Press.
Commission of the Central Executive Committee of the USSR for the Perpetuation of the Memory of V. I. Ulyanov (1924), *Leninu. 21 ianvaria 1924*. Moscow: Goznak.
Davis, Donald E. & Kohn, Walter S.G. (1977), "Lenin's Notebook on Clausewitz," *Soviet Armed Forces Review Annual*, 1, Gulf Breeze: Academic International Press.
Debray, Regis (2007), "Socialism: A Life-Cycle," *New Left Review*, 46, 5-28.
Deleuze, Gilles & Guattari, Félix (1987), *A Thousand Plateaus: Capitalism and Schizophrenia*. Minneapolis: University of Minnesota Press.
Derrida, Jacques (1996), *Archive Fever: A Freudian Impression*. Chicago: University of Chicago Press.
Du Bois, W.E.B. (1953), "On Stalin," *Marxists Internet Archive*. Available online.
Dunayevskaya, Raya (2017), *Russia: From Proletarian Revolution to State-Capitalist Counter-Revolution*. Leiden: Brill.
Ettinger, Elzbieta (1986), Rosa *Luxemburg: A Life*. Boston: Beacon Press.
Gensburger, Sarah, & Truc, Gérôme (2020), *Les mémoriaux du 13 novembre*. Paris: Éditions de l'EHESS.
Giffin, Frederick C. (1975), "The 'First Russian Labor Code': The Law of June 3, 1886," *Russian History*, 2(2), 83-100.
Gómez Velázquez, Natasha (2017), *Palabras de Lenin, conclusiones de hoy*. La Habana: Editorial Félix Varela.
Graeber, David (2012), "Of Flying Cars and the Declining Rate of Profit," *The Baffler*, 19, 66-90.
Gramsci, Antonio (1992), *Selections from the Prison Notebooks*, ed. and transl. by Q. Hoare and G. Nowell Smith. New York: International Publishers.
Gramsci, Antonio (1996), *Prison Notebooks Vol. II*, ed. by J. A. Buttigieg, transl. by J. A. Buttigieg and A. Callari. New York: Columbia University Press.
Gramsci, Antonio (2007), *Prison Notebooks Vol. III*, ed. by J. A. Buttigieg, transl. by J. A. Buttigieg and A. Callari. New York: Columbia University Press.
Guerrero, Amado (1970/71), *Philippine Society and Revolution*. *Marxists Internet Archive*. Available online.
Harding, Neil (1977), *Lenin's Political Thought*. Chicago: Haymarket Books
Haupt, Georges & Jean-Jacques Marie (eds.), *Makers of the Russian Revolution: Biographies of Bolshevik Leaders*. London: George Allen and Unwin.
Hayek, F.A. (1945), 'The Use of Knowledge in Society,' *The American Economic Review*, 35(4), 519-530.

Hazard, John N. (1953), *Law and Social Change in the U.S.S.R.* Toronto: Carswell Company Limited.
Hegel, G.W.F. (1989), *Science of Logic.* Atlantic Highlands: Humanities Press International.
Hegel, G.W.F. (2010), *The Science of Logic.* Cambridge: Cambridge University Press.
Hegel, G.W.F. (2018), *The Phenomenology of Spirit.* Cambridge: Cambridge University Press.
Hill, Robert A. (ed.) (1987), *The Marcus Garvey and Universal Negro Improvement Association Papers, Vol. 5.* Berkeley: University of California Press.
Høgsbjerg, Christian (2009), "The Prophet and Black Power: Trotsky on race in the US," *International Socialism.* Available online.
Jeifets, Víctor L. & Schelchkov, Andrei A. (eds.) (2018), *La Internacional Comunista en América Latina. En documentos del archivo de Moscú.* Moscú-Santiago de Chile: Ariadna Ediciones.
Jovanović, Gordana (2023), "(Childhood) Memories at the Intersection of Coloniality and Decoloniality," *Human Arenas.* Available online.
Klejn, Leo (2012), *Soviet Archaeology: Trends, Schools, and History.* Oxford: Oxford University Press.
Klenner, Hermann (2019), "The 'Classical' Lenin. Justice and Injustice of and in 'The State and Revolution,'" *in* V. I. Lenin *Der Marxismus über den Staat/Staat und Revolution.*
Kohl, Philip (2007), *The Making of Bronze Age Eurasia.* Cambridge: University of Cambridge Press.
Laschitza, Annelies (2010), *Her şeye rağmen tutkuyla yaşamak (Rosa Luxemburg – Im Lebensrausch, trotz alledem).* Istanbul: Yordam kitap.
Le Blanc, Paul (1993), *Lenin and the Revolutionary Party.* Chicago: Haymarket Books.
Leiderman, Daniil & Sokolovskaia, Marina (2021), "'Poor, Poor Il'ich': Visualizing Lenin's Death for Children," *in* Marina Balina and Serguei Alex. Oushakine (eds.), *The Pedagogy of Images. Depicting Communism for Children.* Toronto, University of Toronto Press, 419-443.
Lichtheim, George (1970), *A Short History of Socialism.* New York: Praeger Publishers.
Lih, Lars T. (2008), *Lenin Rediscovered: What Is to Be Done? in Context.* Chicago: Haymarket Books.
Loginov, Vladlen (2019), *Vladimir Lenin. How to Become a Leader.* London: Glagoslav.
Luisi, Paulina (2015), *Bajo el signo de Marte. España. Homenaje a las Democracias Mártires.* Montevideo: Biblioteca Nacional de Uruguay.
Lukács, Georg (1971), *History and Class Consciousness: Studies in Marxist Dialectics.* Cambridge: MIT Press.
Luxemburg, Rosa (1961), *The Russian Revolution: Leninism or Marxism.* Ann Arbor: University of Michigan Press.
Luxemburg, Rosa (2011), *The Letters of Rosa Luxemburg.* Edited by Georg Adler, Peter Hudis, and Annelies Laschitza. Translated by George Shriver. New York: Verso.
Malysheva, Svetlana (2020), "Funeral Wreath to the Leader: Grief for Lenin and the Practices of Soviet Self-Representation," *Bulletin of Perm University,* 4(51), 87-94. In Russian.
Mariátegui, José Carlos (1924), "Lenin." *Marxists Internet Archive.* Available online.
Mariátegui, José Carlos (1971), *Seven Interpretive Essays on Peruvian Reality.* Austin: University of Texas Press.
Mariátegui, José Carlos (1981), *Defensa del Marxismo.* Lima: Biblioteca Amauta.

Mariátegui, José Carlos (2011), "Anniversary and Balance Sheet," *in* Harry E. Vanden and Marc Becker (eds. & trans.), *José Carlos Mariátegui: An Anthology*. New York: Monthly Review Press.
Mariátegui, José Carlos (2011), "Defense of Marxism," *in* Harry E. Vanden and Marc Becker (eds. & trans.), *José Carlos Mariátegui: An Anthology*. New York: Monthly Review Press.
Markwick, Roger (2001), *Rewriting history in Soviet Russia: The politics of revisionist historiography, 1956-1974*. New York: Palgrave Macmillan.
Marik, Soma (2004), "Gendering the Revolutionary Party," *in* Biswajit Chatterjee and Kunal Chattopadhyay (eds.), *Perspectives on Socialism*. Calcutta: Progressive Publishers.
Marik, Soma (2017), "Bolsheviks and Feminists," *Economic and Political Weekly*, 52(44), 81-89.
Marx, Karl (1976), *Capital Vol. I*. London: Penguin.
McCulloch, Jock (2020), *In the Twilight of Revolution: The Political Theory of Amílcar Cabral*. London: Routledge.
Mella, Julio Antonio (2017), *Mella. Textos escogidos. Tomo I & II*. La Habana: Ediciones La Memoria, Centro Cultural Pablo de la Torriente Brau.
Milios, John (1999), "Preindustrial Capitalist Forms: Lenin's Contribution to a Marxist Theory of Development," *Rethinking Marxism*, 11(4), 38-56.
Mishra, Vinod (1988), "Vladimir Ilich Vs. Rosa Luxemburg: A Study Based on Lenin's Writings," *Marxists Internet Archive*. Available online.
Mongait, Alexander (1959), *Archaeology in the U.S.S.R.* Moscow: Foreign Languages Publishing House.
Monogarova, L.F. & B.V. Andrianov (1976), "Lenin's Doctrine of Concurrent Socioeconomic Systems and its Significance for Ethnography," *Soviet Anthropology and Archaeology*, 14(4), 3-26.
Moreau, Alicia (1916), *Correspondencia a Paulina Luisi* (unpublished). Montevideo: Carpeta M del Fondo Paulina Luisi del Archivo Literario de la Biblioteca Nacional del Uruguay.
Mpofu, William (2022), "The Philosophy of Liberation: Troubling the Marxism of the 21st Century in Africa," *in* Sabelo J. Ndlovu-Gatsheni and Morgan Ndlovu (eds.), *Marxism and Decolonization in the 21st Century*. London and New York: Routledge, 31-48.
Neumeyer, Joy (2015), "'The Final Struggle': The Art of the Soviet Death Mask," Berkeley: University of California. Available online.
Nzongola-Ntalaja, George (1984), "Amílcar Cabral and the Theory of the National Liberation Struggle," *Latin American Perspectives*, 11(2), 43-54.
Parker, Clifton B. (2018), "At Stanford, first Cardinal Conversation spotlights technology, politics," *Stanford News*. Available online.
Perriol, Antoine (2010), "Iliazd & L'Imprimerie Union," *Les Carnets de L'Iliazd Club*, 7, 11-86.
Qu Qiubai, "Impressions of the Red Capital," in *Collected Works of Qu Qiubai* (Volume I, Literature). In Chinese.
Qu Qiubai, "Lenin: Tool of History," in *Collected Works of Qu Qiubai* (Volume II, Political Theory). In Chinese.
Radivojević, Miljana, Benjamin Roberts, Miroslav Radić, Julka Kuzmanović Cvetković and Thilo Rehren (eds.) (2021), *The Rise of Metallurgy in Eurasia: Evolution, Organisation, and Consumption of Early Metal in the Balkans*. Oxford: Archaeopress.
Reed, John (1967), *Ten Days That Shook the World*. New York: International Publishers.
Renault, Matthieu (2021), "From Russian colonies to black America ... and back: Lenin and Langston Hughes" *in* David Featherstone and Christian Høgsbjerg

(eds.), *The Red and the Black: The Russian Revolution and the Black Atlantic*. Manchester: Manchester University Press, 81-96.

Rev (2023), "Trump speaks at CPAC 2023 Transcript." *Rev*. Available online.

Rimlinger, Gaston V. (1960), "Autocracy and the Factory Order in Early Russian Industrialization," *Journal of Economic History*, 20(1), 67-92.

Rockmore, Tom (1986), *Hegel's Circular Epistemology*. Bloomington: Indiana University Press.

Rosmer, Alfred (2016), *Lenin's Moscow*. Chicago: Haymarket Books.

Saifulin, M. (ed.) (1972), *Lenin About the Press*. Prague: International Organisation of Journalists.

Santino, Jack (ed.) (2006), *Spontaneous Shrines and the Public Memorialization of Death*. New York: Palgrave Macmillan.

Serge, Victor (1925), "Lenin in 1917," *Marxists Internet Archive*. Available online.

Serge, Victor (2002), *Memoirs of a Revolutionary*. Iowa City: University of Iowa Press.

Serge, Victor (2014), *Birth of our Power*. Oakland: PM Press.

Silina, Maria (2015), "Memorial Industry: V. I. Lenin Commemoration in Soviet Russia from 1924 until today," International Conference "Sites of Memory of Socialism and Communism in Europe," Bern. Available online.

Simon, Joshua (ed.) (2019), *Being Together Precedes Being. A Textbook for The Kids Want Communism*. Berlin: Archive Books

Sison, Jose Maria (2021), "On Internationalism." Available online.

Smith, Michael Nassen (2022), "The Limits of Postcolonial Critique of Marxism: A Defence of Radical Universalism," *in* Sabelo J. Ndlovu-Gatsheni and Morgan Ndlovu (eds.), *Marxism and Decolonization in the 21st Century*. London and New York: Routledge, 49-67.

Society for Military History (1949), "Colonel Rasin's Letter," *Military Affairs*, 13(2), 75-77.

Stalin, J.V. (1924), *The Foundations of Leninism*. Marxists Internet Archive. Available online.

Stalin, J.V. (1946), "Answer to a letter of 30 January, from Col.-Professor Rasin." *Marxists Internet Archive*. Available online.

Stalin, J.V. (1950), "Marxism and Problems of Linguistics," *Marxists Internet Archives*. Available online.

Talaver, Sasha (2020), "When Soviet Women Won the Right to Abortion (for the Second Time)," *Jacobin*. Available online.

Taylor-Stone, Chardine (2021), "Nina Simone Was a Radical," *Jacobin*. Available online.

Tchijevsky, Ivan (2023), "Emma Harris (1871-1940)," *Black Past*. Available online.

Trigger, Bruce G. (2006), *A History of Archaeological Thought. Second Edition*. Cambridge: University of Cambridge Press.

Trotsky, Leon (1967), *History of the Russian Revolution Vol. 3*. London: Sphere Books.

Trotsky, Leon (2017), *History of the Russian Revolution*. London: Penguin.

Tumarkin, Nina (1997), *Lenin Lives! The Lenin Cult in Soviet Russia*. Cambridge: Harvard University Press.

Unknown author (2017), "'Whoever leads in AI will rule the world': Putin to Russian children on Knowledge Day," *RT*. Available online.

Unknown author (2022), "Russian Anarchists on the Invasion of Ukraine," *Crimethink*. Available online.

Vanaik, Achin (2019), "The Question of Organisation: Beyond Marx, the Enduring Legacy of Lenin," *Economic and Political Weekly*, 54(28).

Valentinov, Nikolai (1969), *The Early Years of Lenin*. Ann Arbor: University of Michigan.

Varoufakis, Yanis (2023), *Technofeudalism: What Killed Capitalism*. London: The Bodley Head.
Vergara, Camila (2022), "Lenin and the Materialist Critique of Labor Law," *in* Alla Ivanchikova & Robert R. Maclean (eds.), *The Future of Lenin*. New York: SUNY Press, 257-280.
Viet Nam News (2016), "Women's housework should be part of GDP: researchers." Available online.
Wolff, Larry (1994), *Inventing Eastern Europe. The Map of Civilization on the Mind of Enlightenment*. Stanford: Stanford University Press.
Yurchak, Alexei (2015), "Bodies of Lenin: The Hidden Science of Communist Sovereignty," *Representations*, 129(1), 116-157.
Žižek, Slavoj (2011), *Revolution at the Gates: Selected Writings of Lenin from 1917*. London: Verso.

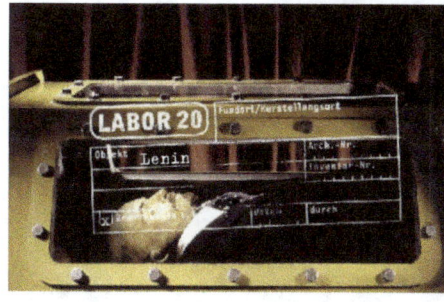

Image created by Johann Salazar.

Related books from Daraja Press

Lenin150 (Samizdat)
January 2021 • 367 pages • $43
https://bit.ly/2QL5jaC

Left Alone
On Solitude and Loneliness amid Collective Struggle
May 2023 • 238 pages • $28
https://bityl.co/IXZ0

October 1917 Revolution
October 2017 • 124 pages • $15
https://bit.ly/3ax0ljwC

Order from darajapress.com
Prices in U.S. dollars

www.ingramcontent.com/pod-product-compliance
Lightning Source LLC
Chambersburg PA
CBHW070307230426
43664CB00015B/2657